# THE CONCISE
# CHILDREN'S
# ENCYCLOPEDIA

KINGFISHER
Kingfisher Publications Plc
New Penderel House
283-288 High Holborn
London WC1V 7HZ
www.kingfisherpub.com

First published by Kingfisher Publications Plc in 2001
2 4 6 8 10 9 7 5 3

1TR/0501/SF/UNV/157MA

A CIP catalogue record for this book is available from
the British Library

ISBN 0 7534 0598 9
Printed in China

# THE CONCISE
# CHILDREN'S
# ENCYCLOPEDIA

KING*f*ISHER

**Editorial Director**
Jennifer Justice

**Managing Editor**
Sarah Allen

**Editorial team**
Trevor Anderson, Max Benato, Jane Birch,
Harry Boteler, Anne Davies, Rebecca Fry, Aimee Johnson,
Tracey Kelly, Sarah Kovandzich, Elizabeth Longley,
Miren Lopategui, Rupert Matthews, Jayne Miller, Brian Williams

**Creative Director**
Val Pidgeon

**Art Director**
Mike Davis

**Art Editor**
David Noon

**Design team**
Liz Black, Pete Byrne, John Jamieson,
Ruth Levy, Emma Skidmore, Nina Tara

**Cover design**
Andy Smith

**Picture Research**
Veneta Bullen, Davina Bullen,
Sophie Mortimer, Yannick Yago

**Maps**
Hardlines

**Contributors & Consultants**
Sue Aldridge, Sarah Angliss, Max Benato,
Martyn Bramwell, Enid Broderick, Tim Brown,
David Burnie, Catherine Halcrow, Jack Challoner, Michael Chinery,
Maria Constantino, Chris Cooper, Sophie Cooper, Alan Cowsill,
Jeff Daniel, David Darling, Dougal Dixon, John Farndon,
Sue Gordon, John Graham, Ian Graham, Catherine Headlam,
Lesley Hill, Caroline Juler, Anne Kay, Robin Kerrod,
J.C. Levy, Keith Lye, Tim Madge, David Marshall, Bob McCabe,
Iain Nicolson, Steve Parker, Jane Parker, John Paton,
Malcolm Porter, Sue Reid, Meg Sanders, Bill Shapiro,
Philip Steele, Richard Tames, John Tipler,
Ian Westwell, Brian Williams

# INTRODUCTION

The word *encyclopedia* comes from the Greek for 'all-round education', and *The Concise Children's Encyclopedia* provides just that, in a way that is both accessible and stimulating.

This all-new encyclopedia covers everything from ancient history to up-to-the-minute developments in technology; from animal and plant life on Earth to plans for the next millennium in outer space. Geography, natural history, religion, the human body – all the topics that children explore at home and at school are included here.

We have rejected the 'sound-bite' approach to children's reference in favour of more in-depth coverage, which makes this encyclopedia perfect for project work and homework assignments. At the same time, the text is broken up into manageable paragraphs, suitable for both confident readers and younger browsers. Colourful photographs and superb illustrations and maps not only enhance the text, but also encourage readers to find out more for themselves.

Easy access is the key to this encyclopedia. Major subject areas such as ELECTRICITY have been arranged alphabetically, but the encyclopedia also has a comprehensive index so that readers can refer quickly to related topics, such as ENERGY and NUCLEAR POWER.

The encyclopedia has been written and checked by a team of specialist authors and consultants, and produced by a team of editors and designers with years of experience in children's reference. We are confident that it is a book in which children, and parents, can put their trust.

*The Editors*

# AFRICA

Africa is the second largest continent and covers about one fifth of the Earth's land area. It includes 53 countries, six of which are islands.

▲ The Tuareg are a nomadic people who inhabit a large area of the Sahara Desert. Some still travel the desert with camel trains laden with goods such as dates and salt.

## KEY FACTS

- **Area:** 30,306,000 sq km
- **Population:** 762,000,000
- **Number of countries:** 53
- **Largest country:** Sudan, (2,505,813 sq km)
- **Smallest country:** Seychelles (455 sq km)
- **Highest point:** Mount Kilimanjaro (5,895m)
- **Largest lake:** Lake Victoria (69,484 sq km)
- **Longest river:** Nile (6,670km)

▼ Chobe National Park in Botswana is home to herds of elephants and impala. Many African countries have set aside large stretches of land as wildlife reserves.

The world's hottest continent, Africa has rainforests and tree-scattered grasslands (known as savanna), which are inhabited by a huge variety of wild animals. A third of Africa is covered by the Sahara, the largest desert on Earth.

### HIGHS AND LOWS

Much of Africa is made up of plateaux, flat areas of land high above sea level. The plateau in East Africa is broken up by two extinct volcanoes – Mount Kenya and Tanzania's Mount Kilimanjaro – and the Great Rift Valley. The Rift is a long crack in the Earth's crust that runs from Mozambique, through East Africa, the Red Sea and into southwestern Asia. Elongated lakes have formed in the valley. Africa's spectacular natural features include the Nile, the longest river in the world, and Lake Tanganyika, the world's longest lake, which stretches for 620km.

### HOT AND DRY

Because Africa lies across the Equator, most of the continent gets extremely hot. The world's highest temperature in the shade was recorded in Libya in 1932 at 58°C. The land around the tropics, each side of the Equator, is starved of rain and more than half of Africa's land has less than 500mm of rain per year.

### RAINFORESTS AND SAVANNA

In some regions, particularly around the Equator in West and Central Africa, rainfall is high and large rainforests grow. Monrovia, the capital of Liberia, has an average of 5,140mm of rain per year. Between the rainforests and the deserts are immense areas of tropical savanna. Savanna is prone to drought, with a mixture of rainy and dry seasons.

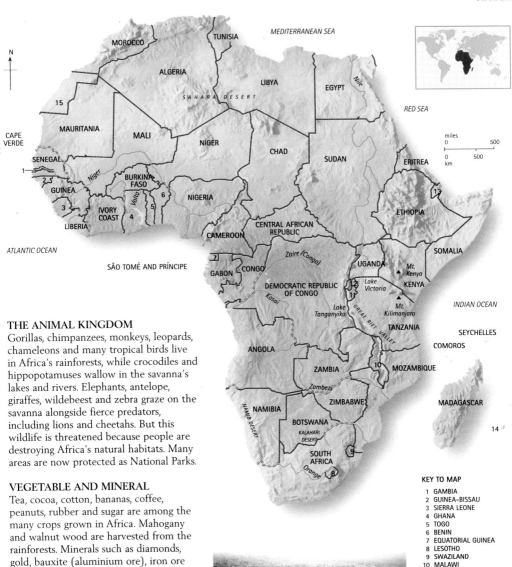

MEDITERRANEAN SEA

MOROCCO
TUNISIA
ALGERIA
LIBYA
EGYPT
SAHARA DESERT
Nile
RED SEA
15
MAURITANIA
MALI
NIGER
CHAD
SUDAN
ERITREA
CAPE VERDE
SENEGAL
Niger
BURKINA FASO
NIGERIA
CENTRAL AFRICAN REPUBLIC
ETHIOPIA
GUINEA
Volta
6
IVORY COAST
5
4
LIBERIA
3
CAMEROON
SOMALIA
ATLANTIC OCEAN
SÃO TOMÉ AND PRÍNCIPE
7
Zaire (Congo)
UGANDA
Mt. Kenya
KENYA
GABON
CONGO
DEMOCRATIC REPUBLIC OF CONGO
Lake Victoria
Kasai
Lake Tanganyika
Mt. Kilimanjaro
INDIAN OCEAN
GREAT RIFT VALLEY
TANZANIA
SEYCHELLES
COMOROS
ANGOLA
ZAMBIA
10
MOZAMBIQUE
Zambezi
ZIMBABWE
MADAGASCAR
14
NAMIBIA
NAMIB DESERT
BOTSWANA
KALAHARI DESERT
SOUTH AFRICA
9
8
Orange

miles
0        500
0    500
km

N

## THE ANIMAL KINGDOM
Gorillas, chimpanzees, monkeys, leopards, chameleons and many tropical birds live in Africa's rainforests, while crocodiles and hippopotamuses wallow in the savanna's lakes and rivers. Elephants, antelope, giraffes, wildebeest and zebra graze on the savanna alongside fierce predators, including lions and cheetahs. But this wildlife is threatened because people are destroying Africa's natural habitats. Many areas are now protected as National Parks.

## VEGETABLE AND MINERAL
Tea, cocoa, cotton, bananas, coffee, peanuts, rubber and sugar are among the many crops grown in Africa. Mahogany and walnut wood are harvested from the rainforests. Minerals such as diamonds, gold, bauxite (aluminium ore), iron ore and copper are mined for export. Oil is exported from Gabon, Libya and Nigeria.

## PEOPLE AND LANGUAGES
Many Africans live in tribal villages with their own cultures. Over 1,000 languages are spoken south of the Sahara alone. Country borders take little account of tribal differences, and in one country there may be many tribal groupings. ▶

KEY TO MAP
1  GAMBIA
2  GUINEA-BISSAU
3  SIERRA LEONE
4  GHANA
5  TOGO
6  BENIN
7  EQUATORIAL GUINEA
8  LESOTHO
9  SWAZILAND
10 MALAWI
11 BURUNDI
12 RWANDA
13 DJIBOUTI
14 MAURITIUS
15 WESTERN SAHARA (occupied by Morocco)

◀ The Korup National Park in Cameroon is one of Africa's densest rainforest areas.

▲ The people of Tahoua in Niger build reed huts from locally available materials. Huts like these are typical of the Sahel region, an area of dry grassland on the edge of the Sahara.

## RELIGIOUS BELIEFS

The people who live in northern Africa are mostly Arabs and Berbers who speak Arabic and follow the Muslim religion. The countries in southern Africa are largely populated by Black Africans. Although most are Muslims or Christians, ancient local traditions still flourish and more than a quarter of Africa's people follow local beliefs.

## THE EARLY DAYS

Many scientists believe Africa is the continent where human beings first evolved, about two to four million years ago, but little is known about this very early history. Around 10,000 years ago, the Sahara had a moist climate and many people lived there, hunting animals, gathering plants for food, and later raising crops and herding cattle.

## ANCIENT EGYPT AND ISLAM

In about 3100BC, Ancient Egypt – one of the world's greatest early civilizations – was formed out of Upper and Lower Egypt in northern Africa. It thrived on the fertile banks of the Nile until, in 30BC, it became part of the Roman Empire. In the 7th century AD, the Arabs conquered northern Africa and converted the people of Egypt and its neighbours to Islam.

## GREAT KINGDOMS

For centuries, people outside Africa knew little about the continent south of the Sahara. Between 1100 and 1500, Arabs trading for gold, ivory and

◀ The Masai people of East Africa are one of many tribal groups that live in Africa. A nomadic people, they raise cattle and hunt wild animals.

▲ The snakes coming out of the nostrils of this 18th-century Benin bronze head represent the belief that those with magic powers could release snakes to destroy their enemies.

slaves brought back news of great empires in West Africa such as Ghana, Mali, Benin, Songhai and Kanem. Kingdoms such as Benin, which was founded in about AD900, produced beautiful bronze sculptures which are highly prized today. Many of the sculptures symbolize the magical aspects of the *obas* (kings) of Benin. Kingdoms arose in the south, such as the huge stone city of Great Zimbabwe. News of Africa's wealth attracted great curiosity among Europeans.

## CONQUERING A CONTINENT

Portuguese explorers were the first Europeans to map the coasts of Africa. In 1498, the navigator Vasco da Gama rounded the tip of southern Africa, the Cape of Good Hope, on a journey that led him to discover a new route to India. Others later sailed on to East Africa. The Portuguese were also the first Europeans to export slaves from West Africa, a trade which continued until the 19th century.

## EUROPEAN INFLUENCE

The Dutch took over many Portuguese trading posts in the 17th century and in 1652 they founded a settlement at Cape

◄ About two thirds of Africa's people live in villages. In some areas, the markets are full of fresh produce, but in others, drought, poverty and civil war have led to food shortages and widespread famine.

Town, which became part of South Africa. By the late 19th century, almost all of Africa was ruled by European powers.

### INDEPENDENCE
Colonial rule continued in Africa until the 1950s, when the colonies began to gain their independence. By the early 1970s, most countries were independent, but economic problems, caused by poverty and ethnic rivalries, have led to instability in many areas. The Organization of African Unity (OAU), set up in 1963, aims to promote economic, political and cultural co-operation across the continent.

▲ Harare, named after the African chief Neharawe, is the capital of Zimbabwe in southern Africa. It is a modern city, with tall skyscrapers and tree-lined streets.

### A HARD WAY OF LIFE
Two thirds of the world's poorest countries are in Africa. Most Africans live in villages and farm the land. Poverty, disease and war in many parts mean that people often do not reach old age. In the mid-1990s, the average age to which a person in Sierra Leone, Uganda or Malawi could expect to live was 45 years.

### BUSY CITIES
Although most Africans live in villages, the continent has some large, bustling cities. Cairo, the capital of Egypt, is the largest, with a population of 9,900,000. Other important cities have grown up around ports, such as Cape Town in South Africa, Casablanca in Morocco and Algiers in Algeria.

### TIME OF EQUALITY
One of the most important events in Africa's history took place in 1994, when South Africa became a democracy under the leadership of Nelson Mandela. This finally ended apartheid, the official policy that separated people of different races from the whites. Since 1948, this policy had given whites power, while denying people of other colours basic rights in education, at work and in everyday life.

▲ Soccer is one of a number of areas in which African countries are increasing their world presence. Cameroon's Roger Miller was one of the stars of the 1994 World Cup in the USA.

### SEE ALSO
Continent, Egypt (Ancient), Grassland, Roman Empire, South Africa

# AMPHIBIAN

Amphibians are cold-blooded animals that are able to live both in water and on land. Most start life with gills, but later develop lungs for breathing.

Like many frogs, the European common frog has smooth, moist skin and long legs for jumping.

Like many toads, the European common toad has dry, lumpy skin and walks rather than leaps.

The long-tailed salamander's bright colour helps it warn off predators.

Newts, such as this smooth newt, are salamanders that spend long periods in water.

Caecilians have no legs and live undergound. They are found only in tropical areas and many are blind.

Frogs, toads, salamanders, newts and caecilians are all types of amphibian. They are cold-blooded creatures that rely on their surroundings for warmth, and are found in most parts of the world. Adult amphibians usually have soft, thin, moist skin that absorbs oxygen from the air, helping them to breathe. But some frogs and toads have thick, warty skin to help them survive in drier conditions.

## JELLIED EGGS

The way amphibians breed and develop is unique in the animal kingdom. Females lay their jelly-covered eggs, called spawn, in water. These hatch into tadpoles, which develop limbs and lungs so that they can live on dry land. Some amphibians need only a small amount of water in which to lay their eggs. The tree frog lays its eggs on moist leaves and the male midwife toad carries the female's eggs on its back legs, dipping them in pools of water. The Australian gastric-brooding frog swallows her eggs. Once they have developed into froglets, they hop out of her mouth.

▲ The extraordinary Mexican axolotl salamander usually spends its life as a tadpole, breathing through gills.

## BIG EATERS

All amphibians are hunters. Many use their bulging eyes to track fast-moving prey, swallowing it whole. Small frogs and salamanders eat insects and tiny fish. Large toads gulp down mice and birds. They usually sit and wait, or crawl towards their prey, before lunging with mouth open. Some frogs and salamanders have a long, sticky-tipped tongue attached to the front of their mouth, which they can flick out to grab insects.

## LEAPING FROGS AND TOADS

Over 80 per cent of all amphibians are frogs and toads, known as anurans. They have long, five-toed back legs for leaping and shorter, four-toed front legs used to cushion the landing. There is no scientific difference between frogs and toads, but anurans with smooth, moist skin that usually jump are called frogs, and those that waddle and have drier, lumpy skin are called toads.

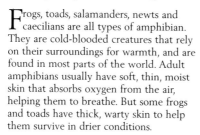

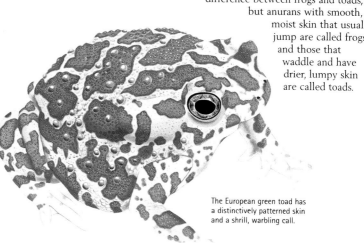

The European green toad has a distinctively patterned skin and a shrill, warbling call.

**THE POISON**
When the fire salamander is attacked by a predator, poison oozes out of the pores in its skin.

▼ All amphibians have glands in their skin that produce slime to help keep it moist. Some also create foul-tasting or poisonous substances as a defence against predators. The fire salamander's bright markings warn predators that it is poisonous to eat.

**THE GLANDS**
Pores that hold the salamander's poison can be found across its back and on the sides of its head.

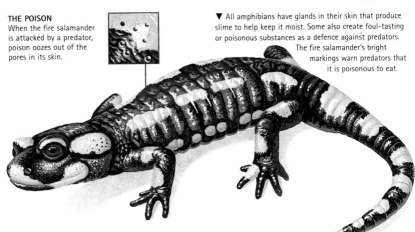

## SALAMANDERS AND CAECILIANS

Newts and salamanders (urodelans) have short limbs and long tails. Salamanders in Europe and North America that spend long periods in water are called newts. Most salamanders breathe with lungs and through their skin, although some have no lungs. Caecilians (apodans) are the third and smallest group of amphibians. They are worm-like, with blunt snouts for tunnelling, tiny eyes and wide mouths. They hunt mainly at night.

▼ The spectacled salamander has a bright red tail that it curls along its back when alarmed.

## THE AMPHIBIAN LIFE–CYCLE

When frogs mate, the male usually sits on the female's back for up to three days. As soon as the female lays her eggs in the water, the male releases sperm to fertilize them. The eggs hatch into tadpoles, which eventually metamorphose (change) into froglets (young frogs) and leave the water for life on land.

**1** The female frog lays her eggs, or spawn, in large masses in a pond or stream. The eggs are protected by a special jelly.

**2** The larvae, or tadpoles, develop inside the eggs. About a week later, the tadpoles hatch out and attach themselves to plants.

**3** The tadpoles breathe through feathery gills and start to swim at about three days old. They feed on waterweeds and algae in the water.

**4** The tadpoles slowly turn into frogs, developing limbs and lungs so that they can live on land. Their tails are absorbed into their bodies.

**5** Fully-grown, the young frogs leave the water. They feed on small insects and will not reproduce themselves until they are a year old.

### SEE ALSO

Animal, Frog and toad, Hibernation

# ANIMAL

**Animals are multi-cellular living creatures that can move, eat food, sense their surroundings and reproduce, usually by mating with a partner.**

The rotifer is one of the smallest animals – seen only through a microscope.

The octopus is a type of mollusc, a group that also includes snails and squid.

The angel fish is just one of 20,000 different species of fish.

The shield bug belongs to the largest group – insects, with over a million species.

The peacock is one of 9,000 species of bird, most of which can fly.

The rabbit is a mammal. Its young are fed on milk produced by the mother.

More than a million kinds of animal live on Earth, and many more are discovered each year. Every animal is unique, but there are common features that set creatures in the animal kingdom apart from other living beings such as plants, fungi and single-celled organisms.

## THE MATING GAME

Like all living creatures, animals must reproduce. Most do this by mating with a partner. It is usually the female that chooses a mate, so many males are brightly coloured or use elaborate courtship rituals to lure a suitable partner to them.

## BILLIONS OF TINY CELLS

All adult animals are multi-cellular, which means they are made up of more than one cell. Some animals, such as rotifers and hydras (aquatic animals), have just a few dozen cells, but large animals, such as humans, are much more complex and can have up to 50 billion cells.

▲ The bushbaby is a nocturnal animal, so it comes out at night to feed. Huge, round eyes, a good sense of smell and an excellent sense of hearing are essential for hunting prey at night.

## FOOD FOR LIVING

Unlike plants, animals cannot make their own food – they must eat ready-made plant or animal food. Most have some sort of mouth, but the way in which the food is broken down inside their body varies. Birds have no teeth, so the food is ground up by stones in their stomach. Snakes swallow prey alive and whole, digesting it slowly with strong juices. The tapeworm has no mouth, but lives in another animal's intestines, soaking up digested food through its skin.

## MOTHERLY LOVE

Many animals go to great lengths to keep their babies alive. For example, the female scorpion, best known for her sting, is a very caring mother. She carries her newborn young on her back for up to 12 days, until they can fend for themselves.

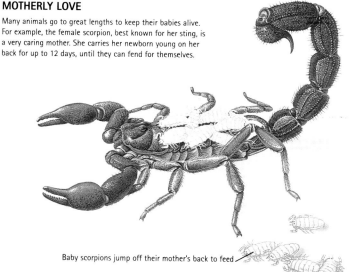

Baby scorpions jump off their mother's back to feed

## NERVES AND SENSES

All animals sense their surroundings with a set of nerves and sense organs that are adapted to suit the way they live. For example, many night hunters have whiskers to find their way in the dark, and some snakes have infra-red sensors to 'see' the body heat of their prey. Sharks can smell blood in the water many kilometres away and home in on it accurately, while migrating animals, such as grey whales, have an extra sense that allows them to travel great distances without getting lost.

## ON THE MOVE

All animals, from the slowest snail to the fastest gazelle, move, usually by using an efficient set of muscles. The way they move varies: some crawl or walk, some slither, while others hop or run – in the case of crabs, sideways. Even a drifting jellyfish pulsates to move itself up or down in the water. This ability to move has allowed some species to spread all over the world. Some animals, such as sponges and corals, can only move when young, but remain in one place as adults. ▶

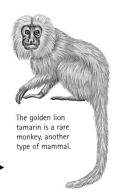

The golden lion tamarin is a rare monkey, another type of mammal.

## THE FASTEST ANIMAL

Predatory animals use many methods to catch their food. Some use stealth, others use camouflage, but the cheetah's strategy is speed. It is the fastest animal on four legs, reaching speeds of 110km/h in mid-chase. Its favourite food is the young antelope that graze on the African savanna. But a cheetah's stamina is poor – if it does not catch the antelope in the first few hundred metres, the prey usually gets away.

1 The cheetah creeps forward slowly, getting as close as possible to its victim before breaking into a high-speed sprint.

2 The cheetah bounds forward, covering several metres in each leap. Its claws do not retract, giving it extra grip on the ground.

3 The antelope suddenly changes direction to confuse the cheetah, but the cat's flexible back allows it to turn sharply.

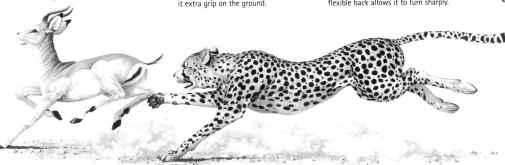

4 The gap closes. The cheetah swipes with strong paws at the antelope's legs to knock it off balance and bring it down, before killing it with a bite.

## A QUESTION OF CLASS

Zoologists divide the animal kingdom into about 30 major groups, or phyla (the largest of which are shown in this chart). Each group, or phylum, can be further divided into sub-phyla, classes (shown), then orders, families, genuses and species (not shown). Animals from different species cannot breed together, except in rare circumstances.

## INVERTEBRATES
### (animals without backbones)

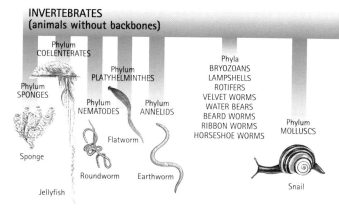

Phylum COELENTERATES

Phylum PLATYHELMINTHES

Phylum SPONGES

Phylum NEMATODES

Phylum ANNELIDS

Phyla
BRYOZOANS
LAMPSHELLS
ROTIFERS
VELVET WORMS
WATER BEARS
BEARD WORMS
RIBBON WORMS
HORSESHOE WORMS

Phylum MOLLUSCS

Sponge

Flatworm

Jellyfish

Roundworm

Earthworm

Snail

▲ The marbled polecat belongs to a family of carnivores (meat-eating mammals) that includes weasels, badgers, otters and skunks. All of these animals have short legs and long, sinuous bodies.

### FAMILY GATHERINGS

Zoologists classify, or group, animals by their common features. For example, all insects have six legs, all birds have feathers, and all mammal mothers feed their young on milk from their own bodies. The grouping of animals in this way is known as taxonomy. It helps zoologists to work out when animals first appeared on Earth, how they have changed over time, and which creatures are closely related.

### WITH BACKBONES

All animals can be divided into two main groups: those with backbones, called vertebrates, and those without backbones, called

invertebrates. Vertebrates include fish, amphibians, reptiles, birds and mammals. All other animals are invertebrates.

### THE MYSTERIOUS BARNACLE

It can be difficult for zoologists to tell if some creatures are animals at all. For example, an acorn barnacle attached to a rock on the seashore does not even look alive, let alone animal-like. By studying its life-cycle, zoologists discovered that before the barnacle attaches itself to a rock, it looks like a young prawn. This proved that barnacles are crustaceans, along with crabs and lobsters.

▲ Acorn barnacles

### WHO IS RELATED TO WHOM?

Scientists study the genetic make-up of animals compared to other animals to reveal who is related to whom. For many years zoologists argued over whether red pandas were related to bears, raccoons or

► The anteater is an edentate. This is an order of mammal with few or no teeth. Other members of the group include sloths, which are herbivores (plant-eaters) and armadillos. The anteater is an insectivore (insect-eater), living solely on ants and termites, which it sniffs out with its snout and licks up with its long, sticky tongue. Its powerful front claws are used for digging.

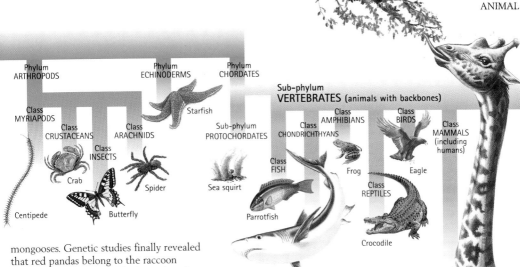

Phylum
ARTHROPODS

Phylum
ECHINODERMS

Phylum
CHORDATES

Sub-phylum
VERTEBRATES (animals with backbones)

Class
MYRIAPODS

Starfish

Sub-phylum
PROTOCHORDATES

Class
AMPHIBIANS

Class
BIRDS

Class
MAMMALS
(including
humans)

Class
CRUSTACEANS

Class
ARACHNIDS

Class
CHONDRICHTHYANS

Class
INSECTS

Crab

Class
FISH

Frog

Eagle

Spider

Sea squirt

Class
REPTILES

Centipede

Butterfly

Parrotfish

Crocodile

Great white shark

mongooses. Genetic studies finally revealed
that red pandas belong to the raccoon
family. In another study, the kiwi, thought
to be one species of bird, was shown to
have two species – they look very similar,
but cannot breed together.

## DEEP-SEA TREASURES
In the 1970s, when scientists sent deep-sea
equipment down to new depths, over 200
new animal types were discovered living
around deep-sea hydrothermal vents (jets
of hot, mineral-rich water spurting out
from the ocean floor). Transparent fish,
2m-long tube worms, plate-sized clams
and blind white crabs were among the
amazing finds.

## SPECIES UNDER THREAT
Many animals in the world are now rare or
nearly extinct. Once an animal species has

died out, it is lost forever, which is
why zoos have breeding programmes
for threatened species. There may be
more than five million animal species
still waiting to be discovered by
science. These too are under threat
as many of the natural areas of the
world, especially the coral reefs
and tropical rainforests, are being
destroyed or polluted by people.

▶ The giraffe is the tallest animal. It is a mammal
and can grow up to 5.5m tall. It lives in Africa and
eats thorny acacia leaves, which it strips from the
branches with its 50cm-long tongue.

▲ Some animals, called detritivores, help to recycle
other animals' waste products. The dung beetle eats
animal dung. Some species eat the dung where they
find it, while others dig a hole and bury it to eat later.

### AMAZING ANIMAL FACTS

• Insects are the most numerous animals on
Earth. It is estimated that for every human
there are 200 million insects

• The largest animal to have lived on Earth
is the blue whale. Belonging to the order of
mammals called cetaceans, blue whales can
grow to over 30m in length

• The fastest-moving animal is the peregrine
falcon, which can swoop at speeds of up to
350km/h

• Unlike most animals, the sponge can regrow
its entire body from a tiny fragment of itself

• The giant squid has the largest eye of any
animal ever to have lived. It is about 40cm in
diameter, or ten times the size of a human eye

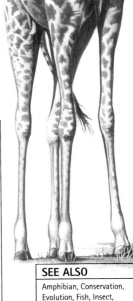

### SEE ALSO
Amphibian, Conservation,
Evolution, Fish, Insect,
Mammal, Micro-organism,
Reptile, Zoology

# ANTARCTICA

Antarctica is the fifth largest continent. It surrounds the South Pole and 98 per cent of it lies buried beneath a thick sheet of ice.

▲ Norwegian explorer Roald Amundsen was first to reach the South Pole on December 14, 1911.

## KEY FACTS

- **Area:** 14,000,000 sq km
- **Population:** no permanent population
- **Number of countries:** none, although some countries claim sections of the continent
- **Highest point:** Vinson Massif (4,897m)
- **Largest ice shelf:** Ross ice shelf (192,000–208,000 sq km)
- **Position of South Pole:** 1,235km from the nearest coastline

Only a few mountains and barren, rocky areas show above the ice that hides Antarctica. The thickness of the polar ice sheet makes Antarctica the highest continent. It is also the windiest continent and largely a frozen desert, with snowfall near the Pole equivalent to less than 150mm of water per year. The world's coldest air temperature, –89.2°C, was recorded there, at Vostok scientific station.

## FIRE AND ICE

A string of mountains cuts across the icy mass. On their eastern side, near the coast, the ice sheet reaches depths of 4,800m. Ross Island, to the west, holds the active volcano, Mount Erebus. Ice flows down to the coast as glaciers and spreads out over the sea, creating huge ice shelves. When the ice becomes too heavy, parts of it break away to form enormous, flat-topped icebergs up to 60m high and many kilometres long.

## FUR AND FEATHERS

Antarctica has few land animals because, even in summer, most of the continent is covered with ice. The animals live mainly in the air or sea and have thick fur,

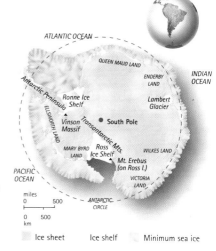

Ice sheet    Ice shelf    Minimum sea ice

◀ Two emperor penguins with their chick. To withstand the winter cold, emperors have very dense feathers and large fat reserves. They also huddle together in groups of up to 5,000 birds to keep warm.

feathers or blubber (fat) to keep them warm. The ocean is home to many types of krill (tiny shrimp-like creatures), squid, fish, seals, whales and eight types of penguin. Antarctic birds include the predatory skua and large-winged albatross.

## STUDIES ON ICE

Antarctica has a temporary population of up to 10,000 scientists from 18 countries. Their interests vary from space research to microbiology, and all must abide by the Antarctic Treaty. This agreement bans the mining of valuable mineral resources buried beneath the ice, and prevents any military or industrial activities on the continent. Up to 10,000 tourists also visit Antarctica each year during the summer.

◀ Icebergs break away from the ice shelves that surround Antarctica. The ice builds up in layers over thousands of years.

## SEE ALSO

Animal, Bird, Climate, Conservation, Glacier, Magnetism

# ARCTIC

**The Arctic is the area within the Arctic Circle – an imaginary line around the northern part of the globe with the North Pole at its centre.**

The Arctic is made up of the frozen Arctic Ocean, the surrounding seas and small islands, and the northern parts of Canada, Alaska, Russia, Finland, Sweden, Norway and Greenland.

## LAND OF THE MIDNIGHT SUN

Temperatures creep above freezing point for only about four months of the year. There are some days during the summer when areas near the North Pole are in constant daylight because the Sun never sets. This is why the Arctic is sometimes known as the Land of the Midnight Sun.

## TUNDRA LIFE

Treeless plains, or tundra, cover the land. In the summer, these plains are home to animals such as reindeer, lemmings, musk ox and Arctic hares, which graze on scrubby plants and shrubs. Migratory birds, such as the Arctic tern, return from winter homes to breed in the short warm season.

▲ Arctic hares live on the tundra. In summer, their fur is brown. They grow a new white coat in winter.

## THE DARK OF WINTER

Wintertime in the Arctic is cold, dark and long. For a short time the Sun does not come above the horizon at all. The ocean is frozen and the tundra snow-covered, with only a few mosses and lichens growing. Most animals and birds migrate south until summer returns. Polar bears thrive in these harsh conditions, hunting seals and catching fish in the icy water.

miles
0    500

0    500
km

BERING SEA

ALASKA (U.S.A.)

CANADA

ARCTIC CIRCLE

ARCTIC OCEAN

Ellesmere Island • North Pole

Baffin Island

Novaya Zemlya

GREENLAND (DENMARK)

BARENTS SEA

ICELAND

NORWAY SWEDEN FINLAND

RUSSIA

▼ An aeroplane arrives with supplies for the store at Savissivik, Greenland. Aircraft are a vital link for scattered settlements around the Arctic.

## PEOPLE IN THE ARCTIC

A number of different peoples live in the Arctic, including the Inuit of Greenland, Canada and northeast Asia, and the Sami (Lapps) of Scandinavia. Those on the coast live by hunting and fishing. Those living inland hunt wild caribou or, like the Nenet tribe from Siberia in northern Russia (below), herd reindeer for a living.

**SEE ALSO**

Asia, Canada, Climate, Magnetism, Native Americans, North America, Ocean and sea, Russia and the Baltic States, Scandinavia, USA

# ASIA

Asia is the world's largest continent. It covers 30 per cent of the Earth's land area and has a bigger population than all the other continents put together.

## KEY FACTS

- **Area:** 31,764,000 sq km
- **Population:** 3,583,000,000
- **Number of countries:** 48
- **Largest country:** Russia, 75% of which is in Asia
- **Smallest country:** Maldives (298 sq km)
- **Highest point:** Mount Everest (8,848m)
- **Largest lake:** Caspian Sea (371,800 sq km)
- **Longest river:** Chang (Yangtze) (6,300km)

The immense size of Asia means it has a huge variety of environments and weather conditions. Its natural habitats include dense tropical forests, fertile plains, Arctic regions and deserts – both hot and cold. The world's ten highest mountains are found in Asia, as well as the lowest point on land: the shores of the Dead Sea, at 392m below sea level.

### NATURAL BORDERS
Asia is separated from Europe by the Ural Mountains in the northwest and from North America by the Bering Strait, a strip of water only 88km wide, in the northeast. The Red Sea and the Suez Canal divide Asia from Africa in the southwest.

### EXTREMES OF TEMPERATURE
Northern Asia is cold and often desolate, with few plants to support people or animals. Noril'sk in northern Russia is the coldest city in the world with average temperatures of –10.9°C. By contrast, Tirunelveli in India, southern Asia, has average temperatures of 29°C.

▲ A dragon boat festival. At the end of the race, the winning team raises its oars. Boats are an important means of transport along Asia's wide rivers.

### WET AND DRY
Ten of the worst floods of the 20th century have occurred in Asia – in China, Bangladesh and India. The monsoon winds from the Indian Ocean bring heavy rain to much of southern and eastern Asia. Vast areas of central Asia, on the other hand, have very little rain, and deserts such as the Gobi dominate the landscape.

### DANGER ZONE
Because Asia lies on faults in the Earth's crust, many Asian countries, especially Japan, have experienced the century's worst earthquakes. The coasts of eastern and Southeast Asia are also prone to typhoons – violent storms that come from the China Sea.

▲ The snow leopard is found in some of the most remote areas of central Asia. Its pale, spotted coat allows it to blend in with its surroundings.

▶ The yak is used in the mountainous regions of Tibet (a region of China since 1950) as a source of food, milk and clothing, and for carrying goods.

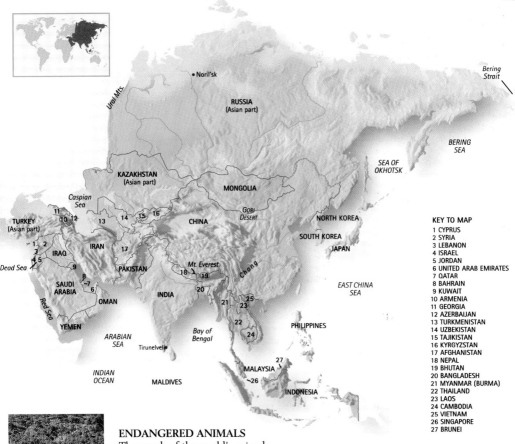

Noril'sk

RUSSIA
(Asian part)

Bering
Strait

BERING
SEA

SEA OF
OKHOTSK

KAZAKHSTAN
(Asian part)

MONGOLIA

Caspian
Sea

GOBI
DESERT

NORTH KOREA

SOUTH KOREA

JAPAN

TURKEY
(Asian part)

11
10  12
13
14   15  16

CHINA

Ural Mts.

1  2
3
4 5
IRAQ
8  7
6

IRAN  17

Dead Sea

9

PAKISTAN

Mt. Everest

18    19

20

INDIA

Chang

21    25
23

22

24

EAST CHINA
SEA

PHILIPPINES

SAUDI
ARABIA

OMAN

YEMEN

Red Sea

ARABIAN
SEA        Tirunelveli

Bay of
Bengal

27

INDIAN
OCEAN

MALDIVES

MALAYSIA

26

INDONESIA

**KEY TO MAP**
1 CYPRUS
2 SYRIA
3 LEBANON
4 ISRAEL
5 JORDAN
6 UNITED ARAB EMIRATES
7 QATAR
8 BAHRAIN
9 KUWAIT
10 ARMENIA
11 GEORGIA
12 AZERBAIJAN
13 TURKMENISTAN
14 UZBEKISTAN
15 TAJIKISTAN
16 KYRGYZSTAN
17 AFGHANISTAN
18 NEPAL
19 BHUTAN
20 BANGLADESH
21 MYANMAR (BURMA)
22 THAILAND
23 LAOS
24 CAMBODIA
25 VIETNAM
26 SINGAPORE
27 BRUNEI

## ENDANGERED ANIMALS

Thousands of the world's animal species live in Asia, especially in the tropical south and southeast. But people clearing the land for farming and hunting animals for their skins have put several species in danger of extinction, including the giant panda, the orang-utan, the tiger and the snow leopard.

## THE LAND PROVIDES

Rice is the main crop of warm, wet southern Asia, while wheat, barley and millet grow in the colder, drier north. Spices such as pepper and cloves have been a source of wealth for India, Sri Lanka and Indonesia for centuries. Other major crops include tea, tobacco, cotton, sugar, coffee, cocoa, jute and fruits. Forests cover a third of Russia's land in Asia, and 20 per cent of the rest of the continent.

N

miles
0        500

0        500
km

## NATURAL RESOURCES

Raw materials are among Asia's most important exports. Asia provides more than half of the world's tin. Coal, gas, aluminium and other metals needed for manufacturing are exported worldwide. The continent includes the five countries with the largest oil reserves: Saudi Arabia, Iraq, Kuwait, the United Arab Emirates and Iran.

## WAY OF LIFE

In the desert areas of Saudi Arabia and Iran, and the steppes (dry, grassy, treeless plains) of Mongolia and neighbouring ▶

▲ Terraces are cut in the hillsides in the Philippines to provide land for growing rice and other crops.

▲ Chinese workers produce many goods, including salt (above). China is also the world's largest rice producer.

▲ Mongolians have traditionally survived off the infertile land of central Asia by herding cattle. Bactrian (two-humped) camels are used as beasts of burden.

▼ San'a, the capital of Yemen, is one of the most beautiful Islamic cities. Handmade goods, such as cloth, leatherware, glassware and pottery, are sold in its bazaars.

countries, there are many nomadic (wandering) tribes. These nomads live by herding camels, goats, sheep and horses. Farming is the most common occupation for the people of many Asian countries, including China, India and Indonesia.

## CROWDED CITIES
In Asia, only one person in five lives in a city, compared to three out of four in Europe and the USA. However, some Asian cities, such as Tokyo, Calcutta and Bangkok, house populations that are among the largest in the world.

## BIG BUSINESS
Industry is a major employer in countries such as Japan and South Korea, and it is becoming increasingly important in Thailand and Malaysia. Other areas such as Singapore and Hong Kong have become important financial centres, while fishing and forestry, as well as manufacturing, are important industries in many Asian countries. Japan is the

world's largest manufacturer of cars and televisions, and shipbuilding is important in Japan. China has one of the world's fastest-growing economies.

## CRADLE OF CIVILIZATION
Asia was the birthplace of some of the world's most ancient civilizations, including Mesopotamia (in modern-day Iraq), China, and the Indus Valley (in modern-day Pakistan). These areas had large cities and were ruled by a small governing class of priests, officials and warriors. Their rich culture attracted both trade and conquering armies.

▲ Followers of Buddhism worship outside a temple in Yangon (Rangoon), the capital of Myanmar (Burma). About 85 per cent of Myanmar's population are Buddhist.

## GAINING INDEPENDENCE

Colonial rule continued until the 20th century, when many of the colonies won their freedom, and created independent nations such as India and Jordan. In other countries, such as the former Soviet Union and China, communism took a firm hold. Since the break-up of the Soviet Union in 1991, republics such as Kazakhstan and Tajikistan have become independent nations once more. New industries have been established, and continued and larger investment by governments has helped to improve the economies of many of the Asian countries.

## MULTI-RELIGIOUS SOCIETY

Asia was where the world's major religions had their roots. Buddhism and Hinduism were spread from India by merchants and missionaries. Islam was carried from Asia to Europe and Africa by conquering armies such as the Mongols in the 12th century. Judaism and Christianity were exported from Asia as well as silk and spices during the Roman period. Today, these five religions still thrive in Asia, although Hinduism has the most followers.

## GLITTERING EMPIRES

By the 16th century, the Ottoman Empire in the Middle East, the Safavid Empire in Iran, the Mogul Empire in India and the Ming Empire in China were the richest and most powerful states in the world. They had grown rich on exports such as silk, spices, ceramics and jewels. But these riches attracted European explorers.

▲ Trade routes, known as the Silk Road, were used to carry goods between Asia and Europe from 1000BC until the 1400s. Luxury items, such as the Ming vase shown here, as well as silks and spices, were carried through Pakistan, Tajikistan, Uzbekistan and Kazakhstan to the Middle East, from where they were taken by boat to Europe.

## COLONIAL RULE

From the beginning of the 19th century, much of Asia was colonized by European powers, whose steamships and modern weapons gave them superior mobility and firepower. The colonists transformed large areas of Asia into plantations for growing tea, coffee, cotton and rubber which they then exported for sale in Europe.

▲ The people of Uzbekistan have their own traditions and customs with distinctive national dress and dances.

## SEE ALSO

China, Communism, Earthquake, Indian subcontinent, Japan, Middle East, Religion, Russia and the Baltic States

# ASTRONOMY

**Astronomy is the scientific study of objects in space, such as planets, stars, comets and black holes, using equipment such as telescopes and space probes.**

Nicolaus Copernicus discovered that the planets orbit the Sun.

Johannes Kepler claimed that the planets move in elliptical (oval) orbits.

Galileo Galilei was the first astronomer to use a telescope.

Early civilizations watched the stars and planets to predict the coming of the seasons. But it was the Ancient Greeks who first studied them as a science. The word astronomy comes from two Greek words meaning 'star laws'.

## COPERNICUS TO EINSTEIN
Modern astronomy began with Nicolaus Copernicus, who realized that the Sun, not the Earth, was at the centre of our solar system. His ideas were published in 1543, the year he died. When Galileo Galilei used his newly invented telescope in 1610, he helped prove those ideas. In 1667, Isaac Newton put forward his laws of gravity, which explained how objects move in

▲ Our galaxy seen through a telescope.
▶ An X-ray picture of our galaxy. The central red and yellow area may be a black hole.

space, and Albert Einstein published a new theory of gravity in 1915, which led to ideas such as black holes and the Big Bang.

## SIGNALS TO THE PLANETS
Today's astronomers can calculate Earth's distance from other planets in our solar system by bouncing radar signals off the planets' surfaces and timing how long they take to return to Earth. The distance to faraway stars can be worked out from their brightness and by using a method called parallax (see diagram far right).

Isaac Newton described how gravity affects cosmic objects.

## THE KECK OBSERVATORY
Observatories are special buildings used to study the skies. The Keck in Hawaii, USA is one of the highest in the world. At the top of an extinct volcano, it is 4,200m above sea level and has two telescopes in twinned domes that track the stars like binoculars.

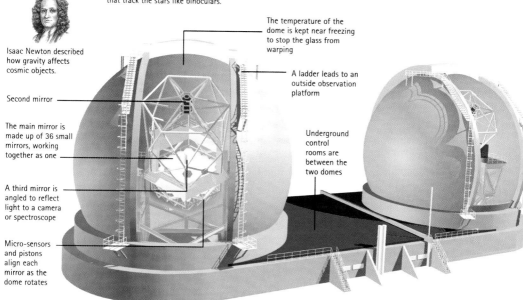

The temperature of the dome is kept near freezing to stop the glass from warping

A ladder leads to an outside observation platform

Second mirror

The main mirror is made up of 36 small mirrors, working together as one

A third mirror is angled to reflect light to a camera or spectroscope

Micro-sensors and pistons align each mirror as the dome rotates

Underground control rooms are between the two domes

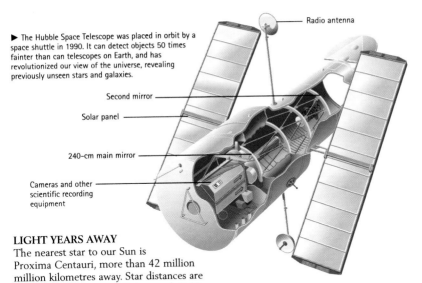

Radio antenna

▶ The Hubble Space Telescope was placed in orbit by a space shuttle in 1990. It can detect objects 50 times fainter than can telescopes on Earth, and has revolutionized our view of the universe, revealing previously unseen stars and galaxies.

Second mirror

Solar panel

240-cm main mirror

Cameras and other scientific recording equipment

Edmond Halley predicted that the comet of 1682 would return in 1758.

Albert Einstein created important theories about space and time.

## LIGHT YEARS AWAY

The nearest star to our Sun is Proxima Centauri, more than 42 million million kilometres away. Star distances are measured in light years (light travels 9.46 million million kilometres in one year). Proxima Centauri is 4.26 light years away, which means its light takes four years and three months to reach Earth.

## SECRETS OF STARLIGHT

The temperature and chemical make-up of objects in space are revealed by the radiation that they give off. This radiation includes light, radio waves, microwaves, infrared, ultraviolet, X-rays and gamma rays. Astronomers use optical and radio telescopes as well as spectroscopes (radiation detectors), set up in observatories, to study cosmic radiation.

## PLANETARY PROBES

Sending unmanned spacecraft to the planets is now the most technically challenging area of astronomy. The spacecraft are launched aboard rockets and either land on the planet or send

down a probe that transmits information back to Earth. In 1997, a probe entered Jupiter's clouds and, in the same year, the first remote-controlled, robotic probe landed and roamed around on the surface of Mars. Saturn and her moons will be visited in 2004 by the *Cassini* spacecraft. It will orbit the planet for four years and release a probe into the dense atmosphere of Saturn's largest moon, Titan.

◀ In 1997, a probe from the *Galileo* spacecraft plunged into Jupiter's gas clouds. It sent back photographs and chemical data to Earth for over an hour before being destroyed.

## KEY DATES

**3000BC** First known records of astronomy made by the Babylonians

**125BC** Hipparchus groups the stars according to their brightness

**1543** Nicolaus Copernicus proposes that the Earth orbits the Sun

**1600** Johannes Kepler discovers that the planets orbit the Sun in ellipses

**1781** William Herschel discovers Uranus

**1846** Neptune discovered

**1908** Giant and dwarf stars first noted

**1930** Clyde Tombaugh discovers Pluto

**1938** Radio waves from space detected

**1955** 76-m radio telescope built at Jodrell Bank, England

**1997** Probe enters Jupiter's atmosphere to collect data;the *Sojourner* probe lands on Mars

## PARALLAX

The distances of nearby stars can be calculated by plotting their positions at different times of the year, and then applying a simple geometric equation. The bigger the parallax angle, the closer the star.

Where the star seems to be on January 1

Where the star seems to be on July 1

Real position of star

Parallax angle

Sun

Position of Earth on July 1

Position of Earth on January 1

## SEE ALSO

Black hole, Galaxy, Gravity, Solar system, Space exploration

# ATMOSPHERE

**The atmosphere is an envelope of gases surrounding the Earth. It shields us from the Sun and contains the air we breathe. Without it life would not exist.**

▲ In the atmosphere above the Arctic and Antarctic, colliding particles from the Sun create flickering bands of light known as auroras.

The gases that form the atmosphere are held in place around the Earth by gravity. They can be divided into four layers: the troposphere, stratosphere, ionosphere and exosphere. Each contains a mixture of gases, which gets thinner the farther away the layer is from the Earth.

## THE WEATHER ZONE
The lowest and densest layer is the troposphere, which extends about 13km above the Earth's surface. It contains 78 per cent nitrogen, 20 per cent oxygen and small amounts of other gases, and is where life exists, clouds form and where most of Earth's weather occurs.

## OZONE LAYER
Above the troposphere, up to about 50km, is the stratosphere. This is where jet planes usually fly, and near its top is the ozone layer, which absorbs most of the Sun's harmful ultraviolet radiation.

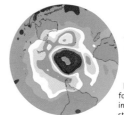

◄ A false-colour satellite image of the atmosphere above Antarctica, showing the hole in the ozone layer (centre). The hole forms each spring, mixing in with the rest of the stratosphere in summer.

The holes developing in the ozone layer have been linked to industrial chemicals such as the CFCs that were used in aerosol spray cans, fire extinguishers and fridges.

## HIGH-ENERGY RAYS
Above the stratosphere is the ionosphere. In this layer, the Sun's rays break up some gas atoms into charged particles, or ions. Temperatures in the upper ionosphere (which is called the thermosphere) can reach 2,000°C.

## MERGING INTO SPACE
Above 500km the ionosphere merges into the exosphere, which stretches away into space to a height of several thousand kilometres. Any gas molecules found here are on their way out towards space.

## EVOLVING ATMOSPHERE
The atmosphere is constantly evolving. At first it was made up of high levels of carbon dioxide. Oxygen appeared about 1,800 million years ago, but advanced life was possible only after the ozone layer formed.

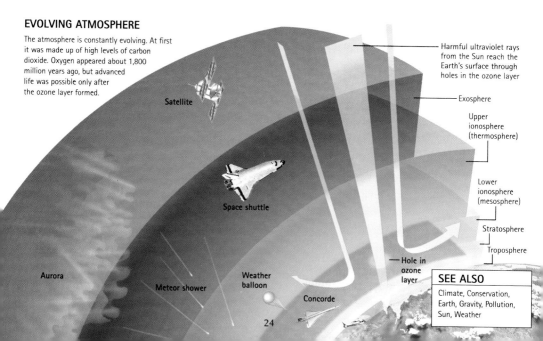

Harmful ultraviolet rays from the Sun reach the Earth's surface through holes in the ozone layer

Exosphere

Upper ionosphere (thermosphere)

Lower ionosphere (mesosphere)

Stratosphere

Troposphere

Satellite

Space shuttle

Aurora

Meteor shower

Weather balloon

Concorde

Hole in ozone layer

### SEE ALSO
Climate, Conservation, Earth, Gravity, Pollution, Sun, Weather

# ATOM AND MOLECULE

**Atoms are the basic building blocks of everything around us, from plants and animals to planets and stars. A molecule is two or more atoms joined together.**

Crystals form regular shapes as their atoms are arranged in fixed patterns.

Pencil 'lead' is soft because its atoms slide easily over each other.

Diamonds are very hard because their atoms are in a rigid framework.

DNA, the basis of life, consists of two coiled strands of molecules.

Every substance in the universe is made of atoms. An atom is the smallest part of any substance that can exist on its own – it is less than ten billionths of a metre in diameter. The full-stop at the end of this sentence contains billions of atoms.

## EMPTY SPACE

Most of an atom is made up of empty space, but at its centre is a tiny nucleus. If an atom were scaled up to the size of a football pitch, the nucleus would be no bigger than a peppercorn.

## THE NUCLEUS

The nucleus is the densest part of the atom and usually contains an equal amount of smaller, 'sub-atomic' particles called protons and neutrons. Electrons are even lighter sub-atomic particles that whiz round the nucleus in all different directions at the speed of light.

▶ A polymer is a compound with large molecules made from thousands of smaller molecules joined together in a long chain. Rubber and plastic are polymers.

## FORMING BONDS

Some substances consist of molecules that are formed from only one type of atom, and these are called elements. But when different types of atoms join to make molecules, they form compounds. A water molecule is a compound of one oxygen atom and two hydrogen atoms.

## SOLID, LIQUID OR GAS

Water is a liquid, which means its molecules can move around (flow), whereas the molecules in a solid such as wood are fixed together in a definite pattern. Gas molecules buzz around randomly, filling all the available space.

### INSIDE AN ATOM

The nucleus of every atom consists of particles called protons and neutrons (except for the hydrogen atom, which has no neutrons). Other particles, called electrons, flit around the nucleus in a random motion, making billions of trips in a millionth of a second.

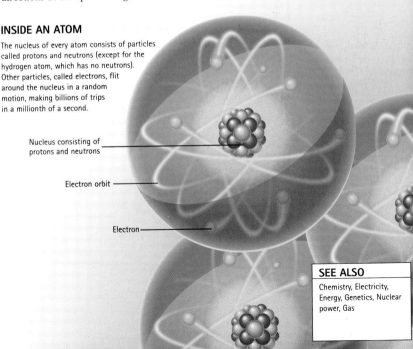

Nucleus consisting of protons and neutrons

Electron orbit

Electron

## SEE ALSO

Chemistry, Electricity, Energy, Genetics, Nuclear power, Gas

# AUSTRALIA

Australia is the sixth largest country in the world, covering about four per cent of the Earth's surface. It is also the smallest, flattest and driest continent.

**Area:** 7,741,220 sq km
**Population:** 18,751,000
**Capital:** Canberra
**Language:** English
**Currency:** Australian dollar

## KEY FACTS

• **Number of states:** six (Western Australia, South Australia, Queensland, New South Wales, Victoria and Tasmania)

• **Number of territories:** two (Northern Territory and the Australian Capital Territory)

• **Highest point:** Mount Kosciuszko (2,228m)

• **Longest permanent river:** Murray (2,589km)

• **Largest Lake:** Eyre (9,583 sq km)

Australia is often referred to as Down Under because it lies below the Equator, in the Earth's Southern Hemisphere. It is both a country and a continent.

### THE GREAT DIVIDING RANGE
With the exception of a few mountain ranges, Australia is low and flat. The mountains of the Great Dividing Range run down the coast of Queensland and New South Wales. Fertile plateaux (flat areas of land high above sea level) lie along the top, where dense forests once grew. Today, many of the forests have been cleared for cities and farms.

### SUNSHINE AND MONSOONS
The weather is cool and wet in the southernmost parts of the country, but most of Australia is hot or warm all year round. There are just two seasons in the far north: wet and dry. The wet season, from November to April, is hot and humid, with monsoon rains that turn huge areas of land into lakes.

▲ Rainforests on the northeast coast of Queensland, where the climate is wettest, are now National Parks.

### THE OUTBACK
The country's vast central region, which the Australians call the Outback, is hot and dry and mostly a desert – the second largest in the world. The temperature at Alice Springs, in central Australia, is often over 38°C. The rest of the interior is made up of land covered in coarse grass, low shrubs and trees, and provides grazing for cattle and sheep.

### LIFE-BRINGING WATER
The many billabongs (waterholes) and rivers in the Outback are dry most of the year, and the parched plants sometimes catch fire. There are occasional heavy rains, however, when the buried seeds of flowering plants come to life and the rivers fill with water. The Australian lung

▼ Uluru (Ayers Rock) is a huge outcrop of sandstone right in the middle of Australia sacred to the Aborigines.

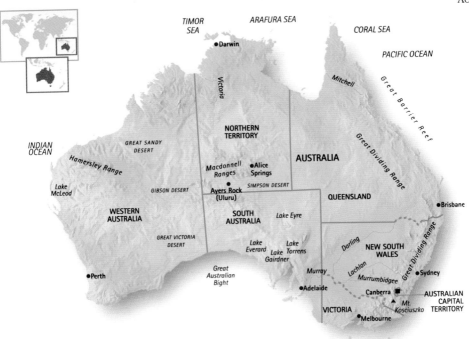

TIMOR SEA
ARAFURA SEA
CORAL SEA
PACIFIC OCEAN
•Darwin
Victoria
Mitchell
Great Barrier Reef
INDIAN OCEAN
GREAT SANDY DESERT
NORTHERN TERRITORY
AUSTRALIA
Hamersley Range
Macdonnell Ranges
•Alice Springs
Great Dividing Range
Lake McLeod
GIBSON DESERT
Ayers Rock (Uluru)
SIMPSON DESERT
QUEENSLAND
•Brisbane
WESTERN AUSTRALIA
SOUTH AUSTRALIA
Lake Eyre
GREAT VICTORIA DESERT
Lake Everard
Lake Torrens
Lake Gairdner
Darling
NEW SOUTH WALES
Great Dividing Range
•Perth
Great Australian Bight
Murray
Lachlan
Murrumbidgee
•Sydney
•Adelaide
Canberra
AUSTRALIAN CAPITAL TERRITORY
VICTORIA
Mt. Kosciuszko
•Melbourne
TASMAN SEA
TASMANIA
•Hobart

miles
0 — 500
0 — 500
km
N

fish has adapted to this changing climate by developing both gills and lungs.

## A LAND ON ITS OWN

Australia has been isolated from any other land mass since about 65 million years ago, when it split from Antarctica. About 130 million years ago, Australia and Antarctica were both part of a great southern continent. Many species of animal that are unique to Australia evolved during this time. These include marsupials (pouched mammals), such as kangaroos, koalas and wombats, as well as two unusual egg-laying mammals, the duckbilled platypus and the echidna (also known as the spiny anteater).

## AUSTRALIA'S EXPORTS

Australia's farms produce wheat, beef, mutton and wool, as well as wine made from grapes grown in the south. Australia is rich in minerals, such as coal, gold, iron ore, bauxite (aluminium ore), uranium, diamonds and opals. Minerals and farm products are the country's main exports, with manufactured goods representing about 20 per cent. Australia's factories ▶

▲ The kookaburra is often seen in parks and gardens. Its strange call, like a chuckling laugh, led to the name 'laughing jackass'.

◀ The Great Barrier Reef is a chain of more than 2,500 small reefs and coral islands that stretch for 2,010km along the northeast coast.

▲ New South Wales and Western Australia produce more than half of Australia's wool.

▼ Sydney is Australia's oldest and largest city, with a population of about 3,770,000. The city is built around a huge natural bay, jutting out into which is the world-famous Sydney Opera House.

produce goods such as motor vehicles, textiles, chemicals and household goods. Australia also has a film industry, which is rapidly expanding.

## SHEEP STATIONS

Most of the Outback is too dry to grow crops, but vast sheep farms, called sheep stations, cover thousands of hectares. Huge beef cattle ranches are known as cattle runs, a few of which are the size of England. The cattle live and breed freely until it is time for market, when the farmer rounds them up, often with a helicopter.

## SCHOOL ON THE AIRWAVES

People living on sheep stations and cattle runs are often hundreds of kilometres from the nearest town. They must rely on flying doctors, who arrive by light aircraft, for medical help. Children in the Outback send and receive schoolwork by mail and listen to lessons broadcast on the radio. They can communicate with their teachers via two-way radios.

## IN THE BIG CITIES

Eighty per cent of people in Australia live in cities, where most of the jobs are to be found. The largest cities – Sydney, Melbourne and Brisbane – lie on the south and east coasts. In Sydney, the population of more than 3.5 million enjoys the attractions of city life, including the world-famous Sydney Opera House, as well as the beach. Bondi Beach lies about 8km south of the centre and attracts many swimmers and surfers.

▲ A favourite pastime in coastal cities is surfboat racing. Lifeguards give demonstrations of their skills at festivals.

## FIRST INHABITANTS

Australia's first inhabitants were Aboriginal people who arrived 50,000 years ago from Southeast Asia. They lived off the land, hunting animals, gathering plants and fishing for thousands of years, until European settlers destroyed their way of life in the 18th century.

## CAPTAIN COOK LANDS

The Dutch were the first Europeans to explore the coast in the 1600s, but they never established any settlements. The first Europeans to settle in Australia were the British. In 1770, Captain James Cook reached the east coast of Australia and immediately claimed it for Britain, calling it New South Wales.

## CONVICTS ARRIVE

The first British fleet landed at Botany Bay in January 1788, with soldiers, convicts and the colony's first governor, Arthur Phillip. The first settlement, named Sydney, was set up nearby, and as more free settlers arrived, other farming settlements grew up around the coast.

## THE GOLD RUSH

In 1851, many more people dashed to Australia with news that gold had been found in New South Wales and Victoria. This became known as the Gold Rush. Melbourne, the capital of Victoria, soon became a wealthy city and Australia's population more than doubled. In 1854, gold miners at the Eureka Stockade rebelled against their colonial rulers, hastening reform and self-government.

## AUSTRALIA – THE NATION

In 1901, Australia became a nation. The colonies became states and united as the Commonwealth of Australia. During World War I, Australian troops helped the British and in World War II they defended their country from Japanese invasion. People from many countries migrated to Australia after both wars and the population rose from five million in 1918 to nearly 18 million today. One in four Australians comes from a family where English is not the first language. Increasingly Australia now looks to Asia and the Pacific countries for trade links, especially to Japan.

▲ Cattle ranches, or runs, can be thousands of kilometres in size. Farmers use helicopters to round up huge herds of livestock.

◄ Tasmania has a cooler, wetter climate than the Australian mainland. Much of the island is unpopulated and covered in thick forest.

◄ Britain sent many thousands of convicts to Australia between 1788 and 1853 under the system of transportation. The early years in prison settlements were harsh.

## SEE ALSO

Continent, Kangaroo

# AZTECS

The Aztecs were members of one of the last great native civilizations of the Americas. They created a large empire in Mexico during the 15th century.

▶ The Aztecs used two calendars: this solar one, divided into 18 months, and a sacred one.

The Aztecs' rise to power began in the 14th century, when they built the city of Tenochtitlán on an island where Mexico City now stands. They began to create their great empire by conquering nearby cities, largely to the south and east.

Quetzalcóatl (meaning plumed serpent) was one of the main Aztec gods.

## THE PEOPLE

The Aztec ruler was an emperor who relied on a warrior class to defend and expand the empire. Next in importance were the priests. Ordinary people were farmers, merchants, craftworkers and slaves. Food was farmed on floating gardens (called *chinampas*) on Lake Texcoco, which surrounded Tenochtitlán. Maize, vegetables and cotton were grown and turkeys and dogs were kept for meat. The Aztecs were among the first to use cocoa beans to

This ceremonial mask was made from precious stones on a human skull.

make a chocolate drink, and the words 'tomato' and 'avocado' come from the Aztec language.

## TEMPLES OF DOOM

The main religious building was the Great Temple at Tenochtitlán, a stone pyramid with sacrificial altars at the top. Each Aztec ruler built a bigger, more impressive temple on the same site. It was rebuilt six times.

## CONQUERED BY A LEGEND

The Aztec Empire was at its height when Montezuma II became emperor in 1502 and built a vast palace. Under his rule the empire stretched across Mexico from the east to the west. In 1519, a small force of Spanish soldiers and bounty hunters, led by Hernán Cortés, arrived in Mexico. Many Aztecs, including Montezuma, believed Cortés was the legendary god Quetzalcóatl, and at first welcomed the Spaniards. By 1521, Cortés' army had completely destroyed Tenochtitlán and Cortés was made governor of Mexico.

## HUMAN SACRIFICE

Religion was very important to the Aztecs. They worshipped many gods – of war, rain, Sun and wind – and carried out human sacrifices to win the favour of their gods. Captives taken in battle were killed by the priests. They cut out the still-living hearts using ceremonial knives made of very sharp stone. The blood was used to bathe statues of the gods.

Stone knives were used to cut out the heart

Feathers from the quetzal bird were used for headdresses

## SEE ALSO
Mexico, Native Americans

# BIRD

Birds are warm-blooded, egg-laying vertebrates (animals with backbones). They have wings, and are the only animals with feathers.

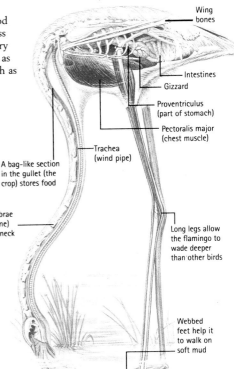

▶ A humming-bird can flap its wings 100 times per second, creating a humming sound as it hovers to drink nectar.

The large beak of the toucan is useful for plucking fruit from trees.

An avocet's long, slender bill probes for shellfish in soft mud.

The eagle uses its hooked beak to tear meat into chunks.

A swift gathers insects in its wide beak while flying.

There are about 8,800 different kinds of bird. They are found all over the world, even on polar ice-caps. Only a few birds cannot fly at all. These include the long-legged, fast-running ostrich of Africa, the rhea of South America, the emu of Australia and penguins in the Southern Hemisphere, which use their flipper-like wings to 'fly' through water.

## HOLLOW BONES
A bird is designed for lightness. Its bones are thin and hollow and its beak is toothless. In the front limb, the upper-arm and forearm bones are long. The wrist, hand and three finger bones are joined together to support the feathers.

## BIRD SENSE
Birds have excellent eyesight and good hearing, but their sense of smell is less developed. A bird's feeding habits vary with habitat and species. Some, such as the parrot, are nut-eaters; others, such as the snipe, feast on worms. Some birds like to scavenge dead bodies. The raven has a reputation as an evil bird because it used to peck at the dead bodies of executed criminals in medieval times.

## CHEWING STONE
As they have no teeth to chew with, seed-eating birds grind their food in the gizzard, a muscular stomach part. Digestion is aided by pieces of stone and grit that they have swallowed for this purpose. ▶

## THE FLAMINGO'S BEAK AND DIET
The shape of a bird's beak depends on what it eats. The flamingo sieves its food from water, so its long beak contains a filter of little hooks to trap tiny plants and crustaceans (shellfish). It is the shellfish that give the flamingo its bright pink colour. If the flamingo doesn't eat them, its feathers turn greyish white.

Wing bones

Intestines

Gizzard

Proventriculus (part of stomach)

Pectoralis major (chest muscle)

Trachea (wind pipe)

A bag-like section in the gullet (the crop) stores food

Sections of short vertebrae (as in a human backbone) allow flexibility of the neck

Long legs allow the flamingo to wade deeper than other birds

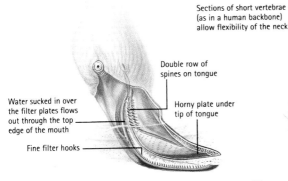

Double row of spines on tongue

Water sucked in over the filter plates flows out through the top edge of the mouth

Horny plate under tip of tongue

Fine filter hooks

Webbed feet help it to walk on soft mud

## NESTS

Birds' nests vary widely, from the bare cliff-ledge of the guillemot, to the stick-and-twig pile of an eagle's eyrie.

Swallows build nests of mud high up on cliffs or on the sides of buildings.

The Indian tailor bird uses spider silk to sew leaves together.

A plover lays its eggs on shingle – their only protection is camouflage.

Some ducks, grebes and other water birds build floating nests.

The ovenbird builds an oven-shaped nest of mud on a branch or fence post.

Down feather

Contour feather

### FEATHERS
Birds have three types of feather. Fluffy down feathers near the body keep the bird warm. Contour feathers give the body a streamlined shape. Flight feathers on the wings have barbs that form smooth, flat surfaces.

Flight feather

## COLOURS AND BREEDING

The colours of a bird's feathers usually help to conceal, or camouflage, it in its natural habitat. Most birds moult (shed) their old feathers and grow new ones each year. This moulting may be linked to breeding, as some male birds, such as the bird-of-paradise and peacock, grow colourful feathers to attract mates. The females, however, tend to be drab in colour so that they are hidden from predators while sitting on the nest.

## COURTING COUPLES

As the spring or mating season arrives, a male and female pair up to mate. Most birds court with a variety of calls and displays. Some males give gifts of food such as insects to the females. Usually the males show off their colours and skills in flight and on perches, or try to out-sing and out-dance rivals. Grebes perform a very elaborate dance that involves crouching, headwagging and swaying.

## LAYING EGGS

Most bird pairs breed alone, but some, such as rooks or puffins, breed in large groups called colonies. The female lays hard-shelled eggs and sits on them to keep them warm until they are ready to hatch. This process is called incubation. The number of eggs laid in one clutch varies – a kiwi lays a single egg, while a North American bobwhite can lay up to 25. Eggs can take at least ten days to hatch; albatross eggs take the longest, up to 70 days.

Quill

Barbs

Barbules

Skin

Feather muscles

### MICROSCOPIC HOOKS
Each feather is made of keratin (found in the hair and nails of humans) and has a long, stiff shaft, or quill, with side parts called barbs, linked by tiny hook-like barbules.

## MATCH-MAKING

Larger, long-lived birds, such as gannets, storks, cranes and albatrosses, often return to the same nest site and the same partner each year. The male ostrich, however, courts several females which all lay eggs in one nest. He then guards all the eggs (there may be as many as 30) and – when they hatch out – the chicks.

▲ Male birds-of-paradise have beautiful feathers. They show off their plumes in a dance to attract a mate.

## HOW A BIRD FLIES

The goose, like other birds in flight, lowers its wings using its strong pectoral (chest) muscles. The wings push the air down and back, thrusting the bird up and forwards in the air. The wing and tail feathers can be twisted and fanned to help the goose manoeuvre as it flies.

**1** The powerful downstroke lifts the bird upwards.

**2** Legs and tail are in line with body to keep the bird streamlined as it flies.

**3** The upstroke is less powerful. Feathers are twisted, letting air through.

**4** The tail is used for steering and for braking.

## MOVING HOUSE

Birds are warm-blooded. Their average body temperature is 41°C – slightly hotter than that of humans. This means they can stay active in cold weather but they need food, so many species leave colder climates and migrate to warmer places somewhere else in the world.

## BETWEEN CONTINENTS

Birds such as geese and waders fly from the Arctic to Europe, Asia and North America. Birds from Europe, such as swifts and bee-eaters, fly south to Africa and India. The Arctic tern is the greatest migrator of all birds, flying an amazing 15,000km all the way to the Antarctic.

### FAST FACTS

• A large bird such as a swan has about 25,000 feathers, whereas a tiny humming-bird has 1,000

• The world's largest bird, the ostrich, is too heavy to fly. The largest flying bird is the Kori bustard, which weighs 18kg

• The pitohui of New Guinea is the only bird that is poisonous

## FEEDING THE CHICKS

The crow belongs to the group known as perching birds, which is the largest of the 28 bird groups. Its toes are designed for gripping, as crows build their nests in trees or on the side of cliffs. The chicks are often born blind and helpless and the parents feed them until they are ready to leave the nest.

The bones are thin and hollow so that birds are very light

The inside of the chick's mouth is bright red to attract the parent's attention

Like all birds, the crow has thousands of feathers

These two-week-old chicks have soft, downy feathers, and their eyes are now open

### SEE ALSO

Animal, Eagle, Zoology

# BLACK HOLE

A black hole is a region of space where the pull of gravity is so strong that nothing can escape from it, not even light.

## INVISIBLE FORCE

When a black hole lies close to another star, its immense gravity sucks particles or gas away from the star. These are pulled into a gassy spiral, called an accretion disc. The gas inside the disc is heated to millions of degrees Celsius and gives off X-rays. It is these powerful, flickering X-rays that reveal the presence of a black hole.

Nearby star

Black hole

Particles, gas and matter spiral downwards

Scientists believe that a black hole forms after a massive, heavy star has exploded at the end of its life. The outer parts are hurled into space but the core of the dead star, with no light and heat left to support it, shrinks very quickly.

## DEAD STARS

The gravity of a dead star is thought to pull all the material left behind inwards, squeezing it tighter to make it smaller and extremely compact. A tiny black hole, the size of a full-stop, could hold enough matter to make a mountain. Vast black holes, thought to exist at the centre of galaxies, may contain as much matter as tens of millions of stars.

## COSMIC VACUUM

Black holes are invisible – they can only be tracked down by their effect on a nearby object. They tug matter away from

the surface of a star, like a vacuum cleaner. This debris enters a whirlpool, which spins around the black hole at speed before disappearing inside, like water going down a giant plug hole.

## THROUGH A WORMHOLE

Some black holes may be the entrances to strange tunnels through space and time known as wormholes. It has been suggested that a spacecraft could travel along a wormhole and reappear in a different part of the universe.

▲ A black hole is shaped like a funnel. Objects are pulled into the funnel and, once inside, never escape.

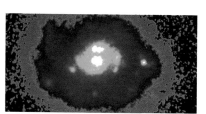

◀ This ultraviolet image shows galaxy M77. Its centre is thought to be a black hole with the mass of several million suns.

### SEE ALSO

Astronomy, Galaxy, Gravity

34

# BLOOD

**Blood is a vital liquid that is pumped through arteries and veins around the body by the heart. Blood carries oxygen, nutrients, hormones and waste products.**

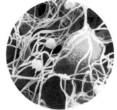

◀ Chemicals in the blood form a net over a wound. The net traps red blood cells, platelets and white blood cells (shown in yellow) to form a clot.

**KARL LANDSTEINER**
This Austrian-born pathologist (1868–1943) discovered blood groups, making blood transfusions safe for the first time.

Most animals have a blood-like fluid. It is red in most vertebrates (animals with backbones), but can be different colours in other animals. Lobsters have blue blood, snails have grey blood, some insects have green blood, and a worms' blood is colourless.

## BLOOD PLASMA
Just over half (55 per cent) of human blood is a pale yellow liquid called plasma. This contains hundreds of substances, including nutrients, sugars, salts, minerals, hormones and chemicals.

## OXYGEN CARRIERS
About 45 per cent of blood is made up of blood cells and platelets. The vast majority of blood cells are small, red and doughnut-shaped. They are made inside the bones and released into the blood, where they carry oxygen around the body. When red cells have plenty of oxygen, as in most arteries, they are bright red. When low in oxygen, as in most veins, they are dark red.

### FAST FACTS

- An average human has about 5 litres of blood
- A blood spot the size of a pin-head contains about 5 million red cells, 10,000 white cells and 250,000 platelets
- Anaemia is a lack of oxygen in the blood

## DEFENDING THE BODY
Less than one per cent of blood is made up of white blood cells and platelets. There are several types of white blood cell, all of which defend the body. Some fight invading bacteria and viruses by bombarding them with chemicals. Others surround invaders and eat them.

## CLOTTING AND HEALING
Platelets are cell fragments that help wounds to heal. They gather around a cut and release chemicals to slow blood loss and form a clot. This stops the blood flow and seals the wound, stopping germs from getting in while new skin grows.

## BLOOD GROUPS
There are several different types of human blood, including A, B, AB and O. The blood group depends on the chemicals that the white blood cells produce. If a person needs blood in an operation, the right blood group must be given as some chemicals do not mix. The wrong chemicals may clot with the existing blood and make the illness worse or even cause death.

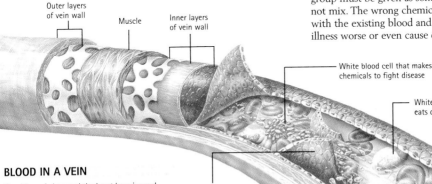

Outer layers of vein wall

Muscle

Inner layers of vein wall

White blood cell that makes chemicals to fight disease

White blood cell that eats dying and dead germs

Red blood cell

## BLOOD IN A VEIN
Blood is carried toward the heart by veins and away from the heart by arteries. Red blood cells returning to the lungs from the heart are dark red in colour because they are no longer carrying oxygen. All blood contains plasma, platelets, red blood cells and several types of white blood cells.

Valve to stop blood flowing the wrong way

Platelets help blood to clot

White blood cell that attacks invaders

### SEE ALSO
Cell, Disease, Heart, Medicine

# BRAIN AND NERVOUS SYSTEM

The brain is the body's control centre, responsible for action, thought, memory, behaviour and emotion. It is linked to the body by the nervous system.

Fish have simple brains, with areas that process smell extending forward to the tip of the nose.

Snakes have brains with large sight areas, showing the importance of sight for hunting.

Birds have brains with large movement centres which control the complex movements used in flight.

Cats, like other mammals, have brains with large cerebrums for complex and adaptable behaviour.

The average adult human brain weighs 1.4kg, looks like a giant, grey walnut and has the texture of blancmange. It is made up of tiny cells that send electrical messages to the body along a network of nerves known as the nervous system.

## IN THREE PARTS

All vertebrates (animals with backbones) have a brain that can be divided into three main areas: brain stem, cerebellum and cerebrum. The brain stem and cerebellum keep the body functioning. The cerebrum deals with thought, memory and sensation.

## BRAIN STEM

The brain stem lies at the bottom of the brain, where it joins the spinal cord (the bundle of nerves linking the brain to the body). The stem controls the body's automatic processes, such as heartbeat, breathing, body temperature, blood pressure, digestion and getting rid of waste.

## THE CEREBELLUM

The cerebellum lies at the back of the brain. When movement instructions come from the cerebrum, the cerebellum sorts them, fills in the details and sends out signals to the muscles to make movements smooth and co-ordinated. The cerebellum also controls posture and balance.

## THE CEREBRUM

About 90 per cent of the human brain is taken up by the cerebrum – the centre of all thought. It is split into two halves, called cerebral hemispheres, which contain grey matter and white matter. Grey matter lies on the surface and is made of nerve cell bodies, which create messages. The inner white matter is packed with nerve fibres carrying the messages to the body.

## CEREBRAL CENTRES

The human cerebrum looks the same all over, but different areas carry out special functions. One area receives and processes nerve signals from the eyes. Another is for touch, processing nerve signals from the skin. Just in front of this is the motor

## HOW NERVE CELLS PASS ON MESSAGES

The brain and nervous system are made of microscopic nerve cells called neurons. Each nerve cell has two parts: a spider-like cell body and a long nerve fibre. The cell body receives signals from other nerve cells and passes these along its fibre, like a tiny telephone wire, to yet more nerve cells, until the message reaches its final destination.

Nerve cell fibre

Nerve cell body

Muscle

1 Messages are sent along a nerve fibre (axon) to another nerve cell.

2 The message has to jump the small gap (synapse) between the two nerve cells.

3 The message travels fast along the axon because it is insulated with a sheath of myelin.

4 The axon joins with other nerve fibres in a bundle creating a pathway.

5 The muscle receives the message from the brain to move.

## FAST FACTS

• About 0.85 litres of blood pass through the brain every minute

• Brain activity uses up one fifth of the body's energy supply

• The longest nerve, the sciatic, runs from the base of the spine to the knee. Some nerve signals travel at up to 400km/h

• Meningitis is the inflammation of the meninges. Encephalitis is inflammation of the brain

## THE BRAIN AND SKULL

The brain is protected by a bony skull, three thin layers of membrane, called meninges, and a pool of fluid. The two sides of the cerebrum (the cerebral hemispheres) are joined by the corpus callosum. The left side of the brain usually controls logic while the right side is more active in creative pursuits.

The hypothalamus is the site of emotion and instinct

The pituitary gland controls the hormones

Bony skull

Fluid

Meninges

Cerebrum

Corpus callosum

Cerebellum

Thought and consciousness

Skilled movement

Touch

Speech

Hearing

Sight

Brain stem

Cerebellum

Spinal cord

centre, which sends nerve signals to the muscles. There are also areas for hearing, taste, speech and other body processes. Consciousness and thought are believed to originate at the front of the cerebrum.

### CROSSING THE DIVIDE
Nerve signals arriving or leaving one side of the brain cross over to affect the opposite side of the body, so signals from the body's right side go to the brain's left hemisphere and vice versa. The two sides are joined by a strip of nerve fibres, the corpus callosum.

### INSTINCTS AND EMOTIONS
Basic instincts, such as hunger, thirst and sleep, as well as strong emotions, such as

fear, anger and joy, come from the hypothalamus, which lies at the top of the brain stem. Dangling beneath it is the pituitary, a pea-sized gland that controls the body's hormones (chemical messages).

### THOUGHTS AND MEMORIES
The human brain contains 100 billion nerve cells and is far more complex than the most advanced supercomputer. One thought or memory involves millions of nerve signals, flashing around billions of brain cells, along trillions of pathways. An electroencephalogram (EEG) machine is used to record these electrical nerve signals.

### A NETWORK OF NERVES
The brain is linked to a branching network of nerves by the spinal cord. Sensory nerves bring information from the senses to the brain. Motor nerves carry signals from the brain to the muscles. The brain and spinal column make up the central nervous system. The nerves in the rest of the body make up the peripheral nervous system.

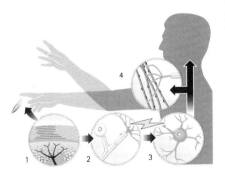

▲ A reflex is an automatic response. The flame's heat stimulates pain sensors in the finger (1) that send a signal to the spinal cord (2). The signal passes to a motor nerve (3), which makes muscles contract (4), pulling away the hand. Signals also pass to the brain, which registers pain.

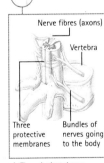

Nerve fibres (axons)

Vertebra

Three protective membranes

Bundles of nerves going to the body

▲ The spinal cord runs through a tunnel formed by vertebrae in the spine. Its nerves are surrounded by protective membranes.

### SEE ALSO
Cell, Hearing, Human body, Sight, Taste and smell, Touch

# BRIDGE

**Bridges are structures that are built to allow people, animals or vehicles to cross rivers, canals, canyons, railways or roads.**

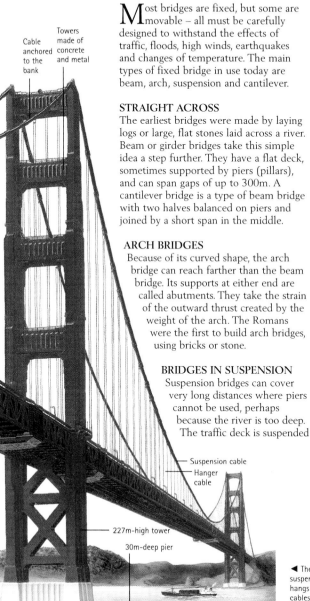

Cable anchored to the bank

Towers made of concrete and metal

Most bridges are fixed, but some are movable – all must be carefully designed to withstand the effects of traffic, floods, high winds, earthquakes and changes of temperature. The main types of fixed bridge in use today are beam, arch, suspension and cantilever.

### STRAIGHT ACROSS

The earliest bridges were made by laying logs or large, flat stones laid across a river. Beam or girder bridges take this simple idea a step further. They have a flat deck, sometimes supported by piers (pillars), and can span gaps of up to 300m. A cantilever bridge is a type of beam bridge with two halves balanced on piers and joined by a short span in the middle.

### ARCH BRIDGES

Because of its curved shape, the arch bridge can reach farther than the beam bridge. Its supports at either end are called abutments. They take the strain of the outward thrust created by the weight of the arch. The Romans were the first to build arch bridges, using bricks or stone.

### BRIDGES IN SUSPENSION

Suspension bridges can cover very long distances where piers cannot be used, perhaps because the river is too deep. The traffic deck is suspended

Suspension cable
Hanger cable

227m-high tower

30m-deep pier

## HOW BRIDGES WORK

Bridges are designed to withstand huge forces (shown by the arrows in the diagrams below). They must be strong enough to carry their own weight, as well as that of the people and vehicles that use them. Bridges must also withstand the strong vibrations set up by high winds.

In an arch bridge, the downward pressure (load) is pushed out towards the foundations on each bank.

In a cantilever bridge, the load on the central span is balanced equally over each supporting pier.

In a suspension bridge, curving cables transfer the bulk of the load to anchored points on each bank.

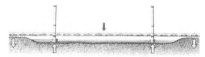

In a cable-stayed bridge, the load is balanced equally over one or more central supports.

→ Load    → Support    ‑ Tension    ‑ Compression

from towers by steel cables. A modern version of this is the cable-stayed bridge, which does not need the heavy anchorages required to stabilize a suspension bridge.

### MOVABLE BRIDGES

Some bridges are built to move so that large ships can pass through. Drawbridges lift up by splitting in the middle or at one end, swing bridges turn sideways, and lift bridges have a central section that can be raised. Deck sections can also be floated on pontoons to create temporary bridges.

◄ The 1,280m-long Golden Gate suspension bridge in San Francisco hangs from two 1m-thick suspension cables, each made of 27,450 wires.

## SEE ALSO

Industrial Revolution, Iron and steel

# BUDDHISM

**Buddhism is a religion that was first practised in Asia about 2,500 years ago. Today, it is estimated that there are around 350 million Buddhists across the globe.**

▲ The Wheel of Life symbolizes the process of change and rebirth. When we reach Nirvana, the process stops and we come off the wheel.

Buddhism was founded in northeast India by a prince called Siddhartha Gautama. Born around 563BC, he left his home at the age of 29 to lead a life of meditation and preaching. He became a great religious teacher before his death in about 483BC.

### THE ENLIGHTENED ONE

While sitting under a fig tree, Gautama entered a peaceful state of mind, called enlightenment, or Nirvana ('absence of sorrow'). He then taught others how to find this peace and gained the title Buddha, which means 'Enlightened One'. The Buddhist religion spread from India to China, Japan and other parts of Asia.

### REBIRTH

Buddhists believe in reincarnation – being reborn until Nirvana is reached. The form of each new life depends on how the being behaved during previous lives. A human might have been an animal in the last life; a male might have been female. This is known as their karma.

▲ A Buddhist monastery in Tibet. Buddhism was introduced into Tibet in AD749. Tibetan monks are called lamas. The chief lamas are the Dalai Lama and the Panchen Lama.

### FOUR NOBLE TRUTHS

Buddha's teachings are based on the Four Noble Truths. These state that all suffering is caused by attachment to the material world. Buddhists believe that

▲ A young Thai Buddhist, in traditional orange robes, sits contemplating under a tree. Buddhists believe that meditation plays a vital role in the path to enlightenment.

they will be free of these attachments, and therefore of suffering, if they follow the Eightfold Path. This consists of eight steps involving wisdom, understanding, morality and meditation.

### TYPES OF BUDDHISM

There are two main types of Buddhism: Theravada is common in Southeast Asia and teaches that Buddha was an ordinary human being who achieved enlightenment; Mahayana is popular in northern Asia and claims that Buddha was the divine spirit in human form. A branch of Mahayana, called Zen Buddhism, was established in Japan in the 1100s.

◄ Many images of Buddha show him sitting serenely with crossed legs in the lotus position. The image reminds followers of Buddha's goodness and helps them to meditate and pray.

### EIGHTFOLD PATH TO ENLIGHTENMENT

- Right views
- Right thought and intention
- Right speech, plain and truthful
- Right action, including never taking a life
- Right occupation, harming no one
- Right effort, always persevering
- Right awareness of the past, present and future
- Right contemplation or meditation

### SEE ALSO
Asia, Japan, Religion

# BUTTERFLY AND MOTH

Butterflies and moths are flying insects with two pairs of wings, which are often brightly coloured. They hatch as caterpillars and change into moths or butterflies as adults.

The turquoise blue has been hunted almost to extinction by collectors for its beautiful wings.

A peacock butterfly's eye spots may help it scare off small birds when it suddenly opens its wings.

The white admiral is a woodland butterfly. Its caterpillar is covered with protective spines.

Swallowtails are large and colourful butterflies, found in North Africa, Europe and across Asia.

The large white is a very common butterfly. Its caterpillars feed in groups, often on cabbage plants.

There are more than 170,000 kinds of butterflies and moths in the world. They form the group of insects known as Lepidoptera, which means 'scale-wing'. Their wings are covered with thousands of tiny scales that give the wings their colourful appearance.

## COLOURFUL BUTTERFLIES

Most butterflies fly by day and have brightly coloured wings, which close together over their backs when they are resting. They have a slim body and thin antennae (feelers) with clubbed tips, which are used to detect smells. The monarch, cabbage white, tortoiseshell and peacock are all types of butterfly.

## DULL MOTHS

Most moths are dull in colour, fly at night, have feathery or hairy antennae and a stout and hairy body. At rest, a moth holds its wings open. A moth's forewing is often linked to its hind-wing on each side by tiny hairs that act like hooks. The hawk moth, ermine, eggar and tussock are all

◀ The back part of the hawk moth caterpillar looks exactly like a viper in order to deceive any predators into leaving it alone.

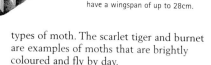

▲ Tropical birdwing butterflies, such as the Rajah Brooke, can have a wingspan of up to 28cm.

types of moth. The scarlet tiger and burnet are examples of moths that are brightly coloured and fly by day.

## SENSING THE WORLD

An adult butterfly or moth sees well with its large eyes. Its sensitive antennae pick up the scents of flowers and fruits and can detect the smell of a mate. Most species of butterfly or moth feed on flower nectar, which is sucked up by a long, straw-like mouth, called a proboscis.

## EGG TO CATERPILLAR

After mating, female butterflies and moths lay their eggs on or near the plant that their caterpillars like to eat. The brimstone butterfly likes buckthorn, while the green oak tortrix moth chooses oak leaves. Some species will feed only on one type of plant.

## LIVING TO EAT

Butterfly and moth eggs hatch into soft-skinned, wingless larvae called caterpillars. Their job is to eat – a large group of caterpillars can destroy crops within a few weeks. A caterpillar sheds its skin (moults) four or five times as it feeds and grows. To protect themselves against predators, some caterpillars are covered in hairs that release a chemical when broken. Others are brightly coloured as a warning.

◀ This peppered moth is a pale, speckled grey in colour to camouflage it against lichen on tree bark.

## LIFE SPAN

Most butterflies and nearly all moths live for just one breeding season or year. A few butterflies, such as peacock and monarch, survive the winter as adults. Their main predators are birds by day and bats at night. The breeding season is usually in the spring or summer, although tropical species can breed at any time of the year.

## ALL CHANGE

When they are ready to become adults, caterpillars enter a pupal stage (chrysalis). Many moth caterpillars spin cocoons of silk. Butterfly caterpillars grow a hard skin. Inside these cases, they gradually change. After a few weeks, or the following spring, the chrysalis splits and the adult winged insect (imago) emerges.

Like all hawk moths, the privet hawk moth is a fast flyer. Its caterpillars have a curved horn at the end.

## CATERPILLAR TO BUTTERFLY

The monarch butterfly lays its eggs on a milkweed plant. A week later a single caterpillar emerges from each egg. First it eats its egg case, then it feeds on the plant. Once fully grown, the caterpillar becomes a chrysalis (pupa). Inside, it metamorphoses (changes form), before emerging as a butterfly. The whole cycle from egg to adult takes about five weeks.

1 The female monarch lays a cluster of eggs on the leaves of a milkweed plant.

2 Each tiny caterpillar (larva) hatches and starts to eat. It grows very quickly.

3 When fully grown, the caterpillar spins a silken thread and firmly attaches itself to a twig.

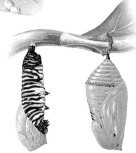

4 The caterpillar sheds its stripey skin, revealing a chrysalis (pupa). It now looks still and lifeless.

5 Inside the chrysalis a new body slowly begins to form. Finally, the skin splits and an adult butterfly emerges.

6 The butterfly clings to the twig of the milkweed plant, letting its new wings hang down to help force blood into them.

7 When the wings have dried and hardened, metamorphosis is complete and the adult monarch butterfly can fly away.

### SEE ALSO

Animal, Flower, Insect

# CANADA

Canada is the second largest country in the world. It is the top part of the continent of North America and a percentage of its area lies within the Arctic Circle.

**Area:** 9,970,610 sq km
**Population:** 30,301,000
**Capital:** Ottawa
**Languages:** English, French
**Currency:** Canadian dollar

▲ Forestry is one of Canada's most important industries. Trees are cut down to make paper as well as to build homes.

## FAST FACTS

• The Yukon Territory is rich in metal ore. During the 1890s, it was the site of the Klondike gold rush

• Alberta has some of the world's best dinosaur remains. *Albertosaurus* is just one example

• The border between Canada and the USA is the longest undefended border in the world

▶ The 553m-high Canadian National (CN) Tower dominates Toronto's skyline. The city is Canada's financial, manufacturing and communication centre.

The Rocky Mountains run down the west of Canada, and four of the five Great Lakes lie on its border with the United States. These, together with other Canadian lakes, contain about a quarter of the world's fresh water.

### CANADIAN FORESTS
Forests cover 40 per cent of the country. British Columbia is the leading province in timber production, with 75m-high trees, such as Douglas fir, growing in its moist, coniferous forests. Maple syrup is collected from maple trees in Ontario and Quebec, and in the southwest there are orchards and vineyards.

### THE GREAT PLAINS
Canada has vast grassland areas called prairies, stretching across its centre. Only about seven per cent of Canada's land is used for growing crops, but these fertile plains produce enough to make Canada the world's second largest exporter of wheat. Cattle ranches on the drier grasslands supply beef and dairy produce.

▲ Moose are just one of the animals living in Canada's forests, which are also home to bears, beavers, bobcats, caribou, foxes, wolves, mountain lions and goats.

### INDUSTRY AND MINING
Canada's manufacturing industries lie mostly in Ontario and Quebec. They make vehicles, aircraft, machinery, steel, chemicals and paper, as well as processing food and minerals. Canada is rich in resources such as gold, iron ore, copper, petroleum and natural gas, many of which are exported. Fishing has long been an important industry in Canada, but overfishing has reduced stocks.

### SPORT AND LEISURE
Most Canadians live in cities around the Great Lakes and St Lawrence River, or on the west coast. They share a love of the outdoors, enjoying ice hockey, baseball, soccer and football. Rodeo enthusiasts flock

◀ In wintertime, temperatures can fall as low as –30°C. Lakes and rivers freeze over, and people play games on the ice.

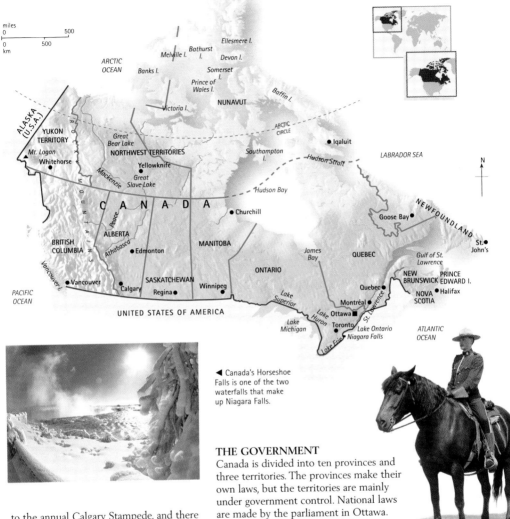

miles
0        500
0        500
km

ARCTIC
OCEAN

ALASKA
(U.S.A.)

Ellesmere I.

Bathurst
I.

Melville I.     Devon I.

Somerset
I.

Banks I.

Prince of
Wales I.

Baffin I.

Victoria I.

NUNAVUT

YUKON
TERRITORY

Great
Bear Lake

NORTHWEST TERRITORIES

ARCTIC
CIRCLE

Iqaluit

Mt. Logan

Whitehorse

Mackenzie

Yellowknife

Southampton
I.

Hudson Strait

LABRADOR SEA

N

Great
Slave Lake

Hudson Bay

C   A   N   A   D   A

Churchill

Goose Bay

NEWFOUNDLAND

St.
John's

BRITISH
COLUMBIA

ALBERTA

Peace

Athabasca

Edmonton

MANITOBA

James
Bay

QUEBEC

Gulf of St.
Lawrence

NEW
BRUNSWICK

PRINCE
EDWARD I.

NOVA
SCOTIA

Halifax

Vancouver I.

Vancouver

Calgary

SASKATCHEWAN

Regina

Winnipeg

ONTARIO

Lake
Superior

Quebec

Montréal

St. Lawrence

PACIFIC
OCEAN

UNITED STATES OF AMERICA

Lake
Michigan

Lake
Huron

Ottawa

Toronto     Lake Ontario

Lake Erie     Niagara Falls

ATLANTIC
OCEAN

◀ Canada's Horseshoe
Falls is one of the two
waterfalls that make
up Niagara Falls.

to the annual Calgary Stampede, and there
are over 30 National Parks.

## CANADIAN PEOPLES

Canada's native peoples are the Inuit and
Native Americans, whose ancestors came
from Asia, probably around 13,000 years
ago. Europeans arrived in Canada in the
1500s, and in the 1700s Britain and France
fought for control of the country. Since
1867, Canada has been self-governing,
with Newfoundland becoming a part of
the country in 1947.

## THE GOVERNMENT

Canada is divided into ten provinces and
three territories. The provinces make their
own laws, but the territories are mainly
under government control. National laws
are made by the parliament in Ottawa.
There is an elected House of Commons
and an upper house called the Senate,
whose job it is to advise parliament.

## TRANSPORT

Canada has a good system of roads,
including the Trans-Canada Highway,
which is more than 7,000km long. The
St Lawrence Seaway, a waterway linking
stretches of river and canals, allows ships
to carry cargoes inland from the Atlantic
Ocean as far as the Great Lakes.

▲ The Royal Canadian
Mounted Police, nicknamed
the Mounties, are Canada's
national police force.

## SEE ALSO

Arctic, Grassland, Native
Americans, North
America

43

# CARIBBEAN

The Caribbean islands lie between North and South America, forming a curving chain about 3,200km long. They include Cuba, Jamaica and Haiti.

▲ Bananas are one of the chief crops. They are picked while still green and exported in refrigerated cargo ships.

**ANTIGUA & BARBUDA**
**Area:** 442 sq km
**Population:** 67,000
**Capital:** St John's
**Language:** English
**Currency:** East Caribbean dollar

**BAHAMAS**
**Area:** 13,878 sq km
**Population:** 294,000
**Capital:** Nassau
**Language:** English
**Currency:** Bahamian dollar

**BARBADOS**
**Area:** 430 sq km
**Population:** 266,000
**Capital:** Bridgetown
**Language:** English
**Currency:** Barbados dollar

**CUBA**
**Area:** 110,861 sq km
**Population:** 11,103,000
**Capital:** Havana
**Language:** Spanish
**Currency:** Peso

**DOMINICA**
**Area:** 751 sq km
**Population:** 73,000
**Capital:** Roseau
**Language:** English
**Currency:** East Caribbean dollar

The region known as the Caribbean includes three island groups: the Greater Antilles and the Lesser Antilles, which lie in the Caribbean Sea, and the Bahamas, in the Atlantic Ocean. These islands are also known as the West Indies because, when the explorer Christopher Columbus first saw them in 1492, he did not know he was off the coast of North America, but believed he was near India.

## TROPICAL ISLANDS
The tropical climate in the Caribbean means that temperatures rarely drop below 25°C, although the hot days are often relieved by coolingy sea breezes. Violent hurricanes sometimes strike the islands, causing great damage to property.

## FOREST ANIMALS
Vegetation on the islands includes palm trees and exotic flowers such as orchids. Some islands also have very dense rainforests – home to parrots and macaws, as well as bats, snakes and insects. In many places, these forests have been cleared to make way for crop plantations.

## HOME-GROWN PRODUCE
Sugar cane is the main crop grown on the islands. The stalks are crushed to produce raw juice or refined to make crystallized sugar. Other important crops are bananas and other fruit, coffee, cocoa and cotton.

## ISLAND INDUSTRY
As well as farming, there is some mining on the islands. Jamaica has bauxite (aluminium ore) and there is gold in the Dominican Republic. Cuba, Trinidad and Barbados all have offshore oil and gas, and there is some manufacturing. Tourism is the largest industry, employing as many as one in five people on many of the islands.

## THE ORIGINAL ISLANDERS
The first settlers in the Caribbean were the Caribs and Arawaks from South America. Most were killed by Europeans who arrived

▼ Large markets, where people sell home-grown goods, are a familiar aspect of island life.

**DOMINICAN REPUBLIC**
**Area:** 48,511 sq km
**Population:** 8,254,000
**Capital:** Santo Domingo
**Language:** Spanish
**Currency:** Peso

**GRENADA**
**Area:** 344 sq km
**Population:** 96,000
**Capital:** St George's
**Language:** English
**Currency:** East
Caribbean dollar

**HAITI**
**Area:** 27,750 sq km
**Population:** 7,647,000
**Capital:** Port-au-Prince
**Language:** French
**Currency:** Gourde

**JAMAICA**
**Area:** 10,990 sq km
**Population:** 2,578,000
**Capital:** Kingston
**Language:** English
**Currency:** Jamaican dollar

N

*ATLANTIC OCEAN*

BAHAMAS

GREATER

CUBA

CAYMAN IS. (U.K.)

JAMAICA

TURKS AND
CAICOS IS. (U.K.)

ANTILLES

HAITI  DOMINICAN
REPUBLIC

HISPANIOLA

*CARIBBEAN SEA*

PUERTO
RICO (U.S.)  ST. KITTS–NEVIS

ANTIGUA &
BARBUDA

MONTSERRAT (U.K.)

GUADELOUPE (FRANCE)

LESSER

DOMINICA

MARTINIQUE (FRANCE)

ST. LUCIA
BARBADOS

ST. VINCENT &
THE GRENADINES

GRENADA

ANTILLES

TRINIDAD
& TOBAGO

◀ This square in Cuba
has architecture typical
of that built by the
European colonials.

**KEY TO MAP**
1 VIRGIN IS. (U.S.)
2 VIRGIN IS. (U.K.)
3 ANGUILLA (U.K.)

*Countries in parentheses are countries of
which that island or group is a dependency.
Aruba (Netherlands) is not shown.*

miles
0       100

0       100
km

soon after Columbus sighted the islands.
The Europeans brought slaves from Africa
to work on sugar and cotton plantations.
After the abolition of slavery in the 19th
century, people from India and China came
to work in the Caribbean.

## A CULTURAL MIX

The people of the Caribbean reflect its mix
of cultures. They speak Spanish, French or
English, often with a local dialect. Religion
is an important part of life. As well as
Christians, Hindus and Muslims, there are
Rastafarians, who worship Haile Selassie
(emperor of Ethiopia until 1974) as a god.
On Haiti, many people practise voodoo, a
blend of African and Christian beliefs.

## SELF-GOVERNING

Most larger islands are self-governing.
Others are dependencies still linked to a
colonial partner. They include Guadeloupe
(France) and the two Virgin Island groups
(UK and USA). The governments of the
Caribbean are working together to develop
the islands, many of which are poor. In the
last 50 years, many islanders have migrated
to Britain, Canada or the USA to find work.

**ST KITTS–NEVIS**
**Area:** 261 sq km
**Population:** 41,000
**Capital:** Basseterre
**Language:** English
**Currency:** East
Caribbean dollar

**ST LUCIA**
**Area:** 622 sq km
**Population:** 152,000
**Capital:** Castries
**Language:** English
**Currency:** East
Caribbean dollar

**ST VINCENT & THE
GRENADINES**
**Area:** 388 sq km
**Population:** 113,000
**Capital:** Kingstown
**Language:** English
**Currency:** East
Caribbean dollar

**TRINIDAD & TOBAGO**
**Area:** 5,130 sq km
**Population:** 1,285,000
**Capital:** Port-of-Spain
**Language:** English
**Currency:** Trinidad dollar

▲ The beautiful sandy beaches and warm waters of the
Caribbean islands lure tourists from all over the world.

**SEE ALSO**

North America

# CASTLE

**Castles are fortified homes that were owned by rich and powerful families during the Middle Ages. Some are still in use, but many are now in ruins.**

Early castles, known as motte and baileys, were made of wood and soil.

Massive stone keeps began to be erected around 1070.

Concentric castles had two or more walls and strongly guarded gatehouses.

In the Middle Ages, castles were used to protect towns, river crossings, and frontiers. They were also used to guard against invasion and prevent rebellion.

## MOTTE AND BAILEY

Castles were first built around A.D. 950 by knights or lords. The castles included a hill or mound surrounded by a ditch and topped by a wooden tower called a motte. A bailey, or courtyard, contained living quarters, stables, granaries, and barns. These early castles were protected by a high wooden fence, called a palisade.

## STONE CASTLES

From about 1070, larger castles had a stone tower called a keep. The Tower of London, the first keep in England, was begun in 1078. Food and weapons were stored inside the tower, and the knight and his staff lived there. Prisoners were kept in dungeons.

## TOWERS AND WALLS

From the 1100s onward, stone curtain walls were built to surround the keeps. Towers were added to the outside of the walls so that attackers could be shot at from different directions. After about 1270, a second outer wall was added to some castles to make them harder to attack. These castles, often built by Crusaders in the Middle East, were called concentric because of their double walls.

## UNDER ATTACK

A castle was attacked with catapults, rams, and siege towers. Boulders and flaming missiles were hurled at it, and its walls undermined. If a castle was not captured quickly it was besieged. Most castles fell because of bribery, disease, or famine.

## CANNON FIRE

By the 1450s, cannons and gunpowder became powerful enough to destroy walls. Castles were no longer safe from attack. Most fell into ruin, but some continued to be used as palaces or luxurious homes.

## UNDER SIEGE

Armies attacked castles by smashing walls with catapults or rams and by digging out foundations so that the walls collapsed. The moat was drained and filled in so that siege machines could be wheeled right up to the walls. Attackers were shielded by frames covered with wet hides.

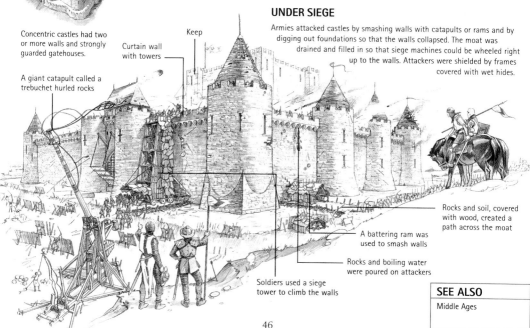

Keep

Curtain wall with towers

A giant catapult called a trebuchet hurled rocks

Rocks and soil, covered with wood, created a path across the moat

A battering ram was used to smash walls

Rocks and boiling water were poured on attackers

Soldiers used a siege tower to climb the walls

**SEE ALSO**

Middle Ages

# CAT

Cats are agile, hunting mammals with keen senses and sharp teeth and claws. Domestic cats make some of the most popular pets.

The long-haired Persian needs regular grooming to keep its coat sleek.

The hairless sphynx was bred in the 1960s from a kitten born without fur.

The Manx cat from the Isle of Man, in the UK, is famous for its lack of a tail.

The blue shorthair has copper eyes and a quiet, affectionate nature.

The Cornish rex has a curly coat of short, thin hair and large, open ears.

The Siamese has long been one of the most popular pedigree (purebred) cats.

## HUNTER IN THE HOME

Even a domestic cat, like this tabby, has the hunting instincts of its wild relations. Cats often toy with their prey, rather than killing it immediately. They hunt mostly at night, catching mice, small birds and insects.

Whiskers are modified hairs with nerves at their base and are ultra-sensitive to touch

Large, sensitive ears pick up sounds too faint for human ears to hear

Pupils open wide to let in a maximum amount of light. A mirror-like layer at the back of the eye intensifies the light

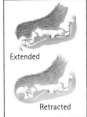

Extended

Retracted

### THE CLAWS

Cats retract (pull back) their claws to keep them sharp when not in use. Each claw is attached to a toe bone. It is retracted by ligaments, which are worked by muscles.

The cat family is divided into two main groups, based largely on size. The first group is made up of big cats such as tigers, lions and leopards. The second includes cougars, bobcats and lynxes, as well as the many small wild cats and the domestic cat. In all there are about 37 species of cat.

## PET CATS

It is thought that the domestic cat was originally a small wild cat living in Africa. By 2000BC it had been tamed by the Ancient Egyptians, who used it to protect their food stores from mice and rats. Today, there are many breeds of domestic cat, including longhaired Persians and Angoras and the shorthaired Manx and Siamese.

## CAT CHARACTERISTICS

Domestic cats resemble their wild relatives in many ways. They are excellent hunters, strong and agile, with a keen sense of hearing and very good eyesight. They have curved claws, strong jaws, sharp teeth and whiskers that are sensitive to touch. Cats are naturally inquisitive and are expert climbers and jumpers. Their flexible backbones allow them to swivel their bodies into a wide range of positions.

## CAT BEHAVIOUR

Cats spend at least an hour a day grooming their fur by licking it with their rough tongues. This helps to keep their fur in good condition and keeps them cool in hot weather. Cats sleep, on average, twice as long as other mammals, spending up to three quarters of the day asleep, usually in short intervals called cat naps.

## HUNTING TACTICS

Although most domestic cats do not have to catch their own food, their instinct (inborn behaviour) is to hunt. A cat's sensitive nose quickly picks up the scent of its prey. With its soft, padded paws, a cat can stalk its prey without being noticed until it is close enough to pounce. Then it grabs the prey with its claws and kills it with a powerful bite – usually at the back of the head, breaking the victim's neck.

### SEE ALSO
Animal, Mammal, Sight, Tiger

# CAVE

**Caves are hollows that are formed in rock and ice by erosion (wearing away), usually by water. The largest, most impressive caves are found in limestone rock.**

Some caves consist of just one hole barely large enough for a person to enter; others are intricate mazes of passageways and chambers. The Mammoth Cave network in Kentucky, USA, is the world's longest. Its labyrinth of caves stretches for 560km.

## ROCK, ICE AND LAVA

Caves sometimes form in sea cliffs, where waves attack weak spots in the rock. The pressure of the water and the salty spray gradually erode (eat away at) the cliff. Long, tunnel-like caves can also develop in glaciers where streams of melted water run beneath the ice. Similar caves can be found in volcanoes, where a crust forms over a liquid stream of molten lava.

## LIMESTONE CAVES

The largest and most impressive caves are found in limestone rock, where rainwater (which is slightly acidic) trickles through cracks in the rock. The rock slowly dissolves and the thin cracks get wider and wider. The trickle of rainwater swells into a stream, which carves hollows in the stone to form caves and pot-holes.

## THE INSIDE STORY

Where streams meet, they carve out very large caves, or caverns. The floor of the cavern may be filled by underground lakes, so that it can only be explored by diving. Water dripping from the ceilings of limestone caves is rich in minerals, such as calcium carbonate, from the dissolved rock. As the water drips, these minerals are often deposited in dramatic columns – long, slender stalactites hang down from the ceiling, while shorter, stumpier stalagmites grow up from the floor. Where they join together, a pillar is formed.

## MAKING CAVES

It takes thousands of years for a limestone cave to form. The process begins when rainwater starts to wear away the stone and seep through cracks. Horizontal caverns are made where the water forms underground lakes. These are left dry when the level of ground water falls.

**1** Rain falls on the ground and seeps through cracks in the rock.

**2** The cracks get wider and form a pot-hole.

**3** Passages appear as the water continues to dissolve the rock.

**4** The water becomes an underground stream, gradually eroding more rock to form a cave.

Stalactite

**5** Stalactites and stalagmites are formed from minerals deposited by the dripping water.

Stalagmite

Underground stream

## SEE ALSO

Glacier, Rock, Seashore, Volcano, Water

# CELL

Cells are the smallest units capable of all the functions of life. Some living things are single cells, while others (such as ourselves) are made up of billions of cells.

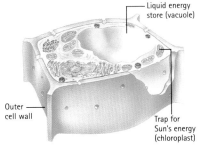

▲ Plant cells have a thick wall of cellulose, which gives them a rigid shape. Up to 90 per cent of their space is taken up by the vacuole – a sack full of sugary water.

Liquid energy store (vacuole)

Outer cell wall

Trap for Sun's energy (chloroplast)

Every living thing is made up of tiny chambers, called cells – the basic building blocks of all organisms. Every cell has its job, but works with the others to keep the plant or animal alive. Some living things, such as bacteria, are just one cell; this contains all they need to survive.

Bacteria have only one cell, and can multiply fast.

## THROUGH THE WALLS

A cell is surrounded by a thin film, or membrane. This gives it shape and allows chemicals and waste to pass in and out. Inside the membrane, tiny structures float in a jelly-like fluid called cytoplasm.

## INSIDE THE CHAMBER

Each tiny structure, or organelle, in a cell has a job. The nucleus, for example, contains genes (instructions that decide the cell's shape and function). Sausage-shaped structures called mitochondria release the energy in food. Other organelles store energy, make proteins, keep the cell clear of debris or defend it against bacteria.

Onions, like most plants, have box-shaped cells.

## PLANT CELLS

Unlike animal cells, plant cells have a thick cell wall and extra structures called chloroplasts. These structures are filled with a green pigment called chlorophyll. This traps the Sun's energy and uses it to make food in a process called photosynthesis.

## SPLITTING IN TWO

Cells multiply by splitting in two. Under a microscope, you can see some bacteria split as fast as once every 15 minutes. Most animal and plant cells multiply much more slowly than this for growth, to repair damage and for reproduction.

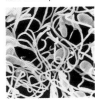

Sperm cells are used in reproduction.

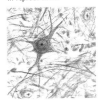

Nerve cells take messages to and from the brain.

Muscle cells are long and thin and lie in bundles.

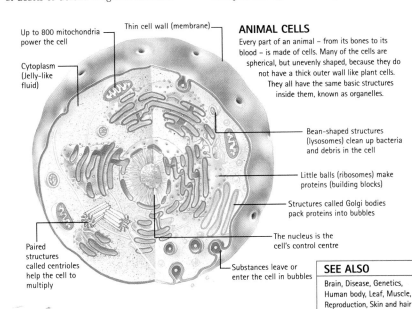

Up to 800 mitochondria power the cell

Thin cell wall (membrane)

Cytoplasm (Jelly-like fluid)

Paired structures called centrioles help the cell to multiply

Substances leave or enter the cell in bubbles

## ANIMAL CELLS

Every part of an animal – from its bones to its blood – is made of cells. Many of the cells are spherical, but unevenly shaped, because they do not have a thick outer wall like plant cells. They all have the same basic structures inside them, known as organelles.

Bean-shaped structures (lysosomes) clean up bacteria and debris in the cell

Little balls (ribosomes) make proteins (building blocks)

Structures called Golgi bodies pack proteins into bubbles

The nucleus is the cell's control centre

## SEE ALSO

Brain, Disease, Genetics, Human body, Leaf, Muscle, Reproduction, Skin and hair

# CHEMISTRY

Chemistry is the study of chemicals. These are substances that are used in, or created by, a reaction involving changes to atoms or molecules.

**ANTOINE LAVOISIER**
(1743–94). Lavoisier was a French chemist. He explained how chemical reactions worked. He was the first to understand the role of oxygen in combustion (burning).

## CHEMICAL ANALYSIS

Chemists use flame tests as a way of identifying chemical elements – by seeing which colour they give off when held in the flame of a Bunsen burner. A compound of an element is burned on the end of a piece of platinum wire or asbestos. The flame burns a distinctive colour and so the element can be identified. This type of chemical analysis is called qualitative and shows what elements a substance contains. To show how much of an element is present, chemists use quantitative analysis.

**Flame colours
of elements**

Barium

Potassium

Lithium

The compound is put into the flame on a platinum wire

Sodium

Copper

Bunsen burner

Calcium

Oxygen is an element. The two atoms that make up its molecules are of the same kind. The chemical formula for oxygen is $O_2$.

Carbon dioxide gas is a compound of two oxygen atoms with one carbon atom. Its chemical formula is written $CO_2$.

A molecule of methane gas has a carbon atom in the middle bonded to four hydrogen atoms. Its formula is written $CH_4$.

Water has one oxygen atom and two hydrogen atoms, giving it probably the best-known chemical formula, $H_2O$.

Chemistry explains the way substances behave and how they combine with each other. Chemists use chemical reactions to create many substances that are used in everyday life, including plastics, dyes, glues, detergents and medicines.

## ELEMENTS AND COMPOUNDS

An element is a substance in which all the atoms are of the same kind. A compound is a combination of two or more elements. The compound sodium chloride (common salt), for example, is a combination of the elements sodium and chlorine. Many compounds, including salt and water, occur naturally. Others, such as nylon and plastic, were first made artificially in laboratories.

## CHEMICAL REACTIONS

When different substances combine to form new materials, a chemical reaction has taken place. A substance's atoms are bonded together into molecules. During a reaction, the bonds between atoms break, allowing new molecules to form. A rusting car is an example of a chemical reaction, as iron in the car and oxygen in the air form iron oxide, or rust. Chemists use symbols (such as Fe for iron and O for oxygen) to record what happens in a reaction.

## ALCHEMISTS TO SCIENTISTS

Medieval alchemists studied reactions, but it was not until the 1770s that Antoine Lavoisier showed how reactions work. In 1869, Russian chemist Dmitri Mendeleyev worked out the periodic table, grouping elements by how they react with each other.

## WEAPONS AND DRUGS

Today, chemical substances of all kinds are mined or manufactured. Chemists search for new reactions to create fertilizers or drugs, which may contain long chains of molecules. Industry mass-produces useful chemicals through large-scale reactions. Poison gas and other chemicals have been used as weapons, but they are now banned.

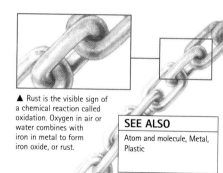

▲ Rust is the visible sign of a chemical reaction called oxidation. Oxygen in air or water combines with iron in metal to form iron oxide, or rust.

### SEE ALSO
Atom and molecule, Metal, Plastic

# CHINA

China is the third largest country in the world and the nation with the largest population. Almost a quarter of the Earth's people live in China.

**Area:** 9,596,961 sq km
**Population:** 1,223,902,000
**Capital:** Beijing
**Language:** Mandarin
**Currency:** Yuan

China is one of the world's oldest civilizations. Its name comes from an ancient Chinese ruling family called Qin (pronounced Ch'in). The Chinese call their country Zhongguo, which means 'middle land'. China's 1.2 billion citizens are ruled by one of the world's few remaining communist governments.

▲ The giant panda lives in the bamboo forests of central and western China. So few now survive in the wild that it has become a worldwide symbol for conservation.

## NATURAL BARRIERS

China lies in the eastern half of Asia, and deserts and mountains form natural barriers with its neighbours. The Gobi Desert, which covers 1,300,000 sq km, straddles China's border with Mongolia. The Himalayas – the highest mountains on Earth, rising to over 8,000m – stretch along the border with India, Bhutan and Nepal. The Chang (Yangtze) river is the longest in Asia and flows from the Tibetan highlands to the East China Sea, dividing the warm, moist southern regions from the drier and cooler north.

## CHINA'S WILDLIFE

Plant life ranges from bamboos and other subtropical plants in the south to coniferous forests in the north. Many garden plants now common around the world, such as the climbing plant wisteria, first came from China. With much of the country covered by mountains and desert, forests have been cleared to make way for villages and farms. This has reduced the habitats of animals such as the tiger (which is also prey to hunters) and the giant panda, making them rare in the wild. ▶

▲ The bicycle is the main method of transport for people in China. More than 17 million bicycles are made there each year.

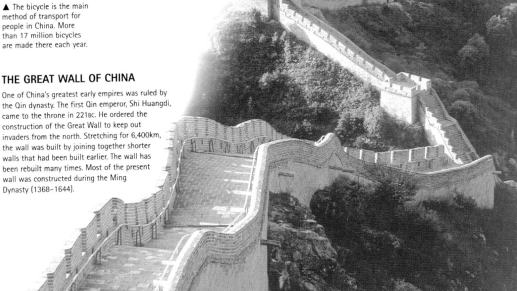

## THE GREAT WALL OF CHINA

One of China's greatest early empires was ruled by the Qin dynasty. The first Qin emperor, Shi Huangdi, came to the throne in 221BC. He ordered the construction of the Great Wall to keep out invaders from the north. Stretching for 6,400km, the wall was built by joining together shorter walls that had been built earlier. The wall has been rebuilt many times. Most of the present wall was constructed during the Ming Dynasty (1368–1644).

## A NATION OF FARMERS

About 70 per cent of people farm the land. Many farms are run as collectives, with people working together and dividing crops between the government and themselves. Important crops include rice and wheat.

## INDUSTRIAL GROWTH

China's industry has grown rapidly in the last 40 years. Chinese factories produce machinery, transport equipment, clothing and electrical goods.

## PHILOSOPHY AND FAMILY

For more than 2,000 years, Confucianism has been China's main religion. It teaches respect for parents and ancestors, and has strongly influenced family life in China. At one time, several generations of a family lived in the same house. Today, families are much smaller.

## RULED BY DYNASTIES

For thousands of years, China was an empire ruled by emperors from royal families called dynasties. Many great inventions were made by the Chinese, including paper, ink, silk, printing and gunpowder. In 1911, dynastic rule ended and China became a republic.

## COMMUNIST RULE

In 1949, China adopted a communist government and was re-named the People's Republic of China, under the leadership of

▲ Preparing food on a street stall. Rice, noodles and vegetables are the main ingredients used in Chinese cooking.

◄ Shanghai is China's largest city, with a population of 13,500,000. It is also China's leading industrial centre.

Mao Tse-tung. His strict policies meant that there were many changes as all aspects of life came under state control.

## CHINA TODAY

Since Mao's death in 1976, China's government has encouraged economic reform and trade with other countries. More people are moving to the cities, attracted by factory jobs and higher living standards.

► This man is performing a traditional form of exercise that develops both mind and body. Called wushu, it is an ancient Chinese martial art.

◄ Farmers bring their produce to sell at a market in southern China. Here, farmers harvest three crops a year – two of rice and one of vegetables.

## SEE ALSO

Asia, Communism, Paper

# CHRISTIANITY

Christianity is a religion based on the teachings of Jesus Christ, who lived in Palestine about 2,000 years ago. Today, it is practised throughout the world.

▲ Upon entering the Christian faith, followers are baptized with water. This symbolizes cleansing and reflects the way Jesus was baptized by John the Baptist.

The most well-known symbol of Christianity is the cross. It represents the cross on which Jesus was crucified.

Greek Christians used the fish as a code. The Greek word for fish spelled out the first letters of 'Jesus Christ, God's Son, Saviour'.

The Christian Bible consists of the Hebrew Bible (Old Testament) and Christ's life and teachings (New Testament).

More people follow the Christian religion than any other. About 1.5 billion people believe that there is only one God and that he sent his son, Jesus Christ, to Earth to proclaim his law and to save people from sin.

## THE LIFE OF CHRIST

The life and teachings of Jesus Christ are contained in the New Testament of the Bible, the Christians' holy book. (The Old Testament of the Bible contains the sacred writings of the Jews.) Jesus is said to have performed miracles and healed the sick. The Roman rulers of Jerusalem crucified him by nailing him to a cross. Christians believe that three days later Jesus was resurrected, or came back to life, and that some 40 days later he rose into Heaven.

## CHRISTIANITY SPREADS

Jesus' teachings were spread by his disciples, or followers, who formed the early church. Despite persecution, Christianity became the religion of the Roman Empire in AD324 and later spread across the world. Today, there are three main divisions in the Christian Church: Roman Catholic,

Protestant and Eastern Orthodox, of which 56 per cent are Catholics.

## THREE-IN-ONE GOD

Christians believe God has three forms: the Father (God), the Son (Jesus) and the Holy Spirit (God's influence on Earth). Together they form the Holy Trinity.

## THE HOLY MEAL

Before his Crucifixion, Jesus ate the Last Supper with his disciples. Christians re-enact this meal with bread and wine in a special church ceremony called Holy Communion, or Mass, when Christ 'becomes present' again. They celebrate Christ's birth at Christmas, his Resurrection at Easter and the coming of the Holy Spirit at Pentecost.

▲ On Palm Sunday (the Sunday before Easter) many Christians carry palms in church. This commemorates Jesus' entry into Jerusalem, when he was greeted with branches of palm.

▶ The leader of the Roman Catholic Church is the Pope. Catholics believe he is God's representative on Earth.

SEE ALSO
Religion, Roman Empire

# CLIMATE

The climate of a region is its weather pattern over a long period of time. The weather may change from day to day, but the climate stays the same.

▼ The world can be divided into different climate zones. These vary from tropical regions, characterized by hot and humid weather, to freezing polar areas.

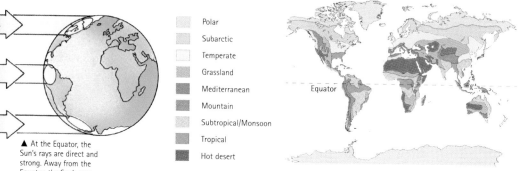

Legend:
- Polar
- Subarctic
- Temperate
- Grassland
- Mediterranean
- Mountain
- Subtropical/Monsoon
- Tropical
- Hot desert

Equator

▲ At the Equator, the Sun's rays are direct and strong. Away from the Equator, the Sun's rays are weaker because they strike the Earth at an angle and must travel farther through the cool air of the atmosphere.

The climate of a region depends on how close the region is to the sea, how high up it is (its altitude) and, most importantly, how far it is from the Equator (its latitude). Climate is usually measured as a combination of the average rainfall in an area and the temperature.

## THE POWER OF THE SUN
The two extremes of climate on Earth are found at the Equator and at the Poles. The climate is hottest in the zones each side of the Equator, known as the tropics, because the Sun is almost directly overhead. The Poles are the coldest areas on Earth: temperatures drop below –50°C.

Polar front

Subtropical jet stream

Wind direction

AFRICA

Warm air from the Equator

## THE TROPICS
The tropics are not only the hottest areas but also the wettest. The Sun is so hot here that it evaporates water from the rivers and oceans, forming rain clouds that drench the region. Some of the world's largest deserts, such as the Sahara in Africa, lie either side of the tropics because the air moving out from the tropics has lost most of its moisture by the time it reaches them.

## COLDER HIGHER UP
Mountainous regions have a colder climate than nearby low areas. This is because air is cooler the higher up you go in the atmosphere. On a mountain, air cools by 6°C for each 1,000m climbed.

## CHANGING CLIMATE
Climates can change over time. Volcanic eruptions may have a sudden, local effect, but deforestation and destruction of the ozone layer by pollutant gases may have long-term effects all over the world.

## WIND CIRCULATION
At the Poles, cold air sinks and disperses and is replaced by warmer air flowing in from above. The cold air moving away from the Poles meets warm winds from the subtropics and pushes the warm air back to the Equator.

### SEE ALSO
Desert, Forest, Habitat, Mountain and valley Pollution, Water, Weather

# COAL

**Coal is a rock formed under the ground from the remains of decayed prehistoric plants. It burns easily and is widely used as a fuel.**

Anthracite is the highest quality coal. It gives the most heat but little smoke.

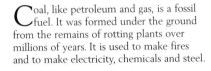

Most coal mined today is used in power stations to produce light and heat.

Some perfumes are made from coal tar – a black liquid produced from coal.

Coal, like petroleum and gas, is a fossil fuel. It was formed under the ground from the remains of rotting plants over millions of years. It is used to make fires and to make electricity, chemicals and steel.

## CARBON CONTENT
Coal is made up of carbon, tar, oils and minerals. There are three different types of coal, depending on the amount of carbon each contains. Lignite, or brown coal, contains less than 50 per cent carbon, bituminous coal around 70 per cent, and anthracite, the most valuable, has about 95 per cent carbon. Over four billion tonnes of coal are mined each year and 4,000 billion tonnes remain underground.

## INDUSTRIAL COAL
In about 1750, the Industrial Revolution led to a huge demand for coal as a fuel for steam engines. Today, many power stations burn coal to produce electricity. The iron industry uses coke – coal which has been heated to make the tar and oils evaporate – to produce iron and steel. The tar and oils are then used to produce dyes, fertilizers and fibres such as nylon.

## POLLUTION
When coal is burned, it releases smoke containing soot and poisonous gases, such as carbon monoxide. These can harm the environment, so power stations usually have filters to clean the smoke.

▲ A great deal of mechanized equipment is used to mine coal. Cutting machines dig out coal at the coal face while a conveyor belt transports it back up the shaft.

## HOW COAL IS FORMED
About 300 million years ago, in an age known as the Carboniferous period, the climate was warm and wet, ideal for swampy forests. Dead plants rotted and formed peat, which was buried under layers of sand and mud as sea levels rose, flooding the swamps. These layers slowly turned to rock. Their weight squeezed the peat, turning it into coal.

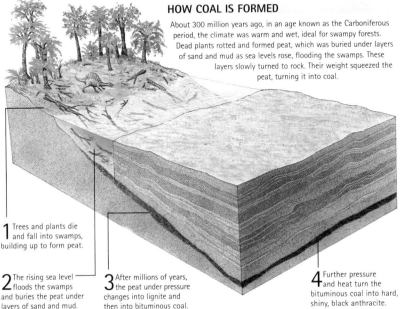

**1** Trees and plants die and fall into swamps, building up to form peat.

**2** The rising sea level floods the swamps and buries the peat under layers of sand and mud.

**3** After millions of years, the peat under pressure changes into lignite and then into bituminous coal.

**4** Further pressure and heat turn the bituminous coal into hard, shiny, black anthracite.

▲ A shaft is dug down to a seam several hundred metres down. A few mines are open-cast – coal is mined at the surface.

### SEE ALSO
Electricity, Fossil, Gas, Industrial Revolution, Iron and steel, Oil, Pollution

# COLD WAR

The Cold War was a period of hostility between
the capitalist and communist countries of the world.
It began after the end of World War II.

▲ The USSR's Nikita Khrushchev (left) and US President
John F. Kennedy, fingers poised over their nuclear buttons,
confront each other in this 1962 cartoon.

For more than 45 years, between 1945
and 1991, two superpowers, the USA
and the Soviet Union (USSR), fought each
other using spies, alliances, trading bans
and local wars as their weapons.

### IRON CURTAIN
After World War II, the USSR and the
USA distrusted each other. As communist
governments took control of Eastern
Europe, the Western nations reacted by
forming a military alliance called the
North Atlantic Treaty Organization
(NATO). The frontier between West and
East became known as the Iron Curtain.

### CONFRONTATION
The Cold War was marked by a series of
crises. The first was the Berlin Airlift in

1948, when the West flew in supplies to a
Soviet-blockaded Berlin, the former capital
of Germany. The superpowers began
stockpiling nuclear weapons. Other
countries took sides. In 1962, people feared
that nuclear war would break out when the
USA demanded that the USSR withdraw
nuclear missiles from Cuba. Eventually, the
Soviets backed down and the crisis ended.

### THE COLD WAR THAWS
After 1970, tension between the
superpowers began to ease. The Cold War
finally ended in the 1990s with the fall of
communism in many European countries,
and the break-up of the USSR.

### NO MAN'S LAND
After World War II, Germany was divided up. The USA, France and
Britain controlled the West and the USSR controlled the East. The
capital, Berlin, was also divided and, from 1949 to 1958, three
million people escaped from East to West Berlin. In 1961, East
Germany close off this escape route by building the Berlin Wall
through the centre of city. It crossed tram lines and roads and
created an area on either side known as No Man's Land.

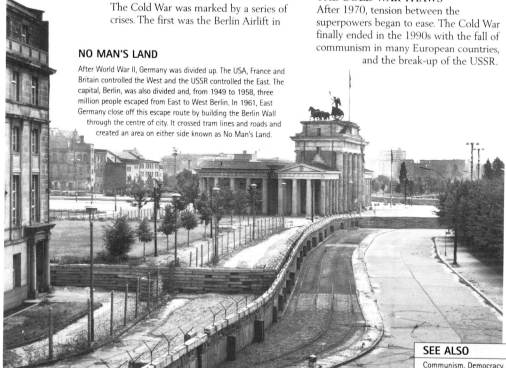

## SEE ALSO
Communism, Democracy,
Germany, Russia and the
Baltic States, USA, World
War II

# COLOUR

Colour is what we see when light from an object reaches our eyes. White light seems colourless, but it is actually made up of a mixture of colours.

When you see a rainbow, you are seeing sunlight split apart by raindrops. The rainbow has seven colours – red, orange, yellow, green, blue, indigo and violet. This range is called the spectrum.

The primary colours of light are red, blue and green. Mixed together they make up white light.

The primary colours of paint are yellow, blue and red. Mixed together they produce black.

▲ Georges Seurat's *The Circus* (1891) is painted using a technique called pointillism. Pure colour is applied as dots, which merge at a distance to create the subtler shades.

## REFLECTING LIGHT

An object only appears to be a particular colour because of the light it reflects. For example, a leaf looks green because it reflects green light and absorbs all the other colours in the spectrum.

## PRIMARY COLOURS

In the 19th century, scientists were amazed to discover that almost any colour of light can be created by combining different amounts of a basic set of three colours – red, blue and green. These are known as the primary colours of light.

## MIXING IT UP

If equal amounts of red, blue and green light are mixed together, they make white light. Mixing just red and green light together makes yellow; blue and green makes cyan (a green-blue); and blue and red makes magenta. In photography, printing, film and television, light is mixed to produce millions of different colours.

## PAINTING A DIFFERENT PICTURE

Pigments (used in paints) have a different set of primary colours. The primary colours are yellow, blue and red, and when they are mixed together they make black.

## SEEING IN COLOUR

We see colour when light falls on the retina at the back of the eye. The retina is full of cells, called cones and rods, that are sensitive to light. Cones are sensitive to particular colours, and rods, which are not colour-sensitive, help us to see in dim light.

## REFLECTION AND ABSORPTION

When light hits an object, the object absorbs (soaks up) some of the colours of the spectrum and reflects (throws off) others. A tomato, for example, looks red because it reflects red light back into our eyes, but absorbs the other colours of the rainbow: orange, yellow, green, blue, indigo and violet light.

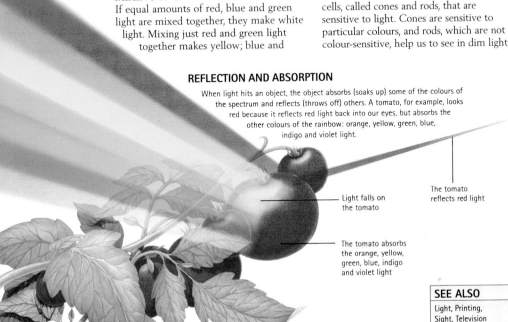

Light falls on the tomato

The tomato reflects red light

The tomato absorbs the orange, yellow, green, blue, indigo and violet light

## SEE ALSO

Light, Printing, Sight, Television

# COMET, METEOR AND ASTEROID

Comets, meteors and asteroids are chunks of ice, rock or metal that circle the Sun. As they travel closer to the Earth, some can be seen lighting up the night sky.

Shooting stars are meteors burning up as they enter Earth's atmosphere.

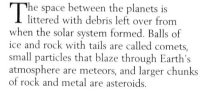

The 19km-long asteroid Gaspra was photographed by the *Galileo* space probe.

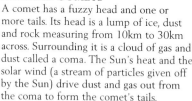

Arizona's Barringer Crater was made by a meteorite over 20,000 years ago.

The space between the planets is littered with debris left over from when the solar system formed. Balls of ice and rock with tails are called comets, small particles that blaze through Earth's atmosphere are meteors, and larger chunks of rock and metal are asteroids.

## ICE-COLD COMETS

A comet has a fuzzy head and one or more tails. Its head is a lump of ice, dust and rock measuring from 10km to 30km across. Surrounding it is a cloud of gas and dust called a coma. The Sun's heat and the solar wind (a stream of particles given off by the Sun) drive dust and gas out from the coma to form the comet's tails.

## SHOOTING STARS AND SHOWERS

Many meteors have been around since our solar system formed, but others are chips off comets and asteroids, or even the Moon and Mars. These can be as small as grains of sand and most

burn up as they hurtle into the Earth's atmosphere, travelling at speeds of up to 40km/second. These are called shooting stars. Some travel in swarms and create a meteor shower in the night sky. Such showers can appear at the same time each year, when Earth crosses the swarm's path. Every year, a few meteors hit the Earth's surface and are called meteorites.

## THE ASTEROID BELT

Asteroids (sometimes called minor planets) are chunks of rock and metal smaller than planets that circle the Sun. More than 4,000 have been found. The largest asteroid, Ceres, is 930km across, but most are much smaller. They are usually found in the asteroid belt between Mars and Jupiter.

## A COMET IN FLIGHT

Comets are surrounded by clouds of dust, called comas, which can be up to a million kilometres across. Comets travel in long loops around the Sun. Each time they approach the Sun, more gas and dust evaporate from their centres, making the comas grow larger and the comets form tails. Comets' tails always point away from the Sun.

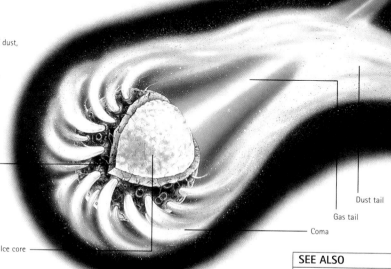

Rocky crust

Ice core

Dust tail

Gas tail

Coma

▲ Halley's Comet is visible from Earth every 76 years. It was closely studied on its last return in 1986.

### SEE ALSO
Astronomy, Moon, Planet, Solar system, Spacecraft, Space exploration, Sun, Universe

# COMMUNICATION

Communication is the process of sending and receiving messages. This can be done by using spoken and written language or recognized signs and signals.

◀ Sign language for the deaf uses hand signals and is based on ideas, not words.

The Sumerians developed the first known writing system in about 3500BC.

From the 1400s, printing became a means of mass communication in Europe.

The telephone, invented in 1876, allowed long-distance communication.

A satellite dish receives images and sounds sent from around the world.

People usually communicate with each other individually or in small groups. However, they sometimes need to relay messages to a much larger audience. This is known as mass communication.

## SIGNS AND SIGNALS
Humans have developed ingenious ways of conveying messages to each other, using signs and signals when language cannot be used. Some Native Americans sent smoke signals and African tribes-people used drumbeats. Signals are still in use today – navies send messages using flags (known as semaphore) and road users rely on roadside signs and traffic lights.

## POSTAL COMMUNICATIONS
One of the earliest, cheapest and most reliable forms of communication is the postal service. The first stamps were used in Britain in 1840. Most letters today are sorted by machine, and then transported by road, rail or air to their destination.

## TELEGRAPH MESSAGES
For a long time, the fastest way to communicate over long distances was to deliver messages on foot, on horseback or by boat. Then in 1840, the American inventor Samuel Morse introduced the first simple telegraph, which used electricity to send messages down wire cables. The messages were coded using a system of dots and dashes. This became known as Morse code.

## FASTER THAN EVER
Since the 1800s, many inventions, such as the telephone, radio and television, have made communication across the world faster and easier. Today, a message can be sent to the other side of the world in seconds by using satellite and computer links. The Internet enables all types of computers to share services and communicate directly. Video conference centres allow people thousands of miles apart to see and talk to each other directly.

## THE PONY EXPRESS
In 1860, the Pony Express was the fastest delivery system in the USA, delivering letters along a 3,164km trail in less than ten days, where previously it had taken over three weeks by boat or stagecoach. The riders rode in all weather, changing to fresh horses at each pony express station – spaced 16-20km apart. The service was closed in October 1861, once the telegraph and Morse code came into use.

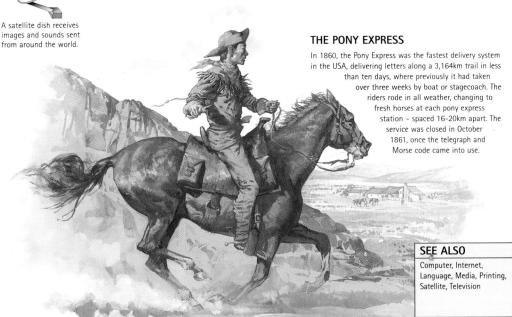

## SEE ALSO
Computer, Internet, Language, Media, Printing, Satellite, Television

# COMMUNISM

**Communism is a political theory based on the idea that everybody should share all wealth, property and industry equally.**

The German journalist Karl Marx developed the idea of communism in the 1800s.

Mao Tse-tung led the Communists to victory in China in the 1940s.

President Fidel Castro has led Cuba since 1959 after a three-year guerrilla war.

Ho Chi Minh led North Vietnam for most of the Vietnam War.

▶ Vladimir Lenin, leader of the Bolshevik Party, led a revolution that overthrew tsarist rule in Russia. He set up the world's first communist regime in 1917.

In 1848, Karl Marx and Friedrich Engels published the *Communist Manifesto*, which stated that private ownership should be replaced by common ownership. Marx wanted to see an end to the way of life in which most people worked for a low wage while a few wealthy people owned the factories and land. He believed that the only way to achieve this was by revolution.

## THE FIRST REVOLUTION

The first successful communist revolution took place in Russia in 1917, after which the Union of Soviet Socialist Republics (USSR) was set up under the leadership of Vladimir Lenin. The state took control of farms, factories and railways in the name of the people. Lenin and his successor, Joseph Stalin, ruled as dictators. Most people were better fed and housed, but personal freedoms were severely restricted.

## SPREAD OF COMMUNISM

After World War II, communism spread to Eastern Europe, China and countries in Africa, Asia and Central America. During

◀ Since North Korea became communist in 1948, many statues to heroic workers have been erected.

the Cold War, there was hostile rivalry between the communist countries and the US-led Western democracies.

## THE COLLAPSE

From 1989 to 1992, communism in countries such as Poland, Hungary and East Germany collapsed. With the break-up of the USSR in the 1990s, China remains the only major nation with a communist government.

### KEY DATES

**1848** Journalist Karl Marx and philosopher Friedrich Engels publish the Communist Manifesto

**1917** Lenin leads Russia's Bolshevik Revolution

**1949** China becomes a communist state under Mao Tse-tung

**1989** Communism collapses in Eastern Europe

**1991** The break-up of the USSR leaves only China, Cuba, Vietnam and N. Korea as communist states

### SEE ALSO

China, Cold War, Democracy, Eastern Europe, Revolution, Russia and the Baltic States

# COMPUTER

Computers are machines that handle information according to sets of instructions. They then give the results in a form that people can understand.

In 1834, Charles Babbage (1792-1871) designed the first mechanical computer, but he never saw it built.

The computer is an electronic device that can do calculations millions of times faster than the human brain. First, the computer receives data, or information, put in by the user, then it processes the data as simple electrical signals according to its program, and produces a result.

## BINARY NUMBERS

All computers use a language called the binary system. Binary numbers are entirely made up of the digits 0 and 1. When a letter is typed on the keyboard or when the mouse or joystick is moved, tiny electric currents are sent to the computer. These currents are stored by the computer as binary numbers.

In the 1960s, computers used transistors and stored data on tape. They could fill a whole room.

## MINIATURIZATION

The first computers took up a whole room, but by the 1960s, electronic components had become much smaller and computers began to shrink in size. The home computer became possible through the invention of the microchip, which contains tens of thousands of electronic components within a space no larger than a fingernail.

The 1981 Sinclair ZX81 was one of the first home computers to be launched on the world market.

## HIGHLY VERSATILE

A PC (personal computer) can tackle jobs from word-processing to 3-D design and animation. Music can be recorded, edited and played back on the PC. Desktop publishing means books and magazines can be designed on the PC.

Portable laptop computers, small enough to fit inside a briefcase, became available in the 1980s.

## HOW IT WORKS

Data (information) in a PC is usually stored in random-access memory (RAM). The central processing unit (CPU) calls it up when it is needed, according to a list of instructions (the program), which is also stored in memory. Data flows to and from the CPU along an electronic pathway called the bus. After processing, data is stored in RAM again.

## SCIENCE FRONTIERS

Computers have revolutionized science and technology. Space probes, satellite TV and weapon detection systems all rely

The process of miniaturization created electronic diaries called personal organizers.

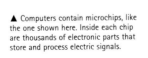

▲ Computers contain microchips, like the one shown here. Inside each chip are thousands of electronic parts that store and process electric signals.

on computers. Computers make it possible to test chemical and nuclear reactions without real-life experiments.

## AUTOMATION
In the car industry, computers are used to design a vehicle and then build it with the aid of robots. Inside the car itself, a computer can check the engine, the brakes and the steering. Computers can even be used in the home to control temperature, lighting and security.

## GLOBAL LINKS
Computers are increasingly changing the way we live by connecting people and places all over the world. The Internet links up computers all over the world, allowing messages and information to be sent across the globe in a matter of seconds.

**BILL GATES** (born 1955) In 1975, American Bill Gates founded Microsoft, now the largest software company in the world.

## HOW THE COMPUTER WORKS

A computer system has four basic parts. An input device such as the keyboard, mouse or joystick enters information into the computer. Then the central processing unit (CPU), acting as the computer's brain, performs the tasks. The information is sent to an output device, such as the screen or printer, to display the results. And finally a memory unit stores programs and data.

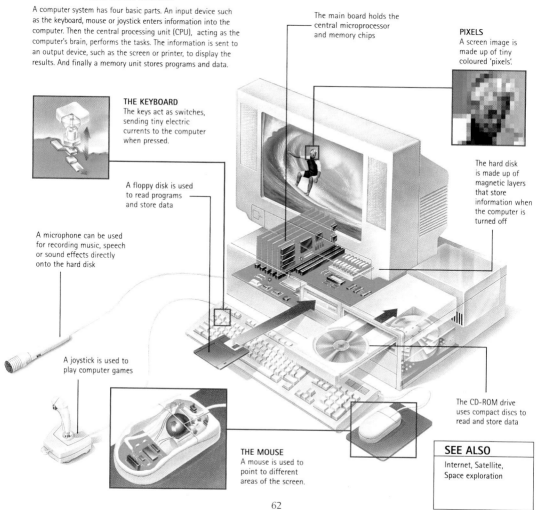

The main board holds the central microprocessor and memory chips

**PIXELS**
A screen image is made up of tiny coloured 'pixels'.

**THE KEYBOARD**
The keys act as switches, sending tiny electric currents to the computer when pressed.

The hard disk is made up of magnetic layers that store information when the computer is turned off

A floppy disk is used to read programs and store data

A microphone can be used for recording music, speech or sound effects directly onto the hard disk

A joystick is used to play computer games

The CD-ROM drive uses compact discs to read and store data

**THE MOUSE**
A mouse is used to point to different areas of the screen.

**SEE ALSO**
Internet, Satellite, Space exploration

# CONSERVATION

Conservation is the protection and careful use of the Earth's natural resources, such as animals, plants and fossil fuels. It also includes care of historical treasures.

▲ Recycling plastics, paper, tin and glass conserves the Earth's resources. In many US states, laws have been passed by which households can be fined for failing to separate rubbish for recycling.

Conservationists try to find a balance between the needs of human beings and care of the environment. There are more than 5,000 million people alive today and they all need land to live on, food to eat and fuel for power. Without care, habitats can be destroyed, resources used up and the Earth damaged.

## GLOBAL AWARENESS

Some conservation issues are local, as when an ancient oak tree is threatened with felling to make way for a new road. Others, such as recycling, saving energy and stopping animals from becoming extinct, are shared worldwide. In 1992, world leaders got together at the Earth Summit in Brazil to draw up the very first global action plan to save the planet. One scheme that was introduced to encourage

◄ The care and preservation of paintings is a painstaking process. An art conservator must understand a painting's history and content in the same way that an animal conservationist must know the habits of an endangered animal.

people to stop destroying their habitats – by logging trees or draining marshes – is the 'debt-for-nature' idea. This means that a poor country has some of its international debt cancelled in exchange for setting aside areas for conservation.

## FACING EXTINCTION

As many as 100 rare plant and animal species become extinct each day – far more than when the dinosaurs died out, 65 million years ago. The tiger, rhinoceros, Asian snow leopard and even some species of insect are all in danger of disappearing forever. The last few hundred mountain gorillas live on the borders of Rwanda, Uganda and Zaire, in Africa. Their rainforest home has been destroyed by farmers and timber firms, and they are killed by hungry villagers.

## NATURE RESERVES

One of the best ways of protecting wildlife is to preserve an entire habitat in a national park. Zoos also help by breeding rare animals, such as the giant panda.

## SAVING THE HELPLESS GIANT

Many species of large whale, such as the humpback whale (below), are threatened with extinction because they have been over-hunted for their blubber, meat, oil and bones. A global conservation body known as the International Whaling Commission (IWC) outlawed the killing of such rare whales in 1985, but not all countries have agreed to stop hunting.

## SEE ALSO

Animal, Asia, Dinosaur, Ecology, Energy, Habitat, Pollution, Rainforest, Whale and dolphin, Zoology

# CONTINENT

Continents are large stretches of land unbroken by sea. There are seven continents on Earth.

## HOW CONTINENTS DRIFT

All the land on Earth is fixed to giant plates which float on a sea of magma (melted rock). As the magma moves slowly, so do the continents, but some towards each other and others apart. Where two giant plates rub together, a crack sometimes appears in the Earth's surface, allowing magma to escape. Two such cracks, known as mid-ocean ridges, run through the Atlantic and Indian oceans.

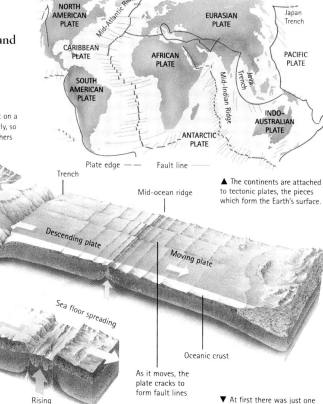

▲ The continents are attached to tectonic plates, the pieces which form the Earth's surface.

Plate edge - - -    Fault line

Trench    Mid-ocean ridge

Continental crust    Volcano    Descending plate    Moving plate

Sea floor spreading    Oceanic crust

Rising magma    As it moves, the plate cracks to form fault lines

The Earth's crust is like a giant jigsaw puzzle made up of eight large pieces and several small pieces, called tectonic plates. On top of these plates sit seven land masses, or continents: Africa, Antarctica, Asia, Australia, Europe, North America and South America. Together they make up 95 per cent of Earth's land surface, with islands forming the rest. The largest continent is Asia, with an area of just over 44 million sq km, and the smallest is Australia, covering about 7.7 million sq km.

## CONTINENTAL CRUST

The continents are the thickest parts of the Earth's outer layer, or crust – in some places reaching down 60km to 70km. At the centre, the continents contain the oldest rocks on the planet, with some dating back three billion years. As newer rocks were added around the fringes of these ancient cores, the continents grew.

## FLOATING WORLD

The tectonic plates on which the continents sit are floating on a hot, molten layer called magma. Heat from deep inside the Earth keeps the magma moving slowly, and as it moves, so do the plates and continents. The slow movement of the continents is called continental drift.

## VANISHED LANDS

More than 300 million years ago, all the land on Earth formed just one continent, called Pangaea. Then, about 180 million years ago, it split into two continents, called Gondwanaland and Laurasia. Slowly, North and South America broke away, India joined Asia, and Australia split from Antarctica and moved northwards, until today's seven continents were created.

## TOMORROW'S CONTINENTS

The movement is still continuing, and the continents we know today will look very different in 50 million years' time. Africa and the Americas, for example, will be even farther away from each other. North and South America will no longer be joined and Australia will have moved farther northwards.

▼ At first there was just one large continent, then two, and finally today's seven continents were formed.

Laurasia

Gondwanaland

180 million years ago

North America    Europe & Asia

South America    Africa    India

Antarctica & Australia

65 million years ago

## SEE ALSO

Africa, Antarctica, Asia, Australia, Earth, Europe, North America, Ocean and sea, Rock, South America

64

# CRAB AND OTHER CRUSTACEANS

Crabs belong to a group of animals called crustaceans. These creatures have no bones and are covered with a hard shell called an exoskeleton.

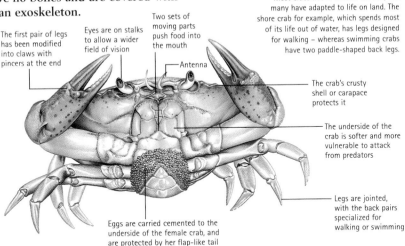

The first pair of legs has been modified into claws with pincers at the end

Eyes are on stalks to allow a wider field of vision

Two sets of moving parts push food into the mouth

Antenna

The crab's crusty shell or carapace protects it

The underside of the crab is softer and more vulnerable to attack from predators

Legs are jointed, with the back pairs specialized for walking or swimming

Eggs are carried cemented to the underside of the female crab, and are protected by her flap-like tail

## LIVING ON THE SHORELINE

Most crabs live in or near the sea, but many have adapted to life on land. The shore crab for example, which spends most of its life out of water, has legs designed for walking – whereas swimming crabs have two paddle-shaped back legs.

The male fiddler crab has a very large claw, which it waves as part of a display to attract the female.

The hermit crab lives in an empty seashell, which it drags around with its two pairs of walking legs.

The lobster has one narrow claw for slicing dead fish, and a heavier claw for crushing clams.

The crayfish grows up to 40cm long, lives in fresh water and has ten legs, like lobsters and crabs.

The water flea is one of the smallest crustaceans, growing to between 0.2mm and 18mm long.

The woodlouse is the only crustacean that lives entirely on land. It can roll itself up for defence.

Crustaceans include shrimps, lobsters, woodlice, water fleas and barnacles. Altogether, there are about 42,000 species of crustacean. Beneath its hard body shell, a crustacean's body is divided into sections, with jointed legs attached. Crabs, lobsters and barnacles have especially thick shells, which contain a lot of chalk-like material. This makes their shells feel like crusts.

### EYES ON STALKS

There are about 4,500 species of crab. The smallest are the tiny pea crabs, which are less than 1cm across. The biggest are spider crabs, which live on the sea bed and measure up to 4m across from the tip of one leg to another. Crabs have ten legs, two of which are claws, and their eyes can move up and down on the end of stalks.

### CRAB HABITS

Crabs usually live in water or close to the shore. Large crabs feed mainly on dead animals, which they tear up with their claws, while small crabs pick tiny scraps of food from the sea bed. Many crabs move sideways on land. The robber crab climbs palm trees to pick young coconuts, which it bores into with its powerful claws.

### WITHOUT A SHELL

A crab's body is armoured by a shell which moults as the crab grows. The hermit crab, however, does not have a shell and must inhabit empty mollusc shells to protect its soft abdomen. As it grows, it searches for a bigger shell to make its home.

### HATCHED FROM EGGS

Crabs and other crustaceans reproduce by laying eggs. On hatching, the tiny larvae drift about in water, passing through several body changes before they become adults. In a few species, such as the woodlouse, the young hatch out looking like mini adults.

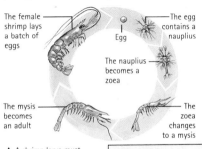

The female shrimp lays a batch of eggs

Egg

The egg contains a nauplius

The nauplius becomes a zoea

The mysis becomes an adult

The zoea changes to a mysis

▲ A shrimp larva must pass through several stages before becoming an adult.

### SEE ALSO

Animal, Seashore

# CUSTOM

Customs are the traditions, rituals and ways of behaving in a society which are passed on from generation to generation and are sometimes turned into laws.

Some Portuguese fishermen paint eyes on their boats to watch over them at sea and bring them back safely.

The *haka*, performed by New Zealand rugby teams before a match, is based on a Maori war dance.

The custom of carving pumpkin faces comes from the Celtic Day of the Dead, celebrated on October 31st.

The *chanoyu*, a Japanese tea ceremony which can last for four hours, came originally from China.

The painting of eggs is a symbol of new life which has been adopted by Christians at Easter time.

## DANCING DRAGON

During the Chinese New Year festival, dancers inside a dragon costume move through the streets while fire crackers are set off. The dragon is believed to bring rain for a successful crop and so has become a symbol of good fortune for the coming year. The fire crackers are to frighten away evil spirits.

Every society has its own set of customs, whether it is waiting in a queue, or wearing a particular costume during a celebration. Learning about different customs helps us to understand people from other countries or cultures.

### RITES OF PASSAGE

Across the world, customs are different, but there are times of life, known as rites of passage, when a person's status changes. Such times include birth, coming of age, marriage and death – occasions that are marked by elaborate customs in every society. The custom of keeping mother and baby secluded from society for a month after birth is a common custom in many countries, probably based on fear of infection. There are also many customs marking a young person's move from childhood to adulthood, ranging from throwing a party to a religious ritual.

### LINKS WITH THE PAST

Customs may be adapted over time, often due to industrialization or contact with other cultures. A custom's original meaning may be forgotten, or it may continue as a way of keeping a link with the past. In the USA, for example, families hold special meals at Thanksgiving to celebrate the first harvest of the Pilgrim Fathers, even though few people today are farmers.

### CUSTOMARY GREETINGS

Everyday customs help people to bond with other members of their society. For instance, every culture has a customary way of greeting – Europeans kiss or shake hands, the Inuit rub noses and the Chinese bow. By taking part in customs, people demonstrate their membership of a group or society.

### GOING AGAINST THE GRAIN

Refusing to follow a custom can offend, and may lead to the exclusion of an individual from a group of society. Customs are not laws, but because they are designed to help us understand what is acceptable behaviour in a society, they are often included in laws or religious codes.

▲ In Hindu weddings, everything is brightly coloured, and the bride usually wears a red sari with lots of gold jewellery.

### SEE ALSO

Judaism

# DEMOCRACY

Democracy is a form of government in which the people take part in ruling the state. The people may rule directly or through elected officials.

◀ Two metal voting discs were given to each man in ancient Athens. They were used in criminal trials to vote guilty or not guilty.

People who live in a democracy either vote for officials who make laws for them, or they vote directly on laws in a meeting known as an assembly. Democracy allows people freedom of speech and the right to choose between competing political parties in regularly held elections.

◀ In some elections today, a person votes by making a mark against the candidate's name on a ballot paper. The papers (votes) are posted in a sealed ballot box, to be counted later.

## POWER TO THE PEOPLE
The first democracy appeared in Ancient Greece in the 6th century BC, when men in cities could vote in assemblies. The word democracy is Greek for 'people-power'.

## ELECTION VICTORY
India is the world's largest democracy and election time plays an important part in the life of the people. Candidates make speeches, distribute leaflets, advertise and design posters to persuade people to vote for them. Most candidates belong to a political party whose members share the same ideas about how the country should be run.

## ELECTED ASSEMBLIES
The reign of Alexander the Great and a succession of Roman emperors gradually put an end to democracy, and the Middle Ages saw the rise of feudalism and monarchy. Democracy reappeared in the 17th century, when elected assemblies, known as parliaments, began to take power in some countries. At first only wealthy men could vote but today nearly every adult in a democracy is allowed to vote.

## MAJORITY RULE
Voters choose people to represent them in legislatures (law-making bodies), such as the British House of Commons or the US Congress. For a new law to be passed, a majority in the legislature must vote for it. On important issues, there may be a vote of all the people, known as a referendum.

## CHOOSING REPRESENTATIVES
Some elections are decided by a 'first past the post' system: the candidate with the most votes wins. Others are decided by proportional representation: each party gets candidates in parliament in relation to the number of votes it receives.

## GOVERNMENTS AND THE LAW
There are many kinds of democracy. In Britain, there is a monarchy, but an elected parliament makes laws. France is a republic with a president and prime minister, as well as a legislature. Russia is becoming more democratic after the fall of its communist government.

### SEE ALSO
Greece (Ancient)

# DESERT

Deserts are dry areas of land with relatively few plants or animals. Most deserts are hot, get very little rain, and are sandy or rocky.

▲ Deserts are not always hot. Some places in Antarctica and Greenland are known as polar deserts because the ground there is so dry. For example, on the western side of Antarctica, there are areas that receive less than 13cm of snow each year.

More than a fifth of the world's land surface is so dry that it is known as desert. Most deserts receive less than 250mm of rain each year. Others receive more rain than this but it evaporates quickly in the strong heat and winds, or sinks into the parched ground. The driest place in the world is the Atacama Desert in Chile, parts of which have less than 0.1mm of rain each year.

## WHERE DESERTS FORM
Most deserts, such as the Kalahari and Sahara in Africa, lie between the tropics of Cancer and Capricorn (25° to the north and south of the Equator). The air in the tropics is often too hot and dry for rain clouds to form. The cold Gobi Desert in central Asia exists, however, because it is far from the sea's moist winds. Other deserts, such as the Atacama, lie behind high mountains which block the rain-bearing winds.

## SURVIVAL TACTICS
Desert plants and animals have developed ways of coping with the lack of water. Plants usually have long, spreading roots to reach any available moisture. Most have spines or small leaves that are rolled or waxy to cut down on water loss through evaporation. Other plants spend most of their lives as seeds – only growing when rain falls. Desert animals often hide during the heat of the day and come out at night. Camels can go for many days without water.

## POCKETS OF WATER
Oases are pockets of fertile land in a desert. These occur where an aquifer, or underground stream, comes to the surface. Plants such as palm trees thrive, and animals and people gather there.

## CREEPING DESERTS
Deserts can spread. This may happen because the climate becomes drier or nearby land is overgrazed by farm animals.

## IN THE SHADOW OF THE SIERRA NEVADA
The deserts of North America are shielded from rain by the towering mountain wall of the Sierra Nevada. In some areas, less than 100mm of rain falls, making the gravelly ground inhospitable except to a few plants and animals. Temperatures during the day can reach 100°C, but at night it is often near freezing because there is no cloud cover.

Scaly skin stops the rattlesnake from drying out

The kit fox sleeps in a cool burrow during the day

The roadrunner gets most of its water from the animals it catches

The prickly pear cactus stores water in its fleshy stem

With its shallow, wide-ranging roots, the saguaro cactus always finds water

Some honeypot ants fill themselves with liquid, and act as reservoirs for the rest of the nest

SEE ALSO
Africa, Antarctica, Climate, Habitat, Plant, South America

# DINOSAUR

**Dinosaurs were a group of reptiles that lived on Earth for over 160 million years. They became extinct about 65 million years ago.**

*Tyrannosaurus rex* was a theropod, or 'beast-footed' dinosaur.

*Diplodocus* was a sauropod, or 'lizard-footed' dinosaur.

*Camptosaurus* was an ornithopod, or 'bird-footed' dinosaur.

*Stegosaurus* was a stegosaur, or 'roofed' dinosaur.

*Sauropelta* was an ankylosaur, or 'jointed' dinosaur.

*Triceratops* was a ceratopsian, or 'horned head' dinosaur.

The dinosaurs evolved 225 million years ago during a geological period known as the Triassic. Some were only the size of a chicken, others were the biggest land animals that ever existed. They roamed the planet throughout the Jurassic period and died out at the end of the Cretaceous period. The Triassic, Jurassic and Cretaceous periods are known as the 'age of reptiles'.

## MORE TO COME

The same dinosaurs did not exist throughout the 'age of reptiles'. For example, *Diplodocus* lived during the Jurassic, and *Tyrannosaurus* reigned in the Cretaceous period. Scientists have found evidence of over 500 types of dinosaur, spanning all the periods, but it is believed that as many as 1,300 types may have existed – most of which are still undiscovered.

## LIZARD OR BIRD-LIKE

There were two main groups, or orders, of dinosaur – the Saurischia (with hip bones arranged like a lizard's) and the Ornithischia (with hip bones arranged like a bird's). The

## KILLING MACHINE

The theropods were the meat-eating dinosaurs, which all had large jaws full of teeth for tearing flesh. *Deinonychus* was a terrifying killing machine equipped with deadly tools, including a slashing claw on the second toe of its back foot which gave it its name – 'terrible claw'.

Saurischia can be divided into two smaller groups known as the theropods and the sauropods. The Ornithischia include four groups: the ornithopods, the stegosaurs, the ankylosaurs and the ceratopsians.

## MEAT-EATERS

The theropods were meat-eaters, all built to the same design. They had long mouths full of meat-tearing teeth, they walked on their hind legs, and had small bodies which they balanced with long, heavy tails. Some, such as *Compsognathus*, were chicken-sized, while the biggest were 12m-long killers, such as *Tyrannosaurus*. ▶

Sharp teeth were used to tear flesh

Each toe and finger had a razor-sharp claw

The second toe of its back foot had a 'terrible claw'

▲ A comparison between the size of mighty *Tyrannosaurus's* feet and those of an average man.

▼ This fossil skeleton of *Tuojiangosaurus* was discovered in China in the 1970s. *Tuojiangosaurus* was a stegosaur that lived in the late Jurassic period, about 150 million years ago.

## DINOSAUR GIANTS

Sauropods were plant-eaters. They had big, heavy bodies and moved around on all fours, using their long necks to reach leaves on trees. They were the biggest land animals that ever lived and included *Diplodocus* and *Brachiosaurus*.

## CHEEKY PLANT-EATERS

The Ornithischia dinosaurs were also all plant-eaters. The only ones that could walk on their hind legs were the ornithopods. They had a more sophisticated chewing system than the long-necked sauropods, with cheeks for holding the food while they chewed it. *Iguanodon* is probably the most famous of the ornithopods.

▲ In 1978, a fossilized nest of 15 young *Maiasaura* was found in Montana, USA. Evidence showed that the young were very small and would have had to be cared for by the mother to survive. *Maiasaura* means 'good mother lizard'.

## BONY ARMOUR

Three ornithischian groups evolved from the ornithopods (bird-footed dinosaurs). They all had armour of some kind, which made them heavy and so they walked on four legs. The first were the stegosaurs – the 'roofed' dinosaurs. They had big bodies and either a double row of bony plates down the back like *Stegosaurus*, or an arrangement of spines like *Kentrosaurus*.

## A SCENE FROM THE LATE JURASSIC

The late Jurassic is the period from 157–145 million years ago. It is known for its many plant-eating dinosaur species, such as spiny *Stegosaurus* and long-necked sauropods, including *Apatosaurus*. The main dinosaur predator was the meat-eating *Allosaurus* – although the reptile *Diplosaurus*, an ancestor of today's crocodile, was pretty fearsome.

*Archaeopteryx* – one of the first birds

# A SCENE FROM THE LATE CRETACEOUS

The Late Cretaceous was a period from 95–65 million years ago. It was dominated by herds of duckbilled *Edmontosaura*, which had replaced the sauropods as the main plant-eaters. Meat-eating *Tyrannosaurus* probably hunted these animals, because other plant-eaters like *Triceratops* and *Ankylosaurus* had developed spectacular defensive armour. Large flying reptiles may have scavenged like vultures on the bodies of dead dinosaurs .

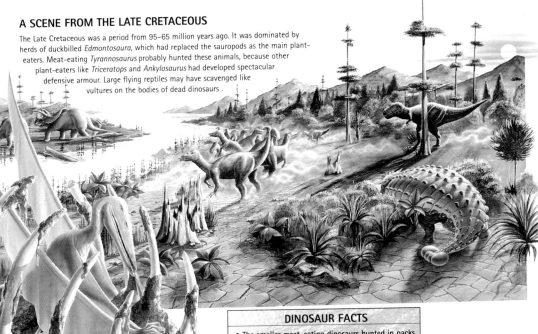

## JOINTED DINOSAURS

The second ornithischian group was the ankylosaurs, or 'jointed' dinosaurs. They had bony armour that lay flat over their broad backs, and were also armed with spikes along the sides, as in *Edmontonia*, or a tail with a club, as in *Euoplocephalus*.

## HORNED HEADS

The last ornithischian group was the ceratopsians. They had armour on their faces and heads, where it formed big bony frills around the neck. These 'horned head' dinosaurs included *Triceratops*, which had a small horn on the nose and two long horns over the eyes, and *Styracosaurus*, which had an enormous horn on the nose and a series of smaller horns around the frill.

## REPTILE NEIGHBOURS

Dinosaurs were not the only reptiles that lived at the time. Many groups of swimming reptiles, such as the fish-shaped ichthyosaurs and the long-necked plesiosaurs, lived in the sea, while pterosaurs flew in the air.

## DINOSAUR FACTS

- The smaller meat-eating dinosaurs hunted in packs like wolves, preying on young or weak plant-eaters
- Large plant-eating dinosaurs like Diplodocus must have had to eat continuously to avoid starvation
- Dinosaurs may have been warm-blooded like mammals and birds
- Many different types of insect and mammal also lived during the time of the dinosaurs
- The dinosaurs' legs were not at the side like reptiles, but under their bodies like mammals

## DEATH OF THE REPTILES

All these unusual reptiles became extinct along with the dinosaurs at the end of the Cretaceous period. Nobody knows for sure how this happened, or why other reptiles, such as crocodiles and turtles, survived. It may have been a gradual process, due to a slow climatic change, or there may have been a sudden catastrophe, such as the Earth being hit by a gigantic meteorite. The dinosaurs did leave some relatives, however. During the Jurassic period, birds evolved from the small meat-eating theropods, which means today's birds are the direct descendants of the dinosaurs.

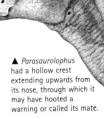

Male

Female

▲ *Parasaurolophus* had a hollow crest extending upwards from its nose, through which it may have hooted a warning or called its mate.

## SEE ALSO

Evolution, Fossil, Mammal, Reptile

# DISEASE

A disease is an illness which disturbs the normal healthy functioning of a plant, animal or person. Each disease produces symptoms (physical changes).

▲ Many diseases have almost been wiped out by the widespread use of inoculation (also called immunization and vaccination). This is when a milder form of the disease is introduced into the body, by injection or via the mouth, so that the person develops long-term resistance to the disease.

The human body may be attacked by thousands of diseases. These range from relatively harmless ones, such as the common cold and athlete's foot, to life-threatening diseases, such as typhoid and some cancers. Plants and animals also suffer from diseases – potatoes suffer from blight and cats can get the flu (influenza).

## VIRUSES AND BACTERIA

Flu, AIDS and tetanus are all types of infectious disease. They are caused by harmful microscopic organisms called germs, which invade the body and multiply. Tetanus is caused by bacteria (living creatures), while flu and AIDS are caused by viruses (bundles of DNA wrapped in protein). Infectious diseases are spread from person to person by, for example, breathing in germs. A sudden outbreak of an infectious disease which affects many people is called an epidemic.

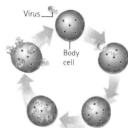

Virus

Body cell

**VIRUS ATTACK**
A virus spreads in the body by using the body's cells to make copies of itself. As the replicas break out, they destroy the body's cell, and each virus starts the process again.

Some infectious diseases can be prevented with vaccinations, and others can be treated with medicines such as antibiotics.

## NON-INFECTIOUS DISEASES

Many diseases are not caused by germs, but are the result of poor diet. An example of this is scurvy, which is the result of not eating enough vitamin C. Others may be caused by an unhealthy lifestyle. For example, smoking and stress can lead to heart disease. Some diseases, such as haemophilia, run in families as a result of faulty genes.

## LOOKING FOR CLUES

Symptoms such as pain or fever tell the person suffering from a disease that something is wrong and give clues to doctors as to the cause. A doctor can also detect signs of disease by taking X-rays or blood tests.

## AFRICAN SLEEPING SICKNESS

The tsetse fly spreads a disease called sleeping sickness in some areas of Africa. When it feeds on human blood, this tiny fly injects some of its saliva into the person's bloodstream. If its saliva contains micro-organisms called *Trypanosoma brucei*, these also enter the bloodstream, and multiply inside the body, causing fever, headaches and sleepiness. The person may die if not treated quickly.

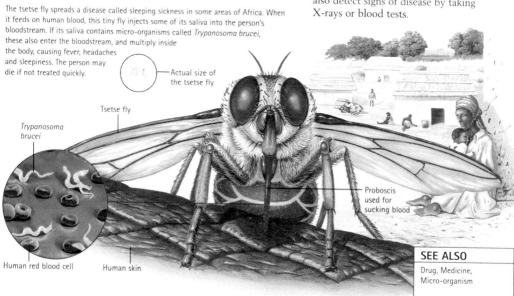

Actual size of the tsetse fly

Tsetse fly

*Trypanosoma brucei*

Proboscis used for sucking blood

Human red blood cell

Human skin

## SEE ALSO

Drug, Medicine, Micro-organism

# DOG

The domestic dog (*Canis familiaris*) belongs to the
dog family, known as Canidae, and is believed
to be descended from the grey wolf.

The chihuahua is the
smallest dog in the world:
only 15cm to the shoulder.

The poodle is an intelligent
dog, used for finding
truffles (fungi) in France.

The greyhound, bred for
speed, can easily reach
57km per hour.

The bulldog was originally
bred for the 'sport' of bull-
baiting in the Middle Ages.

The husky is a powerful
sledge dog, able to pull
twice its own weight.

The Airedale is the largest
breed of terrier, probably
bred for hunting otters.

Dogs do not sweat,
but get rid of heat
via their moist
nose and tongue
(panting)

Adult dogs have
42 teeth in a long
muzzle, originally
adapted for seizing
prey on the run

Muscular, deep-
chested bodies and
long slender legs,
originally designed
for chasing prey

The front paws
have five toes, with
strong, blunt, non-
retractable claws

Dogs have a typical
carnivore's digestive
system, but they can
also eat grain and
cooked vegetables

Pointers have short, smooth coats, but
many sporting dogs have long hair

When a pointer has
located its quarry, its
tail sticks straight out

All dogs' back
paws have four
toes, with a
hidden fifth toe

## SPORTING DOGS

Sporting dogs are bred for their acute sense of smell,
which they use to track down game birds. The pointer
(below) was popular during the 19th century, and gets
its name from the way it stands with its tail straight out
and its nose pointing at the hiding bird. Other sporting
dogs include setters, which crouch down, or 'set', near
hiding birds, and retrievers, which fetch dead game.

Dogs were the first animals to be
tamed. Fossil remains of a domestic
dog dating back to 10,500 years ago have
been found in Idaho, USA. The relationship
between human and dog probably began
because dogs are natural scavengers, and
hung around camps looking for food scraps.

## BREEDS AND GROUPS

Since then, humans have selectively bred
dogs – the American Kennel Club (AKC)
recognizes 138 breeds of dog, and the
British Kennel Club includes about 170.
These breeds are divided into seven groups
by appearance, use and size: Sporting dogs,
Herding dogs, Hounds, Non-sporting dogs,
Terriers, Toy dogs and Working dogs. The
dog's most acute senses – smell and hearing
– were selectively bred early on for guarding
and hunting. Other physical features were
bred for specific uses. For example, the
dachshund's short legs were selected for
going down badger sets, and the bulldog's
set-back nose was selected to help it
breathe while biting. Nowadays, a gentle,
non-aggressive nature is selected for pets.

## A DOG'S LIFE

Most domestic dogs are fully grown by the
age of two, are old by the age of 12, and
rarely live past 20. Bitches (females) can
become pregnant from about seven months,
and give birth to an average of three to six
puppies, although some breeds may have
up to ten puppies. The puppies open their
eyes on the tenth day and are ready to leave
their mother at six weeks. Dogs are pack
animals and follow a leader. This loyalty can
be transferred to a human master, especially
if the dog is trained while young.

▲ The border collie uses
the hunting instincts of
its wild ancestors to
round up sheep.

### SEE ALSO

Hearing, Mammal

# DRUG

Drugs are substances that affect the way in which the body or mind works. Most drugs are used medicinally, to cure or prevent an illness.

Medicinal liquids called syrups make swallowing drugs easy for children.

Tablets and capsules are the most common form of drugs.

A drug is injected into the blood when a quick response is needed.

Eye drops and inhalers act fast by sending the drug to the exact spot.

Creams and gels often contain drugs which disinfect a cut or graze.

Skin patches release drugs slowly through the skin into the blood.

Cigarettes are made from tobacco leaves, which contain the drug nicotine.

Over 4,000 years ago, Emperor Chi'en Nung of China put together a book of more than 300 medicinal plants, many of which are still used in medicine today. But it was not until the 18th century, when the English doctor William Withering studied the heart drug digitalis (extracted from foxgloves), that drugs were looked at scientifically. The modern drug industry began in 1899, when the German company Bayer manufactured the painkiller aspirin.

## TYPES OF DRUG

Doctors use many types of drug to treat patients. For example, antibiotics such as penicillin kill the bacteria that cause infections. Analgesics (painkillers), such as aspirin and codeine, stop pain messages

▶ The foxglove is listed in the oldest surviving book on drugs and their uses, written between AD20 and AD70 by the Ancient Greek doctor Dioscorides.

from reaching the brain. Sedatives have a calming effect and can help a person to sleep. Anaesthetics deaden the body's nerves and are used in operations. Vaccines help the immune system to fight diseases, and insulin is given when the body fails to make enough naturally.

## DANGERS AND ADDICTION

Some drugs, such as heroin or cocaine, are addictive, which means people cannot stop taking them. They are illegal because they are so dangerous. Even medicinal drugs or everyday drugs, such as alcohol, caffeine in tea and coffee or nicotine in cigarettes, can be harmful if taken in large amounts.

## SLOW-RELEASE CAPSULES

Drugs sometimes need to be released into the bloodstream slowly over a few hours, especially if they are painkillers. Slow-release capsules contain hundreds of tiny pellets with coatings of different thicknesses. Some of the pellets release the drug in the stomach, while others release it later in the intestines.

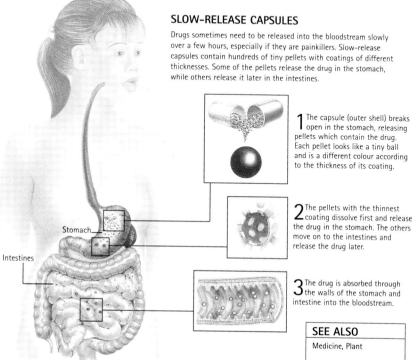

Stomach

Intestines

1 The capsule (outer shell) breaks open in the stomach, releasing pellets which contain the drug. Each pellet looks like a tiny ball and is a different colour according to the thickness of its coating.

2 The pellets with the thinnest coating dissolve first and release the drug in the stomach. The others move on to the intestines and release the drug later.

3 The drug is absorbed through the walls of the stomach and intestine into the bloodstream.

## SEE ALSO

Medicine, Plant

# EAGLE AND OTHER BIRDS OF PREY

Eagles and other birds of prey survive by hunting other animals. They swoop on their prey from the air, grabbing them with their sharp talons.

▶ Unlike hawks and eagles, owls, such as this Little Owl, hunt their prey at night.

Birds of prey are born hunters. They have sharp eyesight to spot far-off prey, sharp, curved talons to catch their food and strong, hooked beaks to tear at flesh. Most have large, broad wings with flight feathers that spread out when they soar in updrafts. As well as eagles, birds of prey include buzzards, falcons, hawks, kites, ospreys and vultures. Owls are also often included, but belong to a different bird group.

## HUNTING SKILLS
Most birds of prey soar high into the air and then swoop down on their prey on the ground at high speed. Some, such as the peregrine falcon, can also attack birds in mid-air. The kestrel is unusual because it hovers just a few metres above the ground before swooping. Vultures usually scavenge dead meat.

## DIFFERENT TASTES
There are more than 50 species of eagle scattered throughout the world, although many are endangered. Most live in wild, remote places where humans cannot disturb them. Eagles eat a wide range of animals. The golden eagle attacks hares, small rodents and other birds, while the bateleur eagle gorges on snakes. Some are experts at snaring fish, and the harpy eagle catches monkeys.

## FISH FOR DINNER
The bald eagle, the national bird of the USA, is one of the most endangered birds of prey. It feeds on birds and small animals, but particularly likes fish. It scoops them from the surface of the water and flies off, gripping them in its sharp talons.

## NEST RECYCLING
Many eagles use the same nest, or eyrie, again and again, adding more material each time they breed. Their nests can become enormous – a bald eagle's can measure 3m across and weigh over a tonne. Most eagles lay just two eggs. Once the young have hatched, they do not leave the nest for up to two months.

The Andean condor is the largest bird of prey. It can weigh up to 12kg.

When peregrine falcons dive, they can reach speeds of over 250km/h.

Northern goshawks can strike in mid-air, often attacking from below.

Vultures, such as this black vulture, feed on the bodies of dead animals.

The golden eagle is the most widespread eagle in the Northern Hemisphere.

**SEE ALSO**
Bird

# EARTH

Our planet, Earth, is one of the nine planets that move around the Sun. It is made up of rock and metal, and is the only planet known to support life.

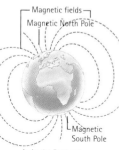

Magnetic fields
Magnetic North Pole
Magnetic South Pole

▲ As the Earth spins, electrical currents beneath the surface turn the planet into a huge magnet, with a north and south pole just like any ordinary magnet.

Planet Earth is an almost perfect ball of rock with a metal core, which travels around the Sun. It is surrounded by a blanket of gases called the atmosphere, has one moon, and as far as we know, is the only planet that supports life.

## NIGHT AND DAY

Approximately every 24 hours, the Earth does a full circle on its axis – an imaginary line joining the North and South Poles. As it spins, one side turns to face the Sun and is in daylight, while the other side turns away, experiencing night. The Earth spins eastward, which is why the Sun seems to rise in the east and set in the west.

## AROUND THE SUN

As well as spinning on its own axis, the Earth is constantly moving around the Sun. One complete path around the Sun is an orbit. The length of a year is determined by the time it takes a planet to make one orbit. This means that the Earth travels 958 million kilometres at an average speed of 30km per second.

## CHANGING SEASONS

The Earth is tilted towards the Sun at an angle of 23.5°. As the Earth orbits, those places that are tilted towards the Sun receive more warmth and light for the part of the year that is known as summer. As these places move further round, they tilt away from the Sun, experiencing winter.

## THE EARTH'S MAKE-UP

Beneath its thin shell, or crust, the interior of the Earth is very hot. Below about 70km, there is a mantle of rock that is semi-molten (partly melted). The outer layer of the Earth's core is molten too, but enormous pressure keeps the inner core (the centre) solid, even though temperatures here reach over 6,000°C. The upper layer of the mantle is made of plates, like pieces of a jigsaw, with the continents on top. Sometimes, the plates rub together, causing pressure which escapes via volcanoes or earthquakes.

## FROM CORE TO CRUST

If we could cut a piece out of the Earth like a giant apple, we would see a planet made in four layers. At its centre is a solid inner core of almost pure iron, surrounded by an outer core of liquid iron and nickel. Enveloping this is a mantle of silicon compounds, crystals and lighter metals, topped with a hard rock crust.

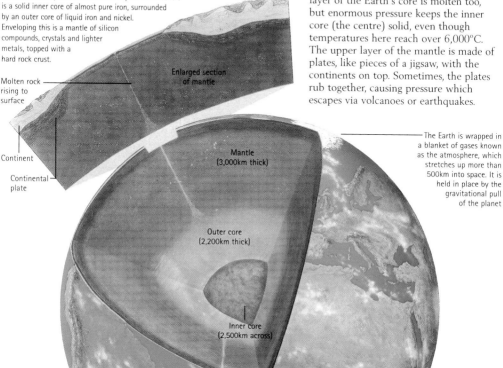

Enlarged section of mantle

Molten rock rising to surface

Continent

Continental plate

Mantle
(3,000km thick)

Outer core
(2,200km thick)

Inner core
(2,500km across)

The Earth is wrapped in a blanket of gases known as the atmosphere, which stretches up more than 500km into space. It is held in place by the gravitational pull of the planet

## THE EVOLVING EARTH

Astronomers believe that the Earth began to form about 4.6 billion years ago, when the solar nebula (a vast cloud of hot debris circling the newly formed Sun) began to cluster together into lumps that eventually became the planets of our solar system. The process took millions of years to complete and Earth, like the other planets, developed a unique chemistry and atmosphere.

**1** Hot clouds of dust and gases spin around the newly formed Sun. As the specks of dust collide, they stick together in lumps.

**2** The forces of gravity pull more passing lumps into the spinning ball. Heavy elements such as iron sink to the centre.

**3** Lighter metals and rocks come to the surface and the red-hot Earth cools enough for a hard shell to form.

**4** Gases escaping from the Earth form clouds and rain falls, creating oceans containing small oxygen-producing plants.

**5** Originally one large mass of land, the Earth's land surface is now split into seven chunks, known as continents.

## LIFE ON EARTH

Why exactly there is life on Earth is still a mystery to scientists. The theories are numerous, but the answer is probably a combination of reasons. Firstly, Earth's distance from the Sun is ideal – not too hot like Venus, nor too cold like Mars. Secondly, Earth is the only planet we know of that has water on its surface – over 70 per cent of it is covered by water. Scientists believe that electrical storms on the newly formed planet caused chemical reactions between gases in the atmosphere. these created the first building blocks of life, which fell into the oceans, where they combined to form simple plant-like creatures. All plants make oxygen, and so an ideal atmosphere was soon created for the evolution of oxygen-breathing life forms.

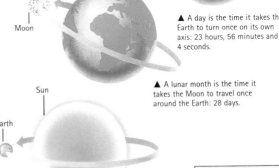

▲ A day is the time it takes the Earth to turn once on its own axis: 23 hours, 56 minutes and 4 seconds.

▲ A lunar month is the time it takes the Moon to travel once around the Earth: 28 days.

Earth

Moon

Sun

Earth

▲ A year is the time it takes the Earth to travel once around the Sun: 365 days, 6 hours and 9 minutes.

## EARTH FACTS AND FIGURES

• The Earth's diameter (the distance from Pole to Pole through the centre) is 12,714km

• The Earth's circumference (the distance around its middle at the Equator) is 40,075km

• As the Earth spins, places near the Equator move much faster than places at the Poles, causing the planet to bulge slightly in the middle and be flattened at the top and bottom

• The temperature of the Earth's inner core may be as hot as 6,200°C

• Of the nine planets in our solar system, Earth is the third closest to the Sun

• The Sun and the Earth are about 150 million kilometres apart

• The Earth's path around the Sun is not a circle but an ellipse (an oval), which means it is closer to the Sun on January 1 than on June 1

## SEE ALSO

Atmosphere, Continent, Earthquake, Evolution, Gravity, Magnetism, Planet, Season, Solar system, Sun, Volcano

# EARTHQUAKE

**An earthquake is a shaking of the Earth's surface. It is caused by the sudden release of pressure through weak parts of the Earth's crust.**

The vast majority of earthquakes do not cause any serious damage. Small tremors can happen with an erupting volcano, an avalanche or a landslide. However, the largest earthquakes occur as a result of pressure or tension deep under the ground being released through weak areas (fault lines) in the Earth's crust.

### TECTONIC PLATES

The Earth's crust is broken into giant slabs called tectonic plates. Sometimes, pressure builds up underground as a result of the plates moving against each other. The pressure is suddenly released, sending out shock waves in all directions and causing the Earth's crust to shake and even crack.

### EARTHQUAKE ZONES

Two great earthquake zones exist. Both are where two tectonic plates meet. One stretches across southern Asia, through the Mediterranean and into East Africa. The other is the 'ring of fire' around the Pacific Ocean, which includes the USA. In 1906, a large part of San Francisco was destroyed by an earthquake in this zone.

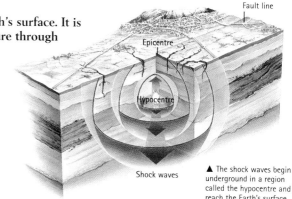

Fault line

Epicentre

Hypocentre

Shock waves

▲ The shock waves begin underground in a region called the hypocentre and reach the Earth's surface directly above, at the epicentre. From here, they radiate out in all directions.

### SHOCK WAVES

Earthquake shock waves are known as seismic waves. They are detected using a measuring instrument called a seismometer. A severe earthquake can be felt as much as 400km away. The intensity of an earthquake is plotted on the Richter scale. An earthquake measuring over 7 on this scale can destroy buildings and take lives.

### DISASTER IN JAPAN

In 1995, the Japanese city of Kobe was devastated by a violent earthquake that killed over 5,000 people. The earthquake measured 7.2 on the Richter scale. It caused houses and apartments to collapse, trains to be derailed and roads to be ripped apart. The shaking lasted for about 20 seconds.

### SEE ALSO

Continent, Earth, Mountain and valley, Ocean and sea, Volcano

# EASTERN EUROPE

Eastern Europe is a geographical region of eight countries that were once part of the communist bloc controlled by the Soviet Union.

▲ Huge expanses of steppe once covered Ukraine but this land, covered with rich soil, is now heavily farmed.

**BELARUS**
**Area:** 207,600 sq km
**Population:** 10,239,000
**Capital:** Minsk
**Languages:** Belorussian and Russian
**Currency:** Rouble

**CZECH REPUBLIC**
**Area:** 78,866 sq km
**Population:** 10,295,000
**Capital:** Prague
**Language:** Czech
**Currency:** Koruna

**HUNGARY**
**Area:** 93,032 sq km
**Population:** 10,114,000
**Capital:** Budapest
**Language:** Hungarian
**Currency:** Forint

**MOLDOVA**
**Area:** 33,851 sq km
**Population:** 4,298,000
**Capital:** Chisinau
**Language:** Romanian
**Currency:** Leu

**POLAND**
**Area:** 323,250 sq km
**Population:** 38,666,000
**Capital:** Warsaw
**Language:** Polish
**Currency:** Zloty

Eastern Europe lies between the Baltic Sea, the Balkan peninsula, the Black Sea and Russia. It makes up more than one sixth of Europe's land area, and is a region of plains, low hills and mountains.

## PEAKS AND PLAINS

To the south lie the rugged Carpathian Mountains and Transylvanian Alps. The highest point is Gerlachovsky Stit, a peak of 2,656m in the Carpathians. To the west is the Hungarian Plain and to the east are the vast rolling steppes (grasslands) of Ukraine.

## A REGION OF RIVERS

The area is watered by some of Europe's major rivers. The Danube, Europe's second longest river (2,858km), forms much of Romania's southwestern border, while the Dnieper and the Dniester both flow through Ukraine. Europe's largest swamp, the Pripet Marshes, straddles the border between Belarus and Ukraine.

## CONTINENTAL CLIMATE

Away from the mountains, Eastern Europe has warm summers with average temperatures reaching 20°C or more in July. Winters get colder as you travel from west to east. Most of the region has moderate rainfall, with 500mm to 1,000mm per year, but the southeast is drier, with less than 500mm of rain a year.

## BREAD BASKET OF EUROPE

In the lowlands, many of the region's forests have been cleared for farming. The fertile steppes, once an area of natural grassland, are also farmed. Ukraine is sometimes called 'the bread basket of Europe' because of its high production of grains and other crops. ▶

▼ The medieval city of Prague, capital of the Czech Republic, has some of Europe's most beautiful and well-preserved architecture.

LATVIA
BALTIC SEA
RUSSIA
LITHUANIA
■Minsk
BELARUS
RUSSIA
*Vistula*
Warsaw■
GERMANY
POLAND
*Pripet Marshes*
Prague■
Kiev■
CZECH REPUBLIC
UKRAINE
*Dnieper*
▲
*Gerlachovsky Stit*
*Dniester*
SLOVAKIA
*Carpathian Mountains*
AUSTRIA
■Bratislava
MOLDOVA
HUNGARY
Budapest■
*Hungarian Plain*
Chisinau■
SLOVENIA
*Danube*
CASPIAN SEA
ROMANIA
CROATIA
*Transylvanian Alps*
BLACK SEA
Bucharest■
YUGOSLAVIA
*Danube*
BULGARIA
*BALKAN PENINSULA*

N
miles
0       100
0    100
km

**ROMANIA**
**Area:** 238,391 sq km
**Population:** 22,503,000
**Capital:** Bucharest
**Language:** Romanian
**Currency:** Leu

**SLOVAKIA**
**Area:** 49,012 sq km
**Population:** 5,391,000
**Capital:** Bratislava
**Language:** Slovak
**Currency:** Koruna

**UKRAINE**
**Area:** 603,700 sq km
**Population:** 50,295,000
**Capital:** Kiev
**Language:** Ukrainian
**Currency:** Hryvna

▶ Old-fashioned factories, such as this one in Romania, cause air, water and soil pollution in many parts of Eastern Europe.

## DISAPPEARING WILDLIFE

As in the rest of Europe, the wildlife in Eastern Europe has been reduced by the destruction of forests and grasslands. A number of large mammals that once grazed on the steppes, such as the saiga antelope, have now disappeared. The rare wisent (European bison) is found in western Belarus and central Poland, while the Danube delta on the Black Sea is a major wetland and home to many birds.

## HEAVY AND LIGHT INDUSTRY

Coal, oil and natural gas, iron ore and other minerals are found in this region. Heavy industry produces machinery,

▲ The practice of Eastern Orthodox Christianity is widespread in Belarus, Moldova, Romania and Ukraine. Here, Holy Communion is celebrated in Kiev, Ukraine.

transport equipment and steel, and the manufacture of electronic goods, clothes and processed food is increasing.

## CITY DWELLERS
Many people live in rural areas, and a few people still follow a nomadic lifestyle. But about two thirds of the people live and work in towns and cities. Kiev, in Ukraine, is the largest city in Eastern Europe, with a population of over 2,651,000.

## RELIGIOUS WORSHIP
Religion is an important part of life for many people in Eastern Europe. The two dominant faiths in the region are Roman Catholic and Eastern Orthodox Christianity. There is a Muslim minority in Romania, which was once part of the Muslim Ottoman Empire.

## FOREIGN POWERS
All of the countries of Eastern Europe have at times in their history been under the influence of a foreign power. In 1793, Poland disappeared after being divided up among Prussia, Austria and Russia. Hungary and Czechoslovakia formed part of the Habsburg Empire until 1918. Romania gained its independence from Turkey in 1878. More recently, Ukraine, Belarus and Moldova were part of the Russian-dominated Soviet Union.

## COMMUNIST RULE
After World War II, all the countries of Eastern Europe came under communist rule, either as part of the Soviet Union or as members of the Soviet bloc. Romania remained outside Soviet control, but under the communist dictator Nicolae Ceausescu.

## THE NEW MAP
In the late 1980s, the countries of Eastern Europe began to abandon communist rule in favour of their own democratically elected governments. Belarus, Moldova and Ukraine gained their independence in 1991, following the break-up of the Soviet Union. In 1993, Czechoslovakia split peacefully into two countries: the Czech Republic and Slovakia.

▲ Holiday-makers in Budapest play chess in one of Hungary's many natural hot springs.

## DEMOCRACY IN HUNGARY
From the end of World War II, Hungary, like the rest of Eastern Europe, came under Soviet communist rule. However, demonstrations in favour of democracy, such as this one in Budapest in 1988, indicated people's unhappiness with the government. In 1989, Hungary was the first Eastern European country to shake off communism. In March 1990, it elected its first democratic government in 42 years.

EUROPA!

CAVE
CANEM

### SEE ALSO
Cold War, Communism, Democracy, Europe, Russia and the Baltic States

# ECOLOGY

Ecology is the study of how plants, animals and humans live together in their natural surroundings, and the ways in which they affect one another.

## THE FOOD CHAIN

Each organism in a food chain feeds on and gets energy from the level above. Ecologists divide plants and animals in a chain into groups, depending on how they get their energy. Plants are energy producers, using the Sun's energy to produce new growth. Animals are consumers, obtaining energy by eating plants or other animals.

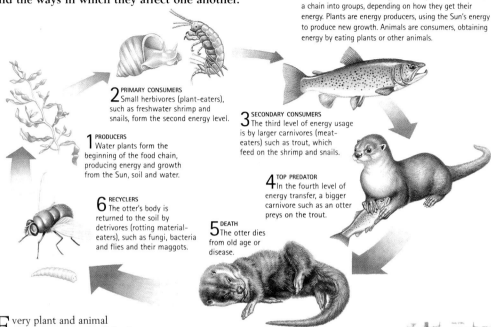

**2 PRIMARY CONSUMERS**
Small herbivores (plant-eaters), such as freshwater shrimp and snails, form the second energy level.

**1 PRODUCERS**
Water plants form the beginning of the food chain, producing energy and growth from the Sun, soil and water.

**3 SECONDARY CONSUMERS**
The third level of energy usage is by larger carnivores (meat-eaters) such as trout, which feed on the shrimp and snails.

**4 TOP PREDATOR**
In the fourth level of energy transfer, a bigger carnivore such as an otter preys on the trout.

**6 RECYCLERS**
The otter's body is returned to the soil by detrivores (rotting material-eaters), such as fungi, bacteria and flies and their maggots.

**5 DEATH**
The otter dies from old age or disease.

Every plant and animal depends on a cycle of food, energy and waste disposal that links it to other plants and animals. Ecologists study how plants and animals are linked to each other in food chains and webs.

### CHAINED TOGETHER

All living things need energy. Plants use light energy from the Sun to turn substances in the soil, air and water into food. Insects eat the plants, and fish, birds and other animals eat the insects. In this way, energy is passed along a food chain. When living things die, their bodies break down and release nutrients back into the ground to start the process again.

### ECOSYSTEMS

An ecosystem is made up of the plants and animals in a certain area, together with the air, soil, climate and other non-living things. A forest is one type of ecosystem, but there are many others. An ecosystem can be as small as a pond or as large as an ocean.

### HUMANS INTERVENE

Humans are part of the biggest ecosystem of all – the Earth itself. Some human actions can affect the entire planet. Logging a rainforest, for example, affects the forest by destroying its plants and animals. Since trees produce the oxygen needed by humans and other life forms, the world's oxygen supply is also affected.

### GREY SQUIRREL INVASION

The introduction of animals or plants from foreign lands can have harmful effects on the ecology of an area. When grey squirrels from North America were introduced to Britain, the native red squirrels were pushed out of the food chain in most areas.

▲ Many timber companies manage their forests ecologically using a process known as artificial reforestation. This means that a constant supply of seeds is sown in a nursery and transplanted to the forest to replace felled trees.

### SEE ALSO

Animal, Conservation, Forest, Habitat, Plant, Pollution

# EGYPT ANCIENT

Ancient Egypt developed along the River Nile around 5,000 years ago. Over the next 2,500 years, it grew into one of the greatest civilizations of all time.

▲ Pyramids were burial monuments for kings. A Sphinx (half man, half lion) stands beside the pyramids at Giza.

The funeral mask of Tutankhamen, boy-king of Egypt (1361–52BC), was discovered in 1922.

The tombs of important officials contained models of items that they might need in the next world.

The Ancient Egyptians chose to settle by the Nile in Africa because each year the river flooded, spreading mud over the banks. This provided them with fertile land to farm.

## PYRAMID BUILDERS

The Ancient Egyptians were the first real engineers and built impressive temples, cities and pyramids. The largest of the pyramids needed over two million blocks of stone, each weighing as much as 2.5 tonnes. Some were cut from distant quarries and floated down the Nile by raft.

## IMPORTANT INVENTORS

The Egyptians used papyrus reeds to make shoes, boats, ropes and writing paper. Papyrus scrolls preserve Ancient Egyptian hieroglyphic writing. The Egyptians also invented a 365-day calendar.

## LIFE AFTER DEATH

Many gods were worshipped, including the sun-god Ra, and Osiris, god of the dead. The Egyptian kings, or pharaohs, were also believed to be gods. When they died, the kings and queens were buried in tombs full of things they might need in the next world – food, jewels, even small statues of servants (*shabtis*). Most royal tombs were later robbed, but in 1922, the tomb of the boy pharaoh Tutankhamen was found with most of its treasures untouched.

## THREE GREAT ERAS

Ancient Egypt included three great ages: the Old Kingdom, the Middle Kingdom and the New Kingdom. In 31BC, Cleopatra died and Egypt fell to the Rome Empire.

## MUMMIFIED BODIES

The Ancient Egyptians believed in life after death. Their bodies were mummified (preserved) before burial to prevent decay. It took 70 days to mummify a body.

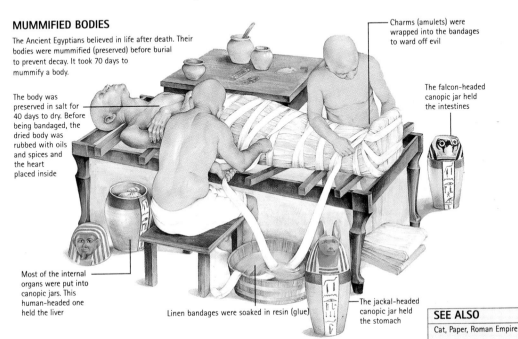

Charms (amulets) were wrapped into the bandages to ward off evil

The falcon-headed canopic jar held the intestines

The body was preserved in salt for 40 days to dry. Before being bandaged, the dried body was rubbed with oils and spices and the heart placed inside

Most of the internal organs were put into canopic jars. This human-headed one held the liver

Linen bandages were soaked in resin (glue)

The jackal-headed canopic jar held the stomach

### SEE ALSO

Cat, Paper, Roman Empire

# ELECTRICITY

**Electricity is a form of energy. It can be stored in batteries or sent along wires to make electric trains, computers, light bulbs and other devices work.**

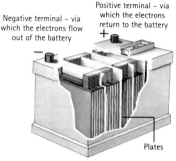

Plates

▲ Wet batteries, like those in cars, store electricity and can be recharged. Six cells contain lead and lead dioxide plates in a solution of dilute sulphuric acid. The battery is first charged by an outside electrical source, but after that a generator, run by the car's engine, keeps it charged.

Electricity is an invisible form of energy created by the movement of charged particles. It flows into our homes along wires and can be easily converted into other energy forms, such as heat and light.

▲ Each light bulb in a circuit creates resistance to the flow of electric current, and so light bulbs wired in series do not glow brightly.

### PASSING ON ELECTRONS
Everything in the world, including humans and the air they breathe, is made of atoms. Each of these tiny particles has a positively charged centre (nucleus), with smaller, negatively charged electrons whizzing around it. Electricity is created when one of the electrons jumps to another atom. This can be caused by the magnetic field in a generator, by chemicals in a battery, or by friction (rubbing materials together).

### THALES THE PHILOSOPHER
The discovery that an electric charge could be created by rubbing two materials together was first made by the Greek philosopher Thales over 2,600 years ago. He found that if he rubbed the fossilized tree sap, amber, with silk, it attracted feathers and dust. We now know that this happened because electrons had been passed between the silk and the amber,

▲ Light bulbs wired in parallel all glow brightly, because each light bulb is connected directly to the battery.

making them electrically charged. In recognition of his discovery, our word electron comes from the Greek word *elecktron*, meaning amber.

### CONDUCTORS AND INSULATORS
The electricity of substances such as amber is called static electricity because the charge stays put once the electrons have moved between the atoms. In other substances, the electrons carry on flowing. These substances are called conductors. Most electrical wires are made of copper because it is a good electrical conductor, as are all metals. Water also conducts electricity, which is why it is dangerous to

## HOW A GENERATOR WORKS

An electric generator works by using the principle of electro-magnetic induction discovered in 1831 by the British chemist and physicist Michael Faraday (1791–1867). He discovered that if a coil of wire is spun between two magnets, electrons begin to flow inside the wire coil. An alternating current (AC) and a direct current (DC) can be created in this way.

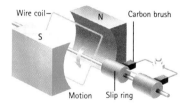

Wire coil
N
S
Carbon brush
Motion
Slip ring

▲ The two magnets naturally produce an alternating current (AC). As the coil spins, the magnetic field inside the coil points first one way and then the other. This makes the electric current change direction, or alternate.

Wire coil
N
S
Carbon brush
Commutator
Motion

▲ To create a direct current (DC), which flows in only one direction, the coil must be attached to a device called a commutator which is able to reverse the current.

▶ Practical DC generators are used to power large industrial motors. Unlike Faraday's simple model, a generator has many coils of wire wound on a rotor.

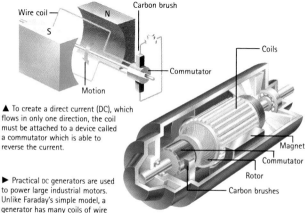

Coils
Magnet
Commutator
Rotor
Carbon brushes

## ELECTRICAL TERMS

**Conductor** Any substance through which an electric current can flow

**Coulomb (C)** The measurement of electric charge

**Current** How fast electrons flow along a conductor – it is measured in amperes (A)

**Insulator** Any substance through which an electric current cannot flow

**Resistance** How hard it is for current to flow through a conductor – it is measured in ohms (Ω)

**Static electricity** Electric charge created by two objects rubbing together and exchanging electrons

**Voltage (V)** A unit of measurement describing how powerfully a battery sends electric current

**Watt** A unit of measurement that describes how much electrical energy can be converted into heat and light energy per second

## PRODUCING ELECTRICITY

All power stations have a generator which produces electricity. In nuclear power stations, the nuclear reactor creates the heat needed to turn water into steam. The steam turns giant wheels, called turbines, which power the generator. The electricity it produces then flows along wires to homes, shops and offices.

### THE POWER STATION
The nuclear reactor splits atoms to create the heat needed to produce steam to spin the turbines.

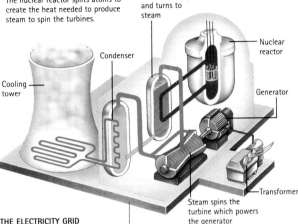

Water heats up and turns to steam

Condenser

Cooling tower

Nuclear reactor

Generator

Transformer

Steam spins the turbine which powers the generator

### THE ELECTRICITY GRID
Electricity from the power station travels via step-up and step-down transformers which convert it to the voltage needed for distribution.

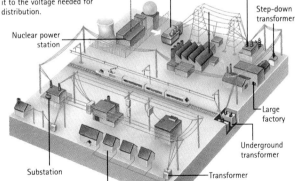

Nuclear power station

Step-up transformer

Substation

Step-down transformer

Large factory

Underground transformer

Substation

Homes

Transformer

operate electrical appliances with wet hands. Other materials are made of atoms between which it is almost impossible for electrons to flow. These materials are known as insulators, and include plastic, wood and amber. A flow of electrons is known as a current, and the term 'resistance' is a measure of how difficult it is for current to flow through a conductor.

### COMPLETING THE CIRCUIT
For an electrical appliance such as a torch to work, its electricity source (the battery) must be connected to the bulb by wires in an unbroken loop. This is known as a circuit. The job of the torch's ON/OFF switch is to open or close a gap in the circuit. When the switch is on, electricity is allowed to flow around the circuit, lighting the bulb. When the switch is off, the circuit is broken and the current cannot flow.

### MAINS SUPPLY
Batteries have a limited amount of chemicals and can only provide a certain amount of electricity. That is why most electrical devices are powered by a mains supply. Wires connect millions of wall sockets to a power station. An electric current flows from the power station along the wires, out of the sockets and into the equipment being used. To complete the circuit, the current returns to the power station through yet more wires.

### ALTERNATING CURRENT
The electricity that comes out of a power station is in the form of alternating current (AC). Unlike a battery, which produces a steady one-way current called a direct current (DC), the mains supply flows first in one direction and then the other. The current changes direction very rapidly (about 50 times a second).

## SEE ALSO
Atom and molecule, Energy, Magnetism, Nuclear power

# ENERGY

**Energy is the ability to do work. An object or substance has energy if it can move or if it can generate such things as heat, sound, or electricity.**

The Sun provides most of the heat and light energy that we use on Earth.

When anything moves, such as a car, it is using kinetic energy.

Dynamite's explosive power comes from stored chemical energy.

A radio produces sound energy by making the atoms in the air vibrate.

A hammer coming down to strike a nail uses the potential energy of gravity.

Nuclear energy takes its most dramatic form in a nuclear explosion.

Energy is everywhere – in sunlight as heat and light energy, in a CD player as sound energy, even in a lump of coal as stored chemical energy. Energy can be converted from one form into another, but it can never be destroyed.

## MOVING OBJECTS
One of the most basic forms of energy is the energy of movement, or kinetic energy. Heavy, fast-moving objects have more kinetic energy than light, slow-moving ones. The kinetic energy of a car is less than that of a lorry travelling at the same speed. A parked car has no kinetic energy at all.

## HEAT ENERGY
Kinetic energy is also closely related to heat energy. An object is hot because its atoms (the tiny particles that it is made of) are constantly in motion. So an object's heat energy can be thought of as the kinetic energy of its atoms. The faster its atoms move, the hotter the object becomes.

## SAVING IT FOR LATER
Energy can be stored to be used later. This energy in storage is called potential energy.

▲ A runner waiting on the blocks to start a race is like a coiled spring ready to expand. When the starter's gun goes, the potential (stored) energy in the runner's muscles is converted into the kinetic (motion) energy of running.

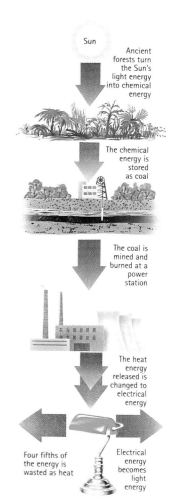
Sun
Ancient forests turn the Sun's light energy into chemical energy

The chemical energy is stored as coal

The coal is mined and burned at a power station

The heat energy released is changed to electrical energy

Four fifths of the energy is wasted as heat

Electrical energy becomes light energy

### ENERGY CYCLE
The Sun is our main source of energy on Earth. Every time it is used, the energy changes form. Other natural sources include oil, gas and coal, but we use them wastefully.

A spring stores energy as it is squeezed. When it is released and expands back to its original shape, the potential energy becomes motion (kinetic energy).

## CHANGING FORM
The law of conservation of energy says that energy can never be destroyed or lost, but will change its form. For example, if a boy gliding on a pair of roller-skates slowly comes to a halt, his kinetic energy will gradually decrease to zero. But the energy

does not vanish, it is transformed into two other energy forms: heat and sound. The heat, created by the friction of the roller-skate wheels rubbing on the ground, warms up both the wheels and the ground. The sound energy can be heard as a swish or squeak of the wheels.

## ENERGY AND POWER

Scientists measure energy using units called joules (J). Power – the rate at which energy is used – is measured in watts (W). The idea of power involves time. If two kettles heat a litre of water from 10°C to 100°C, they both give the water the same amount of heat energy. But if one kettle does the job in half the time, it has twice the amount of power as the other. Nuclear power works by releasing the energy locked up inside the nucleus of an atom and using it to do work.

## MAKING IT WORK

Energy is never lost, but can be wasted if it is not put to work. Heat is the main cause of energy wastage. For example, an ordinary light bulb converts only one fifth of its electrical energy into light – the rest is wasted as heat. Inefficiency of car engines also means that the Earth's natural energy resources, such as oil, are constantly being wasted.

## AN ENERGETIC GAME OF PINBALL

Energy is constantly changing its state. In a game of pinball, potential energy is converted into kinetic energy. The moving ball will tend to slow down through friction as it comes into contact with parts of the machine. Energy is used up in overcoming friction, but it is not lost – it is changed into heat. When the player adds energy to the ball, by pushing it with a flipper, the ball speeds up.

1 Pulling back the plunger coils a spring just behind the ball. In energy terms, the potential energy in the player's hand is transferred to the spring.

2 Letting go of the plunger shoots the ball into play. The spring's potential energy is changed into the kinetic energy of the moving ball.

3 As the ball moves inside the machine, it starts to slow down – its kinetic energy is being changed, mainly into heat. Flippers and obstacles have springs to speed the ball up.

### SEE ALSO

Ecology, Electricity, Force and motion, Light, Magnetism, Nuclear power, Sound

# ENGINE

**Engines are machines which convert energy into mechanical work to power vehicles, to drive other machines or to generate electricity.**

**FRANK WHITTLE**
(1907–87) An officer in the British Royal Air Force, he built the first successful jet engine, known as a gas turbine.

**WERNHER VON BRAUN**
(1912–77) He was head of the team of German scientists that created the V2 – the first rocket-powered guided missile, and the inspiration for later moon rockets.

The main types of engine are steam, petrol, diesel, jet and rocket. Each one is supplied with energy by burning, or combusting, fuels such as coal, petrol and diesel oil. Nearly all engines are internal combustion engines, which means the fuel is burnt inside the engine. The exception to this is the steam engine, which uses external combustion.

### EARLY STEAM ENGINES
In the 18th century, much of the power for the Industrial Revolution was provided by the steam engine. In 1712, Englishman Thomas Newcomen developed the first practical steam engine for pumping water from mines. In 1765, a Scottish engineer, James Watt, began to improve the Newcomen steam engine and developed a much more efficient machine. Soon steam engines were powering factory machinery, as well as railway vehicles such as the *Rocket* locomotive, built by English engineer George Stephenson in 1829.

▲ A microlite is a hang-glider with an engine. It uses a two-stroke engine, which is lighter, cheaper and more powerful for its size than a four-stroke engine.

### THE POWER OF STEAM
In a steam engine, a fire is used to boil water to produce high-pressure steam. As the steam expands, it pushes a piston to and fro in a cylinder, or turns the blades of a fan-like wheel called a turbine. These then drive the machine. Most steam engines have been replaced by internal combustion engines. However, many power station generators today are still worked by steam turbines.

### PETROL ENGINES
Nowadays, cars, trucks, buses and many trains and aircraft use internal combustion

### STEAM LOCOMOTIVE
Steam locomotives powered the railways of the world for over 130 years. Hot gases from the burning coal surround the water tubes, turning the water to steam. The steam passes to the cylinder, driving the piston backwards and forwards. The piston in turn pushes the connecting rod backwards and forwards, which rotates a crank and drives the wheels. Water and coal are carried in the tender.

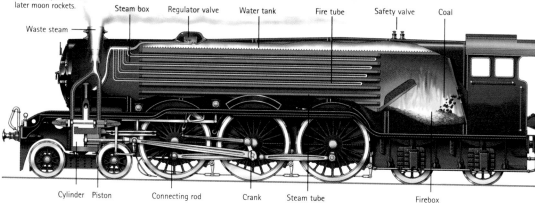

Steam box    Regulator valve    Water tank    Fire tube    Safety valve    Coal

Waste steam

Cylinder    Piston    Connecting rod    Crank    Steam tube    Firebox

## A FOUR-STROKE ENGINE

Cars have internal combustion engines with pistons that work in a four-stroke cycle (the piston makes two movements up and two down). Air and fuel are let into the piston cylinder by valves at the top. The explosion of ignited fuel moves the piston, which turns a crankshaft. This spins the drive shaft.

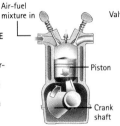

Air-fuel mixture in

Piston

Crank shaft

**1** Induction. As the piston goes down, it draws a mixture of air and petrol into the cylinder.

Valve — Valve

**2** Compression. The piston rises, squashing the fuel and air mixture ready for ignition.

Spark plug

**3** Power. A spark lights the fuel, forcing the piston down and turning the crankshaft.

Exhaust gas out

**4** Exhaust. On the final stroke of the engine, the piston rises to expel exhaust (waste) gases.

engines fuelled by diesel oil or petrol. In a petrol engine, the fuel mixes with air inside a cylinder, and a spark sets the mixture alight, pushing the piston up and down in a four-stroke cycle (see above).

## DIESEL ENGINES

Like petrol engines, diesel engines have cylinders, pistons, valves and a fuel supply, but there are no spark plugs or ignition system. The fuel explodes because of the immense heat created when the piston compresses the fuel and air inside a cylinder. The explosion of fuel pushes the piston up and down, powering the vehicle.

## THE GAS TURBINE

A jet, or gas-turbine, engine does not have pistons. Instead, air is sucked in at the front of the engine and compressed, or squashed, by the rotating blades of the compressor. The air is blown into the combustion chamber and ignited with aviation fuel. The hot gases are expelled from the back of the engine, pushing the plane forward.

## TO THE STARS

Like jet engines, rocket engines also use their exhaust gases to push the vehicle forward. Unlike jets, however, rockets cannot burn fuel by taking in oxygen from the air, as there is no air in space. Instead, they carry their oxygen supply with them, usually as liquid oxygen. The fuel either ignites spontaneously when mixed with the oxygen, or is lit by a spark.

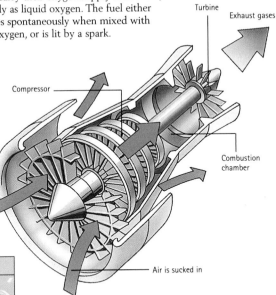

Compressor

Turbine

Exhaust gases

Combustion chamber

Air is sucked in

### A JET ENGINE

In a jet aeroplane engine, air is sucked in at the front of the engine by giant rotating blades. The air is then compressed and passed into a combustion (burning) chamber, where it is ignited. The plane is thrust forward by the exhaust gases. These gases also turn a turbine, which drives the compressor.

### SEE ALSO

Electricity, Energy, Transport

# EUROPE

Europe is the second smallest of the world's seven continents. It has 45 countries, including parts of Russia, Turkey and Kazakhstan.

▲ Iceland in the North Atlantic Ocean is known as the Land of Ice and Fire because of its volcanoes and hot springs set against a landscape of ice fields and glaciers.

## KEY FACTS

- **Area:** 22,986,000 sq km
- **Population:** 704,000,000
- **Number of countries:** 45
- **Largest country:** Russia, 25 per cent (4,309,400 sq km) of which is in Europe
- **Smallest country:** Vatican City (0.44 sq km)
- **Highest point:** Mount Elbrus (5,642m)
- **Largest lake:** Lake Ladoga (17,700 sq km)
- **Longest river:** Volga (3,688km)

Only the continent of Australia is smaller than Europe, but Europe's moderate climate, rich resources and fertile land support a large population. Between them, the people speak about 50 languages and many more dialects. With its 45 countries, Europe is a continent of diverse cultures.

### NEVER FAR FROM WATER
The northwest and west of Europe are bordered by the Arctic and Atlantic Oceans, while the Mediterranean Sea surrounds the south. The coastline is broken up by thousands of fjords and other inlets and only nine European countries have no access to the sea.

### NORTH EUROPEAN PLAIN
Many of Europe's most populated areas lie on the North European Plain, which stretches from the southern part of the United Kingdom through northern France, Germany and Poland to the Ural Mountains in Russia. To the north are forests of coniferous trees such as fir, larch and pine. Deciduous forests of ash, elm and oak grow in central and southern Europe. In the southeast are large areas of dry grassland called steppes.

### SCANDINAVIA
In the far north of Europe lies the cold and mountainous region of Scandinavia, which includes the countries of Norway, Sweden, Denmark and Finland. The climate around the Arctic Ocean is cold and snowy, with temperatures in January averaging below −16°C. Few trees grow in the extreme north, but the forests farther south contain large animals such as brown bears, reindeer and wolves.

▼ Wine is produced throughout Europe, particularly in France (shown here), Germany, Spain, Italy and Bulgaria.

miles
0      500
0      500
km

N

ARCTIC OCEAN

ICELAND

NORWEGIAN
SEA

NORWAY

SWEDEN

FINLAND

Lake
Ladoga

RUSSIA
(European part)

Ural Mountains

BALTIC
SEA

ESTONIA

NORTH
SEA

DENMARK

LATVIA

UNITED
KINGDOM

IRELAND

RUSSIA

LITHUANIA

BELARUS

KAZAKHSTAN
(European part)

PLAIN

EUROPEAN

Volga

ATLANTIC
OCEAN

NORTH

1

2

GERMANY

POLAND

CZECH
REPUBLIC

UKRAINE

Caspian
Sea

SLOVAKIA

Carpathian Mts.

FRANCE

5

AUSTRIA

HUNGARY

16

Mt. Elbrus

Alps

4

10

11

ROMANIA

PORTUGAL

Pyrenees

6

7

9

12

13

BLACK SEA

BULGARIA

Bosporus

8

SPAIN

ITALY

14

TURKEY
(European part)

15

MEDITERRANEAN SEA

GREECE

MALTA

**KEY TO MAP**
1 THE NETHERLANDS
2 BELGIUM
3 LUXEMBOURG
4 SWITZERLAND
5 LIECHTENSTEIN
6 MONACO
7 ANDORRA
8 VATICAN CITY
9 SAN MARINO
10 SLOVENIA
11 CROATIA
12 BOSNIA–HERZEGOVINA
13 YUGOSLAVIA
14 MACEDONIA
15 ALBANIA
16 MOLDOVA

## THE MEDITERRANEAN

The southern part of Europe is divided from the north by three mountain ranges: the Pyrenees, the Alps and the Carpathian Mountains. The Mediterranean countries of southern Europe, including Italy, Spain and Greece, have mild, rainy winters and hot, dry summers.

## A FERTILE CONTINENT

Europe is a fertile continent with farms covering more than half the land. Crops include barley, oats, potatoes and wheat, and citrus fruits and olives in the south. Vast areas of steppes in southern Russia and Ukraine and are farmed for grain.

## OIL, GAS AND COAL

Oil and natural gas are produced in the North Sea, and coal is found in large quantities in Europe. These fuels help power the continent's many factories – Europe produces more manufactured goods than any other continent, including cars, electronic goods, ships and steel.

## A MIXED POPULATION

Most Europeans are the descendants of people who lived on the continent in prehistoric times, but there is a long history of immigration from Africa, Asia and the Caribbean region. About 70 per cent of the population lives in cities and towns, working in factories or service industries, such as finance and tourism. ▶

▲ The number of red squirrels has decreased in Europe in the 20th century, following the introduction of the grey squirrel from North America and loss of large areas of woodland.

▲ Istanbul in Turkey lies on the shores of the Bosporus, which divides Europe from Asia. Its buildings reflect a mixture of Eastern and Western styles.

## BRANCHES OF CHRISTIANITY

Christianity is Europe's leading religion. Many follow the Roman Catholic Church, which has its headquarters in Vatican City. The Vatican covers just 0.44 sq km in Rome, Italy, and is the world's smallest independent country. Protestantism is a branch of Christianity popular in northern Europe, while the Orthodox Church flourishes in the east and southeast.

## HISTORICAL CITIES

Many of Europe's large cities are steeped in history, but are also characterized by modern architecture and a modern way of life. Paris in France contains magnificent buildings dating from the Middle Ages, and is at the same time a leading fashion centre. Moscow in Russia and London in the UK are important international cities, as well as historic sites. Athens and Rome, the capitals of Greece and Italy, have impressive ruins surviving from the days of Ancient Greece and the Roman Empire.

## DEMOCRACY AND LAW

Throughout history, Europe has had an important influence on world politics. The system of democracy – where the government is chosen by the people – was first tried in Ancient Greece about 2,500 years ago. Similarly, many of the

▲ The ruins of Delphi, a sacred site from as early as 1100BC, stand on Mount Parnassus in the southern part of mainland Greece.

laws developed during the Roman civilization (from 590BC to AD476) still influence legal systems today.

## THE RENAISSANCE

From the 1300s, Europe became an increasingly important centre of art and learning, with people interested in new ideas about art, science and literature. This period is known as the Renaissance. At the same time, a desire for trade led European seafarers to set out to explore unknown lands and later to start colonies abroad. In the late 18th century, the continent was the birthplace of the Industrial Revolution, which brought great power and prosperity to the West.

## END OF EMPIRES

The map of Europe has often changed throughout history, largely because of wars between rival countries. In the 20th century, two great world wars were fought between European powers. In the years following World War II (1939–45), the empires created in African and Asia by European countries such as Belgium,

◀ Many European countries, such as Germany, the Netherlands, Romania and Italy, have strong national football teams and attract keen supporters such as these from Switzerland.

Britain, France, the Netherlands and Portugal came to an end. Former colonies became independent countries, but many people living there continued to follow European customs and speak European languages. A large number of them have since made their homes in Europe.

## EAST AND WEST

By the 1950s, Europe was divided between the non-communist countries of the west and the Soviet-backed communist countries of the east. Until the 1980s, the two sides remained armed and

▲ After World War II, about a seventh of Berlin was in ruins. The city was divided between East and West until 1990, when Germany was reunited.

◄ German car-making factories are among the most highly automated in the world, and the cars they produce are exported worldwide.

hostile throughout the period known as the Cold War. But from the late 1980s, the Eastern European countries threw off their communist governments following the break-up of the Soviet Union in 1991. Yugoslavia also split up into five separate countries at this time, and a new map of Europe was shaped, with new countries and partnerships.

## THE EUROPEAN UNION

In the 1950s, a group of countries in western Europe set up the European Community, or Common Market, to encourage greater economic unity in Europe. Over the years, the Community grew into the European Union, with 15 member countries aiming not only for greater economic co-operation, but also greater political unity.

### SEE ALSO

Eastern Europe, France, Germany, Greece and the Balkans, Italy, Netherlands, Belgium and Luxembourg, Scandinavia, Spain and Portugal, Switzerland and Austria, UK

# EVOLUTION

Evolution is the way in which an organism changes over many generations, resulting in a species that is very different from its early ancestors.

**JEAN BAPTISTE LAMARCK**
(1744–1829) was a French biologist who believed, mistakenly, that animals evolved during their own lifetimes. For example, each giraffe, by stretching, elongated its neck.

**CHARLES DARWIN**
(1809–1882) shook the world, and especially the Church, with his theory of natural selection, which he published in *On the Origin of Species* in 1859.

Most scientists believe that the first simple organisms appeared on Earth over 3,000 million years ago and that all today's plants and animals have arisen from these by a process of gradual change. This process, which is constantly happening from one generation to the next, is known as evolution.

## DARWIN'S THEORY
The idea of evolution has been around since the time of the Ancient Greeks. However, the first convincing theory of how evolution works was only provided in the middle of the 19th century by the English naturalist Charles Darwin. He recognized that plants and animals produce lots of offspring but that only a small number of these offspring survive. Darwin concluded that only the individual with the most useful characteristics is able to survive in a process that he called the struggle for existence.

## SURVIVAL OF THE FITTEST
Darwin noticed that individuals that are not well suited to their surroundings die out. This leaves only the fittest individuals

to breed and pass the useful characteristics that have allowed them to survive on to their offspring. In popular terms, this process is known as 'the survival of the fittest'. It explains the enormous variety of plant and animal life that is found throughout the world – because the conditions vary from place to place, animals and plants adapt to fit their environment.

## LITTLE BY LITTLE
With each new generation of plant and animal life, the struggle for existence continues. The result is that, over a long period of time, plants and animals gradually change and become better

## EVOLUTION FACTS AND FIGURES
- Scientists estimate that 99.9 per cent of all the species that have ever lived are now extinct
- The idea of evolution was first suggested by the Ancient Greeks more than 2,500 years ago
- Another naturalist called Alfred Wallace came up with the same theory of evolution as Darwin (and at the same time), but Darwin published his ideas first
- By looking at fossilized animals in different layers of rock, scientists can see how the animals evolved
- When Darwin visited the Galapagos Islands he saw that all the finches had different beaks to suit their food, such as a long, hooked beak for catching insects or a nutcracker-shaped beak for eating seeds

## THE EVOLUTION OF MAN
The earliest human beings probably evolved from ape-like creatures such as *Ramapithecus* (15 mya). *Australopithecus* (3.75 mya) walked upright on his back legs. *Homo habilis* (2 mya) made basic tools from stone and bone, while *Homo erectus* (1.75 mya) was probably the first human being to use fire. The Neanderthal people (*Homo sapiens*, 40,000 ya) lived alongside *Homo sapiens sapiens* who developed into modern man.

RAMAPITHECUS   AUSTRALOPITHECUS   HOMO HABILIS   HOMO ERECTUS   NEANDERTHAL MAN   HOMO SAPIENS SAPIENS

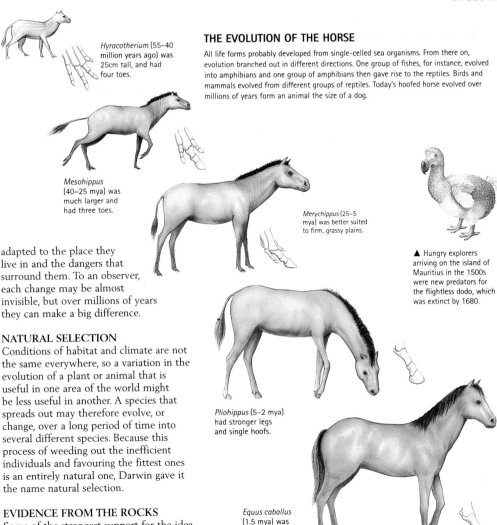

Hyracotherium (55–40 million years ago) was 25cm tall, and had four toes.

Mesohippus (40–25 mya) was much larger and had three toes.

Merychippus (25–5 mya) was better suited to firm, grassy plains.

Pliohippus (5–2 mya) had stronger legs and single hoofs.

Equus caballus (1.5 mya) was similar to today's horses.

▲ Hungry explorers arriving on the island of Mauritius in the 1500s were new predators for the flightless dodo, which was extinct by 1680.

## THE EVOLUTION OF THE HORSE

All life forms probably developed from single-celled sea organisms. From there on, evolution branched out in different directions. One group of fishes, for instance, evolved into amphibians and one group of amphibians then gave rise to the reptiles. Birds and mammals evolved from different groups of reptiles. Today's hoofed horse evolved over millions of years form an animal the size of a dog.

adapted to the place they live in and the dangers that surround them. To an observer, each change may be almost invisible, but over millions of years they can make a big difference.

## NATURAL SELECTION
Conditions of habitat and climate are not the same everywhere, so a variation in the evolution of a plant or animal that is useful in one area of the world might be less useful in another. A species that spreads out may therefore evolve, or change, over a long period of time into several different species. Because this process of weeding out the inefficient individuals and favouring the fittest ones is an entirely natural one, Darwin gave it the name natural selection.

## EVIDENCE FROM THE ROCKS
Some of the strongest support for the idea of evolution comes from the fossilized remains of plants and animals that are found in rocks formed from layers of sand and mud on ancient sea beds. In each layer of rock, the organisms look slightly different from the ones below. This provides the evidence for a process of change over hundreds, thousands or even millions of years.

## A COMMON ANCESTOR
The bone structure of living animals also gives clues to evolution. A human arm, a

bird's wings and a whale's flipper all look very different and have different uses in everyday life. However, their bones are actually very similar. This suggests that these animals have all evolved from a common ancestor, which spread out over a wide geographical area. The arms were then adapted for different jobs according to the demands of the different environments.

### SEE ALSO
Dinosaur, Fossil, Genetics, Horse

# FISH

Fish are vertebrates (backboned animals) which breathe oxygen dissolved in water through their gills. They are found in salty and fresh water around the world.

Mudskippers survive low tides in the swamps of Africa and Southeast Asia by breathing air. They use their strong pectoral fins as 'arms' to climb trees in search of food.

## FOUR TYPES OF FISH
Fish can be divided into groups by body structure. Examples are jawless fish, sharks and rays, and bony fish – primitive and modern.

Lampreys (above) and hagfish are ancient fish. They have no jaws and, like sharks, their skeletons are made of soft cartilage.

Sharks usually have a torpedo-shaped body with a skeleton of cartilage. All have strong jaws, many with several rows of teeth.

Primitive bony fish, such as the coelacanth (above) and lungfish, are related to fish that lived over 400 million years ago.

Perch (above) are modern bony fish. Unlike primitive bony fish they do not have a fleshy lobe at the base of each fin.

Most fish are streamlined for easy movement through water. The tail pushes the fish forward, and the fins are used for steering and balance. Most fish have two pairs of fins on their sides. There is one dorsal fin, running down the middle of the back, and another fin at the base of the tail. The tail is usually forked.

### COLD-BLOODED CREATURES
As cold-blooded creatures, fish stay at the same temperature as the water they live in. If the water is very cold, fish slow down and may stop moving altogether. Apart from using sight and smell, fish also have a row of sensors on their sides known as the lateral line, that picks up vibrations in the water even if the fish cannot see clearly.

### BONE OR GRISTLE
There are over 22,000 known species of fish – more than all other vertebrates put together. Fish can be divided into cartilaginous fish and bony fish. Cartilaginous fish, whose skeletons are made of soft cartilage, or gristle, include sharks, skates and rays. There are only

about 800 species, all of which live in the sea. Bony fish include some of the most colourful animals on earth, and the fastest – sailfish – can reach speeds of 100 km/h.

### BROWN AND GRISTLY
Most cartilaginous fish are brown or grey and have five or more gill slits on each side. Their fins are solid and their bodies are covered with rough, tooth-like scales. Sailors once used shark skins to scrub the decks of wooden ships. The whale shark is the largest fish, measuring 12m long and weighing up to 20 tonnes.

### FISH BONES
Bony fish have smooth, overlapping scales. Their fins are delicate membranes stretched over slender spines. The gills are covered by a flap called an operculum, so there is only one gill opening on each side of the body.

## TEMPERATE SEAS

Fish are adapted to suit their environment. Sea fish constantly lose water and must drink a lot, whereas freshwater fish take in water through their skin. Temperate waters, which get colder in winter, are home to dull-coloured fish, commonly caught for food. These fish often swim deeper or migrate in cold weather.

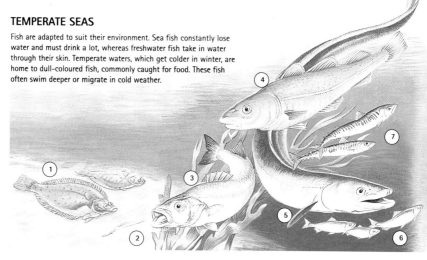

## KEY TO TEMPERATE SEA
1 PLAICE
2 SAND EEL
3 BASS
4 COD
5 CONGER EEL
6 HERRINGS
7 MACKEREL

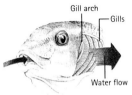

Gill arch
Gills
Water flow

**INSIDE A TYPICAL FISH**

Dorsal fin (for balance)
Spinal cord
Muscle
Brain
Caudal (tail) fin
Barbel
Gill slit
Heart
Anal fin (for balance)
Pectoral fin (for steering)
Swim-bladder (helps the fish to float)
Pelvic fin (for steering)

▲ Oxygen from the water passes through the thin walls of the gills (tiny blood-filled threads arranged in pockets on each side of the throat) and into the blood. The water then passes out through the gill slits.

Most bony fish have an air-filled swim-bladder, allowing them to float motionless in the water. Sharks have no swim-bladder and would sink if they stopped swimming.

## JAWLESS FISH

Another group of fish includes about 70 species of lampreys and hagfish. These are eel-shaped creatures without jaws. Lampreys have round, sucker-like mouths and toothed tongues, used to rasp flesh from other fish. Hagfish have slit-shaped mouths and sharp teeth. They eat dead fish.

## MILLIONS OF EGGS

Some fish give birth to live young, but most species lay eggs. These are usually released into the water by the female, where they are fertilized by the male. Fish lay many eggs, as most of them get eaten. The ocean sunfish may lay 300 million eggs in its lifetime. Fish that protect their eggs do not lay many, and it is often the male that looks after them. The female sea horse lays eggs in a pouch on the male's abdomen, where they can be protected.

## FRESHWATER FISH

About two thirds of all fish live in freshwater streams, lakes, rivers, ponds, marshes and swamps.

Guppies, native to the Caribbean islands, are attractive and popular aquarium fish.

Piranha live in South American rivers, feeding on fish or other animals with their razor-like teeth.

This African catfish is typical of its group, which has long barbels (whiskers) and fins that lock upright.

Rainbow trout are native to North America, but because of trout farming, now live in European rivers.

The climbing perch can be seen taking short 'walks' across land, as it has a gill chamber for breathing air.

## TROPICAL SEAS

The most brightly coloured fish live in the tropics, blending in with the vivid coral reefs, their camouflaged colours hiding them from predators.

8
9
10
11
12
13
14
15
16

**KEY TO TROPICAL SEA**
8 GROUPER
9 CLEANER WRASSE
10 LION FISH
11 FAIRY BASSLET
12 MANTA RAY
13 PARROT FISH
14 BUTTERFLY FISH
15 SEA HORSE
16 TOMATO CLOWNFISH

## SEE ALSO

Animal, Fossil, Jellyfish, Ocean and sea

# FLOWER

Flowers are the reproductive parts of some kinds of plants. They make seeds that will form a new generation of the same type of plant.

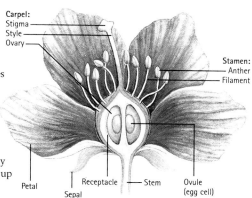

Carpel:
Stigma
Style
Ovary

Stamen:
Anther
Filament

Petal

Receptacle — Stem

Sepal

Ovule
(egg cell)

▲ Flowers have four main parts: sepals and petals (the outer parts), and carpels and stamens (the reproductive parts). The stamens are male and the carpels are female.

Bats are attracted to the nighttime scent and infra-red colours of some tropical flowers.

Flowers are really specialized leaves that have evolved over millions of years to help plants reproduce efficiently. There are more than 250,000 species of flowering plants, called angiosperms, which range from huge, long-lived trees to tiny annuals. Flowers may vary greatly in appearance, but they are all made up of the same basic parts.

## MALE AND FEMALE PARTS

The main reproductive parts of a flower are the female carpel and the male stamens. Each stamen is made up of the anther, which produces tiny powdery grains of pollen, and the filament, or stalk. The carpel has a stigma, which is often sticky and coloured. The stigma is found at the end of a style – a kind of stalk that leads down to the ovary. Inside the ovary are egg cells that develop into the seeds which will later become new plants.

## POLLINATION

For seeds to form, pollen grains from the anther must come into contact with the

Many alpine flowers are tough and lie low on the ground, to help them withstand the cold.

Desert plants, such as cacti, have bright flowers to attract insects for the few weeks they are in bloom.

Water flowers, such as white water-lilies, float above the surface to attract insect pollinators.

stigma. This process is called pollination. Most flowering plants are pollinated by insects. As an insect such as a bee pushes inside the flower looking for nectar, its body gets dusted with pollen from the anthers of the flower. The insect will then transfer the pollen dust to the stigma of the next flower it visits.

## FLOWER APPEAL

The varying colours, scents and shapes of individual flowers have developed to appeal to pollinators – usually insects, but also birds and small mammals, such as bats. Many flowers have glands called nectaries, which produce nectar – a sugary liquid on which the pollinators feed. The pollinators must push past the male and female parts of the flower to reach the nectar.

▲ One of the petals of the bee orchid looks like a real bee. This signals to other pollinators that the flower is a good source of nectar, and they land on it to find food. Other flowers attract bees with ultraviolet markings on their petals that only bees can see.

---

### FLOWER FACTS

• The first flowering plant – thought to have been a magnolia – appeared about 160 million years ago

• The world's largest flower, *Rafflesia arnoldii*, grows in Indonesia and can measure up to 1m in diameter. Its smell of rotting meat is irresistible to the flies that pollinate it

• Opium, which comes from the opium poppy, is used to make pain-killing drugs such as codeine

• The Madagascan periwinkle, once thought of as a weed, is now farmed to produce anti-cancer drugs

---

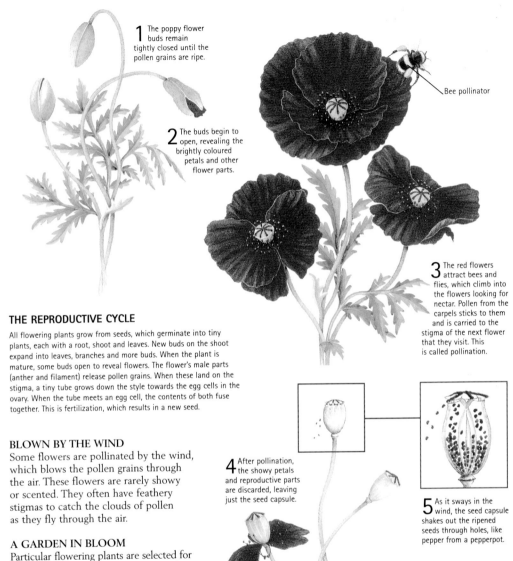

1 The poppy flower buds remain tightly closed until the pollen grains are ripe.

2 The buds begin to open, revealing the brightly coloured petals and other flower parts.

Bee pollinator

3 The red flowers attract bees and flies, which climb into the flowers looking for nectar. Pollen from the carpels sticks to them and is carried to the stigma of the next flower that they visit. This is called pollination.

## THE REPRODUCTIVE CYCLE

All flowering plants grow from seeds, which germinate into tiny plants, each with a root, shoot and leaves. New buds on the shoot expand into leaves, branches and more buds. When the plant is mature, some buds open to reveal flowers. The flower's male parts (anther and filament) release pollen grains. When these land on the stigma, a tiny tube grows down the style towards the egg cells in the ovary. When the tube meets an egg cell, the contents of both fuse together. This is fertilization, which results in a new seed.

## BLOWN BY THE WIND

Some flowers are pollinated by the wind, which blows the pollen grains through the air. These flowers are rarely showy or scented. They often have feathery stigmas to catch the clouds of pollen as they fly through the air.

## A GARDEN IN BLOOM

Particular flowering plants are selected for a garden because of when, and how often, they produce their flowers. This can depend on how long the flowering plants live. Annuals are plants that sprout, mature, flower, produce seeds and die all in the same year. Biennials live for two years, and perennials live for three years or longer. Most garden plants are perennials, because once they have flowered, they flower every year for as long as they live.

4 After pollination, the showy petals and reproductive parts are discarded, leaving just the seed capsule.

Petals fall off to leave seed head

5 As it sways in the wind, the seed capsule shakes out the ripened seeds through holes, like pepper from a pepperpot.

6 Most poppies are annuals (plants that live for one year). This means that the plant puts all its energy into flowering and producing seeds, and then dies.

## SEE ALSO

Desert, Fruit, Grassland, Leaf, Plant, Rainforest

# FOOD

Food is any substance that is a source of nutrition to a living organism. Without it, nothing can live. The food we eat is supplied by plants and animals.

Modern diets contain a wide range of foods. Some, such as fruits and vegetables, are still in the original state in which they were grown. Others, such as bread and hamburgers, are processed foods, which means they arrive at our tables looking very different from the ingredients that were used to make them.

## THE FIRST FARMERS

Until about 10,000 years ago, humans were hunter-gatherers, spending much of their time hunting animals and gathering fruits and vegetables for food. Then, by about 8000BC, people in fertile parts of the world began to manage the land for agriculture. They started to grow food crops and to domesticate animals such as cattle, sheep and poultry for milk, meat and eggs.

## DIFFERENT DIETS

Meat and dairy products are a major part of the diet in developed countries, yet some people in the Far East have lost the ability to digest dairy produce because it has never been part of their diet. In tropical countries, people eat mainly rice, cassava and potatoes, with very few vegetables, while in Mediterranean countries, it is usual to have a high intake of all kinds of different fruits and vegetables.

## FOOD INTAKE WORLDWIDE

Although there is more than enough food to support the world's population, it does not always reach those in need. One in ten people does not get enough to eat, and every year, around 40 million people die of hunger – most of them in the poorer developing countries. In developed countries, people eat 30 to 40 per cent more food than they need, which can cause its own set of health problems.

## STAPLE FOODS

Our food comes from many different sources, either plant or animal. The main foods obtained from plants are grains, fruits and vegetables. Products made from grains, or cereals, such as rice or bread, have been the basis of the human diet for thousands of years. Food from animals includes meat, eggs and dairy products. They cost more to produce than plant foods.

▶ Cereals such as wheat (right), rice and maize together make up about half of the world's food intake.

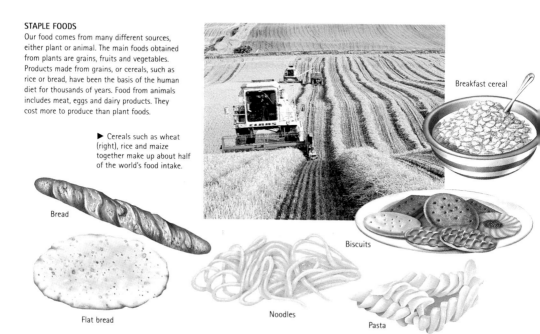

Breakfast cereal

Bread

Biscuits

Flat bread

Noodles

Pasta

## FOOD PROCESSING

Humans have been processing food – by cooking it – ever since the discovery of fire. Today, there are many other ways of processing food, such as milling, freezing, canning and ultra-heat treatment. Processing makes some foods, such as potatoes and wheat, easier to digest. It also stops food from rotting, which encourages germs to grow. Heat treatment kills germs, while chilling and freezing slows down their growth to a safe level.

## ADDITIVES

Substances known as additives are usually added to foods during processing. Some, such as the vitamins and minerals added to bread and cereals, improve the nutritional value of food. Other additives include preservatives, which are added to foods to stop them going rotten, and colourings, such as the natural pigment of beetroot.

## FOOD SAFETY

About six per cent of the population suffers from food poisoning each year, usually caused by food contaminated with harmful bacteria such as *E coli* or *Salmonella*. Preparing food hygienically lowers the risk of food poisoning. Foods such as meat, fish, milk and eggs should be heated and cooked thoroughly before eating to kill any dangerous bacteria.

## RELIGION AND CULTURE

The food people eat often depends on their culture or religion. For example, some Jews eat a kosher diet, governed by religious laws such as cooking and eating meat and dairy produce separately. In the Hindu religion, every living creature is believed to have a soul, so eating animals is often avoided. Many vegetarians believe animals should not be killed for humans to eat.

▲ Paella is a Spanish dish made with rice, shellfish, vegetables and chicken, named after the shallow frying pan in which it is cooked. Each country has unique local ways of preparing food that have often been passed down through the generations, and are usually made from local produce.

### FRUIT AND VEGETABLES

We eat fruits, such as oranges, and vegetables, such as cauliflowers, in their natural state. However, oranges can also be processed to make juice or preserved by canning. Vegetables such as peas can be frozen or dried to last longer.

Picking in an orange grove

Cauliflower

Fresh oranges

Orange juice

### DAIRY PRODUCTS

Dairy cattle produce milk, from which other products such as butter, cheese and yoghurt are made. Beef comes from cattle that have been specially reared for their meat. Beef is cut up into joints or steaks, or minced for foods such as burgers.

Milk

Cheese

Butter

Beefburger

Yoghurt

### SEE ALSO

Nutrition

# FORCE AND MOTION

A force changes the way an object moves. If the object is stationary, a force will set it in motion. If it is moving, a force will change its speed or direction.

Force is a word we use in everyday speech. For instance, we may talk about forcing a door open or forcing a suitcase shut. In both, a force – either a push or pull – is being applied by a person to move the door or suitcase lid.

▲ An object's weight affects how fast it moves and how long it takes to stop. This is called its momentum, and it can be transferred from one object to another, as between two pool balls.

▲ The people on this fairground ride are kept spinning in a circle by two competing forces: centrifugal force, which pulls outwards, and centripetal force, which pulls inwards.

## CHANGING VELOCITY
A force is anything that changes an object's velocity (speed in a given direction). A ball rolling along the ground has a certain velocity, but if it is kicked, the ball increases velocity. An increase in velocity is known as acceleration, and a decrease in speed is called deceleration.

## STATE OF INERTIA
An object that stays at the same velocity – neither speeding up, nor slowing down or changing direction – is said to be in a state of inertia. This rarely happens, however, because moving objects usually slow down because they bump into something, come into contact with the ground or are blown by the wind. The force created by wind, or when two items rub together, is known as friction. It works against motion, slowing things down.

## FAST FACTS
• A bus is harder to push than a car because an object with greater mass (more material) has more inertia, which means it needs a greater force to accelerate

• Two forces that balance each other exactly, producing no movement, are known as static forces. A bridge stays up in this way

## MIGHTY FORCES
Pulling a door open or pushing it shut requires direct force and human strength. But sometimes we are not strong enough (do not have enough force) to move an object. People have invented machines such as levers and pulleys to increase the effect of our force. Powerful natural forces such as electricity and magnetism have also been harnessed to work for us. Another natural force, gravity, literally keeps our feet on the ground.

## NEWTON'S LAWS
Most of the principles of force and motion were first discovered in the 1660s by the English scientist Isaac Newton. Today, in honour of his work, we measure force in newtons (N). One newton is roughly the force that you feel when you hold a large orange in the palm of your hand.

## ACTION AND REACTION
Whenever force is applied to an object, it always creates another force, called a reactionary force, that works in the opposite direction. A canoeist paddling through water moves forward by such action and reaction. The canoeist's paddle pushing the water backwards is the action, while the reaction is the force exerted by the water on the paddle, which pushes the canoe forward through the water.

Action: the paddle pushes against the water

Reaction: the canoe moves forward in the water

## SEE ALSO
Bridge, Electricity, Gravity, Invention, Machine, Magnetism

# FOREST

Forests are large areas of land covered mainly by trees and other plants. Today, they occupy almost 30 per cent of the world's land area.

There are three basic types of forest: coniferous (boreal), broad-leaved deciduous, and dense, tropical rainforests. Many forests include a combination of coniferous and deciduous trees.

## CONIFEROUS FORESTS

Coniferous forests are found in the cold northern areas of Canada, Europe and Asia and include spruce, fir or pine. These trees are evergreens (do not shed their leaves in winter) and carry their seeds in cones.

## DECIDUOUS FORESTS

The temperate regions of the USA and Europe have warm summers, mild winters and rain all year round. Here, the forest trees, such as oak, ash and beech, are all deciduous, which means they drop their leaves in the autumn.

## THE LIFE OF THE FOREST

A forest's highest layer is formed by the tree tops and is called the canopy. Below this are shorter trees, then a layer of bushes and shrubs. Lower still, there are ferns, grasses and wild flowers, and then the mosses and fungi that grow on the forest floor. In addition to the larger animals, such as deer and squirrels, there are thousands of smaller creatures living under the leaves, and in the bark and forest soil.

## THE TROPICS

In the hot, permanently wet regions of the tropics, there are dense rainforests full of teak, ebony, rosewood, mahogany and other evergreen trees. Often the trees grow so closely together that sunlight cannot reach the ground. Other regions in the tropics with both wet and dry seasons have deciduous woodlands and savanna – grasslands with scattered clumps of trees.

## WHY WE NEED FORESTS

Forests provide food and shelter for animals and refresh the atmosphere by turning carbon dioxide into oxygen. More than 2,000 million people use firewood for cooking and heating. There is also a huge trade in forest products: softwood (conifers) for building and making paper, and hardwoods (deciduous) for furniture. Other products include fruits, nuts and spices, gums and resins, rubber and many vital medicines.

▲ In deciduous forests, the fallen leaves form a carpet on the floor, which nourishes new growth.

## FAST FACTS

• Before forests were cleared to make way for farms and cities, forests covered about 60% of the world's land area

• 25% of the forests are boreal, 21% temperate and 54% tropical

• Some rainforests have more than 150 different trees in 100 sq metres

• In the United States, only 5% of the original forests remain

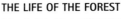

1 At first, there is a grassy meadow, into which pine seeds fall and grow to become seedlings.

2 Pine trees need full sun to grow, so they form the top layer of forest, with deciduous trees beneath.

3 The type of forest changes as old pines die and deciduous trees fill in gaps in the canopy.

4 In the final stage, a totally deciduous forest develops. It is the climax of this ecological succession.

## SEE ALSO

Habitat, Plant, Rainforest, Tree

# FOSSIL

**Fossils are the remains of once-living things found in rocks. They are preserved in different ways and show us what conditions were like in the past.**

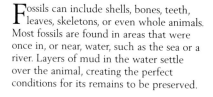

◄ An ancient leaf's shape is often preserved on stone as a black outline, or trace of carbon.

Dead insects can be preserved whole in tree resin (sap) that has turned into amber over time.

Fossils can include shells, bones, teeth, leaves, skeletons, or even whole animals. Most fossils are found in areas that were once in, or near, water, such as the sea or a river. Layers of mud in the water settle over the animal, creating the perfect conditions for its remains to be preserved.

## TYPES OF FOSSIL
A living substance can be preserved whole, but more often is changed in some way over time. It can be replaced by another material, such as stone, or may rot away leaving an empty mould of the organism.

Ammonites (fossilized shells of extinct molluscs) are often found as moulds or casts in rock.

## PRESERVED WHOLE
An insect stuck in resin (sap) oozing from a tree will be preserved whole when that resin turns to the semi-precious stone amber. When larger animals die, usually only the hard parts like bones and teeth, are preserved. Sometimes, pools of natural tar can preserve mammoth bones unaltered since the Ice Age (over 10,000 years ago).

## PETRIFIED WOOD
Fossilized wood is petrified. This means that the wood has been replaced, molecule by molecule, by a stony material. The

A dinosaur footprint, made over 65 million years ago, may be preserved in rock as a trace fossil.

carbon in a leaf can survive as a black outline on a stone surface. Millions of leaves preserved in this way produce coal.

## A STONE REPLICA
Stone copies of plants or animals are created when water seeps through the rock in which they lie, removing all of the remains. This leaves an empty mould in the shape of the living creature, which is filled by minerals seeping into the rock – creating an exact copy of the creature, known as a cast. Seashells are often fossilized as casts in limestone. Trace fossils are marks in the rock that show where an animal once existed, as in the case of worm burrows.

## USEFUL FOSSILS
We can tell how old a rock is from its fossils. Many animals existed for only a short time in history and, when we find their fossils in rock, we can tell the age of that rock. Other fossils tell us about the climate or habitat of an area in the past. For example, finding a fossil palm leaf in a cool region indicates it once had a tropical climate, and fossil seashells found far inland reveal that the area was once under the sea.

## HOW FOSSILS ARE FORMED
When a dinosaur dies, its flesh rots away, leaving only the bones behind. Scavengers may also remove parts of the body, so complete fossilized remains are rare. Over time, the bones are covered by layers of soil, which harden into rock. Millions of years later, the fossil is exposed by wind and rain or movements in the Earth's crust.

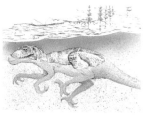

**1** The dinosaur's body falls into a sea, river, lake or swamp. Under water the remains are more likely to be buried fast by soil and sand deposited by the water.

**2** The dinosaur's flesh rots away or is eaten by water animals. Its bones and teeth are covered by many layers of sand and soil, which change to rock over time.

**3** Thousands of years later, the strata of rock shift, bringing the bones to the surface.

### SEE ALSO
Coal, Dinosaur, Evolution, Oil, Rock

# FRANCE

France is Europe's third largest country. Only Russia and Ukraine are bigger. France has a rich cultural tradition and a turbulent history.

**Area:** 551,500 sq km
**Population:** 58,847,000
**Capital:** Paris
**Language:** French
**Currency:** Franc, Euro

▲ Peaceful rural communities across the country are farm-based. Typical crops include wheat, apples and grapes.

Much of the French landscape is either plains or low hills. Three of its borders are high mountain ranges: the Vosges in the northeast; the Pyrenees in the southwest; and the Alps, including France's highest point, Mont Blanc (4,807m), in the southeast. The Massif Central rises in central France. Paris, the capital, lies in flat country on the River Seine. Other big rivers include the Loire, Rhône and Gironde.

## A NATION OF FARMERS

France is Europe's leading farming nation. Its soil and climate are generally good for crops. The north of the country is cool and moist, averaging about 35mm of rainfall per month. The south is drier and hotter, with summer temperatures above 25°C. French farmers grow wheat, barley, oats, flax, sugar beet, fruits and vegetables, and raise cattle and sheep. France is famous for its wines and cheeses, and French cooking is admired and copied all over the world.

## PARIS THE CAPITAL

Paris is the centre of government, arts and fashion. It is France's biggest city – home to about a sixth of the nation's people. Its 2,000-year-long history means the buildings are a mixture of old and new. Visitors come to see the Louvre Museum, the tomb of Napoleon, Notre Dame Cathedral, the Eiffel Tower and other famous sights.

## FRENCH LIFE

Although France is a land of forests and green countryside, three quarters of the French people live in towns and cities. People meet in pavement cafés and restaurants, or enjoy a game of boules (bowls). Favourite sports in France include cycle racing, soccer, rugby football and tennis. There are parades and speeches on Bastille Day (July 14), France's national day, which celebrates the start of the French Revolution in 1789.

## AN INDUSTRIAL GIANT

After Paris, the largest French cities are Marseille (the main seaport), Lyon, Toulouse and Nice. France has a highly developed industrial economy. French factories produce many goods, including cars, aircraft, chemicals, machinery and textiles. Fishing and mining are important. France also has an international reputation for luxury goods, such as perfume and elegant clothes. Europe's fastest trains speed between French cities, and there is a fine road system.

▲ Many French people, and other Europeans, go on winter skiing holidays in the Alps on the border between France and Italy.

▶ This spectacular glass pyramid, finished in 1989, is the entrance to the Louvre Museum in Paris. The Louvre, originally built as a fortress in about 1200, was expanded during the mid-1500s by King Francis I, who wanted to transform it into a palace. It now houses one of the world's largest art collections.

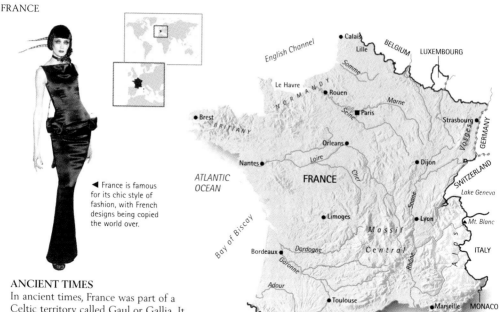

◀ France is famous for its chic style of fashion, with French designs being copied the world over.

## ANCIENT TIMES

In ancient times, France was part of a Celtic territory called Gaul or Gallia. It was conquered by Julius Caesar and was part of the Roman Empire for 500 years, until the fall of the Western Roman Empire in the fifth century. A Germanic people called the Franks then conquered the area, bringing it within their empire. France gets its name from the Latin *Francia*, meaning 'country of the Franks'.

▲ Each summer, the world's top cyclists take part in the Tour de France, a race across the country. The final stage is through Paris, from Disneyland to the Champs Elysées.

## A TURBULENT HISTORY

France became an independent country in the 9th century, but there was no common language until the founding of the French Academy in the 1630s. France has had a turbulent history, including wars with Spain and England and rule by greedy or inept kings. The revolution of 1789 removed the king and many of the old ways, and during the rule of Napoleon Bonaparte (1799 to 1815), France dominated Europe. France suffered great damage and loss of life in two world wars, but recovered to become a founder member of the European Union and a strong voice in world affairs.

## ACROSS THE WORLD

France also ruled colonies overseas, which is why today French language and culture are found in places as far apart as Quebec (Canada) and North Africa. There are still many French dependencies all over the world. The island of Corsica, which lies 170km off the southeast coast, is also an official region of France.

▲ The 300-m high Eiffel Tower in Paris was the winning entry in a design competition for the World's Fair in 1889.

### SEE ALSO
Europe, Revolution, World War I, World War II

# FROG AND TOAD

Frogs and toads belong to the group of animals known as amphibians. Most spend their early life as tadpoles in water, but the adults live mainly on land.

◄ The male edible frog has large vocal sacs to call females in the mating season.

Gliding frogs have rounded sucker pads to help them climb.

Bullfrogs can grow up to 20cm, and may even eat newly-hatched alligators.

Arrow-poison frogs are among the most colourful and poisonous animals.

Frogs are related to toads, but frogs generally have slimmer bodies with a smooth skin, while toads have a drier, warty skin. All amphibians have thin skin, as their lungs are inefficient and they use their skin to breathe through. Oxygen from the air passes through the skin into tiny blood vessels just under the surface. This can happen only if the skin is moist, so frogs and toads are usually found in damp places.

## STICKY TONGUES
Most frogs feed on slugs, insects and worms, which they catch with a long, sticky tongue. Larger frogs, such as the American bullfrog, also feed on prey such as mice, and even small ducklings.

## MUSCULAR LEGS
Frogs are great jumpers. Their long, muscle-packed hind legs can send them shooting over 12 times their own length through the air. Webbed feet help frogs swim, while tree frogs make huge leaps from branch to branch, aided by sticky pads on their toes. Toads have less powerful back legs than most frogs and waddle.

## BRIGHT COLOURS
Green or brown is the typical colour of most frogs, but some tropical frogs are brilliantly coloured. Some species change their skin colour with changes in light or temperature and all frogs shed the outer layer of their skin several times a year, pulling it over their head with their legs.

## NOISY COURTSHIP
Frogs and toads can be very noisy at breeding time, when males croak to attract females. The European marsh frog is one of the noisiest – a colony sounds like a crowd of people laughing.

## INSIDE A FROG

A frog's internal organs are similar to those of higher animals such as dogs. Externally, their bulging eyes help them look around in many directions, while the disc above the eye is the eardrum (called a tympanum). Some frogs have sticky-tipped tongues fixed to the front of their mouths which they flick out to capture prey.

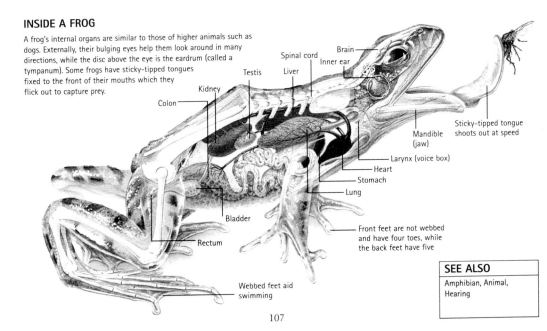

Brain
Spinal cord
Inner ear
Testis
Liver
Kidney
Colon
Mandible (jaw)
Sticky-tipped tongue shoots out at speed
Larynx (voice box)
Heart
Stomach
Lung
Bladder
Front feet are not webbed and have four toes, while the back feet have five
Rectum
Webbed feet aid swimming

## SEE ALSO
Amphibian, Animal, Hearing

# FRUIT

Fruits contain the seeds of flowering plants. They protect the developing seeds and help them to reach a suitable place to grow into new plants.

Pomes are fleshy fruits like pears, which have their seeds in a core formed from the flower stem.

Berries, such as tomatoes, cucumbers and oranges, hold many seeds inside a single fruit with soft pulp.

Drupes have a single stone which contains the seed. Blackberries are a cluster of many small drupes.

Dry fruits range from chestnuts to corncobs, but all are seed-bearing.

For a new generation of plants to grow successfully, the seed must be spread away from the parent plant so that the new plants are not all grouped together. Fruits are the means by which flowering plants ensure that their ripe seeds get to new, fertile locations.

## FLESHY FRUITS
Fruits can be divided into two basic groups: fleshy and dry. Fleshy fruits are juicy and taste good to mammals and birds, which eat the seeds along with the fruit. The seeds pass through the animals bodies undigested and drop to the ground, where they grow into new plants. Strawberries are false fruits. They develop from a swollen stem. The pips on the surface are the real fruits.

## DRY FRUITS
Fruits such as poppy seedheads or walnuts become dry as the seed ripens. Some, such as pea pods, split open so the seed is scattered in all directions. Others, such as the sycamore key, are light and can be blown by the wind. Nuts are also fruits. They have a hard outer casing that rots when the seed inside is ripe and ready to germinate (start growing).

## SEED CONTAINERS
Fruits develop from the ovary of the flower after it has been pollinated. The seeds inside the fruit develop from the fertilized egg cells within the ovary. Some fruits, including peaches, cherries and plums, contain a single seed. However, most fruits, such as apples, raspberries, tomatoes and marrows, contain more than one seed. Occasionally, the sepals (leaves outside the flower petals) remain after the petals of the flower have fallen, and enclose the fruits, as in acorns.

## FRUIT TO EAT
Some fruits are poisonous to humans, but there are many that are delicious and nutritious. Fleshy fruits often contain fruit sugars, which are a useful source of energy, and the fibre provided by the skin, flesh, and sometimes the seeds, ensures healthy digestion. Fruits contain vitamins, minerals and other nutrients that help the body fight off illness. Nuts are also an excellent source of protein.

## EATING THE FRUIT
The bright colour and pleasant smell of fruits such as blackberries attracts birds and animals to eat them. After digesting the soft outer part, they pass the seeds out of their body with the rest of their waste. By this time, they will often be at some distance from the original plant.

1 The dispersed seed falls on fertile soil and the first shoots appear.

2 Flowers on the mature plant are pollinated and produce seeds.

3 The petals drop off and the fruit forms. It is hard and unappealing to birds.

4 The fruit becomes succulent and sweet when it is ready to be eaten.

## SEE ALSO
Flower, Food, Leaf, Nutrition, Plant

# FUNGI

Fungi are neither plants nor animals, but have their own kingdom, which has over 100,000 species and includes mushrooms, toadstools, moulds and yeasts.

◀ The mould on these nectarines comes from airborne spores that have started to breed.

The earth star lifts its fruit body clear of the ground on star-like rays.

The giant puffball is as big as a man's head and makes billions of spores.

Truffles are considered the tastiest of fungi. They grow close to tree roots.

Unlike plants, fungi need a supply of organic food in order to grow and reproduce. Plants have a green pigment, called chlorophyll, which allows them to make their own food using the Sun's energy. Fungi have no chlorophyll, so they take food from plants and animals.

## WHERE THEY LIVE

There are more than 100,000 different types of fungi. Some, like yeast, are only a single cell. Most form masses of threads, called mycelium, which spread inside whatever they feed on. Many live inside plants, or in the soil, where they help to break down dead plant and animal matter.

## HOW THEY BREED

To reproduce, fungi must release minute spores into the air. Some fungi, such as mushrooms and toadstools, grow large fruit bodies to help the spores to travel farther. Others grow tall, thread-like stalks with spore capsules at the end. If they land in a suitable place, the spores will grow to form new fungi of the same type. There are fungus spores around us all the time.

## USEFUL FUNGI

Some fungi are useful as they help to break down the remains of dead plants and animals or make medicines. An example is the antibiotic penicillin. Certain yeast fungi are used to make bread and alcohol. Some mushrooms are good to eat, but others contain deadly poison, and it is difficult to tell them apart.

## NO-FUN FUNGI

Fungi can grow on and spoil food, paper, wood in buildings, and damp clothes. Fungus diseases can damage and even kill plants, including crops such as potatoes and strawberries. Some affect animals and people: athlete's foot is a common fungal disease that causes itchy, flaky skin between the toes.

## HOW FUNGI BREED

Like nearly all fungi, the fly agaric grows a web of thread-like mycelium through which it feeds on decaying matter. In order to reproduce, it releases spores from the surface of its gills into the air. When the spores land, they develop their own mycelium. But they can only grow fruit bodies by joining up with mycelium from the same species of fungi.

Upturned cap allows spores to disperse farther.

Cap

Developing gills

Developing cap

Gills, where spores are produced

— Spores

Stipe (stem)

Mycelium

## SEE ALSO

Medicine,
Micro-organism, Plant

# GALAXY

A galaxy is a huge collection of stars held together by gravity. The Sun is just one of about 200 billion stars contained within our home galaxy, the Milky Way.

Barred-spiral galaxies have a well-defined bar with arms attached to it.

Elliptical galaxies can be round or oval, and have very little gas or dust.

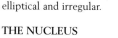

Irregular galaxies are small and shapeless, and contain a lot of gas.

There are probably over a thousand million galaxies in the universe. They come in three basic shapes: spiral, elliptical and irregular.

## THE NUCLEUS

The central part of a galaxy is called the nucleus. Here, stars are crowded much closer together than on the galactic outskirts. Astronomers now believe that massive black holes may lie deep within the nucleus of many large galaxies. There is probably a black hole at the centre of our own galaxy.

## LIGHT YEARS AWAY

Enormous distances separate galaxies. The closest large galaxy to the Milky Way is the Andromeda Galaxy, located about two million light years away. It is the farthest object visible to the naked eye.

## CLUSTERS AND SUPERCLUSTERS

Galaxies are arranged in clusters, which are themselves part of superclusters. The Milky Way and the Andromeda Galaxy are the two largest members of a small cluster of about 30 galaxies known as the Local Group. This, in turn, forms a tiny part of the Local Supercluster.

## ACTIVE GALAXIES

Galaxies vary greatly in the amount of energy they give off. Some galaxies, known as active galaxies, are so called because they give out more energy than is available from all the stars they contain. The extra energy is believed to be supplied by matter falling into a black hole at their centre.

## ELLIPTICAL GIANTS

Elliptical galaxies are round or oval in appearance and usually have very little gas or dust. They vary greatly in size, from giants to dwarfs. Giant ellipticals may contain up to ten trillion stars and are the largest type of galaxy.

## THE MILKY WAY

The Milky Way is a large spiral galaxy measuring about 100,000 light years across (a light year equals 9.46 million million kilometres.) It is about 14 billion years old and takes 225 million years to rotate once. Like all spirals, it contains plenty of gas and dust, from which new stars are formed. The dense nucleus is the oldest part and has no gas left for new stars.

Nucleus

Planet Earth

Gas from which new stars form

Spiral arm

### SEE ALSO

Astronomy, Black hole, Solar system, Universe

# GAS

Gas that is burned for cooking and heating is a fossil fuel consisting mainly of methane. It is usually brought into homes and industries via pipelines.

92% Methane

3.5% Ethane

2.5% Nitrogen

1% Propane

1% Other

◄ The composition of natural gas varies, although its main ingredient is always methane. These are the percentages for North Sea gas.

Gas is useful because it releases heat when it burns. It is used for heating and cooking in homes and many industries burn gas for welding or smelting.

## FOSSIL FUEL

Most domestic gas is natural gas, found underground, often with oil or coal but sometimes on its own. Like oil, gas was formed over millions of years from the remains of plants and animals. These organisms are made up largely of hydrogen and carbon, which change to a hydrocarbon called methane when they decay. The natural gas is then mined. Bottled gas, used by campers, is not natural gas. It is propane or butane, two by-products of oil refining.

## PROCESSING GAS

Most natural gas is found under the sea. It flows under pressure through a pipe connected to a gas terminal on land, although some is made into a liquid and shipped across the sea. There are a few unwanted substances in natural gas, which are removed at the terminal. The resulting gas does not smell, which means that a leak could go unnoticed. For this reason, a smelly chemical called a thiol is added.

## GAS – THE BURNING ISSUE

The Ancient Chinese first used natural gas thousands of years ago to evaporate sea water to obtain salt. In the early 1800s, oil prospectors in the USA set light to wells which produced only gas. Then, in the 1870s, experiments were carried out into piping natural gas into US homes. The UK first began prospecting for gas in the 1930s.

1 Exploration teams search for gas by drilling from rigs in areas with the right rock formation. Gas is often found with oil.

2 The gas reaches terminals in seamless steel pipes.

3 Smaller pipes then supply homes and industries.

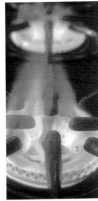

4 The gas is used in cookers and heating systems.

## DRILLING FOR GAS

Gas is usually found thousands of metres below the Earth's surface in a rock such as sandstone. A layer of hard impermeable rock above it prevents the gas from reaching the surface unless it is drilled by a gas or oil company.

## SEE ALSO

Oil, Rock

# GENETICS

Genetics is the science that studies how animals and plants pass their features to their offspring, generation after generation.

Gregor Mendel (1822–84) bred pea plants and studied how they passed features onto offspring.

Nobel Prize-winning scientists James Watson, from the USA and Francis Crick from the UK discovered the structure of DNA in 1953.

Babies look like their parents. This tendency for offspring to resemble their parents was known in ancient times. People selected particular plants or animals with features they wanted, such as cows that gave most milk, and bred them. Over many generations, this selective breeding led to cows which gave even more milk.

## PATTERNS OF INHERITANCE
In the 1850s, an Austrian monk called Gregor Mendel discovered the basics of inheritance by breeding pea plants. He found that some features of pea plants, such as height and colour, were not passed on to the next generation as a blend of both parents' features. Instead, a feature from one parent was dominant.

## IT IS IN THE GENES
We now know that the features inherited by the peas were decided by their genes.

▶ Dolly, an artificially cloned sheep, was created from a cell taken from another adult sheep. This means that both sheep have exactly the same genes.

Genes are the instructions which decide the appearance and function of each living cell or organism. They are arranged on corkscrew-shaped chemicals called DNA (deoxyribonucleic acid), visible only under an electron microscope.

## PASSING ON GENES
When a human or other living thing reproduces, it passes on a copy of half of its genes to its offspring. Each reproductive cell (sperm or egg) contains a different combination of genes, guaranteeing that each offspring will be unique.

## GENETIC ENGINEERING
Scientists can now change animals and plants by genetic engineering. The required gene is extracted from the DNA using chemicals called enzymes and inserted into a host organism to obtain the desired characteristic.

## PASSING ON THE MESSAGE

DNA is made of thousands of chemical sub-units (known as bases), strung in a line like beads on a necklace. There are four different bases, called A, T, G and C, which are arranged along the DNA. Their sequence determines the cell's genetic code, in the same way that letters of the alphabet arranged in a certain order become a sentence.

The DNA is unzipped while the code is copied during reproduction

C = Cytosine, which always links to Guanine

T = Thymine

A = Adenine, which always links to Thymine

G = Guanine

A gene is made up of three pairs of sub-units

Genes are contained inside the nucleus of each microscopic living cell

Nucleus

The DNA strand looks like a twisted ladder – a shape known as a double helix

The DNA strands are coiled up into chromosomes – human cells contain 23 pairs

The DNA is wrapped around a core of proteins

SEE ALSO
Atom and molecule, Cell

# GERMANY

Germany is a large country which lies in the middle of Europe and borders nine other countries. East and West Germany were unified in 1990.

**Area:** 357,022 sq km
**Population:** 82,047,000
**Capital:** Berlin
**Language:** German
**Currency:** Deutsch-Mark, Euro

Germany has a varied landscape, with a broad, flat plain in the north and highlands in the central region. The south is mountainous and includes the South German Hills, Black Forest and Bavarian Alps. The country is crossed by several major rivers, including the Danube, Rhine, Oder, Weser, Ems and Elbe. The climate is rarely severe, with warm summers and mild winters, and most places receive from 500mm to 1,000mm of rainfall a year.

## FARMING AND INDUSTRY

Only about six per cent of Germans are farmers, growing crops such as wheat, barley, rye and potatoes, as well as grapes to make wine. Many more people work in manufacturing or service industries. There are factories almost everywhere, especially in the Ruhr region – the heart of the iron, steel and chemical industries. German goods include cars, cameras, computers and textiles. Factories in the east are being modernized to match those in the west, the most prosperous part of the country.

## GETTING AROUND

Germany has a high standard of living and many people own cars. Motorways, called *autobahns*, were built from the 1930s, and

▲ The Rhine is one of Europe's most important rivers. Its slopes are lined with vineyards and picturesque towns.

the country also has an efficient modern rail system. Barges are used to carry heavy goods along the Rhine and the country's other waterways.

## FESTIVALS, FOOD AND RECREATION

Germans are fond of food and drink. A famous annual get-together is the Munich Beer Festival, held in October. Popular German foods include sausages, such as frankfurters, sauerkraut (a dish made with pickled cabbage), pastries and cheese. For recreation, many people enjoy sports such as soccer, tennis and athletics, and other outdoor activities, including walking, climbing and boating.

## ARTS AND ARCHITECTURE

Many of the world's great philosophers, such as Immanuel Kant, writers, including Goethe, and composers, such as Beethoven and Wagner, have been German. Engineers Daimler and Benz invented the motor car, and German scientists pioneered the jet engine and space rocket. The country is also famous for Meissen china, and for its architecture, which includes many magnificent churches and palaces.

## WARS AND RECOVERY

For hundreds of years, Germany was a patchwork of independent states, each with its own rulers. By the 1700s, Prussia

▲ Many locals wear Bavarian national costume during the famous Munich Beer Festival, held every October. It attracts thousands of people from all over the world.

▶ Germany is the world's third largest producer of cars after Japan and the USA. Car manufacturers from all over the world exhibit their latest models at the Frankfurt Motor Show each year.

emerged as the strongest, uniting most of the other states to form a German empire in 1871. Germany suffered defeat in World War I (1914–18) and was then ruled by the Nazi dictator, Adolf Hitler, who led the country into World War II (1939–45). Defeat in this war left Germany divided. East Germany was under communist rule, while West Germany became the richest capitalist democracy in Europe. In 1990, the two parts – an economically prosperous west and an impoverished east – were reunited, bringing many economic and social problems. However, Germany is still a powerful economic and political force within the European Union.

▲ An East Berlin guard hands a flower to West Berliners sitting on top of the Berlin Wall in 1990 – the year the Wall came down, after dividing the city for over 25 years.

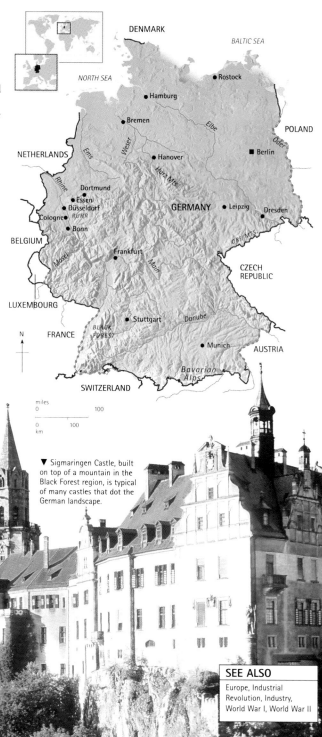

▼ Sigmaringen Castle, built on top of a mountain in the Black Forest region, is typical of many castles that dot the German landscape.

### SEE ALSO

Europe, Industrial Revolution, Industry, World War I, World War II

# GLACIER

A glacier is a mass of ice that flows slowly, under the influence of gravity, either from high in the mountains or in polar regions where it is very cold.

Take a handful of snow and squeeze it hard. It turns to ice in your hand. This is what happens when snow falls, year after year, in the valleys of high mountains. The snow at the bottom of the valley is compressed by the weight of the snow above, until it turns to ice.

### ICE RIVERS
As the ice comes under greater pressure from the snow above, it begins to soften and flow like putty. At this point, a glacier has formed. The movement of the glacier is very slow – only a few metres per year.

### DESTRUCTIVE POWER
A heavy glacier is a powerful force of erosion. As it moves downwards, it grinds the valley into a distinct U-shape. A valley that once held a glacier is obvious from its flat bottom and vertical sides.

### GATHERING RUBBLE
The debris that is worn away by the glacier is carried along, either embedded in the ice or lying on the top. This rubble is called moraine. When it is dropped at the glacier's snout as the ice melts, moraine forms a landscape of irregular heaps of clay, sand and rocks.

### POLAR ICE CAPS
Glaciers that form near the North and South Poles can cover whole countries or continents, and are usually known as ice caps or ice sheets. Snow falls at the centre of the continent and spreads out towards the sea. Antarctica and Greenland are both covered by such ice sheets.

### THE ICE AGE
Between 1,600,000 and 10,000 years ago, the Earth went through periods of intense cold, known as Ice Ages. For thousands of years in each Ice Age, vast glaciers covered much of North America, Asia and Europe as far south as London, England. Many of the lakes, valleys and hills that we see today were carved by these ice sheets. The first people to settle the Americas crossed from Asia to what is now Alaska on 1,000-m high ice bridges.

1 The top of the valley is eroded by the glacier into an armchair shape called a cirque.

2 As the glacier travels, its surface cracks to form crevasses.

3 The glacier picks up rubble (moraine), which piles into ridges.

4 Melting ice forms a lake at the bottom of the glacier.

### SEE ALSO
Antarctica, Arctic, Mountain and valley

# GRASSLAND

Grasslands are large areas of flat or gently rolling land covered by grasses, often with trees and bushes scattered across them or clustered along streams.

▲ Damp long-grass prairies are rich in bluestem, switch grass and needlegrass.

Between dry, rainless deserts and dense, wet forests there are usually areas known as grasslands. These regions have definite wet and dry seasons. The grasses grow quickly, flower, and produce seeds in the wet season, then die back or do not grow in the dry season. Most of a grass plant is below ground. This means that it can survive droughts and fires better than other plants.

## GRASSLAND TYPES
Different types of grass grow all over the world, and grasslands are given different names wherever they exist. In North America, they are called prairies or plains; in Africa they are known as savannas. The cooler grasslands of Argentina are Pampas, and in Russia they are steppes.

## ANIMALS AND PLANTS
Herds of antelope in Africa, kangaroos in Australia and buffalo in the USA graze the grasslands. Marmots, rabbits, and ground squirrels burrow for roots and shelter. These plant-eaters are hunted by lions, wolves and hyenas, and birds of prey, such as hawks and eagles. Invertebrates (animals without backbones), such as insects, are the largest group of grassland animals. These provide food for rodents and small birds.

## HARVESTING THE LAND
Wild grasslands once covered almost a third of the world's land, but most have been changed by humans. Sheep farmers in Australia, cattle ranchers in the USA, dairy farmers in Europe and nomadic goat herders in North Africa, all depend on natural or cultivated grasslands to feed their animals. Grasslands have also been ploughed to produce cereal crops such as wheat, maize, and oats.

### FAST FACTS

• There are more than 7,500 different kinds of grass

• Grasses are very adaptable. They grow in the sea, in marshlands, in deserts, on mountain tops and in the frozen Arctic wilderness

• The biggest grasses are bamboos. They can grow up to 40m tall and 30cm thick at the bottom

## AFRICAN SAVANNA

Temperatures on the savanna are hot all year, but rain falls only during the summer. The long red oat, bluestems and dropseed grasses plus scattered trees produce up to 45 tonnes of vegetation per hectare each year, providing food for animals that include zebra, antelope and ostriches. Frequent fires encourage fresh growth of grasses and trees.

Scattered trees grow where roots can reach deep, permanent water

Waterholes fill during the wet season, storing water for the dry season

Grazing animals wander across the grasslands in herds, usually settling near a source of water

### SEE ALSO
Africa, Animal, Canada, Food, Habitat

# GRAVITY

Gravity is a force that exists between any two objects, pulling them together. On Earth, the force of gravity pulls you towards the ground and gives you weight.

◀ The speed at which a rocket is launched determines whether it escapes Earth's gravity and flies off into space or plummets back to Earth.

▶ Early space rockets used the Earth's gravitational pull to go into orbit around the planet. Today, all satellites use the same principle.

W hen you jump up in the air, you come back down again. This is because the Earth's gravity pulls you down towards the planet. If there were no gravity, we would drift off the Earth and into space. Gravity explains why the stars and planets move in the way that they do and how the Moon affects the tides each day. It is also the force that gives us our weight.

▲ Astronauts and fighter pilots feel the effects of gravity, or G-force, during take-off. Not only does gravity distort their faces, but it can also send all the blood to their legs, often causing them to feel faint.

## FAST FACTS

• Sir Isaac Newton (1643-1727) discovered the Law of Gravity, supposedly when he saw an apple fall from a tree

• Gravity keeps the rings of Saturn in orbit around the planet

• To escape the Earth's gravity, a spacecraft must reach a speed of 11.2km/sec. This is known as the 'escape velocity'

## MASS AND WEIGHT

The less gravity there is, the less you weigh. If you were in outer space, far away from any other objects, you would not feel any gravity. This means you would be completely weightless, even though your mass (quantity of matter) would not have changed. On Earth, the weight of something depends on its mass. A walrus has more mass than a mouse, for example, so it feels a greater force of gravity. That is why a walrus weighs more than a mouse.

## FREE-FALL

Skydivers experience a feeling of weightlessness in a free-fall from a high aeroplane. In fact, they are still being pulled by the Earth's gravity, but the air resistance is pushing against them. Only outside the Earth's atmosphere, in space, are we truly weightless.

## PULLING TOGETHER

We normally think about gravity only as it applies to the Earth, but gravity exists between any two objects. The greater their mass and the closer they are together, the larger the force of gravity between them. Two ships at sea, for example, will attract each other, but their gravitational pull is so small compared to other forces on Earth, that it is not noticeable. However, two nearby spaceships, far away from other objects in space, will create a noticeable gravitational attraction, called microgravity.

## DROPPED FROM ON HIGH

Like all forces, gravity alters the velocity (speed) of objects. Near the Earth's surface, gravity makes all objects accelerate at the same rate ($9.81m/sec.^2$), no matter how heavy they are. If you dropped a full and an empty box from the top of a tall building, they would reach the ground together.

## SEE ALSO

Earth, Force and motion, Moon, Solar system, Spacecraft

# GREECE AND THE BALKANS

Nine countries make up the Balkans, a mountainous region in southwest Europe named after the Balkan mountain range that runs through it.

**ALBANIA**
**Area:** 28,748 sq km
**Population:** 3,339,000
**Capital:** Tirana
**Languages:** Albanian, Greek
**Currency:** Lek

**BOSNIA-HERZEGOVINA**
**Area:** 51,197 sq km
**Population:** 3,768,000
**Capital:** Sarajevo
**Language:** Serbo-Croat
**Currency:** Convertible Mark

**BULGARIA**
**Area:** 110,912 sq km
**Population:** 8,257,000
**Capital:** Sofia
**Languages:** Bulgarian, Turkish
**Currency:** Lev

**CROATIA**
**Area:** 56,538 sq km
**Population:** 4,501,000
**Capital:** Zagreb
**Language:** Serbo-Croat
**Currency:** Kuna

**GREECE**
**Area:** 131,957 sq km
**Population:** 10,515,000
**Capital:** Athens
**Language:** Greek
**Currency:** Drachma

▶ Remains of the Parthenon, a temple built in the 5th century BC to honour the goddess Athena, stand in Athens city centre.

The Balkan peninsula has seas on three sides: the Adriatic and Ionian to the west, the Mediterranean to the south, and the Aegean and Black Sea to the east.

## MOUNTAIN COUNTRY
Apart from the Balkan mountains, there are several other mountain ranges in the region. One of the most famous peaks is Mount Olympus in Greece, which is 2,911m high. The Danube river is the most important waterway, forming the border between Romania and Bulgaria. The Balkans has a mild climate, with summer temperatures reaching 30°C, but winters can be cold and snowy in the mountains.

## LAND OF THE SLAVS
There is a rich cultural and religious diversity as a result of the many invaders to the region. Ancient Greece ruled an empire until the Roman invasion in 146BC. Then, in the 4th century, the Roman Empire became split into east and west, and the Balkans fell into the eastern part, known as the Byzantine Empire. During the 5th and 7th centuries, Slavs came down from the north, scattering into distinct tribes, which are reflected in the languages present today: Bulgarian, Serbian, Croatian, Slovenian and Macedonian. The Ottoman Turks ruled the region from the 1400s, but most Balkan people stayed Christian under Islamic rule.

▲ Fish is important in the diet of many Greek people, especially on the islands. Here, a fisherman rows out from the harbour of Symi, a Greek island near the Turkish coast.

## THE BALKANS TODAY
In 1929, King Alexander I became dictator of Yugoslavia, a nation made up of Bosnia-Herzegovina, Croatia, Montenegro, Serbia and Slovenia, and introduced a common language, Serbo-Croatian. After World War II (1939–45), Yugoslavia, Bulgaria and Albania became communist countries. Josip Tito was leader of the communist Federal People's Republic of Yugoslavia until he died in 1980. Savage civil wars began in 1991, and the former Republic of Yugoslavia broke up. It is now divided into five independent countries. All the Balkan

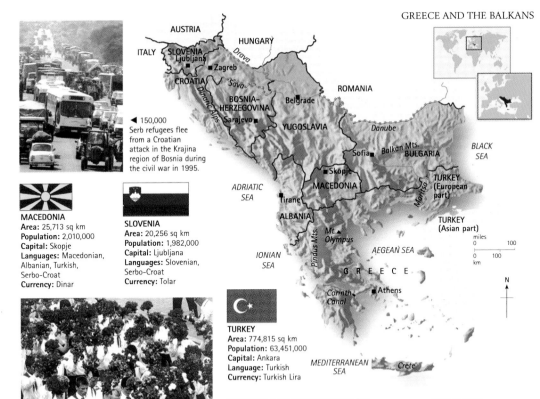

◀ 150,000
Serb refugees flee
from a Croatian
attack in the Krajina
region of Bosnia during
the civil war in 1995.

**MACEDONIA**
**Area:** 25,713 sq km
**Population:** 2,010,000
**Capital:** Skopje
**Languages:** Macedonian,
Albanian, Turkish,
Serbo-Croat
**Currency:** Dinar

**SLOVENIA**
**Area:** 20,256 sq km
**Population:** 1,982,000
**Capital:** Ljubljana
**Languages:** Slovenian,
Serbo-Croat
**Currency:** Tolar

**TURKEY**
**Area:** 774,815 sq km
**Population:** 63,451,000
**Capital:** Ankara
**Language:** Turkish
**Currency:** Turkish Lira

▲ The Festival of Roses is held each year in Kazanluk,
Bulgaria, one day before rose picking begins. The petals are
crushed for their oil, called attar of roses, used in perfume.

countries are striving to modernize their
economies. Several hope to join Greece as
members of the European Union.

## HOW PEOPLE LIVE
Many of the Balkan people are farmers,
living in small towns and villages as their
ancestors did before them. They grow
maize, barley, fruits and vegetables, and
raise sheep, goats, cattle and pigs. Donkeys
and horse-drawn wagons can still be seen
carrying produce to market. There are few
big cities, apart from national capitals such
as Athens (Greece) and Belgrade (former
Yugoslavia), where skyscrapers tower over
older buildings. Factories make vehicles,
textiles, chemicals and electronic goods, and
mines produce coal, iron and lead.

## WHERE EAST MEETS WEST
Along the sunny Balkan coasts, with their
beaches and medieval towns, tourism is an
important industry. New hotels and roads
are being built to cater for the growing tide
of visitors. Eastern and Western building
styles can be seen side by side: here a
Christian church in Byzantine style, there
an Islamic mosque. Bulgaria is famous for
growing roses to make perfume. Visitors
from all over the world visit Greece
to see the wonders of its
ancient civilization.

**YUGOSLAVIA**
**Area:** 102,173 sq km
**Population:** 10,616,000
**Capital:** Belgrade
**Languages:** Serbo-Croat,
Albanian
**Currency:** Dinar

▼ Albanian children
standing in front of one
of the air raid bunkers
built during the rule of
communist dictator
Enver Hoxha from
1946 to 1985.

### SEE ALSO
Europe, Greece (Ancient)

# GREECE, ANCIENT

The Ancient Greeks created one of the world's greatest civilizations. They gave us lasting styles of architecture, art, literature and government.

Not many paintings are left from Ancient Greece, but there are many decorated pots – usually showing myths or festivals.

This silver four-drachma piece, made in Athens, was used all over Ancient Greece. The owl symbolized Athena, goddess of wisdom.

Corrupt politicians were ostracized (sent into exile) if enough voters scratched their name onto an *ostraka* (a piece of broken pottery).

The Greeks moved south into what is now Greece some 4,000 years ago. The Minoans were the first to develop a great civilization around 2000BC, on the island of Crete, but most achievements in the arts, sciences and government were made during the Golden Age. This was a period between 477 and 431BC, when Athens was the ruling city state.

## A RUGGED COUNTRY
The nature of the Greek countryside helped to shape the country's history. Its mountain ranges made travel by land difficult. Fiercely independent and patriotic communities grew up in the fertile pockets between the mountains, and Ancient Greece became a country divided into many city states.

## THE OLYMPIANS
The people were deeply religious. They believed in many gods – all of whom had human form, but possessed superhuman powers and were, of course, immortal. The chief gods were known as the Olympians because they were believed to live at the top of Mount Olympus in northern Greece. Zeus ruled the gods with his wife Hera. Other gods and goddesses included: Aphrodite, goddess of love; Apollo, god of the Sun, music and light; Ares, god of war, and Athena, goddess of wisdom. The Ancient Greeks built temples to their gods, in which they made offerings of food, wine and sometimes live animals. Rich families had shrines in their homes to smaller house gods.

▲ Women were usually married at the age of 13 or 14 to men more than twice their age. They were in charge of the house and wove all the material for the loose-fitting garments, known as chitons, worn by men and women.

## DECORATIVE ARTS AND FESTIVALS
The Greeks decorated their temples and palaces in a new, natural style of marble statues and reliefs. Music, drama, dance and sport were celebrated at festivals, such as the Olympic Games, held every four years from 776BC in honour of the gods.

## LITERATURE AND LEARNING
The poet Homer, who created the epic poems the *Odyssey* and *Iliad*, was just one of many great writers. Dramatists such as Aeschylus, Euripedes and Sophocles wrote plays for open-air theatres. Socrates, Plato and Aristotle discussed philosophy in *agoras* (market places) and academies, while scientific discoveries were made by Pythagoras, Archimedes and others.

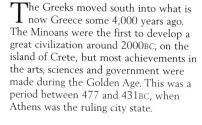

◄ The ruggedness of the Greek countryside meant that most trade and warfare was carried out at sea. Greek warships known as triremes had up to 170 oarsmen, arranged on three decks (above), which gave them great speed.

## ATHENS VERSUS SPARTA

The two most powerful city states were Athens and Sparta, which were constantly at war with each other. They had different approaches to education, the arts and warfare. Athens and other city states had a democratic government where all male citizens could vote, and their children were educated in the arts and sciences. Sparta was a military kingdom with a tough, warlike people. Boys were sent away to military camps at the age of seven, and girls were also trained in gymnastics and warfare – a fact which shocked the Athenians.

## EMPIRE AND LEGACY

Early in the 5th century BC, Athens and Sparta united against a new common enemy, Persia. The Ancient Greeks won, but fighting resumed and the city states began to crumble. Then, in 335BC, Alexander the Great united Ancient Greece once more, and went on to conquer almost the entire Middle East, from Egypt to northern India. In 146BC, the Romans conquered Greece, but adopted much of its culture and ways.

▲ The actors in the amphitheatres wore clay masks so that even people in the top rows could tell the characters apart.

▲ Lyres were stringed instruments made from turtle shells. Athenian boys learned to sing and play the lyre and aulos (flute) at music schools.

▲ Amphitheatres, like this one at Delphi, were carved into the sides of hills. Their clever design meant that a whisper on stage could be heard by the whole audience.

### KEY DATES

2000BC Minoan civilization in Crete flourishes

1600-1200BC Mycenean civilization on the mainland rules Greece

900-800BC Homer writes the Iliad and the Odyssey

490BC Persian army invades Greece – the Greeks win at the battle of Marathon

480BC Battles of Thermopylae and Salamis

431-404BC Peloponnesian war between Athens and Sparta. Plague kills a third of Athenians. Sparta wins

356-323BC Reign of Alexander the Great

146BC Roman Empire conquers Greece

## BATTLE OF THERMOPYLAE

The Greek cities fought frequent wars with each other, but in 480BC they united against an invasion by the Persian Emperor Xerxes. A force of 300 hoplites (armoured infantry) from Sparta held thousands of Persians at the mountain pass of Thermopylae for three days before being wiped out. This gave the Greek fleet of ships time to gather at the Strait of Salamis and defeat the invasion.

### SEE ALSO

Astronomy, Democracy, Europe, Greece and the Balkans, Medicine, Olympic Games, Sculpture, Seven wonders of the world

# HABITAT

A habitat is the home of particular species of animal or plant. It provides them with the food, shelter and conditions that allow them to survive.

◀ Oystercatchers living on the Dutch coast depend on clean seas for the survival of their diet: mussels (left), oysters and limpets.

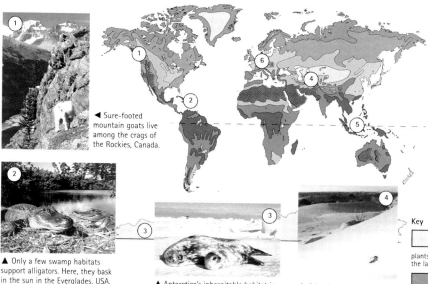

◀ Sure-footed mountain goats live among the crags of the Rockies, Canada.

▲ Only a few swamp habitats support alligators. Here, they bask in the sun in the Everglades, USA.

▲ Antarctica's inhospitable habitat is home to animals with a thick layer of fat, such as this Weddell seal and pup.

▲ A beetle scuttles across the cold desert of Turkmenistan. Its small size helps it keep warm.

▲ An orang-utang sits in a rainforest canopy in Borneo – a threatened habitat.

### Key

**Cold desert:** cold region with little rain. Animals and plants must be able to survive the lack of water and cold.

**Tundra:** treeless plains near Arctic. Snow-covered in winter. Migratory animals, moss and lichens in summer.

**Temperate woodland:** tree-covered areas in climate that changes between winter and summer. Trees usually shed their leaves.

**Coniferous forest:** areas (usually northern) with trees bearing pine cones. Wildlife includes deer, bears, wolves.

**Savanna grassland:** grassland areas with scattered trees, lying between desert and rainforest. Large predators and herbivores.

**Tropical rainforest:** dense forest around Equator in Asia, Africa and South America. Habitat with the most wildlife.

**Steppe and dry grassland:** hot summers and cold winters. Short grasses, with many snakes and rodents.

**Hot desert:** hot with little rain. Can be sandy or rocky. Many animals hide during the day.

Climate, soil, plants and animals – from the tiniest insect to the tallest tree – all create a habitat. Scientists classify them into types, such as grassland, forest, desert, mountain-top, river, marsh or ocean. All these groups show great variation.

## HABITATS AND BIOMES

When scientists talk about a habitat in general, they use the word biome. For example, a grassland is a biome, but a specific grassland such as the Argentinian Pampas is known as a habitat. Within each habitat there are also thousands of small, specialized living spaces, such as the dark, damp world under a rock on a river bank, or a pool of water in the fork of a forest tree. These are known as micro-habitats.

## OCEAN WORLDS

The biggest biome of all is the oceans, which cover 71 per cent of the Earth's surface. This biome is divided into layers according to how warm or salty the water is and how far down the Sun's light reaches. It also varies from place to place – from the warm blue seas of the Caribbean to the cold, windswept Antarctic Ocean. Around the edges of the seas are other special habitats, such as coral reefs, rocky and sandy shores and river mouths.

## UPSETTING THE BALANCE

Each habitat is a complex system, with all the plants and animals perfectly suited to, and yet dependent on, their environment, as well as on one another. When something upsets the balance, a habitat can be badly damaged. Parts of Africa's savannas have been turned into desert because too many people, goats and cattle have stripped off the vegetation. Lakes and rivers in many countries have been poisoned by industrial chemicals. Forests may be damaged by acid rain, and some seashores are being scarred by oil spillages.

### SEE ALSO

Desert, Forest, Grassland, Ocean and sea, Pollution, Rainforest, Seashore

# HEARING

**Hearing is one of the five senses. It depends on the detection of sound waves in the air which are changed into nerve signals and sent to the brain for processing.**

Bats use their high-pitched (100,000Hz) squeaks to locate flying insects to eat.

Frogs can hear only low frequency sounds of 5,000Hz and below.

Dogs hear both high and low-pitched sounds. Dog whistles are 35,000Hz.

Human ears hear frequencies from about 30 to 18,000Hz.

For most people, hearing is the second most important sense, after sight. It allows communication, warns us of danger and gives pleasure, from music to bird song.

## THE OUTER EAR

We hear with our ears. The outer ear is just a skin-covered flap of gristle, or cartilage, that catches sound waves in the air. Most of the delicate working parts are behind it, protected inside the skull.

## INSIDE THE EAR

Sound waves funnel into the ear canal. At its end, they hit a small patch of flexible skin, the eardrum. The sound waves bounce off it and make the eardrum vibrate (shake to and fro). Vibrations pass from the eardrum, along a chain of three tiny bones, called the hammer (malleus), anvil (incus) and stirrup (stapes). These bones pass the vibration to the oval window.

## THE COCHLEA

The oval window is a membrane in the wall of a fluid-filled chamber, the cochlea, which is coiled like a snail, small enough to sit on your fingernail. Vibrations of the oval window push ripples into the fluid inside the cochlea. As the ripples go around the coil, they shake almost two million tiny hairs sticking out from 25,000 hair cells.

## SOUND TO ELECTRICITY

The hair cells send nerve signals, millions every second, along the cochlear nerve to the brain. Here they are analyzed for volume and frequency, and compared with 'soundprints' in the memory. Sound waves travel at about 340m/sec. If the sound comes from the side, the waves reach the nearer ear a fraction of a second before the farther ear. The brain detects this tiny difference and works out the direction of the sound source. This is only possible with two (or more) ears, and is called stereophonic hearing. Frequency of a sound is measured in vibrations per second, Hertz (Hz), and our ears can hear only certain frequencies.

## CAPTURING SOUNDS ON THE AIRWAVES

The outer ear works in the same way as a satellite dish, collecting sound waves in the air and sending them towards the eardrum. They travel through the middle ear, via the hammer, anvil and stirrup to the cochlea, where they become electrical messages that are sent to the brain.

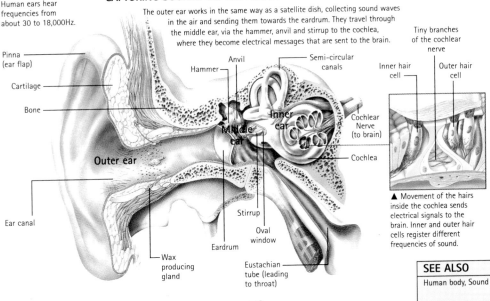

Pinna (ear flap)
Cartilage
Bone
Outer ear
Ear canal
Hammer
Anvil
Semi-circular canals
Inner ear
Middle ear
Cochlear Nerve (to brain)
Cochlea
Stirrup
Oval window
Eardrum
Wax producing gland
Eustachian tube (leading to throat)
Tiny branches of the cochlear nerve
Inner hair cell
Outer hair cell

▲ Movement of the hairs inside the cochlea sends electrical signals to the brain. Inner and outer hair cells register different frequencies of sound.

## SEE ALSO
Human body, Sound

123

# HEART AND CIRCULATORY SYSTEM

The heart is a hollow, muscle-walled pump in the chest. It squeezes at least once every second to pump blood around the body. If it stops, so will life.

**WILLIAM HARVEY**
(1578–1657) The English doctor who showed that blood circulates (moves around the body) in only one direction, along arteries and veins.

The heart is a muscular pump with four chambers (pockets) which drives the blood around the body via a network of arteries, veins and capillaries known as the circulatory system.

### IN AND OUT
As the muscles in the heart contract, blood is squeezed from the heart into arteries, which carry the blood around the body. As the heart muscles relax, blood flows into the heart from the body, via veins. Each squeeze-relax cycle is a heartbeat.

### A TIRELESS MUSCLE
Cardiac (heart) muscle never tires. In an average lifetime, a human heart beats more than 2,500 million times. On average, the heart beats 70 times per minute, although heartbeat rate varies with age or health. Each heartbeat pumps about 70ml of blood. As the body has only about 5,000ml (five litres) of blood, all the blood passes through the heart in one minute. An active body uses more energy and oxygen, so the heart beats faster and pumps more blood with each beat.

### CHECKING THE HEART
Each heartbeat starts in a small patch of the wall in the right atrium. This is the heart's natural pacemaker. It sends tiny electrical signals through the heart's walls, telling them to contract. The action is controlled by nerve signals from the brain and chemicals in the blood called hormones. Electronic sensors placed on the skin can detect the electrical signals of the heart. The signals are displayed as a graph on an ECG (electrocardiograph) machine.

### TWO PUMPS IN ONE
The heart is not one pump but two, separated by a muscular dividing wall. The right pump receives low-oxygen blood from the body, along the main veins. It sends this blood out through the pulmonary arteries to the lungs, where it receives oxygen, and returns to the heart's left pump. This sends it out around the body again.

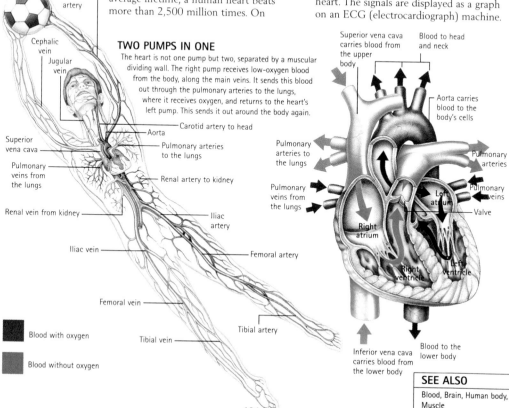

Brachial artery
Cephalic vein
Jugular vein
Superior vena cava
Pulmonary veins from the lungs
Renal vein from kidney
Iliac vein
Femoral vein
Tibial vein

Carotid artery to head
Aorta
Pulmonary arteries to the lungs
Renal artery to kidney
Iliac artery
Femoral artery
Tibial artery

Blood with oxygen
Blood without oxygen

Superior vena cava carries blood from the upper body
Blood to head and neck
Aorta carries blood to the body's cells
Pulmonary arteries to the lungs
Pulmonary veins from the lungs
Pulmonary arteries
Pulmonary veins
Left atrium
Valve
Right atrium
Right ventricle
Left ventricle
Inferior vena cava carries blood from the lower body
Blood to the lower body

### SEE ALSO
Blood, Brain, Human body, Muscle

# HIBERNATION

**In the cooler parts of the world, many mammals pass the winter months in a very deep sleep. This is known as hibernation.**

Many types of bat are active during the night and go into a type of hibernation each daytime.

Some butterflies, such as the monarch, hibernate in large groups in hollow trees or attics over winter.

The deep winter sleep of some bears is hibernation, but their body temperature only drops slightly.

Snakes, such as adders, hibernate under rocks or in holes under the ground when the weather is cold.

Some animals, such as the lungfish, aestivate (become inactive in summer to survive drought).

Many animals hibernate during the winter when it is cold and there is little food about. While hibernating, their body temperature falls greatly until it is little more than that of the surroundings.

## GETTING READY

During the autumn, an animal will eat a lot to increase its body fat, which will give it energy while hibernating. It then looks for a safe spot in which to settle down. Most rodents take food supplies into their sleeping quarters to hibernate.

## ONLY JUST ALIVE

While hibernating, an animal's heart and breathing rates drop until it is only just alive. It may stir and stretch itself from time to time, but does not really wake up until the outside temperature rises in the spring. By this time, most animals have used up all their food reserves and are very thin. They have to look for food right away, and will die if they do not find any.

## WHO HIBERNATES?

Insect-eating bats in cool climates have to hibernate because there are not enough insects for them to eat in the winter. Dormice, hedgehogs and ground squirrels also hibernate. Among the birds, only the American poorwill and some other nightjars are known to hibernate. Small humming-birds also huddle together each night in a type of nightly hibernation.

## COLD BLOODED ANIMALS

Reptiles, amphibians and many fish living in cold climates become inactive in the winter. As the air or water temperature falls, the animals get slower and slower and then come to a complete stop. But there is not such a dramatic change as in the hibernating mammals because they are cold-blooded animals and their temperature is always similar to that of the surroundings.

## WARM WINTER SLEEP

Before hibernating, the chipmunk tunnels underground and builds a nesting place. It also collects seeds and nuts, which it stores in the tunnel. After it has pushed the earth out, it often loosely plugs up the entrance with earth. The chipmunk sleeps through most of the winter but may wake up on warm winter days, when it will eat some of its food.

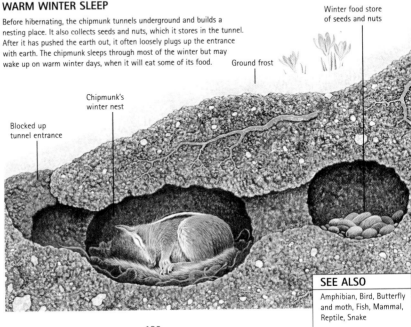

Winter food store of seeds and nuts

Ground frost

Chipmunk's winter nest

Blocked up tunnel entrance

### SEE ALSO
Amphibian, Bird, Butterfly and moth, Fish, Mammal, Reptile, Snake

# HINDUISM

Hinduism is one of the oldest existing religions. It began in north India about 4,000 years ago and is now the most popular religion in southern Asia.

▲ Many small shrines exist by the sides of roads as well as at most Hindu homes. Here food and flowers are offered and incense and candles burned.

Today, about 80 per cent of Indians are Hindu and there are over 800 million Hindus worldwide. Much of Hinduism was developed by people called Aryans, who settled in India from about 1500BC.

### EARLIEST WRITINGS
The Aryans produced the earliest Hindu writings, called the *Vedas*, in about 1000BC. Later there were the famous epic stories, the *Ramayana* and *Mahabharata*. Other important writings led to the creation of the Indian caste system. This is a social and religious system where people are divided into different groups by birth.

### MANY GODS
Hindus have three main gods: Brahma (the creator of the universe), Shiva (the destroyer) and Vishnu (the preserver). But they also worship many other gods

and goddesses and believe that all kinds of people and objects can become divine. The cow and the crow, for example, are sacred to Hindus and cannot be killed.

### CYCLE OF LIFE
Like Buddhists, all Hindus believe in reincarnation, or being born again after death. They also believe in the importance of living a good life, and in karma, which means that one is punished or rewarded for one's past actions in the next life.

### HINDU TEMPLES
Like most Hindu temples, this one in India's capital city, Delhi, is highly ornate. The goddess of good fortune, Lakshmi, is worshipped here in religious rituals, which are usually led by Hindu priests and teachers, who are members of the Brahman caste.

▲ Shiva is one of the most important of Hindu gods and represents destruction and rebirth.

## FAST FACTS

• Unlike Buddhism, Hinduism does not have a founder or a rigid system of beliefs

• There are all kinds of religious festivals and pilgrimages. Thousands travel to bathe in the sacred waters of the River Ganges every year

• Hindu wedding celebrations are very colourful and elaborate. When Hindus die, they are cremated

## SEE ALSO
Buddhism, Religion

# HORSE

Horses are four-legged, plant-eating mammals with a single hoof on each foot. Long ago they were wild but today almost all horses are domesticated.

**THE HORSE FAMILY**
All animals that have a single-toed hoof on the end of each leg belong to the group called Equidae.

The common zebra has black and white stripes and lives wild in Africa.

The ass is smaller than the horse, has long ears and is usually coloured grey.

The Shetland pony is a hardy breed of horse with thick coat and long mane.

Przewalski's horse, found in Mongolia in 1870, is the only truly wild horse left.

Most grazing mammals are cloven-hoofed, which means that their feet end in a pair of hoofed toes. Horses' feet, however, end in a large single hoof. This feature, combined with long and powerful legs, makes horses fast and tireless runners. They are therefore perfectly suited to life in open places, where there is nowhere to hide from danger.

## WILD HORSES
Horses are sociable animals, and in the wild live in herds about 10 to 20 strong. Mares (female horses) usually breed at the age of about two or three years, and normally have one foal a year. At one time, herds of wild horses roamed across the grassy plains of eastern Europe and central Asia. They were preyed upon by wolves and other predators, and hunted by people for food. But about 6,000 years ago, humans began to tame horses. From that moment, the history of the horse abruptly changed.

## PRZEWALSKI'S HORSE
Domesticated horses soon outnumbered wild ones, which became increasingly rare. There were originally three different kinds of wild horse. But by the late 1800s, only one was left, Przewalski's horse, which lived in a remote part of Mongolia. Today, there are over 700 Przewalski's horses in zoos around the world.

## PULLING POWER
Horses have been bred for a wide variety of purposes. Some of them were originally bred for their pulling power, and were used by farmers to pull ploughs and farm carts in the days before tractors were invented. Today, there are nearly 200 different breeds of horses. They include huge shire horses, which can measure as much as 2m high at the shoulder, child-sized Shetland ponies, and the Falabella horse from Argentina, which is smaller than many dogs.

▲ Many North American rodeo events such as steer wrestling have evolved from working with cattle.

## HORSES TODAY
Today, horses are used in every continent except Antarctica. In many countries, they still carry on traditional roles of providing transport and a livelihood for their owners. In North America, they have played a vital role in cattle herding since the mid-1800s, while Australians still use the hardy horses called Walers that were bred by early settlers. Other uses today include policing, ceremonial and sports events, hunting and riding for fun. But one of the most popular events is horse-racing. For this, thoroughbreds descended from 18th-century Arabian stallions are mostly used.

▲ Horses used for show jumping need to have a combination of power, stamina, boldness and agility in order to be able to handle the tough demands of the sport.

# PARTS OF THE HORSE

The overall shape and appearance of a horse is called its conformation, while the parts of the horse's body are called the points. A horse's skeleton gives clues about its breed. For example, a cart-horse has large, thick bones which it needs to support its weight whereas a racehorse has long, fine bones that help it to run swiftly.

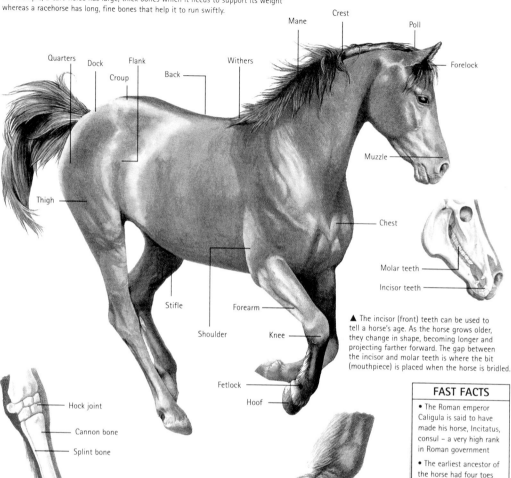

Quarters · Dock · Flank · Croup · Back · Withers · Mane · Crest · Poll · Forelock · Thigh · Muzzle · Chest · Molar teeth · Incisor teeth · Stifle · Forearm · Shoulder · Knee · Fetlock · Hoof · Hock joint · Cannon bone · Splint bone · Long pastern bone · Short pastern bone · Coffin bone · Heel · Frog · Hoof wall · Sole · Shoe

▲ The incisor (front) teeth can be used to tell a horse's age. As the horse grows older, they change in shape, becoming longer and projecting farther forward. The gap between the incisor and molar teeth is where the bit (mouthpiece) is placed when the horse is bridled.

▲ The modern horse stands on only one toe (its hoof), but the two splint bones on either side of the cannon bone are remnants of the early horse's other toes.

▲ Horses have metal shoes nailed to their hooves to protect the hoof wall from wearing down on rough or hard ground. Shoes must be replaced every few weeks. Before they can be fitted, the new growth of hoof has to be trimmed and the hoof reshaped.

## FAST FACTS

• The Roman emperor Caligula is said to have made his horse, Incitatus, consul – a very high rank in Roman government

• The earliest ancestor of the horse had four toes and was the size of a fox

• Horses are measured in hands from the ground to the top of the withers. A hand is 10cm

• A horse goes through four paces, from slow to fast: walk, trot, canter and gallop

## SEE ALSO

Animal, Evolution, Mammal, Sport, Transport, World War I

# HUMAN BODY

**The human body is made up of a skeleton, organs, outer skin and specialized systems, all of which work together to make it one of the most complex of all life forms.**

▼ Different ethnic groups vary in appearance, often as a result of adapting over thousands of years to climates and conditions.

Arabian

African

European

Chinese

Indian

The human body is similar to the bodies of other large mammals, especially apes. But it is also unique in many ways. It can walk upright on its two back legs. Its fingers are capable of precise, delicate movements, and its large brain is far more complex than that of any other creature. These features make humans a separate species in the animal kingdom, called *Homo sapiens*.

### BUILDING BLOCKS
The human body is made up of more than 50 million million tiny building blocks, called cells. These are all microscopic in size and vary in shape and structure according to their functions. Every second, the body makes more than five million cells of various kinds, to replace those that wear out and die.

### BODY TISSUES
Cells of the same kind are grouped together to form tissues. For example, bone tissue is strong and stiff, to provide the body with an inner supporting framework – the skeleton.

▶ Athletes train hard in order to build up their muscles and reach peak body fitness.

▶ Through regular stretching exercises, the human body can become very supple and capable of bending and twisting in extreme ways.

Cartilage tissue is also strong, but softer and smoother. It covers bones where they join, and is found inside bendy parts of the body such as the nose and ears.

### BODY ORGANS
Groups of tissue make up the main parts of the body, called organs. Examples are the intestines, which absorb digested food into blood; the kidneys, which filter waste products from blood; and the heart, which pumps blood. Several organs work together as a major body system.

### BODY SYSTEMS
Each system has a very important job to keep the body alive and healthy. For example, the respiratory system consists of the nose, windpipe and lungs. It breathes in air and absorbs oxygen from the air into the blood. Oxygen is needed to release the energy from digested food substances in order to power life processes. ▶

## DIGESTIVE SYSTEM

The body needs to maintain its cells and tissues, and repair worn-out parts. The raw materials for growth and repair come from food, which is processed by the digestive system: the mouth, teeth, gullet, stomach and intestines. Food is broken down into nutrients and energy-rich chemicals, which pass into the bloodstream. Waste matter passes out of the body as faeces.

## URINARY SYSTEM

The life processes inside cells produce waste products, some of which are removed by the urinary, system. This consists of the kidneys, which filter the wastes from the blood to form urine; and the bladder, which stores the urine before it is removed from the body.

## CO-ORDINATION AND CONTROL

The body parts and organs do not work on their own. Two main control systems keep them functioning together in a co-ordinated fashion. The hormonal system consists of body parts called endocrine glands that make substances named hormones. These pass into the blood and around the body. Each hormone affects the chemical activity of certain cells and tissues, making them speed up or slow down.

## NERVOUS SYSTEM

The second control system, the nervous system, is a network of wire-like nerves throughout the body, with the brain as the control centre. The brain receives information as tiny nerve signals from the sensory system – mainly the eyes, ears,

## SKIN AND MUSCLES

The skin protects the inside of the body from dirt, too much dryness or wetness, injury, harmful rays and germs. It also helps to keep the body warm in cold weather and cool in hot conditions. The muscular system consists of more than 640 muscles. In most cases, each end of a muscle is joined to a bone. When the muscle shortens or contracts, it pulls on the bones and moves that part of the body.

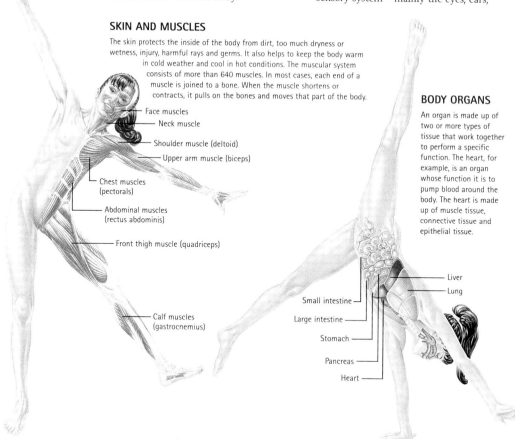

Face muscles
Neck muscle
Shoulder muscle (deltoid)
Upper arm muscle (biceps)
Chest muscles (pectorals)
Abdominal muscles (rectus abdominis)
Front thigh muscle (quadriceps)
Calf muscles (gastrocnemius)

## BODY ORGANS

An organ is made up of two or more types of tissue that work together to perform a specific function. The heart, for example, is an organ whose function it is to pump blood around the body. The heart is made up of muscle tissue, connective tissue and epithelial tissue.

Liver
Lung
Small intestine
Large intestine
Stomach
Pancreas
Heart

nose, tongue and skin. These sense organs detect what is happening around the body. The brain also sends signals to muscles, telling them when and how to contract and produce movements. It is also the site of mental processes such as thoughts, feelings, emotions and memories.

◄ The average body reaches its peak physical power and maximum size around the age of 18 to 25 years. After this it begins to age. Signs of ageing include wrinkled skin, grey hair, balding in men, shrinking, weaker muscles, slower reactions and less sharp senses.

## REPRODUCTION
The human body reproduces like any other mammal. The reproductive system consists of either female or male sex organs. The male ones make sperm cells. The female ones contain egg cells. When a sperm cell fertilizes an egg cell, the egg begins to multiply rapidly. Over a period of nine months, it grows and develops within the mother's body into an embryo, then a foetus, and is born as a baby.

## GROWING UP
Some animals are active and independent within minutes of birth. But a human baby needs food, warmth and care for many months. As it grows into a child, it learns to sit, stand, walk, talk, read, write and acquire many other skills. This takes years because human society is very complex, with many customs, traditions, rules and laws.

## CIRCULATORY AND LYMPHATIC SYSTEMS
The circulatory system consists of the heart, blood vessels and blood. It transports oxygen from the lungs, nutrients and energy-rich substances to all parts of the body. The lymphatic and immune systems produce antibodies which are released into the bloodstream to fight off disease.

■ Oxygenated blood
■ Deoxygenated blood
□ Lymphatic system

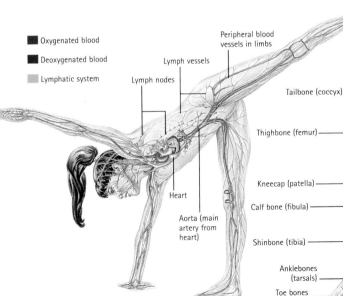

## THE SKELETON
The human skeleton consists of 206 bones. These are rigid and tough, and provide a strong supporting framework inside the body. They are linked at joints, which allow the bones to move in certain ways without coming apart.

### SEE ALSO
Blood, Brain, Heart, Kidney, Lungs, Reproduction

# INCAS

The Incas were people who lived in the Andes Mountains of South America from about 1200 to the mid-1500s. They ruled a rich and sophisticated empire.

The Inca Empire was centred around Cuzco – a highland valley in the Andes mountains of Peru. The empire stretched into present-day Ecuador, Colombia, Bolivia, Argentina and Chile. Although made up of many tribes, its ruling emperor and nobles were members of the Inca tribe. The empire collapsed after the Spanish invaded in 1532.

The Incas had no writing system. They used knotted, coloured strings, called *quipus*, to keep records.

## GOD ON EARTH
The first great Inca emperor was Pachacuti Yupanqui, a warrior who came to power in 1438. His son, Tupac, and grandson, Huayna Capac, extended the empire. The emperor was known as the 'Inca'. He was considered a god, a descendant of the Sun.

## RUNNING AN EMPIRE
The empire was strictly governed. The ordinary people worked many days each year for the emperor, planting crops, fighting battles or building bridges and roads. The roads ran throughout the empire, crossing mountain ravines

Gold, silver and precious stones were used to craft beautiful objects used by noble families and in religious rituals.

by rope bridges. In places, roads were carved from rock, elsewhere they were paved. The roads were mostly used by *chasquis*, the royal messengers, and merchants, who used llamas to carry goods. There were no wheeled vehicles.

## EVERYDAY LIFE
Most of the 12 million people were farmers. They kept llamas and alpacas for wool and meat, and grew maize, potatoes and other vegetables in terraced fields. Wool and cotton cloth were woven by hand and pots made from clay. Stone fortresses guarded cities and roads, but most families lived in houses made from mud bricks.

## GREAT FESTIVAL OF THE SUN
The Capac Raymi, the Great Festival of the Sun, was held in Cuzco on the longest and shortest days of the year. At dawn, the emperor offered a golden cup of sacred beer and sacrificed a white llama to Inti, the Sun god, to gain his help and protection. Other important gods included the supreme deity Viracocha and the goddesses of the earth and the sea.

### SEE ALSO
Aztecs, South America

# INDIAN SUBCONTINENT

The Indian subcontinent is a huge land mass which includes the countries of India, Pakistan, Bangladesh, Nepal and Bhutan. It makes up one tenth of Asia.

**BANGLADESH**
**Area:** 143,998 sq km
**Population:** 125,629,000
**Capital:** Dhaka
**Language:** Bengali
**Currency:** Taka

**BHUTAN**
**Area:** 47,000 sq km
**Population:** 759,000
**Capital:** Thimphu
**Language:** Dzongkha, Nepali, English
**Currency:** Ngultrum

**INDIA**
**Area:** 3,287,263 sq km
**Population:** 979,673,000
**Capital:** New Delhi
**Languages:** Hindi, English
**Currency:** Rupee

**MALDIVES**
**Area:** 298 sq km
**Population:** 263,000
**Capital:** Male (Male Island)
**Language:** Divehi
**Currency:** Rufiyaa

**NEPAL**
**Area:** 147,181 sq km
**Population:** 22,851,000
**Capital:** Katmandu
**Language:** Nepali
**Currency:** Rupee

Three quarters of the Indian subcontinent is covered by India itself. As well as Pakistan, Bangladesh, Nepal and Bhutan on the mainland, there are two island nations in the south – Sri Lanka and the Republic of the Maldives.

## FROM HIGH TO LOW
High mountain ranges lie in the north of the region, including the Himalayas, which contain the world's highest peak, Mount Everest (8,848m), on the border between Nepal and China. Southern India consists largely of a plateau called the Deccan. Bordering the Deccan are two low mountain ranges, the Eastern and Western Ghats, fringed by narrow coastal plains.

## WATER AND WINDS
The longest river in the region, the Indus (2,897km), flows from the Himalayas through Pakistan, where its waters are used by farmers. The Rivers Brahmaputra (2,704km) and Ganges (2,494km) join together in Bangladesh and flow across the world's largest delta, into the Bay of Bengal. Cherrapunji, near Shillong, just

▲ Religion and festivals play an important part in Indian life. Many people go on pilgrimages to holy places like the city of Varanasi on the banks of the River Ganges. The waters of the river are considered sacred.

north of Bangladesh, is the rainiest place on Earth receiving an average of 10,820mm a year. Most rain comes between June and October, when moist monsoon winds blow from the sea. These have little effect on the dry northwest – the Thar Desert along the Pakistan-India border has less than 250mm of rain a year.

## TROPICAL TREES
Few plants grow in the northwest, except on the wetter mountain slopes, but most of the Indian subcontinent has plenty of farming and grazing land. Valuable trees in tropical forests include ironwood, rosewood and teak. Bamboo also grows in many areas.

▼ Spices provide a major industry for India and are sold at markets like this one in Udaipur.

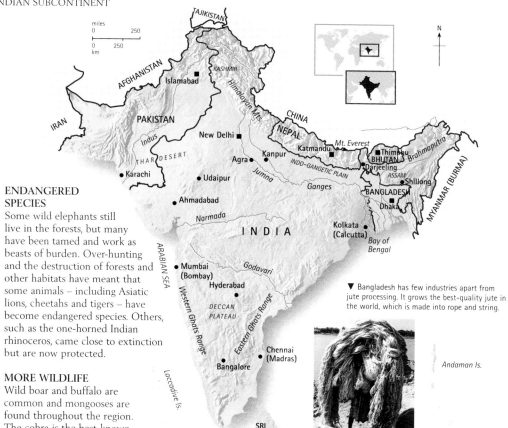

## ENDANGERED SPECIES

Some wild elephants still live in the forests, but many have been tamed and work as beasts of burden. Over-hunting and the destruction of forests and other habitats have meant that some animals – including Asiatic lions, cheetahs and tigers – have become endangered species. Others, such as the one-horned Indian rhinoceros, came close to extinction but are now protected.

## MORE WILDLIFE

Wild boar and buffalo are common and mongooses are found throughout the region. The cobra is the best-known reptile, and the region's many birds include the myna bird, which can imitate human speech. Mountain animals include brown and black bears, deer, the rare snow leopard, the markhor (a kind of wild goat), various kinds of wild sheep and wild yaks.

▲ Ihuhu Island is one of 1,200 coral islands that make up the Maldives. Most are just 2m above sea level.

▼ Bangladesh has few industries apart from jute processing. It grows the best-quality jute in the world, which is made into rope and string.

## GROWING POPULATIONS

With its population likely to pass the billion mark soon, India has more people than any other country apart from China. Pakistan, with a population of almost 132 million, ranks sixth in the world and Bangladesh, with 126 million people, is the world's eighth largest country.

## INDIA'S LANGUAGES

India has 19 major languages and more than 1,650 dialects and minor languages. The two main language groups are the Indo-European, which includes Hindi – the most widely spoken language – and the Dravidian languages, including Tamil, which are spoken mainly in the south. English is also spoken by some Indians. ▶

**PAKISTAN**
**Area:** 796,095 sq km
**Population:** 131,582,000
**Capital:** Islamabad
**Language:** Urdu, English
**Currency:** Rupee

**SRI LANKA**
**Area:** 65,610 sq km
**Population:** 18,778,000
**Capital:** Colombo
**Languages:** Sinhala, Tamil
**Currency:** Rupee

## URDU AND BENGALI

Pakistan's official language is Urdu, but less than a tenth of the people speak it as their first language. Instead, they speak the language of their community. The largest communities are the Punjabi, Sindhi, Pushtun and Baluchi. In Bangladesh, more than 95 per cent of the people speak the official language, Bengali.

## RELIGIONS OF INDIA

Beautiful temples, mosques and other religious buildings are everywhere. In places such as Udaipur, India, there are spectacular palaces built hundreds of years ago for princes. Today, Hindus make up 82 per cent of India's population, with Muslims forming another 12 per cent. India also has large numbers of Christians, Sikhs, Buddhists and Jains. Islam, the Muslim religion, is the chief religion in Pakistan, Bangladesh and the Maldives.

## INFLUENCE OF BUDDHA

Hinduism is the official religion of Nepal, but the country was the birthplace of Buddha, so many Nepalese have combined the

▲ Agriculture is Sri Lanka's main economic activity. Important crops, including tea, are grown on large plantations.

beliefs and practices of the two religions. Buddhism is the chief religion in Bhutan and of the Sinhalese in Sri Lanka, although a minority group in Sri Lanka, the Tamils, mainly follows Hinduism. Differences between these groups have led to fighting between government troops and Tamil guerrillas.

## FARM LIFE

More than three fifths of the people of the Indian subcontinent are farmers who live in villages and farm the land around them. Farming is the leading activity and rice is the main food crop in India, Bangladesh and Sri Lanka. In Pakistan, wheat is the leading food crop. Tea is grown in northeast India, around Darjeeling and in Assam, as well as in Sri Lanka. Most farmers have a

▼ Nepal's Sherpa people live on the southern slopes of the Himalaya mountains where the spectacular landscape, which includes Mount Everest, attracts many tourists. Timber is used for cooking and heating by locals and tourists, and more than a third of the country's forests have been cut down since the 1950s.

▲ In Bhutan, local women make cheese from yaks' milk.

## CITY LIFE AND EDUCATION
The region has six cities with more than five million people. These are the four Indian cities of Mumbai (formerly Bombay), Kolkata (formerly Calcutta), Delhi (made up of the walled city of Old Delhi and the capital New Delhi) and Chennai (formerly Madras), as well as the Bangladeshi capital Dhaka and Karachi in Pakistan. Sri Lanka has a good education system, but in the rest of the Indian subcontinent there are millions of people who cannot read or write. The education system in India is, however, gradually improving.

## EARLY TIMES
From the late 18th century, India, Pakistan and Bangladesh formed part of a huge colony called British India. In 1947, British India became independent, splitting into two parts – modern India and Pakistan, which was created for Muslims. In 1971, East Pakistan broke away and became the separate country of Bangladesh. Sri Lanka became independent from Britain in 1948, as did the Maldives in 1968.

**GANDHI**
Mohandas K. Gandhi was born in India in 1869. From the 1920s he used peaceful protests to lead India to independence. He became known as Mahatma, meaning 'Great Soul'. He was assassinated in 1948.

low standard of living and live in houses made of mud and straw. India has more cattle and buffalo than any other country but these animals are considered sacred by Hindus and cannot be killed for food. Fishing is also a major activity.

## DEVELOPING INDUSTRY
The Indian subcontinent has plenty of coal, iron ore and other minerals. There is some oil, and petroleum refining is an important industry. Textiles are leading products, and Mumbai and Delhi are developing large electronics industries.

## DIFFICULT DIVISION
At the time of the partition of British India, the status of Kashmir in the north was not satisfactorily settled. Part of the territory now falls within northeast Pakistan, but the bulk lies within the Indian states of Jammu and Kashmir. Guerillas and governments are in dispute over whether Kashmir should remain part of India, become part of Pakistan, or become independent.

◀ Pakistan's national cricketers are world famous. Children play the game from an early age.

## SEE ALSO
Asia, Buddhism, Hinduism, Islam, Mountain and valley

# INDUSTRIAL REVOLUTION

**The Industrial Revolution is the name given to the great changes that took place when people began to use steam power to make goods in factories.**

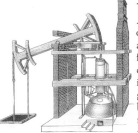

Thomas Newcomen built the first steam engine in 1712 to pump water.

In the 1700s, society in Britain began to change from being based on agriculture, with people working at home, to being dominated by factories and industrial cities. The changes were caused by the invention of machines that made goods faster and more cheaply than before. The owners of the new machines employed other people to work on them. In this way, the factory came into existence, surrounded by houses for the workers. Often several factories were built together, from which a new town developed.

## WOMEN'S WORK

Factory jobs often required skill rather than strength. Women were as good as men for such work, and many single women gained independence by earning a wage for themselves. Most women gave up work when they married, to run the household and family.

The spinning jenny of 1764 could spin several threads at one time.

In 1777, the world's first iron bridge was erected in Shropshire, England.

Eli Whitney's cotton gin of 1794 separated cotton seeds from fibre at speed.

Locomotives, such as the German *Der Adler* of 1835, powered the rail boom.

## KING COTTON

The Industrial Revolution began around 1760, when new machines that could spin cotton thread very quickly were invented in Britain. These made thread so fast that hand weavers could not keep up. So weaving machines were invented. At first, water wheels powered the machines, but by 1780, these could not cope. In 1785, the British clergyman Edmund Cartwright (1743-1823) invented a power loom that used steam power to drive it.

## THE POWER OF STEAM

Simple steam engines were already being used to pump water out of mines. Between 1764 and 1790, the Scottish engineer James Watt (1736-1819) improved the steam engine so that it used heat more efficiently and could drive machines. By 1800, there were about 500 steam engines at work in Britain. For the first time, people had an artificial source of power, which was cheap and efficient. ▶

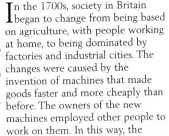

**BRUNEL**
The British engineer Isambard Kingdom Brunel (1806–59) built railways, bridges and the world's largest ship.

## RAW MATERIALS

The Industrial Revolution required iron for machines, coal to burn in steam engines and money to pay for them both. By 1750, Britain had all three and became the first country to industrialize. The iron industry grew quickly after 1709, when Abraham Darby first used coke to smelt iron (melt the iron ore). This was cheaper and more efficient than the old way using charcoal. New coal mines were dug to supply coal for steam engines and coke for ironworks.

## CANALS AND RAILWAYS

The new industrial products required a transport system to move them to people. Between 1750 and 1830, canals were dug, linking major cities and rivers. Most roads remained poor, but in 1804, Richard Trevithick built the world's first steam locomotive. By the 1830s, Britain had embarked on a railway craze, and railways were soon built across countries in western Europe and North America. By 1870,

most of these nations had linked their cities by rail. Belgium, France, Germany and the USA began industrializing after 1815. By 1900, the USA and Germany had overtaken Britain in steel production.

## BUSINESS BOOM

The new machines made goods faster and more cheaply. Factory and mine owners made huge profits, some of which they spent on more machines, so creating new jobs. Investors saved small amounts of money in banks, which then lent large amounts to industrialists. This developing 'capitalist' system raised money to build factories, offices and houses.

## A HARD LIFE

For many workers, life in the factories and mines was hard and dangerous. Men, women and children worked 13 or more hours a day, often for low wages. Many workers

## DEVELOPING INDUSTRIAL AREAS

New factories were built near canals and railways so that raw materials could be brought in and finished goods taken to markets easily. To begin with, the houses that were built to accommodate the workers in many industrial became slums, with no running water, drains or other basic services.

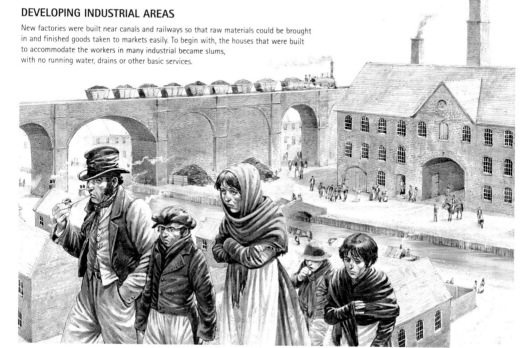

## KEY DATES

**1709** Abraham Darby uses coke to smelt iron
**1764** The spinning jenny is invented for cotton
**1770** The first factories begin producing cotton
**1789** The first steam-powered factory opens
**1804** Richard Trevithick builds first steam locomotive
**1825** The first public railway is opened
**1820s** Rapid growth of industrialization in USA

were killed or injured by unsafe machinery before new safety laws were enforced. Towns grew rapidly and without proper planning, leaving some areas without drains or clean water. Diseases that were caught from unclean water (such as cholera) or in crowded conditions (tuberculosis) became common and killed thousands of people. These conditions caused social unrest and even riots.

### CAMPAIGNERS AND REFORMERS

Gradually, laws to shorten working hours and stop child labour were introduced. Trade unions, at first banned, campaigned for better pay and conditions for workers.

In time, reformers won improved working conditions and schooling for all children. Slums were cleared and new laws controlled factory and housing development.

### LONG-TERM EFFECTS

During the Industrial Revolution, cities grew rapidly as people began to leave the countryside to find work. Industrialization spread worldwide in the 20th century, and the world economy today is geared to the production of goods, though some countries in Africa and Southeast Asia remain dependent on agriculture or services. People now enjoy higher standards of living than ever before, but at a high cost to the environment. Industrialization has caused pollution and used up resources such as coal, oil and minerals. However, new technology is being developed to solve some of the problems created by industrialization.

### URBAN DEVELOPMENT

Rows of terraced cottages were built around factories to house the workers. Gradually, some factory owners or town councils improved conditions for the workers by building schools and churches.

**CHILD LABOUR**
In the 1700s and 1800s, factory owners employed children, many of them under ten years of age, to work in factories and mines. They had to work long hours in dangerous and unhealthy conditions. However, by 1900, most industrialized countries had banned child labour.

## SEE ALSO

Coal, Engine, Iron and steel, Machine, Transport

# INDUSTRY

**Industry covers all the different kinds of work people do, from producing raw materials and manufacturing goods to providing services.**

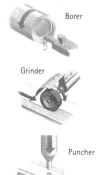
Borer

Grinder

Puncher

Turning machine

▲ Machine tools such as these are widely used to manufacture machinery and motor components.

Manufacturing industries, such as the aircraft and automobile industries, make goods for people to buy. The electronics industry, for example, produces tiny wafers of silicon that are the brains of our desk-top computers, and the chemical industry manufactures a wide range of chemicals, from fertilizers to life-saving antibiotics. The steel industry is one of the most important of all industries because it produces the metal that many other industries rely on. The construction industry uses steel to build towering skyscrapers and massive dams and bridges.

## PRIMARY INDUSTRIES
Mining produces the raw materials, such as ores and petroleum, on which the manufacturing industries depend. It marks the beginning of the industrial production process and is therefore called a primary industry. Agriculture, forestry and fishing are also primary industries. Manufacturing is next in the production chain, and is called a secondary industry.

## GETTING SERVICE
When the manufacturing industries have produced the goods, they have to be sold to the consumer. This is the job of shops and stores. They do not produce goods

► Researchers in the chemical industry develop new materials such as drugs and plastics.

themselves, but provide a service by buying goods from the manufacturers and selling them on to customers. Shops are an example of a service industry, often called a tertiary (third) industry. Other examples of service industries include transport and tourism, insurance and banks, restaurants and hotels, hospitals and local government.

## MASS PRODUCTION
A key feature of modern industry is mass production – the manufacture of goods in large quantities at a relatively low cost. In a typical mass production operation, goods are built up piece by piece on an assembly line, with people often working side by side with industrial robots.

▲ Some industries, such as this shoe factory in India, involve hundreds of people working together. Others have people working in smaller groups, or alone at home.

## AUTOMATION TAKES OVER
Today, many assembly lines are fully automated, with machines now controlled by computers instead of humans. Robots are increasingly being used, particularly in the automobile industry. They are ideal for performing highly repetitive, hazardous or awkward tasks, such as spot welding or paint spraying. Fitted with a gripper, they can also be used to move objects about.

| SEE ALSO |
| --- |
| Industrial Revolution |

# INSECT

Insects belong to the large group of animals called arthropods, which means 'jointed feet'. An insect's legs are made up of small segments and flexible joints.

Male stag beetles have large jaws that look like the antlers of a stag.

A cricket has long hind legs for hopping and scrapes its wings to 'sing'.

Earwigs are flat with pincers at their tail and wings that fold away.

Aphids have soft brown or green bodies about 2–3mm in length.

A human louse, like all sucking lice, feeds on the blood of mammals.

## IDENTIFYING AN INSECT

Adult insects, such as the wasp below, have a body that is divided into three parts: the head, the thorax (where legs and wings are joined) and the abdomen (where the insect digests its food and makes its eggs). They also have three pairs of legs, and a tough body case, or exoskeleton.

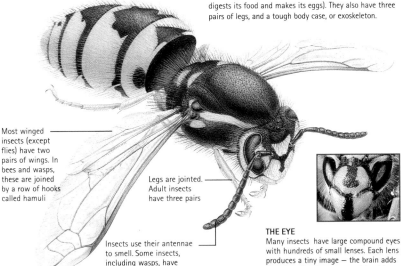

Most winged insects (except flies) have two pairs of wings. In bees and wasps, these are joined by a row of hooks called hamuli

Legs are jointed. Adult insects have three pairs

Insects use their antennae to smell. Some insects, including wasps, have taste organs in them too

### THE EYE

Many insects have large compound eyes with hundreds of small lenses. Each lens produces a tiny image — the brain adds these together to see a complete picture.

---

More than a million kinds of insects have been found on Earth. That's more than all the other types of animals put together. They are split into around 29 groups and include grasshoppers, beetles, butterflies, flies and bees. Insects have no backbone or skeleton inside the body, but the whole insect is covered with a tough, horny material called chitin. This forms an external skeleton rather like a suit of armour. It is made up of segments, some of which are loosely connected by soft membranes so that the insect can move.

## WITH OR WITHOUT WINGS

Most insects have two pairs of wings, but some, including fleas and worker ants, never have wings. Flying ants only have wings for a short time, then lose them. Beetles and many bugs look as if they have no wings because their front wings form hard cases and completely cover the delicate hind wings.

## BREATHING WITH TUBES

Insects do not have lungs. They breathe by way of a system of fine tubes, called tracheae. These branch through the body and carry air and oxygen. In most insects, air enters the tubes through small holes on the sides of the body – mainly on the abdomen. The openings are called spiracles and they are best seen in large caterpillars, which are the young stages of butterflies and moths.

## WATER BUGS

Insects that live in water usually have to come to the surface to renew the air in their breathing tubes, but many young insects can absorb dissolved oxygen straight from the water into their tracheae. ▶

▶ Beetles form the largest insect order, with more than 250,000 species.

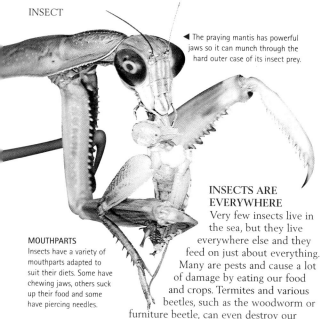

◀ The praying mantis has powerful jaws so it can munch through the hard outer case of its insect prey.

### MOUTHPARTS
Insects have a variety of mouthparts adapted to suit their diets. Some have chewing jaws, others suck up their food and some have piercing needles.

Tiger beetles are fierce carnivores (meat-eaters), with prominent biting mandibles (or jaws).

Weevils' mouthparts are extended into a snout. They can be serious pests, infesting flour and grain.

A fly's proboscis is like a straw with a sponge tip. It dribbles on food to dissolve it, then sucks it back up.

## INSECTS ARE EVERYWHERE
Very few insects live in the sea, but they live everywhere else and they feed on just about everything. Many are pests and cause a lot of damage by eating our food and crops. Termites and various beetles, such as the woodworm or furniture beetle, can even destroy our houses. Fleas and mosquitoes suck our blood and carry dangerous diseases. But there are also some very useful insects. Honey bees pollinate many of our crops and give us honey, silkmoths give us silk, ladybird beetles eat huge numbers of greenflies (aphids) and other plant pests, and dung beetles and their grubs help to keep the countryside clean by eating up cow-pats and other animal dung.

## AN INSECT GROWS UP
Most insects start life as eggs, but the insect that hatches from an egg does not usually look much like its parents. A caterpillar, for example, looks nothing like an adult butterfly or moth: it has no wings and instead of sipping nectar from flowers it munches its way through leaves with its biting jaws. Before it becomes an adult, the caterpillar has to pass through a chrysalis, or pupa, stage, during which its body is broken down and re-built in the adult form. Bees, flies and beetles pass through similar stages as they grow up.

#### THE EMERGING INSECT
Insects, such as this lacewing, moult several times as they grow up, because their tough outer coats, or exoskeletons, cannot grow. At each moult, the old skin splits open, and the insect crawls out.

### INSECT LIFE-CYCLE
Advanced insects, such as flies, have a four-part life-cycle. The eggs hatch into larvae which change their skins twice as they grow. Then comes the pupa stage where they change into the adult form.

Young insects at the worm-like stage are called larvae, and this way of growing up is called a complete metamorphosis, meaning 'a complete change'.

## SMALL ADULTS
Grasshoppers, dragonflies and bugs have a slightly different kind of life-cycle. The young insects do not have wings, but they do look fairly like the adults apart from being smaller. They are called nymphs, and they gradually turn into adults without passing through a chrysalis stage. This way of growing up is called an incomplete metamorphosis – 'an incomplete change'.

# INSECT HOMES

Ants are the most successful social insects. In the leaf-cutter ant's communal home, the queen lays the eggs, nursery workers look after them, larger workers cut leaves and bring them back to the nest, leaving scent trails by touching the ground with the tips of their abdomens. Soldier ants have a big head with strong jaws and bite to protect the nest; while smaller workers build new tunnels and tend the fungus gardens to feed the others.

Nursery worker

Soldier ants use their sting and powerful jaws to defend the colony

A queen ant can lay one egg every ten seconds.

Ants chew the leaves to pulp and mix it with their droppings. A fungus grows on the mixture and the ants eat the fungus.

Smaller worker protects leaf

A large leaf-cutter can grow up to 2cm and carry a gigantic weight in its mouth.

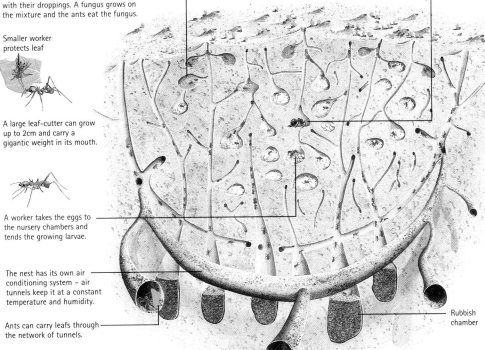

A worker takes the eggs to the nursery chambers and tends the growing larvae.

The nest has its own air conditioning system – air tunnels keep it at a constant temperature and humidity.

Ants can carry leafs through the network of tunnels.

Rubbish chamber

## GETTING FATTER

As insects grow they shed their old body cases – but not before growing a soft new one. The insect pumps itself up with air or water for a few hours until the new skin has hardened, and then gets rid of the air or water to leave enough space for the next stage of growth. Most insects moult between four and ten times as they grow up, but some may moult as many as 50 times before they are fully grown adults.

## LITTLE AND LARGE

The heaviest insect is the African Goliath beetle, which is about as big as a man's fist and weighs about 100g. Some stick insects are much longer, but their bodies are all quite thin. The tiniest insects are smaller than a full-stop on this page.

## HOME ALONE

Most insects are solitary – living alone and finding a safe place to lay their eggs. This may be inside the body of another insect, as in the case of the tarantula hawk wasp which lays an egg on a paralyzed but living spider. Social insects, such as ants, live together in large groups. Each insect has its own job and only the queen lays eggs.

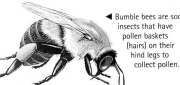

◄ Bumble bees are social insects that have pollen baskets (hairs) on their hind legs to collect pollen.

## FAST FACTS

• Ants and bees recognize members of their own colony through smell

• The number of lenses in an insect's eye varies from about six in a worker ant to 30,000 in some dragonflies

• A single swarm of locusts can contain twice as many insects as the entire human population!

## SEE ALSO

Butterfly and moth, Disease, Fossil

143

# INTERNET

**The Internet is a globe-spanning computer network, giving people rapid access to information, knowledge, entertainment and opinions from around the world.**

▲ Cybercafés allow people who are not on the Internet to make use of it in comfortable surroundings.

The Internet, or 'Net', is often referred to as the Information Superhighway. It allows vast amounts of information to stream around the world from computer to computer, letting the general public have easy and quick access to it.

### WHAT THE INTERNET CAN DO

School students can call up pictures and information from galleries in, for example, France, Japan and Britain. They can check unfamiliar words and historical dates in computerized reference libraries based in any country. Alternatively, they can listen to a clip from an album while printing out the guitar chords to go with it. A major use of the Internet is to carry electronic mail, or email. An email message can include pictures and audio clips, as well as words, and can be sent to hundreds of computers as easily and as cheaply as to one.

### BIRTH OF THE INTERNET

The Internet began as a military network for communications. In the early 1970s, American engineers designed a system that could keep working even if a nuclear attack knocked out some of the computers. Signals could automatically be re-routed through the surviving computers. This design was later used to set up computer networks linking universities and now it is used in the Internet.

### THE WORLD WIDE WEB

The World Wide Web was invented in 1990 so that users could 'surf the Net' quickly. By clicking on hot-spots on the screen with the mouse, the user jumps to pages of information consisting of words and pictures located on various computers around the world. Each of these has its own hot-spots which lead to further pages.

▼ Search engines greatly speed up the process of finding Web pages and specific pieces of information on the Web.

▲ Many goods and services can be ordered and paid for over the Internet.

▶ Using email, people can send letters and pictures to one another across the world within minutes.

▼ People can view live video clips of a current US space mission from NASA.

◀ Information on shows, films, zoos, circuses and many other forms of entertainment can be found on the Internet.

## SEE ALSO

Communication, Computer

144

# INVENTION

An invention is the creation of something new. In the past 200 years, the number of inventions has boomed, changing the world dramatically.

▲ Wheels were used in Mesopotamia about 3200BC. The cart wheel was developed from the earlier potter's wheel.

Civilization has been driven forward by inventions. Each invention has been based on those that came before it, and has made further progress possible.

### GETTING THE BASICS RIGHT

Prehistoric people were the first inventors. They learned how to farm and to make fire, pottery, the wheel and metal tools. One invention often leads to others. Without the wheel, for example, there could be no carts, watermills or machines driven by gears. Key inventions of the 19th century included photography, electric light, plastics and motor vehicles. In 1946, the first electronic computer started up, changing the way we live.

### THE INVENTORS

Some people stand out as lone inventors. In the late 1400s, the Italian Leonardo da Vinci designed a flying machine, but could not build it because there was no suitable engine. The American Thomas Alva Edison (1847–1931) is credited with more than 1,000 inventions, among them the light bulb and the phonograph. Other pioneers who worked alone were Alexander Graham Bell (the telephone), Guglielmo Marconi (the radio) and Karl Benz and Gottfried Daimler (the motor car). More recent inventions, such as the television and computers, were developed by large research teams with many specialists.

### GOOD OR BAD?

Most people would agree that pain-killing drugs are 'good' inventions and that poison gas is 'bad', but poison gas can be put to good use to kill pests that eat our food. It is how inventions are used that makes them useful or harmful.

The flushing toilet was developed in the 1840s.

Safety matches were invented in 1844.

An early experimental photocopier of 1940.

John Logie Baird invented the television in 1926.

Alexander Graham Bell invented the telephone in 1876.

### PHONOGRAPH
Thomas Edison's phonograph of 1877 used a cylinder of tin foil to record sound.

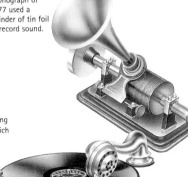

### RECORDED SOUND

Sound recording has traditionally been by analogue means. The sound waves in the air are reproduced as peaks and troughs in a groove on a solid object. These were read by passing a needle along the groove. Modern CDs treat sound as digital computer data which is recorded as a series of pits on the disk.

### 78RPM GRAMOPHONE
In 1921, a flat plastic disc, or record, with sound fed through electric speakers gave better-quality sound.

### COMPACT DISC
The compact disc, or CD, of the early 1980s contained digital music, read by a laser beam for accurate reproduction.

### HI-FI VINYL
In 1958, stereo sound from long-playing records produced high fidelity sound, or hi-fi, for the first time.

### SEE ALSO
Industrial Revolution, Nuclear power, Printing

# IRELAND, REPUBLIC OF

The Republic of Ireland occupies 80 per cent of the island of Ireland, which lies off the west coast of Britain. It is also called by its Gaelic name, Eire.

**Area:** 70,273 sq km
**Population:** 3,705,000
**Capital:** Dublin
**Languages:** Irish Gaelic and English
**Currency:** Punt (Irish pound)

Ireland is a land of green fields, rolling hills, lakes, known as loughs, and winding rivers. The centre of the country is flat while low mountain ranges line the coasts. The Shannon (386km) is the longest river in the British Isles and is used to produce hydroelectric power. Ireland has a mild, moist climate and rich green grass grows on the limestone that forms much of the country, giving it the name Emerald Isle.

## FARMING AND EUROPE

Ireland is a farming country famous for dairy foods such as butter. Wide bogs in the midlands are full of peat (decayed plants), which is cut and dried for fuel. After joining the European Union (EU), the Republic prospered as EU money helped it to modernize farm machinery and farming methods.

▲ Live music, traditional and modern, is a large part of Irish culture. The country has also produced many great writers.

## INDUSTRY AND CITIES

Irish factories make electronic equipment, textiles, plastics and other goods. The country also brews alcoholic beverages. Industry is centred mainly around Dublin, Cork and Limerick – three fifths of the people now live in towns or cities, where they are more likely to find work.

## IRELAND AND BRITAIN

England gained control of Ireland in the 1500s, after which Protestants from England and Scotland settled there. When Ireland became self-governing in 1921, the six Protestant-dominated counties of Northern Ireland stayed part of the United Kingdom. In the Republic, most people are Roman Catholics. The division of the island causes continuing tensions.

▼ The city of Dublin is popular with tourists. Landmarks include the Ha'penny Bridge over the River Liffey.

▲ The Irish are famous for breeding horses. Their thoroughbred yearlings are most often used as racehorses.

## SEE ALSO

Christianity, Europe, UK

# IRON AND STEEL

Iron is one of the most common metals in the Earth's crust. It is often used mixed with other ingredients in the form of steel – a cheap, strong building material.

Steel can be shaped in various ways. It can be rolled into tubes...

... or drawn through a hole to make wire.

A series of rollers shapes solid steel into girders.

Steel is used for a wide range of everyday objects.

In its natural state, iron is found combined with other elements, such as oxygen, as a rocky material called iron ore. Before it can be used, the iron has to be extracted (removed) from its ore by a process called smelting.

### EXTRACTING THE IRON
The iron ore is mixed with coke (a form of carbon) and limestone (a chalky rock). Then it is blasted with hot air until it reaches a temperature of over 1500°C. The iron melts and most of the impurities (unwanted materials) float to its surface. The impurities, known as 'slag', are then removed. The iron remaining is called pig iron. This still contains some impurities, especially carbon, but after further heat treatment, it can be poured into moulds to make cast-iron parts such as engine blocks.

▲ Glowing red-hot, molten iron is poured from a giant ladle into moulds and left to cool as ingots.

### MAKING STEEL
Most pig iron goes for refining, or purifying, to make steel. This involves mixing it with scrap steel and blasting it with oxygen so that most of the carbon burns off. Steel is a tough, strong material that is used to make bridges, buildings and many other objects that carry heavy loads. Manufacturers often add other elements to steel to give it special properties. Adding chromium and nickel makes stainless steel – a material that never rusts. This is used to make such things as engine parts and surgical tools.

### PROCESSING THE IRON
Iron is extracted from its ore in a blast furnace. The resulting pig iron contains about four per cent carbon, which comes from the coke in the furnace. This carbon makes the iron very brittle, so the iron is processed again before it is used. Steel is made by blasting the pig iron with oxygen inside a furnace called a converter. The oxygen combines with the carbon in the iron to form gases that are easily removed.

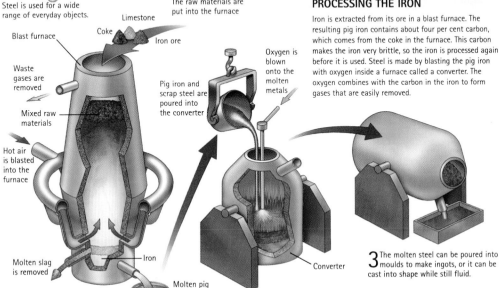

The raw materials are put into the furnace

Limestone

Coke

Iron ore

Blast furnace

Waste gases are removed

Mixed raw materials

Hot air is blasted into the furnace

Molten slag is removed

Iron

Molten pig iron pours into ladle

Pig iron and scrap steel are poured into the converter

Oxygen is blown onto the molten metals

Converter

**1** As the coke burns inside the furnace, it removes the oxygen from the iron ore to leave pig iron.

**2** Inside the converter, oxygen is used to burn off most of the carbon, leaving steel.

**3** The molten steel can be poured into moulds to make ingots, or it can be cast into shape while still fluid.

## SEE ALSO
Bridge, Earth, Metal

# ISLAM

Islam is the second most common religion in the world after Christianity. People who follow Islam are called Muslims.

▲ The crescent and star are the symbols of Islam.

There are more than one billion Muslims across the world, many in the Middle East and Africa. They believe in one all-powerful god, who created everything. Their name for God is Allah. Islam means 'submission' in Arabic, and devout Muslims try to live their lives according to Allah's word.

### THE STORY OF MUHAMMAD

Islam began with the prophet Muhammad, an Arab born in about AD570 in the city of Mecca (in what is now Saudi Arabia). When he was 40, Muhammad was called by Allah to preach his words, and he spread Islam throughout much of the Arab world. He died in 632.

▲ Islam has no organized Church and no priests. Instead, there are holy men and teachers.

### PILGRIMAGE TO MECCA

The pilgrimage to Mecca, called the hajj, takes place during the 12th month of the Muslim year. About two million Muslims from across the world converge on Mecca to perform rituals, such as walking round the holy shrine, or Kaaba (the black structure seen below), which contains a black stone dating from ancient times.

## THE FIVE PILLARS OF ISLAM

There is no god but Allah, and Muhammad is God's messenger

A formal prayer must be said five times every day, while facing the holy city of Mecca

Those who can afford it should give to the poor each year

Followers must fast during the month of Ramadan

Followers must make a pilgrimage to Mecca, if possible, at least once during their lifetime

### LAWS OF ISLAM

Islamic Law, or the Shariah, is very important to Muslims. It was laid down by early Islamic teachers and tells Muslims how they should live their lives. The holy book of Islam is the Koran (or Qur'an), said to be Allah's exact words, as told to Muhammad. A Muslim's main religious duties are the 'Five Pillars of Islam'– faith, prayer, almsgiving, fasting and pilgrimage.

### MUSLIMS AT PRAYER

The Muslim place of worship is called a mosque. Five times a day, criers known as *muezzins* call the people to prayer from minarets, or towers, on the mosques. Muslims do not have to go to the mosque to pray, except on Fridays, but can pray in any clean place.

## SEE ALSO

Middle East, Religion

# ISRAEL

Israel occupies a narrow strip of land in southwest Asia, on the eastern shore of the Mediterranean Sea. It makes up most of the area once called the Holy Land.

**Area:** 21,056 sq km
**Population:** 5,963,000
**Capital:** Jerusalem
**Languages:** Hebrew and Arabic
**Currency:** Shekel

▲ The Dome of the Rock shrine, sacred to Muslims and Jews, stands in East Jerusalem. It is on the site where Muhammad is said to have risen into heaven.

The hills of Galilee lie in northern Israel, while lowlands and fertile plains lie to the west. Most of the south is made up of the Negev Desert.

## SALTY SEA
The Jordan river flows along the country's eastern border from the north, into the Sea of Galilee and then into the Dead Sea. The Dead Sea is actually a lake and contains useful minerals, such as potash, used to make soap. The water is so dense that swimmers can float easily.

## WATERING THE LAND
Summers in Israel are dry and hot, while winters are cool. Irrigation schemes have brought water to dry land, making it lush with crops. On collective farms called kibbutzim, families live and work together growing fruit such as oranges – Israel is a major producer of citrus fruits. Other crops include vegetables, cotton and olives. Israel is a highly developed country, however, and about 90 per cent of Israelis live in towns and cities. Many of them work in factories or service industries.

▲ The Dead Sea is the saltiest body of water in the world. The salt crystallizes to form lumps in the water.

## THE HOLY LAND
Jews, Christians and Muslims all regard Jerusalem as a holy place. Its religious sites include the Wailing Wall, part of the Jews' holy temple from biblical times. When the Romans conquered the land and called it Palestine, most Jewish people were forced to leave. Modern Israel was founded in 1948 as a homeland for the Jews. Several wars between Jews and Palestinian Arabs followed, involving neighbouring Arab states. Today, some 900,000 Arabs live in Israel and an uneasy peace is maintained.

◀ Since 1993, Palestinians have had limited control over the West Bank and Gaza Strip. Jewish children attend separate schools.

### SEE ALSO
Asia, Christianity, Islam, Judaism, Middle East

# ITALY

As the seat of the Roman Empire and cradle of the Renaissance, Italy has been at the centre of European civilization for centuries.

**Area:** 301,318 sq km
**Population:** 57,589,000
**Capital:** Rome
**Language:** Italian
**Currency:** Lira, Euro

▲ ▼ Venice's annual carnival is a major event, and carnival-goers dress flamboyantly for the occasion. Boats known as gondolas are used for transport in Venice, where the main 'streets' are canals – the Grand Canal at the Rialto Bridge has been the scene of many regattas.

▲ Italy has many old and beautiful churches. Even a tiny country church, like this one in Siena, may have a priceless medieval wall painting or carving.

Some of the highest mountains in Europe, the Alps, tower across northern Italy. Another mountain chain, the Apennines, stretches from north to south. The independent state of San Marino lies at the bottom of Mount Titano in the Apennines – it is the oldest republic in Europe, founded in the 4th century, and has an area of just 61 sq km.

## POWER FROM WATER
Rushing mountain streams are used in hydroelectric schemes to provide much-needed power for a country with little coal or oil of its own. Italy's largest rivers, the Po, Arno and Tiber, are all in northern Italy, as are lakes Garda, Como and Maggiore. Southern Italy, which includes the islands of Sardinia and Sicily, is hotter and drier than the north.

## FOOD AND DRINK
Italy is the world's largest wine producer. Italian dishes vary from north to south, and range from veal in subtle, light sauces to seafood in rich, spicy tomato sauces. Italian recipes have inspired cooking around the world, and pizzas and pasta have become international dishes.

## AGRICULTURE
Many Italians are farmers. The major crop is wheat, used to make pasta and bread. Others are olives, grapes, maize and sugar beet. Cattle are reared mainly in the north, and many sheep and goats are kept on rough pasture in Sardinia and Sicily.

## INDUSTRIOUS NORTH
In northern Italy, industry is based around the cities of Turin, Milan and Genoa. Factories make a wide range of goods including motor vehicles, clothing, machinery and chemicals. Milan is particularly famous for its fashion houses, where clothes are designed. Many raw materials have to be imported and Italy has a large fleet of merchant ships.

## SPEAKING ITALIAN
Almost everyone in Italy speaks Italian, although a few communities speak another language – German is the first language of people

▲ Italy is rich in artistic treasures, spectacular buildings and historic remains such as those of the Colosseum, an ancient amphitheatre in Rome.

living near the Austrian border. Most Italians are Roman Catholics and the head of the Catholic Church, the pope, lives in Vatican City, in Rome.

## VATICAN CITY
Vatican City is the smallest independent state in the world, with an area of only 0.44 sq km. St Peter's Basilica stands at its centre. It was built during the fourth century and rebuilt in the 16th century.

## VARIETY FOR VISITORS
Tourism is one of Italy's main industries. Every year, millions of people visit the country to enjoy its peaceful countryside, sunny beaches, snow-capped mountains and historic cities such as Venice, Florence, Naples and Rome.

## ROME TO RENAISSANCE
Italy was where the Roman Empire was founded. Roman rule ended in AD476, but Rome remained the headquarters of the Roman Catholic Church. Italy broke up into smaller city states, and in the 15th and 16th centuries, it was the centre of the Renaissance. The country has produced explorers such as Marco Polo, artists such as Leonardo da Vinci and scientists such as Galileo.

## UNITING THE STATES
From the 1500s, France and Austria tried to control Italy. In the 19th century, Giuseppe Garibaldi and others led the fight to unite the Italian states. They drove out the Austrians and, in 1861, Italy became an independent and united kingdom.

## MODERN ITALY
During the 1920s and 1930s, the fascists, led by Benito Mussolini, held power. After World War II (1939–45), Italy held its first free election for 20 years and a republic replaced the monarchy. The country has prospered as a member of the European Union, despite having had many changes of government. Today, the south of Italy is poorer than the north, but as a whole, modern Italy is a major industrial nation.

▲ Modern opera began in Italy in the early 1600s, with the composer Claudio Monteverdi. Today, Italian singers such as Luciano Pavarotti are popular all over the world.

◀ Motorbikes are a popular form of transport with young Italians, meeting here at the Piazza del Popolo in Rome.

## SEE ALSO
Christianity, Europe, Renaissance, Roman Empire, Volcano

# JAPAN

Japan is an island country in northeast Asia, off the east coast of China. The Japanese call their country Nippon or Nihon, which means 'source of the Sun'.

**Area:** 377,829 sq km
**Population:** 126,410,000
**Capital:** Tokyo
**Language:** Japanese
**Currency:** Yen

By area, Japan is Asia's 18th largest country. Its largest island is Honshu, followed by Hokkaido, Kyushu and Shikoku. There are also thousands of small islands, such as the Ryukyu island chain.

▲ Today, Japan's leading industries include the manufacture of electrical goods such as televisions.

▲ Japan is a leading fishing nation. It supplies not only its own people but also many other countries.

▼ Many beautiful temples, like the Kinkaka Ji, with its spectacular gardens, can be found in Japan's former capital, Kyoto.

## ERUPTIONS AND EARTHQUAKES
Most of Japan is hilly or mountainous and the rivers are fast flowing, providing water power for making electricity. Japan's highest peak, Mount Fuji (3,776m), is a volcano which last erupted in 1708. More than 60 of Japan's volcanoes are active and earthquakes are also common.

## VARIED CLIMATE
The northernmost island of Hokkaido, just south of Russia's Sakhalin Island, is cool, and snow is common in winter, while Kyushu in the south is much warmer. Most of Japan has plenty of rainfall.

## PINK-FACED MONKEYS
Forests cover about two thirds of the land and many animals, including bears, wild boar, deer and foxes, live in them. Pink-faced monkeys called Japanese macaques live as far north as the northern tip of Honshu. They have long, thick fur and swim in hot springs in the snow to keep warm.

## FIRST ARRIVALS
The first people in Japan were probably descendants of a group of people called the Ainu, a few thousand of whom live in Hokkaido today. The ancestors of most modern Japanese people probably reached the islands from mainland Asia around 2,200 years ago. The country ranks seventh in the world by population.

## SHARED RELIGIONS
Over three quarters of the people live in crowded cities and towns. The largest city is Tokyo, and other large cities include Yokohama and Osaka, all situated on Honshu, where 80 per cent of the people live. There are two main religions in Japan: Shintoism (the oldest religion) and Buddhism.

## MEETING ITS NEEDS

Although it lacks natural resources, Japan is a wealthy country. Because it is so hilly, only about 15 per cent of the land is farmed. But Japan produces about 70 per cent of the food it needs. Rice is the leading crop and food. Fruit, sugar beet, tea and vegetables are also important.

## MADE IN JAPAN

Manufacturing is the most valuable activity, and Japan ranks second only to the United States among the world's top industrial countries. Its products are sold around the world and include chemicals, electrical goods and electronic equipment, iron and steel, machinery, ships, textiles, transport equipment and it produces more cars than any other country.

## POWERFUL NATION

Japan became a powerful nation in the late 19th century. It won some important battles against China in 1894 and defeated Russia in 1905. In 1937, it attacked China and, in 1941, it attacked the American naval base in Pearl Harbor, Hawaii. This act drew it and the USA into World War II.

## MOVING TO DEMOCRACY

In 1945, after the United States had dropped atomic bombs on Hiroshima and Nagasaki, Japan surrendered. The United States occupied Japan until 1952. During this time, Japan became a democratic country and the once all-powerful emperor became head of state with only ceremonial duties. The country is now ruled by an elected prime minister and government and is one of the world's great economic powers.

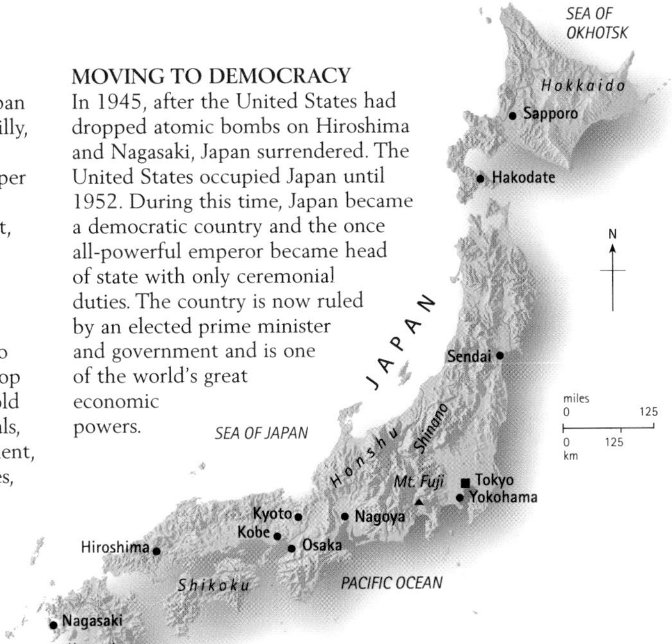

▶ Sumo, a Japanese style of wrestling in which opponents try to push each other out of a ring, is a popular national sport.

◀ Japan's bullet train, seen here against Mount Fuji, is one of the fastest in the world. It runs on the island of Honshu.

### SEE ALSO

Asia, Buddhism, China, Industry, Volcano, World War II

# JELLYFISH AND OTHER COELENTERATES

Jellyfish, sea anemones and corals belong to a group of animals called coelenterates. They all have soft bodies armed with stinging tentacles.

▶ Jellyfish move by pumping water backwards with their bodies.

A Portuguese man-of-war is not a true jellyfish. Like corals, it is a colony of animals living together.

The hydra is a freshwater coelenterate. It forms new buds that break off and grow into new animals.

Tube-shaped sea anemones attach themselves, with their sucker-like base, to rocks in the sea.

Coelenterates are invertebrates – which means 'no backbone'. In fact they have no trace of a skeleton at all – except for corals, whose soft bodies are surrounded by a hard limestone case. Coelenterates have no brains, but have simple nerves and muscles. The largest individuals are found among the jellyfish, which are nearly all umbrella- or bell-shaped animals with a mouth on the underside. There are about 250 different kinds. Most of them are no bigger than a saucer, but there are a few real giants, with bodies up to 2m across and tentacles as long as 70m.

## STINGING STRINGS

Most coelenterates use tentacles to catch prey. Even corals are carnivorous, using stinging cells on their tentacles to paralyze microscopic animals in the water. The stings of some jellyfish are very dangerous to swimmers. Those of the Australian sea wasp jellyfish can kill a person within a few minutes.

## ENTANGLING PREY

The jellyfish's tentacles are covered with potent stings and are used to catch and kill fish, prawns, and other small animals. The lion's mane jellyfish, here, has a 2-m body and tentacles reaching 40m. The tentacles pull the victim into the mouth, which is hidden under its bell-like body.

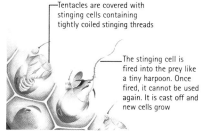

Tentacles are covered with stinging cells containing tightly coiled stinging threads

The stinging cell is fired into the prey like a tiny harpoon. Once fired, it cannot be used again. It is cast off and new cells grow

## A STICKY END

Some jellyfish have bodies covered with sticky slime that traps any small animals they bump into. Aurelia, the common jellyfish found washed up on beaches, uses stinging cells and then envelops its paralyzed prey in mucus.

## BREAKING UP

Jellyfish scatter eggs or tiny babies into the water, but these do not grow directly into jellyfish. The tiny creatures that hatch from the eggs of common jellyfish settle on a rock or seaweed and grow into cone shapes. They gradually divide until they look like piles of miniature saucers. Each saucer floats away and grows into a new jellyfish.

## SEE ALSO

Animal, Evolution, Ocean and sea

# JUDAISM

Judaism is the religion of the Jewish people. It teaches that there is one true God, who revealed himself to the Jews and has given the human race rules to live by.

The six-pointed star became a symbol of Judaism during the Middle Ages. It signifies the protection of God given to David, king of Israel, in about 970BC.

Jews believe that there is one eternal, invisible God who created the universe. There are about 18 million Jews living in Israel and all over the world.

## MOSES AND THE HEBREWS
The first followers of Judaism were the Hebrews of the Middle East. According to the Bible (Old Testament), the Jewish holy book, God promised Abraham and his descendants land to live in and protection around 1900BC. In about 1200BC, God sent Moses to lead the Hebrews out of slavery in Egypt. God revealed his teachings, about how to live and serve God, to Moses. These teachings are the basis of Judaism and are contained in the Torah, laws based on the first five books of the Bible. Later works, the Talmud, interpret the Torah. They tell people how to lead good lives and how to observe rituals.

## THE HOLY SABBATH
The Hebrews worshipped at the Temple in Jerusalem, but this was destroyed in a war with the Roman Empire in AD70. Modern Jews study their faith in buildings called synagogues. Here, they are guided by teachers known as rabbis. The most religious day of the week is the Sabbath, which lasts from sunset Friday to sunset Saturday. Jews cannot work on this day, because they believe that this was the day when God rested after creating the world.

Jewish women pray at Jerusalem's Western Wall (Wailing Wall), at the site of the ancient Temple.

Jews light a candle a day during the eight days of Hanukkah, to celebrate the rededication of the temple in 165BC.

▲ A rabbi preparing to sound the *shofar* (ram's horn) at Yom Kippur wears a *tallith* (prayer shawl).

## BAR MITZVAH
When a Jewish boy officially becomes a man, at the age of 13, the bar mitzvah ceremony is held. The boy reads from the books of the prophets during the Sabbath service. The service is often followed by prayers and a family celebration.

## KOSHER RITUALS
Jews observe various festivals, including Yom Kippur in September or October, when sins are confessed and forgiveness asked. At Passover, in March or April, the departure from Egypt is celebrated. Orthodox Jews have strict rules about what they eat, how their food is prepared and the way ritual objects should be treated. These rules are called kosher.

## PERSECUTION
For centuries, Jews have lived among other nations, which have sometimes persecuted them. During World War II, the Nazis murdered millions of Jews in what is called the Holocaust. After this, many Jews created a new homeland, Israel, in the area where the Hebrews lived. But they still face conflict with neighbouring states.

### SEE ALSO
Israel, Religion, World War II

# KANGAROO AND OTHER MARSUPIALS

**Marsupials are mammals that normally carry their babies in pouches. There are about 250 kinds, most of which live in Australia, New Guinea and the Americas.**

Koalas live in and feed off eucalyptus trees.

Common opossums live in Central and North America.

Wombats are nocturnal burrowing animals.

The Tasmanian devil is stocky with sharp teeth.

Kangaroos are the biggest of the marsupials, some of them reaching nearly 2m high. They are Australia's equivalent of the herds of antelope that live on the African plains. Kangaroos are not hoofed animals and they move by leaping instead of running, but they graze and browse like antelope and they have a similar head and jaws. Farmers do not like kangaroos because they eat the grass intended for sheep.

## ALL KINDS OF KANGAROO

There are about 60 kinds of kangaroo. The smallest are about the size of a rabbit and are called rat kangaroos. The middle-sized ones are often called wallabies. The red kangaroo and the grey kangaroo are the biggest species. They usually live in small groups called mobs. Although they are about as tall as a man when they stand upright, their young, called joeys, are only about 2.5cm long when they are born.

## THE LONG JOURNEY

A kangaroo is born blind and helpless, and looks more like a grub than a kangaroo. As soon as it is born it has to climb up to its mother's pouch, where it starts to feed and grow. It develops long back legs and a long tail, and by six months it is ready to leave the pouch for the first time.

## A WIDE VARIETY

Not all marsupials are grazers. Just like the mammals in other parts of the world, Australia's marsupials have adopted all sorts of habits. Possums and gliders live in the trees like monkeys and squirrels, while the koala is like a small bear. There is even a marsupial mole. There are also many carnivorous, or flesh-eating, marsupials, including the dog-like Tasmanian devil.

## EXTINCT SPECIES

The Tasmanian wolf, or thylacine, is another dog-like marsupial, but it has not been seen alive since 1936 and is probably extinct. Farmers hunted it because they thought it killed their sheep. Many other Australian marsupials have died out because they were killed by cats and dogs and other mammals introduced by man.

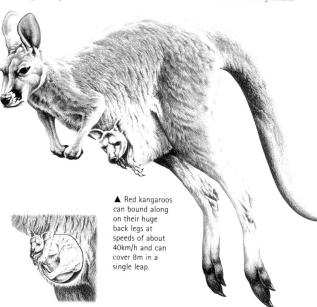
▲ Red kangaroos can bound along on their huge back legs at speeds of about 40km/h and can cover 8m in a single leap.

**1** The newly born kangaroo crawls over its mother until it reaches the security of the pouch.

**2** Inside the pouch, the baby suckles on its mother's milk and starts to grow rapidly.

**3** By six months, the joey is old enough to leave its mother's pouch, but it soon jumps back inside if danger threatens.

## SEE ALSO

Animal, Australia, Mammal, Zoology

# KIDNEY

The kidneys are vital organs that clean the blood by filtering out unwanted substances and excess water. These are then removed from the body as urine.

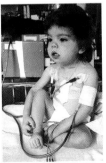

▲ A young girl whose kidneys are not working properly is given regular 'dialysis' treatment. This involves linking her up to a special machine called a hemodialyzer which filters out the waste materials in her blood. Once a suitable donor has been found, she can be given a kidney transplant.

Body processes, such as digesting food or burning energy, produce various waste substances. These are collected from all parts of the body by the blood system and are carried to the kidneys, where they are filtered out. The kidneys are the most important part of the body's excretory system, which is responsible for getting rid of, or excreting, liquid wastes.

## A MILLION MICRO-FILTERS

Inside each kidney are two layers. The outer layer – the renal cortex – contains about a million tiny filtering units, called nephrons. Each nephron has a tiny knot of microscopic blood vessels, or capillaries, called a glomerulus, which is surrounded by a double-layered cup – the glomerular, or Bowman's, capsule. As blood flows through the glomerulus, water, minerals, salts and wastes seep out into the glomerular capsule. These substances ooze from the capsule through a long, thin, U-shaped tube, called the nephron loop, or

loop of Henlé, which lies in the kidney's inner layer – the renal medulla.

## KEEPING USEFUL SUBSTANCES

Each nephron loop is surrounded by more capillaries, so that useful substances such as minerals and salts can pass from the loop back into the blood. A certain amount of water is also taken back, or reabsorbed. The amount depends on the body's water supplies and is controlled by chemical messengers called hormones.

## COLLECTING THE WASTES

The unwanted substances that are left form the urine. This trickles into larger tubes, or collecting ducts, and gathers in the renal pelvis – a space in the middle of the kidney. From here it dribbles into a tube called the ureter and is carried down to the bladder, a stretchy-walled bag in the lower body. The bladder empties by squeezing its muscular wall to force the urine along another tube, the urethra, to the outside.

## THE KIDNEYS AT WORK

The kidneys, which are bean-shaped, are positioned centrally in the rear of the body, on either side of the backbone. They receive blood via the renal arteries and, after the blood has been filtered, it is carried away by the renal veins. All the body's blood flows through the kidneys about 350 times a day – that's more than 1,700 litres! It is constantly cleaned and filtered to produce about 1.5 litres of urine each day.

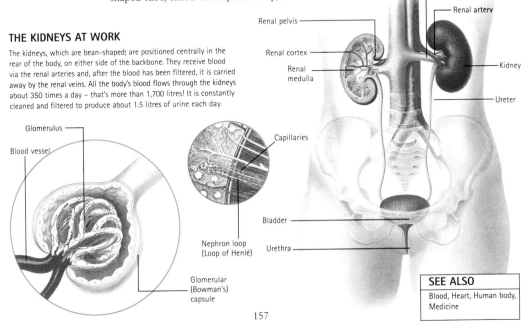

Glomerulus

Blood vessel

Capillaries

Nephron loop (Loop of Henlé)

Glomerular (Bowman's) capsule

Renal vein

Renal artery

Renal pelvis

Renal cortex

Renal medulla

Kidney

Ureter

Bladder

Urethra

### SEE ALSO
Blood, Heart, Human body, Medicine

# LANGUAGE

Language is how humans communicate with one another, either through speech, writing or sign language. It comes from the Latin word *lingua*, meaning 'tongue'.

▲ 'Happy New Year' written in a number of different languages.

Language started as a collection of sounds, arranged so that they mean something. Over thousands of years, people developed different languages and then organized the sounds into alphabets. An alphabet is a collection of signs that represent the sounds we use.

▲ The Rosetta Stone, found in Egypt in 1799, helped scholars to read Ancient Egyptian hieroglyphics (left) as the same inscription was written in three languages, including Ancient Greek.

## WORLD LANGUAGES
Today, there are between 4,000 and 5,000 languages in the world. Mandarin Chinese is the language spoken by the largest number of people. Next comes English, which is spoken in more countries than any other language. About 845 languages are spoken in India. People have tried to make up artificial 'universal' languages. The best known is Esperanto, invented in 1887, the most widely used international language.

## HOW LANGUAGES CHANGE
Languages constantly change. New words, such as 'Internet', come into use. Old words disappear, for example 'bombard', a cannon. Latin, the language of the Romans, is not spoken but people can read it. Words can also move from one language to another. English contains many such words, such as 'video' from Latin and 'planet' from Greek.

## LANGUAGE FAMILIES
Languages belong to families – groups of related languages which developed from an original parent language. English belongs to the Germanic branch of the large Indo-European language family, while French belongs to the romance branch.

**ABCDE**
Roman

ج ح ث ت ب ا
Arabic (read right to left)

**АБВГД**
Cyrillic (Russian)

**ΑΒΓΔΕ**
Greek

בגיד
Hebrew (read right to left)

▲ The first five written symbols (letters) of five different alphabets.

香氣治療
Chinese characters

▲ Chinese has no alphabet, but uses up to 50,000 characters, each of which represents an object or idea.

## SIGNS AND CODES
Language is not just confined to spoken or written words. Deaf people use sign language, while blind people read Braille, a special alphabet using raised dots. Even codes, such as those used by computers, are called languages.

◄ *The Tower of Babel* is the story of how people tried to build a huge tower to reach Heaven. God stopped it from being built by making everyone speak different languages so that they could not understand each other.

### SEE ALSO
Communication, Internet, Media

# LEAF

**Leaves use energy from sunlight to make food for plants and are themselves a source of food for animals. They also produce the oxygen we need to breathe.**

The horse chestnut has a compound leaf made up of separate leaflets.

Maple leaves are hand-shaped, or palmate, with no separate leaflets.

The ash leaf is made up of several pinnate (spindle-shaped) leaflets.

The cherry has a simple pinnate leaf with tiny saw-like serrations at the edges.

Pine needles are long, thin evergreen leaves that grow in clusters.

Leaves are the food factories of green plants. They come in a variety of shapes and sizes, and help us to identify the different species of plants. The branching pattern of veins on the surface of a leaf is part of a network of tubes that carry water and food to all parts of the plant. The large vein that runs across the centre of the leaf is called the midrib.

## MAKING FOOD

The main function of leaves is to make food for the plant. This process, known as photosynthesis, takes place in tiny bodies, called chloroplasts, in the leaf cells. These contain a green-coloured substance called chlorophyll that absorbs light energy. The energy is used to turn water and carbon dioxide gas from the air into food molecules, such as starch and sugar. The by-product of this process is oxygen gas, some of which is used by the plant for respiration. The rest passes into the air. Nearly all living things need oxygen to survive.

## TRANSPIRATION

Leaves also help the plant to draw water up from the soil, by a process called transpiration. As the water evaporates (dries) from tiny pores, or stomata, in the leaf's surface, more water is sucked up from the roots to replace it. Each pore is bound by two 'guard' cells that can open or close the opening to control water loss. The water moves up the stem through fine tubes called xylem vessels. Another set of tubes, the phloem vessels, carries food around the plant.

## LEAF DESIGN

Leaves are designed to catch as much sunlight and lose as little water as possible. Stiff veins hold the leaf out to the light, and cells are transparent so that light can reach the chloroplasts. The outer layer, or cuticle, is waterproof, and most of the stomata are on the underside of the leaf, shielded from drying breezes.

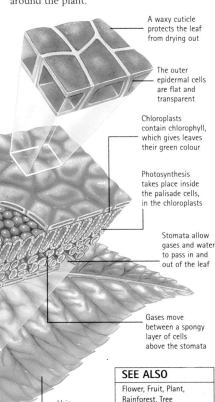

A waxy cuticle protects the leaf from drying out

The outer epidermal cells are flat and transparent

Chloroplasts contain chlorophyll, which gives leaves their green colour

Photosynthesis takes place inside the palisade cells, in the chloroplasts

Stomata allow gases and water to pass in and out of the leaf

Gases move between a spongy layer of cells above the stomata

Sunlight

Oxygen

Carbon dioxide

Midrib

Water

Blade

Vein

### SEE ALSO
Flower, Fruit, Plant, Rainforest, Tree

# LENS

Lenses are transparent objects with at least one curved surface that help us focus on an image by bending rays of light. They are usually made of glass or plastic.

Glasses help us see if our eye lenses don't work properly.

The lens in a camera focuses light onto the film inside.

Optical microscopes use lenses to magnify objects from 100 to 2,000 times.

Lenses in a pair of binoculars help you see things that are far away.

Some periscopes use lenses to enlarge the image reflected from the mirrors at either end.

When light travels through a lens, it slows down. This is because light travels faster through air than through other transparent substances like water, glass and plastic. As it slows down it bends off course. This effect, called 'refraction', is why a straw put in a glass of water at an angle looks bent. The bending distorts the image seen by the eye and can be used to make an object seem bigger or smaller.

## DISTORTED IMAGES
If you put a magnifying glass close to the page of a book, you'll see a larger-than-life version of the page below it. This happens

## BENDING LIGHT
There are two kinds of simple lens: convex (or converging) lenses which enlarge the image and concave (or diverging) lenses which are thicker at the edges than the middle and reduce the image.

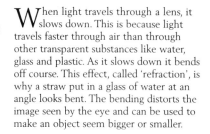
Focal length – distance from lens centre to the focus

Actual image

Virtual image

Virtual image

Virtual image

Actual image

**CONVEX LENS**
Rays of light passing through the lens are bent inwards. A magnified image is produced behind the object.

**CONCAVE LENS**
Light rays are bent outwards, so they spread out (diverge) producing a reduced image between the object and the lens.

▶ A magnifying glass has a convex lens — a lens that's thicker at the middle than the edges. The image seen depends on how close you hold the glass.

because light rays from the page have been bent away from each other by the lens. Light rays from distant objects are bent towards each other by a magnifying glass. If it's dark enough, you can catch these rays on a sheet of paper. If you put the paper the right distance from the lens, they will form a focused (sharp) image.

## GETTING FOCUSED
The distance from the lens to the piece of paper is called the 'focal length' of the lens. In general, a thick lens bends light more than a thin one, so it has a shorter focal length. A camera uses a convex lens to produce sharp images on a sheet of film. Specialist cameras also use concave lenses – that are thicker at the edges than the middle. These are used to reduce large images, like landscapes, onto a photograph.

## EYE LENSES
Our eyeballs act like giant convex lenses that focus (bend) light onto the backs of our eyes. The muscles of our eyes pull the lenses flatter when we want to focus on objects in the distance, or make the lenses thicker to help us focus on nearby objects.

**SEE ALSO**
Astronomy, Light, Microscope, Sight

# LIGHT

Light is a visible form of energy. It moves faster than anything else in the universe, travelling 300,000,000 metres in a single second. Without light we cannot see.

▲ The Moon has no light of its own – it shines only because it reflects the Sun's light. Stars, however, are luminous because they produce their own light.

**SIR ISAAC NEWTON**
The English scientist and mathematician (1642–1726) demonstrated that light was broken into different colours by shining light through a prism.

The Sun, our nearest star, is our main source of light. Although it is nearly 150 million kilometres away, the light it makes reaches the Earth in only eight minutes and is so strong that it damages our eyes if we look straight at it. At night, when our part of Earth faces away from the Sun, we have to use light bulbs or candles for light. Compared to the Sun, the light energy made by these is tiny. They can only light up objects a few metres away.

## CASTING SHADOWS

Light can travel through air, water and other transparent (see-through) materials. Unlike sound, it can also travel through a vacuum, or empty space. Materials that only allow some light through, and are not transparent, are said to be translucent. Many

▲ When light shines through a prism (a glass triangle), it splits into the colours of the spectrum.
▶ This also happens when light shines through water (rain) causing a rainbow.

materials, like wood and metal, are opaque – they block light. If you shine a light at an opaque object, you will see a dark patch behind it – the shadow. This has exactly the same outline as the object because light travels in straight lines.

## INVISIBLE ENERGY

There are many other types of energy, including radio waves, microwaves and X-rays, that travel just like light. In fact, light is only one tiny part of a huge range of energy forms, called the electromagnetic spectrum. Over the last 100 years, people have built a variety of machines, such as scanning equipment, microwave ovens and radios, that can detect or make use of the invisible parts of this spectrum.

▲ There are two basic ways to produce artificial light: through heat (known as incandescence), as in an electric light bulb, or by making a gas glow, as in a fluorescent light.

▲ Glow worms, the glowing larvae of fireflies, have light organs under their abdomen which produce a heatless light known as bioluminescence.

▶ Many deep-sea fish have similar light organs on their sides to help them find food and mates in the dark.

## SEE ALSO

Colour, Electricity, Energy, Lens, Microscope, Moon, Sun

# LUNGS AND RESPIRATORY SYSTEM

The lungs are two pinkish-grey, spongy, cone-shaped organs inside the chest. The respiratory system consists of the nose, throat, windpipe, lower airways and lungs.

Breathing in    Breathing out

▲ When breathing in, the rib cage expands and the diaphragm is lowered. These actions happen in reverse when breathing out.

### FAST FACTS

• Adult lungs hold three to five litres of air

• At rest, an average person takes about 12-15 breaths each minute. Each breath consists of about half a litre of air

• After great activity, the breathing rate can rise to 60 breaths per minute with over three litres of air per breath

Oxygen is essential for almost every living thing, including the human body. When we breathe in, our lungs take in fresh air, absorb oxygen from it and pass it to the blood, which carries it to all the parts of the body. Fresh air is taken into the lungs by breathing, or respiration. This process is powered by two sets of muscles – the diaphragm below the lungs and the intercostal muscles between the ribs, in front of the lungs.

### IN AND OUT

To breathe in, the diaphragm tenses, shortens and flattens. The intercostals also shorten and pull the ribs upward and forward. These movements stretch the lungs, making them larger, and suck fresh air in through the nose and mouth, down the throat and windpipe, into the lungs. To breathe out, the diaphragm relaxes and the stretched lungs spring back to their normal size, pushing stale air out.

### OXYGEN IN

Dark bluish-red, low-oxygen blood flows to each lung along the pulmonary artery. This divides many times to form a vast network of microscopic blood vessels, or capillaries, which enclose tiny balloons called alveoli. Oxygen from the air inside each alveolus seeps easily through its thin lining and the thin capillary wall, into the blood. This makes the blood bright red. The capillaries join to form the pulmonary vein, which carries the high-oxygen blood away.

### CARBON DIOXIDE OUT

In addition to taking in oxygen, the respiratory system also removes one of the body's waste products, carbon dioxide. This seeps the opposite way to oxygen – from the blood into the alveolus – and is breathed out as stale air.

Pulmonary vein

Oxygen-rich blood flows away from the lung

Pulmonary artery

Oxygen-poor blood flows to the lung

Bronchiole

Alveolus lining

Alveoli

Capillaries

Alveoli cluster

Air intake

Windpipe (trachea)

Upper lobe of lung

Bronchus

Lower lobe of lung

### INSIDE THE LUNGS

Air flows along the windpipe into a branching system of tubes called bronchi. These divide many times, becoming smaller and thinner. Deep in the lungs they form very fine tubes, or bronchioles, each of which ends in a tiny clump of microscopic air sacs, called alveoli. There are over 350 million alveoli in each lung.

### SEE ALSO

Blood, Heart, Human body, Muscle

# MACHINE

**A machine is a device that makes work easier by enabling us to use force to complete a task. It can be simple, like a screwdriver, or complicated, like a car.**

Corkscrews make use of screw and lever actions. The screw's spiral thread gives a tight grip.

A pair of scissors is a double lever. The screw is the fixed point or fulcrum; the blades pivot around it.

A can opener acts as a wedge, forcing its way into the lid while cogged wheels turn the cutter.

Simple machines make work easier and can be used as parts of more complex devices. There are six main types of machine: the lever, pulley, and wheel and axle (which are all forms of levers), and the screw, inclined or sloping plane, and wedge (all forms of inclined planes).

## BASIC MACHINES

By using a lever, you can increase the effect of the force, or effort, you apply. The machine needs a fulcrum (a fixed point) to support it. By positioning the fulcrum carefully, a small effort applied at one end of the lever, can raise a big load at the other end. Heavy weights can be moved using an inclined plane (pushing goods up a ramp is easier than lifting them), or on rollers, like the logs used by pyramid builders to move slabs, or by a wheel turning on an axle.

## MAGNIFIED FORCE

A screw can either pull things together or push them apart (like a jack). A pulley system uses wheels to change the direction of a force produced by pulling on a rope. The wedge (an axe, for example) can be used to split materials.

## RAISING THE LOAD

The simplest type of pulley is a wheel with a grooved rim. A rope or chain is passed around the groove. The pulley changes the direction of a force, so by pulling down on the rope, a person can raise a heavy weight. The more pulleys there are with one rope running through them, the greater the load that can be lifted with the same effort.

## THE FIRST MACHINES

The potter's wheel, invented around 3500BC, was one of the earliest machines. Others include the spindle, for spinning fibres into yarn; the loom, for weaving yarn into cloth; the plough, for turning heavy soil; and bellows, for blowing air into fires.

## WAR AND WORK

Early war inventions include the battering ram (a wedge), and the catapult (a lever). An important development of the wheel was the gear. A gear wheel combines the principles of wheel and lever. As it turns, its teeth, or cogs, mesh with other toothed wheels. In this way it can change the speed and direction of the force applied, depending on the number and spacing of the teeth.

## INVENTIVE PAST

The Ancient Greeks used screws, lathes (used for turning wood), construction cranes and watermills – the first machines to use non-animal power. They discovered that steam could be used to drive machines. But neither the Greeks nor the equally inventive Chinese were interested in labour-saving machines, because slaves were cheap and plentiful. ▶

Pulley wheels

Having four wheels allows four times the load to be lifted with the same effort

—— Effort

Load ——

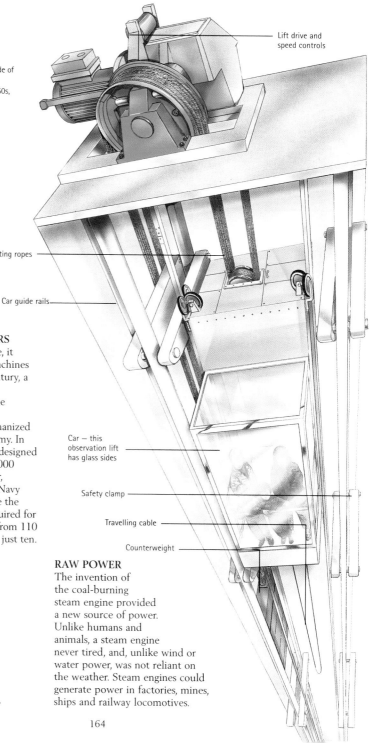

Lift drive and speed controls

## TAKING THE STRAIN

Lifts can be hydraulic or operated by electric traction, like the one here. Hoisting ropes, made of steel cables, are raised or lowered by a pulley wheel, turned by an electric motor. In the 1850s, engineer Elisha G. Otis invented the first lift featuring an automatic safety device – a safety clamp – which would prevent the lift from falling if the rope broke.

## MEDIEVAL MACHINES

Important mechanical inventions of the Middle Ages included the crossbow, windmill, clockwork and the printing press. In the 13th century, the English monk Roger Bacon predicted the use of cars, aeroplanes and submarines long before the technology and materials required for such inventions were even available.

Hoisting ropes

Car guide rails

## MACHINES REPLACE WORKERS

As labour became more expensive, it made economic sense to make machines do more work. From the 18th century, a new kind of mechanized industry developed. In the United States, the Federal Armory in Springfield, Massachusetts, pioneered the mechanized manufacture of muskets for the army. In Britain, the engineer Marc Brunel designed 43 machines that could make 10,000 pulley-blocks a year, enabling the Royal Navy dockyard to reduce the workforce required for the task from 110 to just ten.

Car – this observation lift has glass sides

Safety clamp

Travelling cable

Counterweight

▲ From the invention of the potter's wheel, someone got the idea for the cartwheel. Fitted with pots, a wheel could also raise water from one level to another, for irrigation.

## RAW POWER

The invention of the coal-burning steam engine provided a new source of power. Unlike humans and animals, a steam engine never tired, and, unlike wind or water power, was not reliant on the weather. Steam engines could generate power in factories, mines, ships and railway locomotives.

## THE FACTORY AGE

To make machines for manufacture, machine tools were needed to stamp out metal plates, cut screws and gears, and shape metals by cutting, drilling, grinding or polishing. Standardization of parts made it easier to keep machines working and repair them quickly. Important new inventions included the dynamo, the electric motor, and the hydraulic press and ram. The clothing and shoe-making industries were transformed by the sewing machine, invented in 1846.

## THREAT TO JOBS

The use of machines in industry greatly increased output and made factory goods cheaper. But there was a human cost. Workers, including women and children, toiled for low pay in bad conditions. In the 1880s, social critics like the Englishman William Morris complained that machines were destroying craftsmanship, reducing people to a form of slavery. Some people smashed machines they thought would take away their work.

## WORK REVOLUTION

The machine revolution affected farming, where machines took over harvesting, baling and threshing. Transport and trade were revolutionized in the mid–1800s by the locomotive, steamship and conveyor belt. Machines invaded offices and shops, at first in the form of typewriters and cash registers.

## THE MODERN WORLD

New machines, such as the car and the aeroplane, began to transform the world at the beginning of the 20th century. The invention of the jet engine and the rocket allowed people to travel at speeds that had been unimaginable before. In the home, ancient devices like the butter churn and the washboard were discarded, and the washing machine, vacuum cleaner and the food processor took pride of place. In industry, robots and increasingly efficient computers took over many basic production processes. New materials, such as plastic, ceramics and carbon fibres, are today replacing metals to make machines that are smaller, yet more efficient.

▲ Car jacks can be manual (like the screw car jack above) or hydraulic. They are machines that are designed to raise and support a heavy load, like a car, little by little. By turning a handle many times, the operator applies a small force pushing a long way; this force is converted to pushing a large force (the car) a short way.

▶ A forklift truck is a machine that raises weights using liquid pressure (hydraulics). Simple hydraulic machines have a cylinder with a large and a small piston inside. The cylinder is filled with fluid. A force applied to the small piston is transferred to the larger one, increasing the force.

◀ A snowblower has two engines: one drives the truck, the other turns the drum. As it turns, blades on the drum churn the snow, forcing it upward through the chutes. As the truck moves forward, it takes in more snow.

## SEE ALSO

Engine, Industrial Revolution, Industry, Invention

# MAGNETISM

Magnetism is a force that pulls objects made of iron, nickel or cobalt towards magnets. Scientists do not fully understand how this force is created.

▶ Industrial electro-magnets are powerful enough to lift heavy pieces of scrap iron.

The horseshoe magnet has a pole at each end.

So does the simple bar magnet.

A ring magnet has one pole on its outer surface and another pole on its inner one.

If you have ever moved a magnet towards a pin, you have experienced magnetism. Pins are made of steel – a material that consists mainly of iron – and they feel a strong force pulling them towards the magnet, which may even be strong enough to make them stick to it. Any material, like steel, that is attracted towards a magnet in this way is called a magnetic material.

## MAGNETIC POLES

When an object is attracted to a magnet, it sticks to its ends – this is where the magnet exerts, or gives out, the greatest force. The two ends of the magnet are called its poles. One of them is north-seeking and the other is south-seeking. They need to be marked in some way so you can tell them apart. If you bring the same poles of two magnets face to face, they will repel each other; if you bring different poles of two magnets face to face, they will attract each other.

## ELECTRO-MAGNETISM

In 1820, a Danish physicist, Hans Christian Oersted, discovered that magnetism was produced by an electric current. This led to the development of the electromagnet – a temporary magnet formed when an electric current passes through a conductor such as wire, which is wrapped around an iron core. Electromagnets are useful because they can be turned on or off and altered in strength. They can produce magnetic fields strong enough to drive generators and electric motors. Smaller ones are used to make doorbells and buzzers work.

## MAGNETIC EARTH

The Earth itself acts like a huge magnet with magnetic poles at its north and south ends – known as the magnetic north pole and the magnetic south pole. These poles act like the ends of a magnet and make compass needles point north. They are close to the geographic North and South Poles, which are at the top and bottom of the imaginary line, or axis, around which the earth spins.

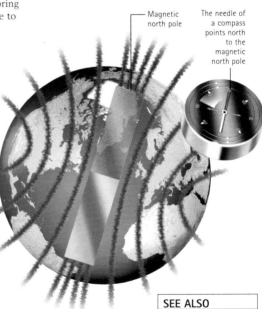

Magnetic north pole

The needle of a compass points north to the magnetic north pole

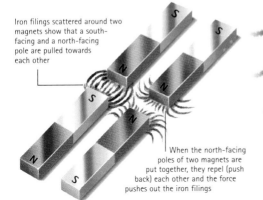

Iron filings scattered around two magnets show that a south-facing and a north-facing pole are pulled towards each other

When the north-facing poles of two magnets are put together, they repel (push back) each other and the force pushes out the iron filings

## SEE ALSO

Antarctica, Arctic, Earth, Electricity, Iron and steel, Metal

# MAMMAL

Mammals are vertebrates (they have backbones). They have adapted to a wider range of habitats and show a greater variety of forms than any other animal group.

Orang-utans are one of about 180 primates. This group includes humans.

The bat is the only mammal that can fly. Its forelimbs act as wings.

There are about 250 types of marsupial, mostly found in the Australian region.

Flesh-eating mammals like the hyena have strong teeth called canines.

Marine mammals like the seal have short fur and streamlined bodies.

The duck billed platypus is one of only three species of egg-laying mammal.

A ll mammals are warm-blooded, which means they can keep their bodies warm and stay active even in the coldest weather. The only other animals that can do this are birds. Most mammals are covered with hair or fur, which helps keep them warm. Unlike other animal babies, young mammals feed on their mother's milk. Mammals also have larger brains than other animals.

### A SUCCESSFUL GROUP
The first mammals appeared on Earth about 200 million years ago as small, insect-eating creatures. When dinosaurs died out about 65 million years ago, mammals began to explore different habitats and try different foods. They became larger and took on many different shapes. Thousands of 'experimental' mammals have come and gone during the last 50 million years, but only about 4,200 different species live in the world today.

### VARIETY OF HABITAT
Mammals are not as numerous as birds or fish, but they can be found in almost every

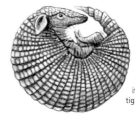

◄ The armadillo is covered in bony plates that protect it from predators. When attacked, it curls up into a tight ball.

habitat: some live in seas and rivers; some spend their lives high up in the trees of the forest; antelopes and other grazing mammals form huge herds on grasslands. Some mammals manage to survive in the driest deserts and on the coldest mountain tops. Bats have taken to the air; seals, whales and dolphins to the seas.

### THE RIGHT TEETH
Mammals eat a wide range of foods and most have teeth designed to suit their diets. Most plant-eating mammals (herbivores), such as horses and elephants, have large grinding teeth at the back of the mouth. Rodents have sharp, chisel-like front teeth for gnawing nuts and other hard foodstuffs. Flesh-eating mammals (carnivores), such as lions and wolves, have large, sharp canines for stabbing and seizing prey, and sharp-edged cheek teeth for slicing off flesh.

### CARE OF THE YOUNG
Young mammals learn many of their survival skills during the period that they are with their mother, feeding on her milk. At birth, lion cubs are blind and helpless, weighing only about 1.5kg. The mother carries them in her mouth, one at a time, from one hiding place to another; the male protects his family from intruders. Only when the cubs are between 18 and 24 months old will the lioness have another litter.

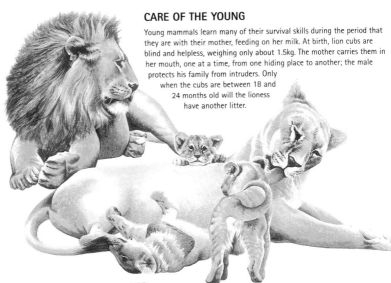

## MAMMAL OF THE DESERT

The two-humped Bactrian camel of central Asia is well adapted to life in the desert. It can travel for days or even weeks with no food or water because it carries a large store of fat in its humps, which it converts into food. At the end of a long period without food, the humps lose much of their firmness, and may even flop to one side. With its bushy eyebrows and long lashes, the camel can shield its eyes from the sand. It can even close its nostrils during a sandstorm. A close relative of the Bactrian camel is the Arabian camel, or dromedary, which has only one hump.

**COVERED IN FUR**
One of a mammal's main characteristics is its fur. A Bactrian camel's fur can grow to 25cm on its head, neck and humps. Camels grow a new coat once a year.

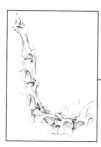

**NECK BONES**
All mammals, apart from the manatee and sloth, have seven cervical vertebrae (bones that make up the neck).

**A MOTHER'S MILK**
Mammals are the only animals to feed their young with milk – produced in special glands called mammae.

## LICKING AND SIFTING

Omnivorous mammals, which include humans, eat plants and animals. Insect-eaters, such as shrews and hedgehogs, have lots of small, sharply pointed teeth, but anteaters have no teeth at all: they lap up ants with their sticky tongue. Some whales have no teeth: they sift tiny creatures from the water through plates of horny material called baleen or whalebone.

## EGGS AND POUCHES

A tiny number of mammals, such as the duck billed platypus, are unusual because they lay eggs. Others, called marsupials, are also known as pouched mammals, because the female nurses her babies in a pouch or pocket on her body. About 50 million years ago, marsupials lived all over the world, but they are now found mainly in the Australian region, with a few in North and South America. All other mammals, known as placental mammals, give birth to live young.

## THE LARGEST GROUP

Placental mammals are by far the biggest group of mammal. While the baby is inside its mother, it gets food and oxygen from her blood through a structure called the placenta. A placental mammal baby can stay inside its mother's body for much longer than a marsupial baby. A baby elephant, for example, grows inside its mother for about 22 months and is well developed when it is born. Some baby mammals can run about soon after they are born, but many others, including human babies, are quite helpless at birth.

### FAST FACTS

• With their relatively large brains, mammals have a greater ability to learn than other animals

• Special mammal senses include the bat's sonar and the mole's ultra-sensitive whiskers

• The largest mammal is the blue whale, which grows up to 30m long

### SEE ALSO

Animal, Cat, Dog, Horse, Kangaroo, Monkey, Rat, Tiger, Whale and dolphin, Zoology

# MAP

Maps show the Earth, or a part of it, on paper. They may show travellers a route, or they may display weather patterns, land use and other information.

A pedometer is used to measure distance.

A theodolite gives the direction of distant objects.

Stereo viewers give a 3-D image from aerial photos.

From the earliest times, people have drawn sketch maps to describe a route or place. Only in the past 400 years has science made it possible to draw accurate maps of the entire world.

## CHARTS IN CLAY

The first maps were drawn on clay tablets about 2300BC in Mesopotamia. They showed nearby towns and how to reach them, but were not at all accurate. In about AD140 the scientist Claudius Ptolemy produced a book on geography which contained many maps. Soon afterwards, the Roman army produced a map of cities and forts based on accurate measurements of the roads in between.

## SEA CHARTS

The European sailors who travelled to other continents from the 1450s onwards needed charts that included information such as depth of the sea, strength of currents and how best to enter a harbour.

## READING THE MEANING

Maps may contain many different types of information. The most familiar maps are those showing road and rail routes for travellers. Scientists may create maps showing how many people live in different areas, what land is used for, or the types of soil to be found. Maps showing temperatures and air conditions are used for weather forecasting. All maps rely on accurate surveying, the collecting of information by people on the ground and the transferring of this to the maps.

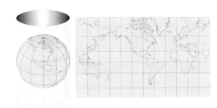

▲ Maps using Mercator's projection, invented in 1569, allow sailors and pilots to plot their course accurately, but distort areas close to the North and South Poles.

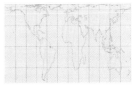

► Maps using Peter's projection, developed in 1973, give accurate areas but distort shapes.

Modern charts contain similar information, together with locations of lighthouses and radio beacons.

## MAPS TO SCALE

Cartographers (map makers) often use computers to draw maps. Most maps are made to a scale, meaning that distances on the map are related to distances on the ground. A map of scale 1:100,000 means that 1cm on the map equals 100,000 cm, or 1km, on the ground. Some maps are deliberately inaccurate. For example, a map of a motorway does not need to show corners or distances, but only which towns can be reached from each exit.

▲ Relief maps show physical features, such as rivers, plains, hills and mountains.

▲ Here, population density is shown by colours. Dark colours are the areas with the most people.

▲ Route maps may show roads, railways and built-up areas to help travellers find their way.

| SEE ALSO |
| --- |
| Navigation |

# MAYA

The Maya Indians dominated Central America from about AD250 to AD850, building cities deep in the rainforest. Their descendants still live in the region.

The Maya were great astronomers and carved dates of religious ceremonies on stones.

Maya people wrote using glyphs (picture symbols) to show sounds of words or to convey ideas.

The Maya were among the most highly developed civilizations in Central America. Their achievements in art, architecture and mathematics were outstanding. That is why it is a mystery that their civilization collapsed so suddenly.

## MIGHTY MAYA

The first Maya lived in city states, probably led by priest kings. Evidence of these states dates back to around AD250 with stone pillars erected by the rulers to record their achievements. Within a few generations, the Maya were building vast cities, such as Tikal (now in Guatemala) with populations of up to 50,000 people. These spread across the Yucatán Peninsula south to the Pacific Ocean. This was known as the Classic era.

## WEALTH FROM THE EARTH

The wealth of the Maya was based on trade and farming. As early as 1500BC, people in the area were growing maize, the basic

▲ Modern Maya selling their wares at a market on the steps of a church in Guatemala.

food of the Maya. The seeds were often boiled, but were also ground into a powder to make a porridge. Maya farmers grew tomatoes, runner beans, avocados and sweet potatoes. They had no farm animals, but hunted wild game and fish. Most people lived in forest huts, only coming into the city for markets or religious ceremonies.

## SCIENCE OF THE STARS

Mayan priests learned how to calculate the solar year, lunar months and even the movements of the planet Venus. For these calculations, the Maya developed complex mathematical skills and used writing more skilfully than any other American peoples.

## DEATH OF A CULTURE

In about AD800, some of the southern cities began to be abandoned; historians are not sure why. By AD950, most of the great cities had collapsed. People continued to live in their homeland, but in villages. There was a revival around 1200, then, in the 1500s, the Maya were conquered by Spanish invaders.

## MAYAN MONUMENTS

With only stone hand tools, the Maya managed to build great pyramids and palaces. The Castillo pyramid in Chichén Itzá reached 30m above the ground. Chichén Itzá survived longer than most Mayan cities – it was inhabited until about 1440.

The Castillo is 55m square at the base

Four staircases each had 91 steps. These, plus the step at the temple entrance, added up to 365 – the number of days in the Mayan year.

SEE ALSO

Mexico

# MEDIA

The media are the channels through which news and views are publicized. They include radio, television, newspapers, magazines, teletext and the Internet.

▲ Paparazzi photographers spy on celebrities and take photographs for international papers and magazines.

The media offer a window on the world, bringing events from other countries close to home. Media can be printed (newspapers, magazines or books), broadcast (on radio, television or cinema) or electronic, such as the Internet. It can be aimed at informing and entertaining, or advertising something or someone.

## CENSORSHIP

News put out through media can affect public opinion. Some governments try to censor the media, others use them for propaganda. The freedom of the press to print or broadcast what it likes, so long as it is true, is an important civil right. In democratic countries such as the USA, there are laws to protect the press from pressure to print a particular thing. A free press can question the actions of a government and make it difficult for dictators. Most dictators or one-party states allow only news favourable to themselves to be broadcast.

## CONTROLLING THE MEDIA

Usually the media are owned by private businesses. Reporters or programme-makers may do as they please, as long as their work fits in with the style and tone of the programme or publication, which may support a particular political party.

## MEDIA INFLUENCE

Companies and personalities may try to influence what appears in the media by offering gifts, trips or parties. Journalists may also be threatened with being sued for libel or having access to events withdrawn if unpleasant stories are broadcast.

## COVERING AN EVENT

A news event will be covered in different ways by the various media: newspapers send a reporter and photographer; radio shows may have just one broadcaster with an outside broadcast unit; television needs visual images and sound.

### Game, set and match to Rusedski

British tennis ace Greg Rusedski wowed spectators with his powerful style on court yesterday to win through to the finals.

By JANE SMITH

CANADIAN-BORN Rusedski beat his opponent 6-0, 6-4 in straight sets, then faced a gruelling fifth set when he eventually took match point on 14-12.

GIRLFRIEND IN CROWD
Rusedski's girlfriend Lucy Connors was among the crowd cheering ecstatically on centre court. He now heads Britain's hopes to take the Grand Slam.

### NEWSPAPER
A reporter and photographer will go along to a match to record results and comments from players.

### TELEVISION
Television coverage of a news event demands camera operators, sound technicians and a commentator on site.

### RADIO
Results are given during a radio news bulletin, while sports programmes are recorded live from events.

### THE EVENT
Major sports attractions, such as the Wimbledon or the US Open tennis tournaments, give press passes to TV and radio stations and accredited journalists.

## SEE ALSO

Internet, Television

# MEDICINE

Medicine is the scientific study of human disease. It covers the causes, prevention, diagnosis and treatment of all types of different illnesses.

The name of the Ancient Greek Hippocrates (c.460–377BC) lives on in the Hippocratic Oath, a code of principles for doctors.

The Greek physician Hippocrates is often called the 'founding father of medicine'. He examined patients and recorded their symptoms. He also prescribed many remedies, including willow bark tea – later shown to be the source of aspirin. But medicine could not progress in a scientific way until doctors understood how the body works.

## UNDERSTANDING THE BODY

The 16th-century Belgian anatomist Andreas Vesalius was the first to show where bones, muscles, blood vessels and organs were situated in the body. Then William Harvey (1578–1657), a British doctor, discovered that the blood was pumped around the body by the heart. When 19th-century scientists showed that microbes (microscopic organisms such as bacteria) could cause disease, medicine began to progress as a modern science.

French chemist Louis Pasteur (1822–95) invented pasteurization – a process of killing germs in liquids such as milk.

## MAKING A DIAGNOSIS

The identification, or diagnosis, of a disease begins with the doctor taking a history of the illness. This includes asking about symptoms, previous illnesses and details of the patient's lifestyle. Then the doctor carries out a physical examination. This may include listening to the sounds

English surgeon Joseph Lister (1827–1912) introduced antiseptics into surgery, reducing the risk of bacterial infection.

Alexander Fleming (1881–1955) was a British bacteriologist who discovered the antibiotic drug penicillin.

### MILESTONES IN MODERN MEDICINE

**1905** First blood transfusion

**1922** Frederick Banting and Charles Best first treat a diabetic patient with insulin

**1928** Discovery of penicillin by Alexander Fleming

**1938** First artificial hip replacement

**1943** First renal dialysis or artificial kidney machine

**1955** Polio vaccine introduced by Jonas Salk

**1967** First heart transplant operation done by Dr Christiaan Barnard in Cape Town, South Africa

**1979** World declared free of smallpox following worldwide vaccination programme

**1981** First cases of AIDS diagnosed

of the patient's chest and abdomen with a stethoscope, feeling organs such as the liver, and looking into the eyes, ears and throat with special instruments. Most illnesses can be diagnosed from the history and physical examination alone. The doctor may also send blood, urine and other samples to a hospital laboratory for testing. Sometimes the patient will need to have an X-ray or a scan. These create pictures of the inside of the body which can give a better idea of what is wrong.

## MEDICAL TREATMENT

Most illnesses are treated by drugs or surgery. There are around 6,000 drugs available today, including painkillers, antibiotics, anti-cancer drugs and drugs

◀ Computer technology is widely used in the development of new drugs. Here, a 'virtual reality' system is being used to create a 3-D image of a drug, which can then be manipulated by the researcher.

for mental illness. Surgery is often used in the treatment of heart disease and cancer to remove or repair diseased tissue. It is now also possible to replace major organs such as the heart, lungs, kidneys and liver by transplant surgery.

## PREVENTATIVE MEDICINE
Prevention is always better than cure. Doctors and nurses use what they know about the causes of disease to help stop patients getting ill in the first place. Smoking is known to cause both heart disease and lung cancer, so the medical profession tries to discourage patients from smoking. Smokers can attend anti-smoking clinics, for example, and there are health warnings on cigarette packets. People can also look after themselves by eating a healthy diet, exercising, getting enough rest and having regular check-ups. Vaccination protects people from diseases such as polio.

## ALTERNATIVE TREATMENT
There are also complementary or alternative medicines, which take a different approach to healing. Acupuncture comes from the Chinese medical tradition. It depends upon balancing the body's life-force, or *chi*, which flows along invisible channels in the body called meridians. During treatment, an acupuncturist uses needles to help the chi flow more freely. This and other alternative medicines, such as reflexology, homeopathy and aromatherapy, are popular with patients, although their effects may not be scientifically proven.

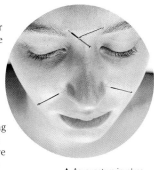

▲ Acupuncture involves thin metal needles being inserted into selected points in a patient's body. In China, where the technique originated, it is used as an anaesthetic during surgical operations.

## VIEWING THE BODY IN CROSS-SECTIONS

One of today's fastest and most accurate forms of imaging (to help diagnosis) is the computerized tomography (CT) scanner, which creates a 'virtual reality' image of the patient's body. The patient is moved slowly through the scanner, inside which an X-ray source rotates around the body. A ring of detectors relay the information to a powerful computer for processing. The information is then displayed on screens on the main console as a series of cross-sections, or slices, through the patient's body.

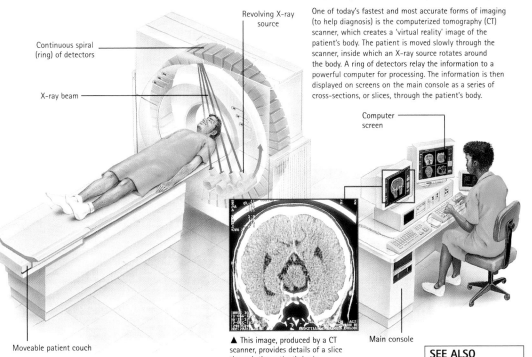

Revolving X-ray source

Continuous spiral (ring) of detectors

X-ray beam

Computer screen

Moveable patient couch

▲ This image, produced by a CT scanner, provides details of a slice through the patient's brain.

Main console

### SEE ALSO
Disease, Drug, Human body, Nutrition, X-ray

173

# METAL

**A metal is a shiny material such as iron, gold or copper. Most are solid at room temperature, easy to shape when hot and good at conducting heat and electricity.**

▲ Metals can be joined by welding – the application of heat, pressure or both. Here an electrical current is being used to heat steel in a process called arc-welding.

▼ Aluminium alloys are used in aircraft construction because they are light but strong.

The Earth has a huge supply of some metals such as tin and iron – used to make tools, machines and large structures. Other metals, such as gold and platinum, are rare. They are usually used in small quantities.

## WORKING WITH METAL
People have known how to extract and use metals since about 8000BC. If a metal is heated until it becomes molten (liquid), it can be poured into a mould. As soon as it cools, it hardens and keeps its shape until melted again. Metals can also be hammered into any shape or pulled into long strands. Most solid metals are very strong and hard, which is why they are used to make things like building frames and engine parts that have to keep their shape when put under pressure.

## METALS THAT RUST
If something made of iron is left outside, it will go rusty. This is because the surface of the iron reacts with oxygen in the air to form a new compound – iron oxide. Many other metals react with oxygen or other elements, so are not found in their pure state in the ground. Instead, they are found as ores – compounds of metal and oxygen. A common way of extracting metal from oxide ores is to heat them with charcoal to remove the oxygen, leaving the pure metal.

## ALLOYS
People have discovered many ways to mix metals with each other, and with non-metals, to make useful materials. These mixtures are called alloys. Steel is an alloy made from iron and small amounts of carbon and other metals. It is harder and stronger than pure iron. Bronze is a hard alloy made from copper and tin.

## METAL FATIGUE
You need a large force to break a lump of metal apart in one go. But some metal objects break when bent many times by a small force. This way of breaking a metal, called metal fatigue, can be a real hazard. Machines like aeroplanes that must not fail are checked for signs of metal fatigue.

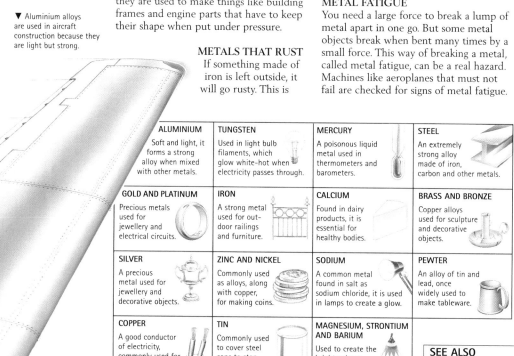

| ALUMINIUM | TUNGSTEN | MERCURY | STEEL |
|---|---|---|---|
| Soft and light, it forms a strong alloy when mixed with other metals. | Used in light bulb filaments, which glow white-hot when electricity passes through. | A poisonous liquid metal used in thermometers and barometers. | An extremely strong alloy made of iron, carbon and other metals. |
| **GOLD AND PLATINUM** | **IRON** | **CALCIUM** | **BRASS AND BRONZE** |
| Precious metals used for jewellery and electrical circuits. | A strong metal used for out-door railings and furniture. | Found in dairy products, it is essential for healthy bodies. | Copper alloys used for sculpture and decorative objects. |
| **SILVER** | **ZINC AND NICKEL** | **SODIUM** | **PEWTER** |
| A precious metal used for jewellery and decorative objects. | Commonly used as alloys, along with copper, for making coins. | A common metal found in salt as sodium chloride, it is used in lamps to create a glow. | An alloy of tin and lead, once widely used to make tableware. |
| **COPPER** | **TIN** | **MAGNESIUM, STRONTIUM AND BARIUM** | |
| A good conductor of electricity, commonly used for electrical wiring. | Commonly used to cover steel cans to stop them rusting. | Used to create the bright colours in fireworks. | |

**SEE ALSO**

Iron and steel, Mineral and gem

# MEXICO

Mexico, North America's third largest country, lies between the United States to the north and Central America to the south.

▲ At Christmas, children try to burst a hollow papier-mâché *piñata*, full of sweets.

**Area:** 1,958,201 sq km
**Population:** 95,846,000
**Capital:** Mexico City
**Language:** Spanish
**Currency:** Mexican peso

In north and central Mexico, mountain ranges called *sierras* enclose a high plateau. This plateau, the country's most thickly populated region, contains active volcanoes. Mexico's highest peak, Mount Orizaba (5,700m), also called Citlaltepetl, is a dormant volcano.

### DESERTS AND FORESTS
Seven tenths of Mexico has little rainfall. The north is largely desert, but rainforests grow in the south. Temperatures vary according to the height of the land. Acapulco on the coast is much warmer than Mexico City, which is 2,300m above sea level. Mexico City was built on the site of the ancient Aztec capital founded around 1325.

▲ Tourists visit Mexico to see ancient ruins such as the Great Pyramid and *Chac-mool* figure in the Yucatán Peninsula.

### MESTIZOS
Many Mexicans are *mestizos*, of mixed European and Native American origin. Most white people are descendants of Spaniards who arrived in Mexico in 1519. Spanish is the official language but some Mexicans speak Native American languages. Most Mexicans are Roman Catholics and about three quarters of the people live in cities and towns.

### TRADE AND FOOD
Mexico is rich in minerals, including silver, while oil, gas and oil products are the main exports. Factories also produce chemicals, clothing, iron and steel, processed food and vehicles. Food crops include maize (used to make flour for traditional pancakes called *tortillas*), beans, rice and wheat. Coffee, cotton, vegetables and fruits are also important.

### MODERN TIMES
Mexico became independent from Spain in 1821. It lost land to the United States in the Mexican War (1846–48) and this war ruined Mexico's economy. There were revolutions between 1910 and 1921, but since then Mexico has been mainly at peace. Poverty has led many people to enter, illegally, Mexico's rich neighbour, the United States, in search of jobs.

◀ Cattle are reared in the northern part of Mexico's plateau, where there is little rainfall.

### SEE ALSO
Aztecs, Maya, Native Americans, North America

# MICRO-ORGANISM

Micro-organisms are tiny living creatures that cannot be seen without a microscope. They can be bacteria, viruses, protists (protozoans), or tiny algae or fungi.

The Ebola virus is long and worm-like in shape. It is often deadly.

Yeast cells are fungi and can be used to ferment alcohol and make bread.

A colony of rod-like, food-poisoning bacteria growing on cooked roast beef.

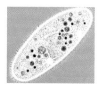

*Paramecium* protists are abundant in water and soil and feed on bacteria.

Many varieties of single-celled algae form colonies in or on top of water.

Bacteria are single-celled specks of living matter, mostly well under one hundreth of a millimetre long. There are three main shapes: rods, spheres and spirals. Bacterial cells differ from other cells because their DNA, which controls all living things, floats free through the cells instead of being contained in a nucleus. They get food and energy by breaking down all kinds of living or dead substances and, unlike most other living things, many of them can survive without oxygen.

## GOOD AND BAD
Bacteria reproduce by simply splitting into two. This can happen every 15 minutes in good conditions, so bacteria exist in huge numbers. Many bacteria cause illnesses, including tuberculosis, cholera and food-poisoning. These are often called germs or microbes. But not all bacteria are harmful. Some help to keep the soil in good condition, while others can be used to manufacture yoghurt and other foodstuffs.

## PROTISTS

Protists are single-celled organisms in which the DNA is wrapped up in a nucleus near the cell's centre. They live everywhere, especially in watery surroundings. The best known members of the group are amoeba, which continually change shape as they move. Some live harmlessly in water and swallow bacteria by simply flowing over them. Others live inside animals and cause illness. Many protists cause illnesses such as malaria and sleeping sickness.

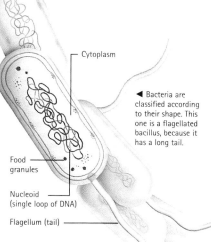

Cytoplasm

◄ Bacteria are classified according to their shape. This one is a flagellated bacillus, because it has a long tail.

Food granules

Nucleoid (single loop of DNA)

Flagellum (tail)

## VIRUSES
Viruses are even smaller than bacteria. On the border between living and non-living things, most consist of a piece of DNA inside an envelope of protein. Viruses can form crystals like salt and other chemicals, and can survive in this state for a long time. But they can reproduce only when they get inside other living things. In such cases, the DNA of a virus invades the cells, forcing them to make more viruses. All viruses therefore cause disease in other living things. Human illnesses caused by viruses include measles, AIDS and the common cold. Prions are even smaller than viruses and have only recently been discovered. BSE, or mad-cow disease, is thought to be caused by prions.

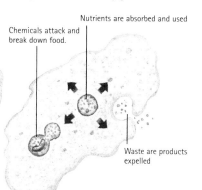

Nutrients are absorbed and used

Chemicals attack and break down food.

Waste are products expelled

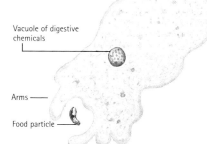

Vacuole of digestive chemicals

Arms

Food particle

## SEE ALSO
Cell, Disease, Fungi, Genetics, Microscope

# MICROSCOPE

Microscopes are instruments that magnify tiny objects or reveal fine details on larger objects. They have opened up a whole world that is invisible to our eyes.

▲ In an electron microscope, the electrons are invisible, so a fluorescent screen is used instead of an eyepiece.

An electron scan (x20) of velcro, used as a clothes' fastener, showing the nylon hooks and loops.

The first microscope was made by the Dutch spectacle-maker Zacharias Janssen in 1609. The first scientist to see bacteria was the Dutchman Anton van Leeuwenhoek, who made his own microscopes in the 1670s. The first microscopes were optical, which means that the object, or specimen, being studied was viewed through an eyepiece. For this to work, the specimen needed to be thin enough to let light through.

## ELECTRON MICROSCOPES

Electron microscopes were first used in the 1930s. Instead of light, they use a beam of electrons controlled by magnetic fields. Electron microscopes are very powerful and can show details 1,000 times larger than optical microscopes can. However, the specimen must be dried out

A false-colour electron scan (x200) of a sweat pore from a blister on the palm of a man's hand.

## OPTICAL MICROSCOPES

In an optical microscope, light shining through an object is bent as it passes through a lens. This makes the object appear much bigger. Adding a second lens makes the magnification even greater. Optical microscopes with several lenses are called compound microscopes and can magnify things by up to about 2,000 times their real size.

and sliced very thinly (about a thousandth – the thickness of this page). In addition, the air must be removed from inside an electron microscope and from around the specimen, as electrons are easily scattered.

## OTHER MICROSCOPES

Scanning electron microscopes move a beam of electrons over the surface of the specimen. The electrons that bounce off are collected to make an image. Scanning probe microscopes and atomic force microscopes were invented in the late 1980s. They can magnify a million times, showing up individual atoms. An extremely sharp probe moves over the surface of the specimen, 'feeling' its shape in tiny detail. A computer turns signals from the probe into a 3-D image, which is displayed on a television screen.

An electron scan (x 500) of individual fibres that make up a single thread of cotton.

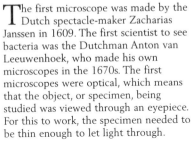

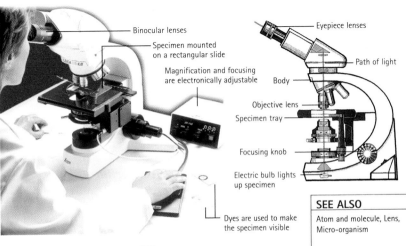

Binocular lenses
Specimen mounted on a rectangular slide
Magnification and focusing are electronically adjustable

Eyepiece lenses
Path of light
Body
Objective lens
Specimen tray
Focusing knob
Electric bulb lights up specimen
Dyes are used to make the specimen visible

An electron scan (x1,300) of human hairs protruding from the surface of the scalp (coloured pink).

### SEE ALSO
Atom and molecule, Lens, Micro-organism

# MIDDLE AGES

The Middle Ages was the period in European history which began in about AD750 and ended in the 1400s with the dawn of the period known as the Renaissance.

► During the 1400s in France, Christine de Pisan wrote for a living — this was unusual in an age when few people, particularly women, knew how to read and write.

Society was divided into three estates: the clergy and the nobility ...

... and the third estate, made up of farm workers, traders and craftsmen.

Following the collapse of the Roman Empire in the 5th century AD, western Europe was overrun by pagans (non-Christians). By 1400, Europe shared a common Christian culture and was about to begin centuries of expansion through exploration, trade and conquest.

## EMPEROR AND POPE
In 800, Charlemagne, king of the Franks, was crowned emperor by the pope. This was an attempt to reunite Europe under a Christian ruler. The power of pope and emperor dominated the Middle Ages.

## FEUDAL SOCIETY
In this period, Europe was divided into many kingdoms, dukedoms, bishoprics and other states. The source of most wealth was farmland. The feudal system of controlling land and people was developed in France in the 10th century. Kings gave land to lords

and knights in return for military services. Each lord had to swear fealty (loyalty) to his overlord. The lord's land was farmed by peasants, who paid him in labour and surplus crops. The Church also held a lot of land and many monasteries used their wealth to encourage learning and the arts.

## A VIOLENT PERIOD
After the defeat of invading Vikings, Muslims and Avars, the rulers of Europe fought each other for power and wealth. The Hundred Years' War (1337–1453) was fought between the kings of England and France over who should rule France. The Habsburg family of Austria and the Hohenzollerns of Germany fought long wars to conquer new lands.

## TRADE AND INDUSTRY
After about 1100, Europe became increasingly wealthy. Merchants and craftsmen formed guilds – organizations that imposed regulations and controlled prices. They helped spread skills and encourage trade between regions. By 1400, a growing number of people were working in manufacturing and trade.

## MEDIEVAL BANQUETS

The wealthy lords and ladies of the Middle Ages held banquets for special occasions. These formal meals began early in the day — around 10 or 11am — and continued for several hours. Guests ate with their fingers or with knives and spoons (forks had not yet been invented). The food included a great many meat dishes and was often heavily spiced.

### SEE ALSO
Castle, Renaissance, Roman Empire

# MIDDLE EAST

The Middle East is a group of countries in southwest Asia lying between Africa and Europe. It has great economic importance and is an area of unrest.

**AFGHANISTAN**
**Area:** 652,090 sq km
**Population:** 25,051,000
**Capital:** Kabul
**Languages:** Pashtu and Dari
**Currency:** Afghani

**BAHRAIN**
**Area:** 694 sq km
**Population:** 643,000
**Capital:** Manamah
**Language:** Arabic
**Currency:** Bahraini dinar

**CYPRUS**
**Area:** 9,251 sq km
**Population:** 753,000
**Capital:** Nicosia
**Languages:** Greek and Turkish
**Currency:** Cyprus pound

**IRAN**
**Area:** 1,633,188 sq km
**Population:** 61,947,000
**Capital:** Tehran
**Language:** Farsi
**Currency:** Rial

**IRAQ**
**Area:** 438,317 sq km
**Population:** 22,328,060
**Capital:** Baghdad
**Language:** Arabic
**Currency:** Iraqi dinar

Much of the Middle East is desert, with rugged mountain ranges in eastern Turkey, Iran and northern Afghanistan. Afghanistan contains the region's highest peak, Nowshak (7,485m), in a range called the Hindu Kush. Most people live along the coasts, in inland valleys or around oases.

## ANCIENT RIVERS

The main rivers, the Tigris and Euphrates, rise in Turkey and flow through Syria and Iraq. They join to form a river called the Shatt al Arab, which empties into the Persian Gulf. The world's first city-states were founded along these rivers in Mesopotamia, by a people called the Sumerians, in around 3500BC. The Middle East's most famous inland body of water is the Dead Sea, which lies in a deep valley between Israel and Jordan. Its shoreline is the world's lowest point on land, 400m below sea level.

▲ The Elburz mountains run along Iran's northern border close to the Caspian Sea, and make up one of the Middle East's many mountain ranges.

## RAIN, SNOW AND DESERT

The areas with the highest rainfall are in the northeast: the Turkish city of Istanbul has an average rainfall of more than 800mm a year, while Saudi Arabia's capital Riyadh has only 80mm. Snow falls on the mountains and temperatures drop below freezing in winter. The desert plains are hot. Few plants grow in the deserts, though date palms flourish around oases. ▶

▼ The Middle East has been transformed by the discovery of oil. In Kuwait, the oil industry provides jobs for women as well as men.

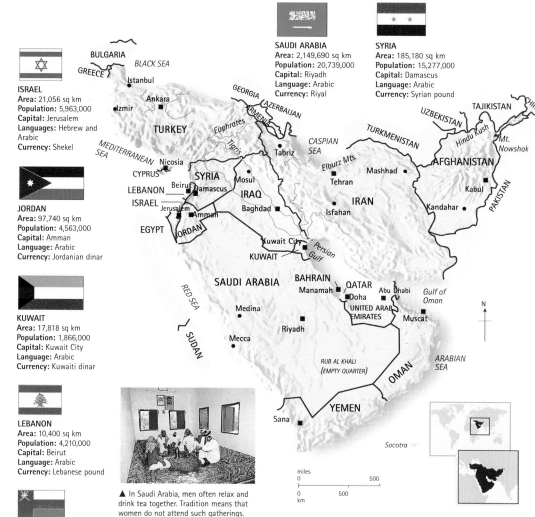

**ISRAEL**
Area: 21,056 sq km
Population: 5,963,000
Capital: Jerusalem
Languages: Hebrew and Arabic
Currency: Shekel

**JORDAN**
Area: 97,740 sq km
Population: 4,563,000
Capital: Amman
Language: Arabic
Currency: Jordanian dinar

**KUWAIT**
Area: 17,818 sq km
Population: 1,866,000
Capital: Kuwait City
Language: Arabic
Currency: Kuwaiti dinar

**LEBANON**
Area: 10,400 sq km
Population: 4,210,000
Capital: Beirut
Language: Arabic
Currency: Lebanese pound

**OMAN**
Area: 212,457 sq km
Population: 2,302,000
Capital: Muscat
Language: Arabic
Currency: Omani rial

**QATAR**
Area: 11,000 sq km
Population: 742,000
Capital: Doha
Language: Arabic
Currency: Qatar riyal

**SAUDI ARABIA**
Area: 2,149,690 sq km
Population: 20,739,000
Capital: Riyadh
Language: Arabic
Currency: Riyal

**SYRIA**
Area: 185,180 sq km
Population: 15,277,000
Capital: Damascus
Language: Arabic
Currency: Syrian pound

▲ In Saudi Arabia, men often relax and drink tea together. Tradition means that women do not attend such gatherings.

## DESERT ANIMALS

In some areas, nomadic tribes herding camels, goats and sheep move around in search of pasture. The best-known animal of the Middle East is the camel, which can go for long periods without water. Another desert animal, the Arabian oryx, once lived throughout the Arabian peninsula and in Lebanon, Iran and Iraq. By 1972, it was extinct in the wild because people had overhunted it in their cars. Arabian oryxes bred in captivity have now been released in Oman and are increasing in number.

## PEOPLE AND RELIGION

Many of the people of the Middle East are Arabs and Arabic is their chief language. There are also Afghanis, Armenians, Greeks, Iranians, Jews, Kurds and Turks. The Middle East was the birthplace of Judaism, Christianity and Islam, and all three religions regard Jerusalem in Israel as a holy city. Muslims also make pilgrimages to Mecca and Medina in Saudi Arabia. Islam is now the main religion, although Christians live in Cyprus and Lebanon, and Judaism is the chief religion in Israel.

◀ In cities such as Damascus in Syria, hand-crafted goods are sold at markets called *souks*.

## MIDDLE EASTERN WARS

The boundaries of many countries in the Middle East were fixed after World War I (1914-18). Israel was created in 1948, leading to a number of Arab-Israeli wars. Civil war occurred between rival religious and political groups in Lebanon between 1975 and 1991, while Cyprus has been divided since 1974 into a Turkish-speaking Muslim area and a Greek-speaking Christian area. Another conflict involves a people called the Kurds, who live in parts of Armenia, Iran, Iraq, Syria and Turkey. They are fighting to have their own country, Kurdistan.

**SADDAM HUSSEIN**
Saddam Hussein (born in 1937) became Iraq's president and prime minister in 1979. He led Iraq into a war with Iran which lasted from 1980 to 1988. In 1990, Iraq invaded Kuwait, but an international force drove the Iraqis out during the Gulf War in 1991.

## HOW PEOPLE LIVE

Until about 50 years ago, most people lived on farms or in farming villages. Today, three fifths of the people live in cities and towns. The largest cities are Istanbul in Turkey and Tehran, capital of Iran. Many cities have tall modern buildings as well as older areas.

## OIL POWER

The region's chief resource is oil, and Saudi Arabia has about a quarter of the world's known oil reserves. Other leading oil producers are Iraq, Iran, Kuwait, Oman, Qatar and the United Arab Emirates. Bahrain also depends on oil exports. Money from oil sales has been used to build new cities and roads, and to develop new industries to make oil products such as chemicals and plastics.

## INDUSTRY AND FARMING

Iran and Turkey have many other industries, while Israel, the most developed country in the Middle East, is known for its aircraft, electrical goods, electronics, precision instruments and textiles. About two fifths of the people are employed in agriculture. Barley, citrus fruits, cotton, sugar cane and wheat are leading products.

▶ Kuwait's water towers are part of a desalination plant, where fresh water is produced by removing salt from sea water.

**TURKEY**
**Area:** 774,815 sq km
**Population:** 63,451,000
**Capital:** Ankara
**Language:** Turkish
**Currency:** Turkish lira

**UNITED ARAB EMIRATES**
**Area:** 83,600 sq km
**Population:** 2,724,000
**Capital:** Abu Dhabi
**Language:** Arabic
**Currency:** Dirham

**YEMEN**
**Area:** 527,968 sq km
**Population:** 16,599,000
**Capital:** San'a
**Language:** Arabic
**Currencies:** Rial

**SEE ALSO**

Asia, Christianity, Europe, Islam, Israel, Judaism, Oil

# MINERAL AND GEM

Minerals are the natural elements or compounds that make up rocks in the Earth's crust. Gems, metal ores, sand, salts and even talc are all forms of minerals.

Jade is a hard, often green, semi-precious gemstone that can be carved to form fine ornaments.

Turquoise ranges in colour from blue to grey-green. Sky blue specimens are popular as gems.

The gem opal shows a characteristic play of colours, known as opalescence.

There are over 3,000 different minerals, but only 30 of them make up the majority of rocks, soils and sand on Earth. Some minerals form glassy crystals, others are like brightly coloured rocks. They vary in colour, density and hardness, and also in their ability to reflect light, and conduct heat or electricity.

## MINERAL COMPOUNDS

Some minerals, such as gold, consist of one pure element. Many others are made up of two or more elements, combined to form a compound. The most common mineral – quartz – is a combination of silicon and oxygen. Most grains of sand are quartz, which is used for making glass.

## MINERAL ORES

Many mineral compounds contain metals. The mineral hematite, for example, is iron oxide, and galena is lead sulphide. Minerals such as these, from which the metals can easily be removed, or extracted, are called ores, and are widely mined.

## FORMING CRYSTALS

Many minerals form distinct three-dimensional shapes called crystals. The shapes are the result of the neat arrangement of atoms and molecules inside the mineral. Minerals that produce fine, hardwearing crystals that can be cut and polished to a beautiful finish are called gemstones.

## PRECIOUS GEMS

Gems are most commonly worn as jewellery. They include diamonds, rubies, sapphires and emeralds. Diamonds, which are incredibly hard, are also used in industry and mining for drilling, cutting and grinding. Industrial-grade diamonds can now be made artificially.

### SCALE OF HARDNESS

An Austrian scientist, Friedrich Mohs (1773–1839), devised a scale to grade the hardness of minerals. His scale ranges from grade 1 for talc, the softest, to grade 10 for diamond, the hardest.

On Mohs' scale, a fingernail rates as 2.5, a copper coin as 3.5 and a steel penknife as 5.5.

## A SELECTION OF MINERALS

Galena has a metallic grey colour and forms cubic crystals. It is the main ore of lead, and is commonly found with quartz.

The iron ore hematite often forms kidney-shaped lumps, which earns it the name kidney ore.

Talc (magnesium silicate) is the softest mineral on Mohs' scale. It is widely used as talcum powder.

Gold is a soft, malleable (easily worked) metal which has been used since ancient times to make jewellery.

Malachite is a copper ore, well known for its bright green colour. It is often granular, and rarely forms crystals.

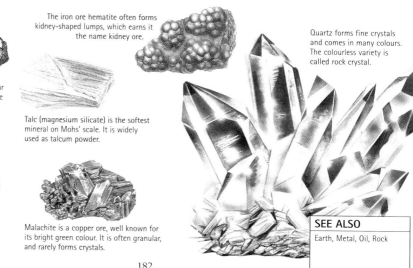

Quartz forms fine crystals and comes in many colours. The colourless variety is called rock crystal.

### SEE ALSO
Earth, Metal, Oil, Rock

# Money

Money is used to buy things or to save wealth for future needs. Money may take the form of notes, coins, or anything accepted as payment.

Before there was money, trade took place through barter, the exchange of one commodity or service for another. Barter only works if the person with one item wants what the other has to offer. Money allows people to sell things for money, then swap the money for what they want. It also makes borrowing possible, so that exchanges can be spread over time.

Native Americans used beads and shells made into decorative patterns.

## BEADS TO COINS

Many things have served as money. Useful products, such as salt or knives, have been used, as have decorative beads or even natural items such as shells or cattle. Coins made of precious metal and stamped with a design to show how much metal they contain were probably invented in Lydia (part of modern Turkey) around 700BC.

The Ancient Chinese used bronze cast into spade, knife and other shapes.

## PROMISES TO PAY

Paper money is not valuable itself, but is a promise to pay real money. It was invented in China in around AD1000. Until the 20th century, notes could be exchanged for gold. Most modern notes represent promises made by a bank or government, as do cheques or credit cards.

Coins are popular as they are easy to produce and last a long time.

Paper money began as promises by banks to pay a certain amount of coins.

Credit cards and cheques are convenient substitutes for cash.

▶ In 1923, German money lost value rapidly. Money became so worthless that bundles of notes were used as toys.

## MAKING COINS

Coins are made from metals such as bronze or copper, which are stamped with a design showing how much they are worth and which country produced them. An artist draws the design on paper.

The design is engraved, in reverse, onto metal dies.

The metal for the coins is melted into thin sheets

Round 'blanks' are cut from the metal sheet.

The dies stamp the coin design onto the blanks.

## THE MEASURE OF WEALTH

Money can be used to store and measure wealth, but the value of money is not stable. Wars may cause governments to collapse, so that their money becomes worthless. If a government prints too many notes, or allows excessive borrowing, the money loses value and inflation occurs.

## HIGH FINANCE

Large sums are lent and borrowed by governments and large companies in the money markets. Brokers and banks arrange loans or sell shares allowing businesses to grow and trade.

| SEE ALSO |
| --- |
| Metal |

# MONKEY AND OTHER PRIMATES

Monkeys and apes belong to a group of mammals
known as the primates, which also includes lorises,
lemurs and bushbabies, as well as human beings.

Monkeys differ from apes in having a
tail, although this is sometimes very
short. Both have their eyes at the front of
the head, giving them human-looking
faces. They are intelligent creatures with
good brains, and they learn quickly. They
live in family groups or larger colonies and
spend a lot of time grooming each other
and looking after their babies. Apes are the
nearest living relatives of human beings.

The woolly monkey is a New World monkey.

## LIFE IN THE TREES
Monkeys and apes are very active and
nimble animals, with excellent eyesight.
Except for the South American night
monkey, or douroucouli, they feed in the
daytime and sleep at night. Most of them
live in the trees, where they can run along
branches and swing from branch to branch
with amazing ease. They grasp branches
with hands and feet, and some South
American monkeys can even hold on to
the branches with their tail. Baboons, the
largest of the monkeys, live mainly on the
ground, although they usually sleep in the
trees at night. With their pointed muzzle
and large teeth, they look more like
domestic dogs than monkeys.

The South American spider monkey uses its tail as an extra hand.

## TWO MONKEY GROUPS
There are about 130 kinds, or species, of
monkey, nearly all of which live in the
tropical and subtropical parts of the
world. They fall into two main groups –
the New World monkeys of South and
Central America and the Old World
monkeys of Africa and
Asia. New World
monkeys, which include
the little tamarins and
marmosets, have a

The Old World colobus monkey rarely comes down from the trees.

The mandrill is one of the largest Old World monkeys.

▲ Ring-tailed lemurs walk on the ground holding their
long tail up in the air. The word lemur means 'ghost', a
name derived from the weird cry of some species.

broad nose with the nostrils facing to the
sides. Old World monkeys have a narrower
nose with the nostrils pointing downwards.

## THE BIGGEST APE
Thirteen different kinds of ape live in the
forests of the Old World; no apes are
found in the Americas. The gorilla, the
chimpanzee and the bonobo, or pygmy,
chimpanzee live in Africa. Weighing up to
200kg, the gorilla is the largest and
strongest of all the primates. It usually
walks on all fours, with its knuckles on the
ground. Gorillas are not the fierce
creatures that people once thought them
to be. In fact, they live peacefully in the
forest in small family groups.

◄ Baboons live in close family
groups called troops. Like other
monkeys and apes, the female
carries her babies until they are
old enough to look after
themselves.

▲ An adult chimpanzee, closely observed by its young,
uses a stick as a tool to probe for termites. Chimpanzees
are among the most intelligent apes, able to imitate
humans and solve simple problems.

## INTELLIGENT CREATURES

Chimpanzees look like small gorillas, but usually have a paler face. They live in large communities, often with over 100 individuals. They are probably the most intelligent of the apes, often using simple tools to help them find food.

## ORIENTAL APES

The orang-utan and the nine species of gibbon live in Southeast Asia. Orang-utans reach up to 1.3m when standing upright, and their bodies are covered in rather sparse, reddish-brown hair. Gibbons are small apes, rarely weighing more than 6 or 7kg, and they are wonderful acrobats. They use their very long arms to swing and leap through the branches at high speed. Unlike chimps, gibbons and orang-utans rarely come down to the ground.

## FAMILY LIVING

Gorillas live in family groups, or troops. Each group is made up of one or more males and several females with their young. The group is ruled by a large mature male, known as a silverback because of the silver-grey hairs on his back. Gorillas are vegetarian, eating a diet consisting mainly of leaves and shoots but also of bark, stems, roots and fruit. They may live for up to 37 years.

## VEGETARIAN DIETS

Monkeys and apes are basically vegetarian, although they often eat insects and other small animals. Chimpanzees even catch monkeys and small antelopes. Fruit is plentiful at all times of the year in the tropical areas and is the main food of most monkeys and apes. The gorilla and a few monkeys feed mainly on leaves and shoots.

## OTHER PRIMATES

Bushbabies, lorises and lemurs have smaller brains than monkeys and apes, and are often called 'lower' primates. Their snouts are more pointed than those of most other primates. They live mainly in the trees and feed mostly on fruit, leaves or insects. Bushbabies live in tropical Africa and lorises in southern Asia. Both are active at night and have very large eyes. Lemurs are found only on the island of Madagascar, off the east coast of Africa.

▲ The loris is a slow-moving primate that lives in Southeast Asia. It has huge, forward-pointing eyes and broad grasping hands and feet.

▲ The orang-utan is an endangered species. Special rehabilitation centres in Sumatra and Borneo care for young animals and introduce them back into the wild.

### SEE ALSO
Animal, Conservation, Mammal

# MOON

The Moon is the Earth's only natural satellite. Its diameter is 3,476km and it lies at an average distance of 384,400km from the Earth.

Crescent Moon (waxing)

Half Moon (first quarter)

Full Moon (appears round)

Half Moon (Last Quarter)

Crescent Moon (waning)

The Moon shines because it reflects light from the Sun. The phase of the Moon (how much of its surface we can see) depends on the position of the Moon in its orbit.

## SOLAR ECLIPSE

Sometimes the Moon passes exactly between the Earth and the Sun. When this happens, there is a total solar eclipse and, for a few minutes, the Sun's bright disc is blotted out. Since the Moon takes exactly the same time (27.3 days) to complete one orbit of the Earth as it does to spin around once on its axis, it always keeps the same side facing towards us.

## BLEAK AND LIFELESS

The Moon is a bleak place with no atmosphere which means there is no weather – no clouds, rain, nor wind. There is no life, although ice has now been found on the dark side. The Moon consists mostly of solid rock with a small central core of molten rock or iron. A thin layer of dust covers its surface. During the day, the surface temperature may climb to 127°C (more than the boiling point of water), but at night it can plunge to as low as –173°C.

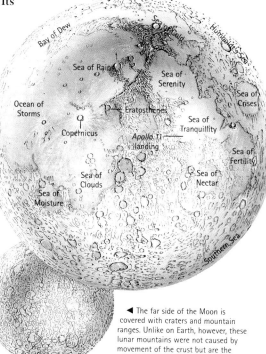

Bay of Dew · Sea of Gold · Humboldt's Sea · Sea of Rains · Sea of Serenity · Sea of Crises · Ocean of Storms · Eratosthenes · Sea of Tranquillity · Copernicus · Apollo 11 landing · Sea of Fertility · Sea of Clouds · Sea of Nectar · Sea of Moisture · Southern Sea

◄ The far side of the Moon is covered with craters and mountain ranges. Unlike on Earth, however, these lunar mountains were not caused by movement of the crust but are the surviving walls of huge, ancient craters.

## ORIGIN OF THE MOON

The Moon was formed just over four and a half billion years ago. It may have been gouged out of our own world when a large object struck the Earth. Another possibility is that the Moon has always been a separate body and was captured by the Earth when it strayed too close.

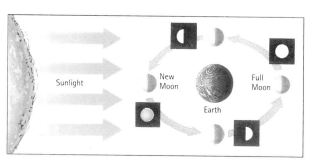
Sunlight · New Moon · Full Moon · Earth

◄ At New Moon, the unlit side of the Moon, which is invisible, faces the Earth. It grows (Crescent Moon) until half, then all, the unlit side becomes visible (Full Moon). The phases then continue in reverse until the Moon is new again.

## PLAINS AND CRATERS

The dark regions of the Moon's surface, known as maria (seas), are low-lying plains of solidified lava surrounded by brighter, mountainous areas. Craters, formed by the impact of meteorites and asteroids, occur everywhere on the Moon, but are

▼ The Collision Theory suggests that a large body struck the Earth.

◄ This body added its own material to the debris thrown off into space (1). The debris formed an orbiting cloud (2), which finally solidified into a solid mass – the Moon (3).

1

2

3

especially common in the highlands. They range in size from a few metres to 1,100km across (Imbrium Basin in the Sea of Rains).

## PULL OF THE MOON

Just as the Moon is held in orbit around the Earth by gravity, so the Earth itself is affected by the Moon's gravity. This is noticeable in the movement of the oceans and seas, which are pulled up when the Moon is directly above them. As the Earth rotates, these tidal bulges shift from east to west twice daily, causing high tides.

## MYTHS AND LEGENDS

For centuries, the Moon has given rise to various myths and legends. Early peoples saw it as a god or goddess, while some philosophers thought that it was linked with birth and death, because it waxed and waned. It was also feared that eclipses signalled famine or war. In astrology, the Moon is believed to have an important influence over our lives and destiny.

▶ The Capture Theory suggests that the Moon was a passing body caught by the Earth's gravity. This explains its different composition, although calculations show that a collision with

Moon's new orbit

Original path of Moon

Moon     Earth

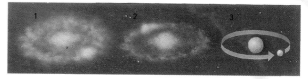

▲ The Earth and Moon may have formed together as a double planet from the cloud of debris left over after the formation of the Sun. However, this argument does not explain why their surface rocks are so different and why the Moon has such a small iron core compared with the Earth.

▼ Moon rock brought back from the *Apollo* missions ranges in age from about 4.5 billion years, just after the Moon was formed, to 3.1 billion years, when the lava plains were created.

Anorthosite

Vasicular basalt

Typical basalt

## SEE ALSO

Earth, Gravity, Planet, Solar system, Space exploration

# Mountain and Valley

A mountain is a mass of land that is much higher than its surroundings, pushed upwards by movement of the Earth's crust. Valleys are formed on mountain slopes.

As glaciers melt, they leave behind deep, U-shaped valleys gouged by the ice.

A mountain is higher than a hill, but there is no strict distinction between the two. Mountains are natural barriers to communications, while valleys offer trade routes, places for settlement, and pastures for farming. Some mountains are found under the sea. One of them, Mauna Kea in the Pacific Ocean, is higher than Everest.

### HIGHEST PEAKS

Mountains are formed over millions of years through plate tectonics – movement of the Earth's crust. The crust is made up of rigid plates which are continuously moving. The highest mountains are the youngest. The longest mountain range on Earth, the Andes (7,200km long), is being formed as the Pacific plate plunges beneath the South American plate. The highest, the Himalayas, is being formed as the Indian plate crushes up against the Asian plate.

Erupting volcanoes build up mountains made of lava and ash.

### FOREVER WEARING AWAY

All the time a mountain is being pushed up, forces of erosion (such as wind and water) are wearing it down. Water flowing down the slopes gathers in streams and rivers, which carve out deep V-shaped valleys. Flat-bottomed, U-shaped valleys are formed by glaciers. Some straight valleys, like the Great Rift Valley, in East Africa, are formed along a crack or fault in the Earth.

### MOVING THE EARTH

The highest mountains are fold mountains. These are found in chains, or ranges, and are formed like folds in a blanket when the ends are pushed together. They are pushed up when rocky plates of the Earth's crust collide. When one plate plunges beneath another, the rocks of the uppermost plate crumple up, making the mountain range.

Block mountains form along breaks, or faults, in the Earth's crust.

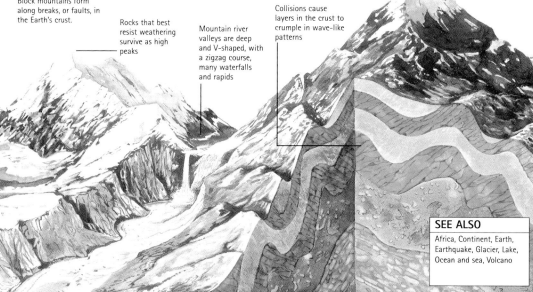

Rocks that best resist weathering survive as high peaks

Mountain river valleys are deep and V-shaped, with a zigzag course, many waterfalls and rapids

Collisions cause layers in the crust to crumple in wave-like patterns

### SEE ALSO

Africa, Continent, Earth, Earthquake, Glacier, Lake, Ocean and sea, Volcano

# MUSCLE

The body has 640 muscles, each specialized to contract (become shorter) to make the body move. All body actions, from blinking to sprinting, are muscle-powered.

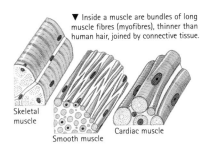

▼ Inside a muscle are bundles of long muscle fibres (myofibres), thinner than human hair, joined by connective tissue.

Skeletal muscle

Smooth muscle

Cardiac muscle

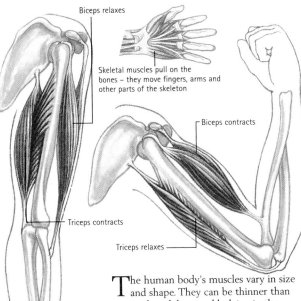

Biceps relaxes

Skeletal muscles pull on the bones – they move fingers, arms and other parts of the skeleton

Biceps contracts

Triceps contracts

Triceps relaxes

The human body's muscles vary in size and shape. They can be thinner than cotton thread, long and bulging in the middle, or wide and slab-like. The largest, the gluteus maximus, is in the buttocks. Most are firmly attached to the skeleton by their tapering ends, called tendons.

### WORKING IN PAIRS
Muscles can only pull, not push. So they are arranged in opposing pairs. One of the pair pulls the body part one way. To move the part back again, its opposing partner pulls it the other way. Animal muscles have the same structure, and work in the same way, as human muscles.

### INSIDE A MUSCLE
Muscles are made up of bundles of long fibres called muscle fibres or myofibres. Each one of these contains bundles of even thinner microscopic parts – muscle filaments or myofilaments. In turn, muscle

▲ When you bend your arm, the biceps muscle in the upper arm pulls the forearm, and so bends the elbow. Its opposing partner, the triceps, pulls the forearm the other way and straightens the elbow.

filaments are made of bundles of thread-like structures, called actin and myosin.

### MUSCLE POWER
For a muscle to pull, each myosin 'grabs' its neighbouring actin and makes it slide past, like pulling in a rope with a hand-over-hand movement. Millions of myosins and actins doing this make the whole muscle shorten. The amount and strength of contraction are controlled by nerve signals to each muscle from the brain.

### THREE MUSCLE TYPES
Skeletal muscles have a striped appearance under the microscope, so they are known as striped, or striated, muscles. As we can make them contract when we want to (by thinking), they are called voluntary muscles. Cardiac muscle (called the myocardium) forms the thick walls of the heart. It contracts regularly to pump blood. Visceral muscle forms layers and sheets in the walls of the body's inner parts – viscera – such as the stomach, intestines and bladder. Both of these work automatically, so they are known as involuntary muscles.

The eye has six muscles which help rotate the eyeball in its socket

Ligaments

Tendons and ligaments are tough elastic tissues. Ligaments connect one bone to another, tendons connect a muscle to a bone

Achilles tendon

Tendons

### SEE ALSO
Heart, Human body, Lens, Lungs, Sight, Touch

# MUSICAL INSTRUMENT

Musical instruments create vibrations that are turned into sound. Most have their own range of pitched (high or low) notes. All have their own tone, timbre or 'voice'.

Irish harps were carried from town to town by wandering minstrels.

The 1.8m-long serpent was very popular during the 1600s and 1700s.

From the 1100s, the hurdy-gurdy accompanied singers at feasts and dances.

The Jew's harp is placed inside the mouth, while a finger plucks its tongue.

Musical instruments may be classified scientifically as: aerophones, in which the air itself vibrates; chordophones, in which one or more strings vibrate; membranophones, in which a stretched skin, or membrane, vibrates; and idiophones, in which the whole body of the instrument vibrates as one. The better-known way of classifying them is: strings, woodwind, brass, percussion, as well as keyboard instruments, electronic instruments and the voice.

## STRINGED INSTRUMENTS

Stringed instruments produce their sounds from vibrating strings. With violins, violas, cellos and double-basses, the strings are usually scraped with a bow to make them vibrate. In other stringed instruments, notably the guitar, the strings are plucked. The player presses down on the strings with his or her fingers to change their 'playing length', which is the section that vibrates. This is called 'stopping'. The wooden body vibrates in sympathy with the strings, giving them volume and tone.

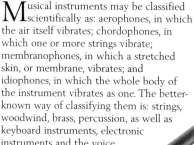

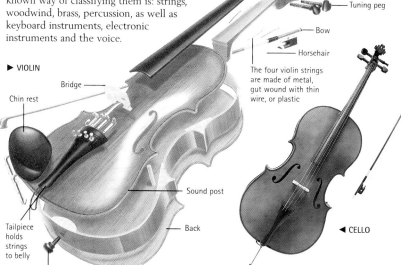

▶ VIOLIN

Bridge

Chin rest

Tailpiece holds strings to belly

End pin

Sound post

Back

Fingerboard

Scroll

Tuning peg

Bow

Horsehair

The four violin strings are made of metal, gut wound with thin wire, or plastic

◀ CELLO

## SYMPHONY ORCHESTRA

A typical orchestra includes a string section of violins, violas, cellos and double-basses; a brass section of French horns, trumpets, trombones and tuba; a wind section of clarinets, oboes, bassoons, flutes and piccolos; and a percussion section of timpani, gong, glockenspiel, bass drum, and various other percussive instruments.

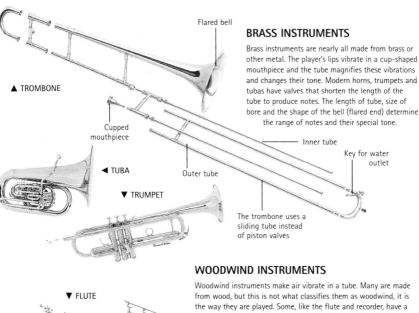

▲ TROMBONE

◀ TUBA

▼ TRUMPET

Flared bell

Cupped mouthpiece

Inner tube

Key for water outlet

Outer tube

## BRASS INSTRUMENTS

Brass instruments are nearly all made from brass or other metal. The player's lips vibrate in a cup-shaped mouthpiece and the tube magnifies these vibrations and changes their tone. Modern horns, trumpets and tubas have valves that shorten the length of the tube to produce notes. The length of tube, size of bore and the shape of the bell (flared end) determine the range of notes and their special tone.

The trombone uses a sliding tube instead of piston valves

The electric guitar has a flat, solid body and electric pick-ups under each string.

## WOODWIND INSTRUMENTS

Woodwind instruments make air vibrate in a tube. Many are made from wood, but this is not what classifies them as woodwind, it is the way they are played. Some, like the flute and recorder, have a mouth-piece that turns the player's breath directly into vibrations. The oboe, clarinet and bassoon have small vibrating reeds. The player sounds different notes by opening or closing holes in the tube's side, so changing the length of the tube in which the air vibrates.

▼ FLUTE

Finger key

Foot joint

Finger hole covered by key

Cork pads make airtight seal

Head joint

Body joint

Lip plate

Blow hole

The saxophone has a flared bell, single-reed mouthpiece and is very popular in jazz.

▼ CLARINET

▼ OBOE

Single (clarinet) reed

Double (oboe) reed

The rock drumkit includes a bass drum, floor toms, cymbals and snare drum.

## PERCUSSION INSTRUMENTS

Percussion instruments are struck. Drums have a tight membrane across a frame, which the player strikes with hands, fingers or sticks. The air inside the frame, or the frame itself, makes the vibrating membrane sound louder. Bells, cymbals and gongs are all made from a single piece of material and vibrate as a whole when struck. Some percussion instruments, such as drums and bells, sound notes of definite pitch. But with gongs and cymbals it is difficult to place the pitch.

▼ TIMPANI (KETTLEDRUM)

Drumhead

Tightening screws

Tuning gauge shows pitch

Tension rod

Supporting strut

Foot pedal changes pitch of drum

Copper bowl

The powerful church organ has one or more keyboards and several banks of pipes.

| SEE ALSO |
|---|
| Sound |

# NATIVE AMERICANS

Native Americans were the first peoples to settle in North America, before the discovery and settlement of those lands by Europeans.

The Tlingit lived along the northwest coast.

Navajo farmed the south west of North America.

▲ This thriving smoked fish business in Wisconsin shows how traditional skills have been adapted to modern times.

Native Americans developed into many different tribes and cultures, but were overwhelmed by European invaders after the 15th century. Today they make up a minority of the North American population.

### EARLY ARRIVALS
Before 20,000BC, humans crossed into the Americas along a land bridge that stretched from eastern Asia across the Bering Strait. By about 10,000BC, they had spread south to the tip of South America. The Inuit of Canada and Alaska came from Asia only 3,000 to 5,500 years ago.

### NATIVE CULTURES
The earliest Native Americans hunted wild animals and gathered wild plants. In about 1500BC, some peoples began farming. Maize, beans and squashes were grown in most areas. Few animals were domesticated and Native Americans relied on wild game for meat. The great plains were dominated by tribes hunting bison, buffalo and other animals. Southwestern tribes were farmers and sheep herders. In the eastern woodlands, tribes lived off the game that was plentiful there. Along the northwest coast, cultures based on fishing developed.

The Creek lived in the eastern woodlands area.

### DISEASE AND MASSACRE
In 1492, Christopher Columbus sailed to the Americas from Europe. Over the next 400 years, the European settlers spread over most of the Americas. European diseases killed many Native Americans, who had no immunity. About 80 per cent of the Mandan tribe in the northern plains died of smallpox.

◄ The Cheyenne were one of the plains tribes. During war, the warriors were organized into seven societies, with the 'dog soldiers' acting as scouts and forward troops.

**CULTURES**
- Arctic
- Subarctic
- Northwest coast
- California
- Plains
- Eastern woodlands
- Southwest

Many other surviving tribes were driven from their lands or killed in warfare. The last battle of the Indian Wars was fought at Wounded Knee, South Dakota in 1890.

### TRIBAL LANDS
In the late 1970s, some tribes started legal battles against the US federal government to try to reclaim land that had been taken from them. Today, North America is home to about two million Native Americans. Many live on reservations and keep alive traditional cultures. Some are poor, while others run thriving businesses.

**SEE ALSO**

Aztecs, Canada, Incas, Maya, North America

# NAVIGATION

Navigation is the science of finding the way. It is used mainly to guide ships, aircraft and spacecraft, but can also be used for vehicles on land.

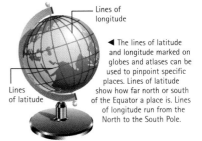

Lines of longitude

◀ The lines of latitude and longitude marked on globes and atlases can be used to pinpoint specific places. Lines of latitude show how far north or south of the Equator a place is. Lines of longitude run from the North to the South Pole.

Lines of latitude

The magnetic compass was invented in China around AD1000.

For thousands of years, ever since people began to travel by sea, navigation has been necessary. Early navigators relied on skill and guesswork, but today are helped by satellite technology and computers.

## ANCIENT ARTS

Many early peoples travelled for trade or war, but the first to navigate seriously were the Phoenicians and Greeks, who sailed throughout the Mediterranean from about 750BC. By 300BC, some Greeks could find latitude by studying the stars, but after the fall of the Roman Empire, most navigational skills were lost.

The backstaff helped find latitude by measuring the height of Sun and stars.

## HENRY THE NAVIGATOR

In 1418, Prince Henry of Portugal set up a school of navigation, which made many advances in exploration and navigation.

## MODERN NAVIGATIONAL SYSTEMS

The idea of bearings from beacons is used with satellite technology. The US military Geostat system has satellites in orbit around the Earth positioned so that at least two are within radio range from any place on Earth. It is claimed a soldier with a computerized hand-held receiver can find his position to within 2m.

The astrolabe was used by navigators before the invention of the sextant.

The tools developed depended on compass readings and sightings of the stars and Sun. Although this early equipment underwent many changes, it remained the basis of navigation until well into the 20th century.

## PINPOINTING A TARGET

World War II brought a major boost to navigation. Bomber aircraft needed to find their way to a target accurately. One way was to direct two radio beams into enemy territory so they crossed over the target. Aircraft followed one beam until they found the second. Another system was based on radio beacons. By taking a bearing on two beacons, the navigator could find his position to within a few hundred metres. The system was adapted to cover shipping lanes as well as air routes, and remains in use today as a major navigational aid for boats and ships.

The sextant, which also determines latitude, is still in use today.

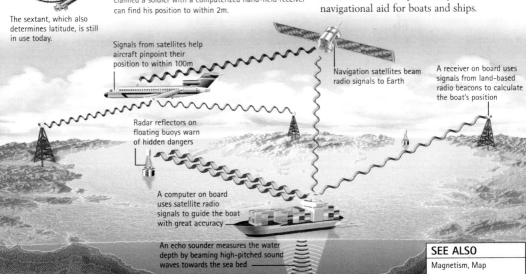

Signals from satellites help aircraft pinpoint their position to within 100m

Navigation satellites beam radio signals to Earth

A receiver on board uses signals from land-based radio beacons to calculate the boat's position

Radar reflectors on floating buoys warn of hidden dangers

A computer on board uses satellite radio signals to guide the boat with great accuracy

An echo sounder measures the water depth by beaming high-pitched sound waves towards the sea bed

### SEE ALSO
Magnetism, Map

# NETHERLANDS, BELGIUM AND LUXEMBOURG

The Netherlands, Belgium and Luxembourg make up a group of countries in northwest Europe called the Low Countries. The Netherlands is also known as Holland.

**BELGIUM**
**Area:** 30,528 sq km
**Population:** 10,204,000
**Capital:** Brussels
**Languages:** Dutch and French
**Currency:** Belgian franc, Euro

**LUXEMBOURG**
**Area:** 2,586 sq km
**Population:** 427,000
**Capital:** Luxembourg City
**Languages:** French, German, Letzebuergesh
**Currency:** Luxembourg franc, Euro

**NETHERLANDS**
**Area:** 41,526 sq km
**Population:** 15,698,000
**Capital:** Amsterdam
**Language:** Dutch
**Currency:** Guilder, Euro

The name Netherlands means 'lowlands' – two fifths of the country lies below sea level and the countryside is criss-crossed with canals. Half the country's freight is carried on the inland waterways. The landscape is dotted with windmills, originally built for controlling the water level. Belgium is also low lying and mostly flat, rising to hills called the Ardennes in the south, which extend across the border into the small country of Luxembourg.

## TRADE AND NEW LAND
From the 1500s, the Dutch became seafarers, growing rich from fishing and trade, and built up an empire in Southeast Asia. Rotterdam is now the world's largest port. The Dutch became experts at flood control, draining the land and reclaiming it from the sea, by building dykes and using pumps. This has created rich farmlands – cheese and butter are major exports.

## INDUSTRIES AND CITIES
Belgium's textile industry dates back to the Middle Ages. Today, the country is a heavily industrialized nation. Belgium and Luxembourg are both leading steel producers. The city of Luxembourg is a major centre of banking, and Luxembourg is one of the wealthiest

nations in Europe. The Netherlands is Europe's most densely populated country. Amsterdam, its largest city, is the national capital, although the government sits at The Hague.

## HISTORY AND HERITAGE
The Netherlands fought for freedom from Spanish rule in the 16th century. Belgium and Luxembourg were part of the Netherlands until the 19th century. These three countries remain closely linked as members of the European Union, which has its headquarters in Brussels.

◀ Cut flowers and bulbs are important crops in the Netherlands, as well as fruit and vegetables.

| SEE ALSO |
| --- |
| Europe |

# NEW ZEALAND

New Zealand lies in the South Pacific, 1,900km southeast of its nearest neighbour Australia. It has two main islands, both of which are long and narrow.

**Area:** 270,534 sq km
**Population:** 3,792,000
**Capital:** Wellington
**Language:** English
**Currency:** New Zealand dollar

◄ Most of New Zealand's landscape is hilly, but there are fertile valleys and plains, such as South Island's Canterbury Plains.

miles
0    100

0    100
km

TASMAN SEA

Great Barrier I.
Auckland
Manukau
Bay of Plenty
Hamilton
Rotorua
Mt. Egmont
Lake Taupo
North I.
Mt. Ruapehu
Palmerston North
Tasman Bay
Wellington
Buller
Clarence
Cook Strait
NEW ZEALAND
South I.
Mt. Cook
SOUTH PACIFIC OCEAN
Christchurch
Southern Alps
CANTERBURY PLAINS
Clutha
Lake Te Anau
Dunedin
Invercargill
Stewart I.

N

▲ In the greeting *hongi*, Maoris rub noses. Other traditions include carving, weaving and tattooing.

Over four fifths of New Zealanders live in towns or cities. Three quarters of the population live on North Island, where it is warmest, but South Island is the largest of the two main islands.

## NATURAL HAVEN
The coasts are ideal for sailing, surfing and fishing, and the mountains attract many skiers. There are active volcanoes, geysers and pools of bubbling mud. Because New Zealand has been isolated from other land masses for millions of years, it has developed distinct native wildlife such as the kiwi, a flightless bird, and many different kinds of fern. Farm animals (mostly cattle and sheep) outnumber people by 20 to one.

## EARNING A LIVING
Most of New Zealand's wealth comes from farming, but this employs fewer than one in six people. Major exports include cheese, fruits, meat, wool and wine, as well as seafood, timber products and aluminium. There are large reserves of coal and gas, and industry is concentrated around Auckland, the largest city. Tourism is a fast-growing business.

## TWO TRADITIONS
New Zealand was first settled by Maoris from Polynesia around AD900, and they still account for about an eighth of the population. Permanent British settlement began in 1840. Settlers transformed the country by founding cities and introducing cereal crops, sheep and cattle. Independence came in 1907, but ties between New Zealand and Britain remain close through trade and sport.

◄ The All Blacks is New Zealand's national rugby football team. It is one of the best in the world.

| SEE ALSO |
| --- |
| Custom |

# NORTH AMERICA

North America is the third largest of the world's seven continents and the fourth largest in population. It stretches from the Arctic Ocean to Central America.

▲ In the province of Quebec in Canada, average January temperatures range from −12°C to −29°C.

## KEY FACTS

- **Area:** 21,517,000 sq km
- **Population:** 467,000,000
- **Number of countries:** 23
- **Largest country:** Canada
- **Smallest country:** St Kitts-Nevis
- **Highest point:** Mount McKinley (6,194m)
- **Largest lake:** Superior (82,103 sq km)
- **Longest river:** Missouri (4,090km)

▼ The world's first skyscraper was built in Chicago, USA, in 1884. It no longer stands, but two other early skyscrapers, the Wrigley Building (left) and the Tribune Tower (right), are still Chicago landmarks.

The largest part of North America is made up of Canada and the United States. The rest consists of Mexico, the seven countries in Central America and the islands in the Caribbean Sea, which include 13 independent countries and 11 overseas territories still linked with a colonial partner. The UK territory of Bermuda lies in the North Atlantic Ocean and is also part of North America.

### LARGEST ISLAND
Greenland, in the north, is a self-governing territory linked with Denmark and is the world's largest island.

### MOUNTAINS AND PLAINS
In the western half of the continent are the Rocky Mountains, the world's second longest mountain chain. The continent's highest peak, Mount McKinley (6,194m), is in Alaska. There are smaller mountain ranges in the east, including the Appalachians. The Canadian Shield is a huge area of ancient rock with poor soils but rich in minerals. Across the centre of the continent is a vast grassland region, known as the prairies.

### GREAT LAKES AND RIVERS
The five Great Lakes – Superior, Huron, Erie, Ontario and Michigan – form the world's largest grouping of this kind. The thundering waters of Niagara Falls, on a strait between Lakes Erie and Ontario, are an impressive spectacle. The Mississippi, Missouri and Ohio rivers together form the continent's longest river system, more than 7,500km long.

### COLD AND HOT
North America has every kind of climate. The north has bitterly cold winters – in the Arctic regions of Canada and Alaska it is too cold for trees to grow. In the south, huge forests of evergreen and deciduous trees cover the land. Still farther south, there are hot deserts and tropical forests.

### GIANT TREES
Some of the world's tallest trees, the giant redwood and the sequoia, grow on the west coast of North America. In the eastern forests, the leaves of maple, hickory and other deciduous trees provide a brilliant colour show in the autumn. Mesquite, prickly pear and saguaro cactus grow in desert regions. ▶

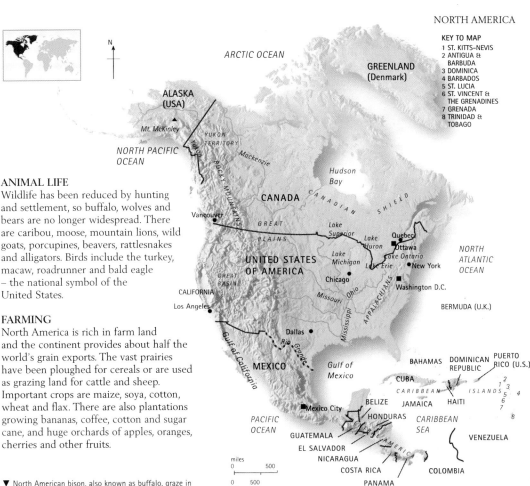

KEY TO MAP
1 ST. KITTS–NEVIS
2 ANTIGUA &
  BARBUDA
3 DOMINICA
4 BARBADOS
5 ST. LUCIA
6 ST. VINCENT &
  THE GRENADINES
7 GRENADA
8 TRINIDAD &
  TOBAGO

## ANIMAL LIFE

Wildlife has been reduced by hunting and settlement, so buffalo, wolves and bears are no longer widespread. There are caribou, moose, mountain lions, wild goats, porcupines, beavers, rattlesnakes and alligators. Birds include the turkey, macaw, roadrunner and bald eagle – the national symbol of the United States.

## FARMING

North America is rich in farm land and the continent provides about half the world's grain exports. The vast prairies have been ploughed for cereals or are used as grazing land for cattle and sheep. Important crops are maize, soya, cotton, wheat and flax. There are also plantations growing bananas, coffee, cotton and sugar cane, and huge orchards of apples, oranges, cherries and other fruits.

▼ North American bison, also known as buffalo, graze in Yellowstone National Park. These animals live mostly in reserves. Their numbers have been greatly reduced by overhunting and strict laws now exist to protect them.

## GOODS AND RESOURCES

Only Europe makes more factory goods than North America, which is a major producer of vehicles, aircraft, electronics and chemicals. It is rich in minerals, including silver, natural gas, oil, copper and coal. Some of the world's leading companies are based here.

## CITIES AND TRANSPORT

Most North Americans live in towns and cities. The continent has some of the world's largest cities, including Mexico City, New York and Los Angeles, where skyscrapers make dramatic skylines and

▲ At carnival time in Mexico, people dress in traditional costume. Many Mexicans are of Spanish ancestory, but there are also descendents of the Ancient Aztec and Mayan people living in Mexico and Central America.

where cars and trucks move along multi-lane highways. In this huge continent, trains and aeroplanes carry passengers and freight long distances. Many North Americans enjoy a high standard of living, but in the inner cities of the United States and in Mexico and parts of the Caribbean, people are relatively poor.

## VARIED ROOTS

North America has been a melting pot for peoples from many parts of the world. English is the main language but French is used in parts of Canada, while Spanish is spoken in Mexico and by many people in Central America and the United States. Many North Americans have European or Asian roots. African Americans are the descendants of black people who were brought from Africa as slaves.

## THE FIRST AMERICANS

People came to North America from Asia, possibly as early as 30,000BC and settled across the continent. They were hunters, some of whom, over the ages, became farmers and town-builders. Another group was the ancestors of the Inuit people, who settled in the far north. The Maya and Aztecs of Mexico created civilizations of which impressive ruins still remain.

## EUROPEANS ARRIVE

Vikings came to North America about 1,000 years ago but did not settle for long. In 1492, the explorer Christopher Columbus discovered the American continent, which soon became known as the New World. He was followed by other explorers from Spain, who came seeking gold. From the 1600s, the British and French settled in Canada and along the east coast. Spain ruled Mexico, Florida and Central America. Canada and Mexico became independent in the 19th century.

## THE UNITED STATES

The United States was created in 1776 when 13 colonies broke away from Britain. It grew rapidly into an industrial giant. Native Americans were driven from their lands as settlers moved west across the Great Plains and reached the Pacific coast. Immigrants from Africa, Europe, Asia and Central America have helped to shape the modern United States.

▲ Sequoias, growing on the west coast of the continent, are some of the world's tallest trees.

◀ Grenada is one of 13 independent island nations in the Caribbean. Its capital, St George's, lies on the southwest coast among forested hills.

## SEE ALSO

Arctic, Aztecs, Canada, Caribbean, Maya, Mexico, Native Americans, USA, Vikings

# NUCLEAR POWER

**Nuclear power is the generation of electricity using heat released by changes in the nuclei of atoms. The process is known as a controlled nuclear reaction.**

Lise Meitner (1878–1968) proved that heavy atoms can be split into lighter ones – a process she called 'nuclear fission'.

Otto Hahn (1879–1968) worked with Meitner to split the atom, for which he was awarded the 1944 Nobel Prize for Chemistry.

Enrico Fermi (1901–54) built the first nuclear reactor in a squash court in 1942 and later worked on the atomic bomb project.

The centre of an atom is called the nucleus. Radioactive elements such as uranium have nuclei which sometimes split, releasing energy including heat. When these nuclei split, they throw out two or three tiny particles called neutrons. These can hit other nuclei, making them split, shooting out more neutrons.

## AN IDEAL FUEL

Compared to coal, oil or gas, very small amounts of uranium can make a lot of electricity, and it does not pollute the air with chemicals or solids. Nuclear power is ideal for spacecraft and submarines: a nuclear-powered spacecraft can keep its instruments working for years, while a

▲ The mushroom cloud from a nuclear explosion is made up of particles of rock, soil, water and other materials that eventually fall back to Earth as radioactive 'fall-out'.

nuclear-powered submarine can travel around the world without refuelling and does not pollute the air with waste gases.

## HOPEFUL SOLUTION

In the 1950s, nuclear power was seen as the solution to the world's energy needs. The world's first commercial nuclear power station, Calder Hall, in the UK, started generating electricity in 1956. Some countries, such as France, rely heavily on nuclear power. But few nuclear power stations are now being built because of the dangers.

## NUCLEAR HAZARDS

Nuclear waste is hard to dispose of, remaining dangerously radioactive for thousands of years. Making old nuclear reactors safe is expensive. There is also the chance of an accident, such as the one in 1986 at Chernobyl in the Soviet Union, when an explosion contaminated thousands of square kilometres. Nuclear fusion, which releases energy by joining nuclei together rather than splitting them apart, may provide safe and clean energy in the future.

## THE NUCLEAR REACTOR

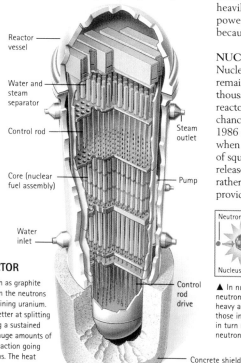

Reactor vessel

Water and steam separator

Control rod

Core (nuclear fuel assembly)

Water inlet

Steam outlet

Pump

Control rod drive

Concrete shield

In a reactor, a moderator such as graphite or water is used to slow down the neutrons released from fuel rods containing uranium. Slowed neutrons are much better at splitting other uranium atoms, causing a sustained chain reaction that releases huge amounts of heat. Control rods stop the reaction going too fast by absorbing neutrons. The heat boils water into steam, which turns turbines to make electricity.

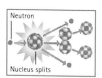

Neutron

Nucleus splits

▲ In nuclear fission, neutrons are used to split heavy atoms, such as those in uranium, which in turn release more free neutrons and energy.

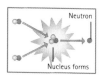

Neutron

Nucleus forms

▲ In nuclear fusion, two nuclei of a lightweight substance such as hydrogen combine to form heavier ones, releasing a further neutron and energy.

### SEE ALSO

Atom and molecule, Electricity, Energy, World War II

# NUTRITION

Nutrition is the process by which we take in and use food. Chemical substances found in food, called nutrients, provide energy and help the body function.

There are five important nutrients – carbohydrates, proteins, fats (in small quantities), vitamins and minerals. We also cannot live without water.

▲ Children in the Sudan collecting ants to eat during famine. Not eating enough food can result in malnutrition, draining energy and lowering resistance to disease.

Fruit and vegetables are rich in vitamins. We should eat five portions each day.

Carbohydrate foods contain natural sugars and starches for energy.

Fats can be animal (butter, milk, cheese) or vegetable – from plants and nuts.

Meat, fish, cheese, pulses and nuts are all sources of protein.

## ENERGY AND GROWTH
Carbohydrates and fats provide the body with energy. Proteins are necessary for growth and repair of cells. Vitamins and minerals like calcium, potassium and iron are essential for the health of nerves, skin, bones, muscle and brain. Research has shown that eating food rich in vitamins A, C, E and beta-carotene can help protect against the cell damage that causes cancer.

## FIBRE AND WATER
Fibre, the indigestible part of fruits and vegetables, is essential in the diet. It adds bulk to food and helps it move through the large intestine during digestion. Water is vital. The human body is made up of about 65 per cent water. Its cells need water to keep chemical reactions going. We need about two litres of water a day.

## A BALANCED DIET
The energy value of food is measured in calories. The more work your body does, the more calories you need. A man needs, on average, 2,700 calories a day and a woman 1,900; a 16-year-old boy needs 3,200 calories a day and a girl 2,100.

## FOOD SHORTAGES
Many people do not get enough to eat. Malnutrition (not getting sufficient nutrients) causes weakness and disease, accounting for around 54 per cent of deaths in under-fives in developing countries, which is about 6.6 million deaths a year.

## A BALANCED DIET
A healthy meal can take many forms. Most national diets are based on locally grown produce, animals or fish and a traditional staple food that is usually starchy and relatively cheap, such as rice, bread or pasta.

▼ Pasta is a good energy source, adding cheese increases protein. Tomato sauce provides Vitamin C.

▼ The traditional Thanksgiving dinner in America is a typical well-balanced meal.

◀ Research shows the Japanese diet is especially beneficial to long-term health. Tofu (beancurd) contains protein, calcium and other minerals. Raw fish is used to make sushi.

◀ A healthy meal in one bowl. In parts of West Africa, meat, beans and nuts are mixed in a stew (gumbo) along with yam, a root vegetable.

▶ Many of our most popular foods originally come from South America.

▲ Fresh, raw vegetables are simply prepared in hot countries like Australia. Grilling meat reduces fat.

### SEE ALSO
Food, Fruit

# OCEAN AND SEA

Seventy-one per cent of the Earth's surface is covered by water. Nearly all of this vast area is made up of salt water oceans and seas.

High spring tides are caused by the combined gravitational pull of the Sun and Moon when they are in line with the Earth. This occurs at the full Moon and new Moon.

Weak neap tides occur during the Moon's first and third quarters, when the gravitational forces of the Sun and Moon are at right angles and their combined force is less.

The Earth's crust is of two types: dense oceanic crust and lighter continental crust. The continental crust forms the great land masses of the Earth and these, being relatively light, stand high above the general level of the Earth's surface. The water-filled hollows that lie between the continents are called oceans.

## OCEAN FOUNDATIONS
The ocean floor is made of denser crustal material, which is constantly being created and destroyed through the process of plate tectonics. Along each ocean lies a volcanic ridge, forming a vast underwater network that encircles the Earth. This is where new crustal material is generated. The old material is destroyed along the edges of some of the oceans as one crustal plate is drawn down and swallowed up beneath the edge of another.

## OCEAN FEATURES
All this movement gives the basic features of any ocean – the oceanic ridge, which can rise to about 1,000m beneath the surface; the abyssal plains, which comprise the greatest area of ocean floor and average 5,000–6,000m deep; and the oceanic trenches, many of which are over 9,000m deep with the deepest – the Marianas Trench – plunging to over 11,000m.

## THE SOFT COVERING
The sediments of the ocean floor consist of oozes, which are made up of tiny skeletons and shells, volcanic dust and mud that has washed off the land. Sediments are very thin close to the oceanic ridges, but thicker farther away. This is because the new ocean crust close to the ridges has not had enough time to collect much debris.

## SHALLOW SEAS
Seas differ from oceans in that they are much shallower. They are the areas of the continents that happen to be below sea level – the continents' flooded edges. Sea floors tend to be thickly covered in sediment, such as sand and mud, brought

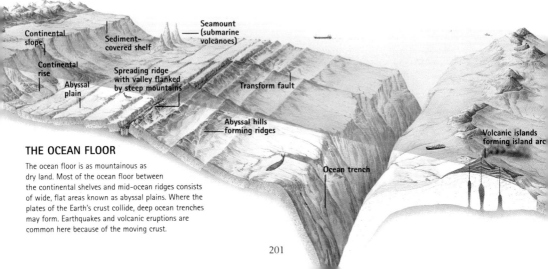

Continental slope

Sediment-covered shelf

Seamount (submarine volcanoes)

Continental rise

Spreading ridge with valley flanked by steep mountains

Abyssal plain

Transform fault

Abyssal hills forming ridges

Volcanic islands forming island arc

Ocean trench

## THE OCEAN FLOOR
The ocean floor is as mountainous as dry land. Most of the ocean floor between the continental shelves and mid-ocean ridges consists of wide, flat areas known as abyssal plains. Where the plates of the Earth's crust collide, deep ocean trenches may form. Earthquakes and volcanic eruptions are common here because of the moving crust.

down by the rivers. Some seas do not lie on the continental shelf but are inland. The Caspian Sea is completely landlocked, and the Black Sea is only narrowly connected with the Mediterranean Sea. The Red Sea is an oddity – although it is small and almost landlocked, its floor is true oceanic crust and it has a central ridge.

## LIVING THINGS

Most ocean life is found within a layer of water about 100m deep, where sunlight penetrates. Plankton is the mass of tiny plants and animals that drifts in the sea and is the basis of the entire ocean food chain. All sea creatures depend directly on plankton for food or on animals that feed on plankton. Planktonic plants

## MARINE LIFE

Life forms in the ocean are more varied than those on land. New creatures are often discovered in the deep sea.
**1** Herring **2** Sperm whale **3** Prawn **4** Kat-tail **5** Angler fish **6** Grenadier **7** Cod **8** Gulper eel **9** Sea spider, tube worms, clam, white ghost crab **10** Tripod fish **11** Viper fish **12** Swallower **13** Lantern fish **14** Swordfish **15** Yellowfin tuna **16** Giant squid **17** Hammerhead **18** Barracuda **19** Portuguese man-of-war **20** Plankton **21** Green turtle **22** Sea lion **23** Common dolphin

(*phytoplankton*) grow here, and also planktonic animals (*zooplankton*), which include one-celled animals, baby crabs and fish. Larger creatures feed upon these animals, and even larger predators feed upon them in turn. The final link in the food chain is humans – the sea provides a source of food for much of the world's population.

## MYSTERIOUS DEPTHS

Scuba divers and submersibles are still exploring the sea, studying its creatures and geological features and discovering submerged cities and ship-wrecks. Although the oceans have been travelled by many generations, the sea has always retained its mystery. It has been the source of many legends, such as that of the mermaid and the sea serpent, and has inspired artists throughout the centuries.

### ATOLLS

An atoll begins as a coral reef surrounding a volcanic island. As the island sinks, the reef grows upwards to keep pace. Eventually, the island disappears completely and all that remains is a ring-shaped reef, or atoll, surrounding a lagoon.

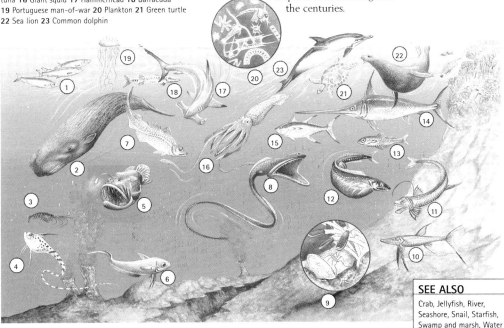

## SEE ALSO

Crab, Jellyfish, River, Seashore, Snail, Starfish, Swamp and marsh, Water

# OIL

Oil, or petroleum, is a thick, black liquid, sometimes called crude oil. It is a valuable raw material for fuels such as petrol, and in the chemical industry.

▶ In a refinery, parts, or fractions, of the crude oil are separated out in a process called fractional distillation. Fuels such as paraffin and petrol are made by mixing these fractions. Other fractions are sent to chemical plants to be made into drugs, paints, plastics and other products.

**OTHER OIL SOURCES**
Many oil products are derived from animal and vegetable sources.

Animal fats, such as pig lard, are used for cooking.

Vitamin-rich cod liver oil is used in medicine.

Most of the world's olive crop is grown for its oil.

Oil from sunflower seeds is used to make margarine.

Oil is a complex mixture of chemical compounds consisting of the elements hydrogen and carbon. These hydrocarbons release heat when they burn. This is what makes them useful as fuels.

### THE ORIGINS OF OIL
The story of oil began millions of years ago, with plants and animals that lived in the ancient seas. After they died, the bodies of these plants and animals decayed and gradually turned into oil. The oil has remained trapped in rocks ever since. Like coal and gas, oil is a fossil fuel.

### FINDING OIL
The search for oil is called oil exploration. Crude oil is always found in certain patterns of rock, so geologists look for these patterns in areas where oil is likely to be found. They use magnetic and seismic surveys (which send sounds from explosions at ground level to bounce off rocks underground) to find rock formations that may contain oil.

### DRILLING FOR OIL
To get the oil out, a hole is drilled down through the rocks. This is an oil well. The most expensive method is using oil rigs at sea (offshore), although onshore drilling is also common. The oil is sent by pipeline or by ship to an oil refinery for processing.

### THE FUTURE OF OIL
Like other fossil fuels, oil pollutes the environment when it is burned. It also contributes to acid rain and to global warming. The modern world uses increasing amounts of oil for vehicles, power generation, heating and industry. New oil finds are being made but known reserves may only last about 50 years. In future, alternative fuels will be needed so that the world's oil reserves do not completely run out.

### OFFSHORE DRILLING
An offshore oil rig is more dangerous to work on than a land rig as storms can damage the structure. It also costs about ten times more to build. The rig itself has to be floated out to sea in sections and then assembled, while the equipment and crew are carried out to the site by helicopter. Because of the huge expense involved, several test drillings are carried out to make sure that there are enough oil reserves to justify the cost of setting up a permanent rig.

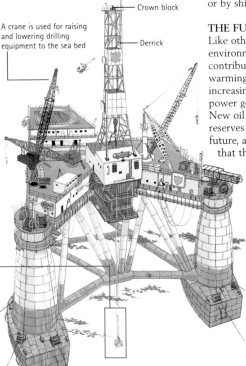

A crane is used for raising and lowering drilling equipment to the sea bed

Crown block

Derrick

◀ A large-toothed bit is used to drill through soft rock.

▶ The drill shaft rotates within an outer casing. Mud is pumped down to clean the bit and bring up the rocks.

### SEE ALSO
Coal, Gas, Medicine, Plastic, Pollution

# OLYMPIC GAMES

The Olympic Games are a world athletic and sports competition that takes place every four years. About 200 nations enter competitors in about 270 events.

The first modern Olympic Games were opened by King George I of Greece in Athens on April 5, 1896. They were a huge success, but it took several attempts to get it established as a successful global event. The modern Olympics were inspired by the ancient Olympic Games, which were first held in Olympia, Greece in 776BC.

▲ The ancient Olympians, such as this discus thrower, competed naked.

## OLYMPIC SPIRIT
The aim of the Olympic Games is to promote peace, equality and friendship, and to inspire athletes around the world. Competition between individuals rather than countries is encouraged and on the scoreboard at every Olympic Games is the message: "The most important thing in the Olympic Games is not to win but to take part…"

▲ The Olympic symbol of five linked rings represents the five continents of Africa, Asia, Australia, Europe and North America. It was designed so that at least one of the six colours in the symbol (including the white background) would appear in all the flags of the competing nations.

## OPENING CEREMONY
At every Olympic opening ceremony, the parade of nations is led by Greece, the founder nation, with the host country coming last and the nations in between appearing in alphabetical order. During the celebrations, the athletes and officials take the Olympic oath, the Olympic torch is lit and the Olympic flag raised. As a sign of peace, doves are released into the stadium. ▶

## FAST FACTS

• Since 1896, only five countries have been at all the Games – Australia, France, Greece, Great Britain and Switzerland

• The marathon used to be 25 miles, but in the 1908 London Games it was extended to over 26 miles so that Princess Mary could see it start from the nursery window at Windsor Castle

• The newest Olympic sports include beach volleyball, women's football, tae kwondo and the triathlon (introduced for Sydney 2000)

• The Roman Emperor Nero was so desperate for Olympic victory that he introduced music and poetry competitions and announced himself winner in six events

## THE 1996 ATLANTA GAMES

The 1996 Games, which marked the 100th anniversary of the start of the modern Olympics, was held at Atlanta in Georgia, USA. The opening ceremony was the most spectacular to date, and new events for the Games included mountain biking, beach volleyball, women's football and women's fencing.

▲ US athlete Jesse Owens became the star of the 1936 Games at Berlin, Germany, when he walked away with four gold medals. In the face of Nazi propaganda for white superiority, Owens's victory was a huge embarrassment for Nazi officials.

▲ Not all Olympic events go smoothly, as was the case when Britain's Zola Budd (right) collided with America's Mary Decker in the women's 3,000m event in 1984 at Los Angeles. Mary Decker fell and was robbed of the chance of victory. This caused a great uproar.

## RECORD BREAKERS

• The first men's gold medallist was James Connolly, from the USA, in 1896 in the triple jump

• The first women's gold medallist was British tennis player Charlotte Cooper in 1900

• Johnny Weissmuller of the USA won five gold medals altogether for swimming, in 1924 and 1928, and went on to play Tarzan in 18 Hollywood movies

• America's Jesse Owens in 1936 and Carl Lewis in 1984 are the only two athletes to win four gold medals at one Games

• Swimmer Mark Spitz of the USA has won more medals in one Olympics than any other competitor. In 1972, he won seven swimming medals

• Swimmer Kristin Otto of East Germany was the first woman to win six medals at one Olympic Games, in 1988

### THE OLYMPIC TORCH

Four weeks before the start of the Games, the Olympic flame is lit in Greece by magnifying the Sun's rays with mirrors. It is then carried across the world in a torch by a series of runners. On the opening day of the Games, the last runner enters the stadium and the arena flame is lit. It stays burning until the close of the Games.

### THE ANCIENT GAMES

The ancient Olympic Games were first organized as a religious, sporting and cultural festival held in honour of Zeus, the most powerful of the Greek gods. Every four years, Greek athletes travelled from all over the country to Olympia, a village near Mount Olympus (home of the gods) in Greece. Only Greek citizens could compete, although no women were allowed to take part in or even watch the Games on pain of death. The Games were taken so seriously that a truce between any warring states within Greece was called so that competitors could travel safely to Olympia.

### BANNING OF THE GAMES

At the first ancient Olympic Games in 776BC, there was only one event, a 200m stadium race. Gradually, more events were added, including chariot racing in 680BC. The Games were finally banned in AD394 by the Roman Emperor Theodosius. The Romans had conquered Greece and Theodosius banned all pagan festivals, including the Olympic Games.

### THE WINTER OLYMPICS

The modern Olympics falls into two parts: the Winter and the Summer Olympics. The first Winter Olympics were held in Chamonix, France in 1924. Until 1994, they were always held the same year as the Summer Olympics but is now

Thomas Burke (USA) wins the 100m event in the 1896 Olympics in Athens, Greece.

The Canadian ice hockey team triumphs in the first-ever Winter Olympics in Chamonix, France in 1924.

Attilio Pavesi (Italy) wins the cycling road race in the 1932 Games in Los Angeles, USA.

Dawn Fraser (Australia) wins 100m freestyle swimming event in Melbourne, 1956.

Joe Frazier (USA) is heavyweight boxing champion at the 1964 Games in Tokyo, Japan.

held two years earlier. Winter Olympic sports include ice hockey, luge (small toboggan), skating, skiing and bobsleigh.

## THE SUMMER OLYMPICS

The Summer Olympics include nearly 30 sports: combat sports include judo and boxing; ball games include volleyball and handball; court games include tennis and badminton; and water sports include rowing and swimming. Athletics is classified as one sport in the Olympics, but includes 24 men's events and 20 women's events. As well as running events, athletics includes the high jump and long jump, the discus and javelin, and the decathlon (ten athletic events spread over two days).

## POLITICAL PROBLEMS

Because the Olympic Games are the world's greatest sporting event, they have sometimes been used as a political tool. In 1972, Israeli competitors were attacked and killed by Arab terrorists at the Olympics in Munich, Germany. Eight years later, the Games in Moscow were boycotted by the USA and its allies because of the Soviet invasion of Afghanistan. In 1984, the Soviet Union and its allies refused to compete in the Olympics in Los Angeles because of fears over security arrangements.

## TODAY'S GAMES

At recent Games, there have been problems over athletes taking drugs. In 2000, a gymnast, four weightlifters and a wrestler were stripped of their medals because they had taken drugs. Despite such controversies, the Olympic Games are still considered to be the ultimate sporting event and attracts athletes from all over the world.

▲ The Paralympics is a competition for disabled competitors. It is separate from, and held after, the main Olympics, although it takes place in the Olympic stadium and is no less competitive. Here, the 4 x 400m wheelchair relay event at Atlanta was won by the German team.

▲ Yaping Deng, from China, was winner of the women's table tennis singles competition at Barcelona, Spain in 1992 and at Atlanta in 1996.

14-year-old Nadia Comaneci (Romania) is gold medallist in the combined athletics event in the 1976 Games in Montreal, Canada.

Steffi Graf (Germany) wins the women's tennis singles event in the 1988 Games held in Seoul, South Korea.

Jan Zelezny (Czech Republic) wins the javelin event in the 1996 Games in Atlanta, USA.

| SEE ALSO |
| --- |
| Greece (Ancient), Sport |

# PAPER

Paper is a material made from plant fibres that are webbed together to form sheets. It is used for many different purposes, including writing and packaging.

Waxed paper can be used to make cartons for holding liquids.

Filter paper is used inside cars to stop grit from entering the engine.

Furnishings such as lampshades and wallpaper can be made from paper.

Paper is used for communication – it can be printed or written on.

Paper is used to mop up liquids, both in industry and in the home.

People have known how to make paper for over 2,000 years. The earliest paper-makers lived in Ancient China. They made thick, coarse sheets of paper by flattening and drying out a pulp (mush) of water, chopped bark, plants and fishing nets. Some 500 years before them, the Egyptians had discovered they could make something like paper by pressing papyrus strips together. Our term 'paper' comes from the word papyrus.

## STRONG FIBRES
Like Ancient Chinese paper, modern paper is made from a pulp, but most of it contains shredded, softened wood from conifer trees such as pine, spruce or fir. The fibres in wood, or any other plant, are made of a strong material called cellulose. This makes the paper very strong, so that it does not fall apart easily when pressed, folded or stretched.

## MAKING PAPER TODAY
In a modern paper-making machine, wood chips are boiled with caustic soda or another chemical to soften them and strip them of everything but their long, stringy fibres. This pulp is spread over a conveyor belt, blasted with air, then squeezed between rollers to turn it into dry paper.

## DIFFERENT SOURCES
Over the years, people have experimented with cellulose from sources other than wood. Bank notes and expensive writing paper often contain fibres from cotton rags, which are made from cotton plants. The fibres make the paper very smooth and tough.

## WASTE PAPER
On average, every person in the United States uses about 300kg of paper a year. About half the paper we use is recycled to make newspapers, toilet rolls and other low-quality papers. The rest is dumped in landfill sites.

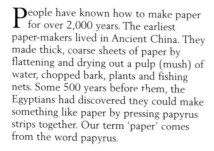

Pulp from recycled paper added

Bark removed

Wood chipped

Water and chemicals added and wood chips cooked into pulp

Pulp beaten to break down fibres so they will mat together easily

Pulp cleaned and bleached to make it white

Pulp drained on fine mesh belt

Heated rollers dry paper and press fibres firmly together to form a sheet

Finished paper is wound on to reel

### SEE ALSO
Egypt (Ancient),
Conservation

# PLANET

Planets are the largest objects that circle around stars. They may be rocky, like the Earth, or made mostly of gas and liquid, like Jupiter.

Sir William Herschel (1738–1822) discovered Uranus in 1781.

The Sun is orbited by nine planets, most of which have moons. They range in size from Pluto, less than one fifth as wide as Earth, to Jupiter, which is 11 times wider than Earth.

In 1846, Urbain Le Verrier (1811–77) found the position of Neptune.

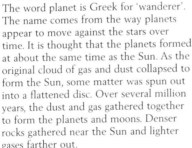

## PLANET SYSTEMS

Planets in the solar system and around other stars share several features. The solid centre is often surrounded by layers of gas forming an atmosphere. Circling the planet may be smaller planet-like objects called moons. Around the equator may be found bright rings consisting of tiny particles of rock and ice.

John Couch Adams (1819–92) predicted in 1845 that an eighth planet existed.

## THE WANDERERS

The word planet is Greek for 'wanderer'. The name comes from the way planets appear to move against the stars over time. It is thought that the planets formed at about the same time as the Sun. As the original cloud of gas and dust collapsed to form the Sun, some matter was spun out into a flattened disc. Over several million years, the dust and gas gathered together to form the planets and moons. Denser rocks gathered near the Sun and lighter gases farther out.

Percival Lowell (1855–1916) began the search for Pluto in 1905.

## MERCURY

Mercury is the planet closest to the Sun,

at an average distance of 58 million km. With a diameter of just 4,878km, Mercury is the smallest planet apart from Pluto. During the day, its temperature soars to 430°C, hot enough to melt lead, but at night it cools down to –170°C. Mercury's day, the time it takes to spin around once on its axis, is equal to 59 Earth days. Its year, the time it takes to go once around the Sun, is equal to 88 Earth days.

### PLANETARY NAMES

Mercury The Roman god of merchants and travellers
Venus The Roman goddess of love
Mars The Roman god of war
Jupiter The king of the Roman gods
Saturn The Roman god of seeds and sowing
Uranus The Greek and Roman god of the sky
Neptune The Roman god of the sea
Pluto The Roman god of the dead

## VENUS

With a diameter of 12,142km, Venus is nearly the same size as Earth. However, most of Venus's atmosphere consists of carbon dioxide, a gas that traps the Sun's heat. This 'greenhouse effect' makes Venus hotter than Mercury, although it is about twice as far from the Sun. Most of its surface is covered in lava that flowed out of giant volcanoes millions of years ago. Venus is the only planet to spin the opposite way to the direction of its orbit. It spins so slowly that one of its days lasts for as long as 243 days on Earth. ▶

Clyde Tombaugh (b. 1906) discovered Pluto in 1930 near its predicted position.

## MARS

The fourth planet from the Sun, Mars is only about half the size of the Earth and is much cooler. Its strong red colour is due to rust in the rocks on its surface. Its atmosphere consists mostly of carbon dioxide and is about 100 times thinner than the Earth's. The largest volcano and the largest canyon ever discovered are to be found on the Martian surface. There are also features on Mars that look like dried-up river beds. This suggests that Mars was once warmer and wetter than it is now. Under these conditions, life may have developed and there is even a chance that primitive life may exist there today. Mars has two tiny moons: Phobos and Deimos. The larger of these, Phobos, is only about 24km across.

## JUPITER

The biggest of the planets, Jupiter, could swallow up over 1,000 Earths. It has a

▲ The space probe *Voyager 2* was launched in 1977 and by 1989 had passed close to Jupiter, Saturn, Uranus and Neptune, sending data back to Earth.

**MERCURY**
The surface of Mercury is rocky, often covered in sand and marked by large meteorite craters. There is no atmosphere and the planet is roasted by the nearness of the Sun.

**VENUS**
Venus has broken slabs of rock and some dust on its surface. Most sunlight is blocked by the clouds of sulphuric acid in the atmosphere of carbon dioxide and nitrogen.

**EARTH**
Only Earth is known to support life. The rocky surface is covered by water and soils. The atmosphere of nitrogen and oxygen contains clouds of water vapour.

**MARS**
The reddish surface of Mars is made up of rock and sand. The atmosphere is thin and consists mostly of carbon dioxide. Both poles are covered with caps of ice.

**JUPITER**
As a gas giant, Jupiter has no surface. Instead, dense layers of gas surround a core. Io, one of 16 moons, has a rocky surface dyed red by sulphur from its many volcanoes.

**SATURN**
Like Jupiter, Saturn is a gas giant. The 91 per cent hydrogen atmosphere has dense clouds of ammonia, water and methane coloured by phosphorous and other elements.

**URANUS**
Hydrogen and helium make up most of the gas giant Uranus. The planet is surrounded by rings of blackish particles 'shepherded' in place by two small moons.

**NEPTUNE**
The blueness of the gas giant Neptune is due to methane gas. The surface of the moon Triton is frozen methane and nitrogen. Geysers of nitrogen gas erupt to 8km.

**PLUTO**
Pluto is made of frozen nitrogen and methane. Its moon Charon is almost large enough to be a twin planet. The Sun is so far away that it appears as a bright star.

diameter of 142,800km, but most of this is made of gases and liquids rather than solid rock. Like the Sun, Jupiter contains a great deal of hydrogen. Jupiter spins so fast that its day lasts less than ten hours. But a year on Jupiter is nearly 12 times longer than one of ours. Jupiter has a single ring and 16 satellites. One of these, Ganymede, is the largest moon in the solar system – bigger than Mercury.

## SATURN

Measuring 120,000km across, Saturn is second only to Jupiter in size. Like Jupiter, Uranus and Neptune, it is a gas giant. It is famous for its bright rings, made of billions of particles of rock and ice. The rings are more than 272,000km across, but they are very thin. Saturn has at least 18 moons. The largest of these, Titan, is the only moon known to have an atmosphere.

## URANUS

Orbiting the Sun 19 times farther out than the Earth, Uranus receives very little heat. The temperature at the top of its clouds is –220°C. With a diameter of 52,000km, Uranus is less than half the size of Saturn but still four times bigger than the Earth. It was the first planet to be discovered through a telescope. Uranus has a set of thin, dark rings and 15 moons.

## NEPTUNE

Similar in size and appearance to Uranus, the blue-green planet Neptune orbits the Sun at an average distance of 2.8 billion km. It is bitterly cold and 85 percent of its atmosphere is hydrogen, while violent winds blow at over 1,000km/h. Neptune has several thin rings and eight moons.

## PLUTO

With a diameter of about 2,300km, Pluto is the smallest planet in the solar system. It is also the coldest and the farthest from the Sun, lying on average 40 times farther out than the Earth. One year on Pluto lasts about 248 Earth years. Pluto's moon, Charon, was discovered in 1978, and has a diameter of about 1,300km.

## PLANETS OF OTHER STARS

Although planets around other stars have never been seen, scientists know they exist as they cause the stars they orbit to wobble slightly. As more and more are found, the chances grow that billions of planets may exist, and that there may be life on some of them. In 1961, astronomers at the Green Bank Observatory in West Virginia, USA, estimated that the nearest intelligent life should exist within about 300 light years of Earth. Radio telescopes are used to monitor stars with planets for radio broadcasts.

▲ Life from other planets has featured in the movies. The alien in the movie *E.T.* was friendly, but other movie aliens are warlike.

## GREAT RED SPOT

The Great Red Spot on Jupiter has existed since at least 1665. It is a circular storm with winds blowing at about 80m per second. The red colour may be due to sulphur in the clouds.

▲ Saturn's rings are made up of dust, ice crystals and rocks up to 10m across. The rings are 66,000km wide, but only 1km deep. As Saturn orbits the Sun, the rings are seen from different angles from Earth.

### SEE ALSO

Astronomy, Moon, Solar system, Spacecraft, Space exploration, Sun

# PLANT

Plants are living organisms that harness the energy of the Sun to feed themselves. Without plants for animals to feed on, there would be no animal life on Earth.

Ferns are among the oldest plants, appearing about 350 million years ago.

The dodder is a parasitic plant. It inserts suckers into other plants to get food.

The carnivorous Venus flytrap feeds on insects that it traps in its leaves.

We make textiles from the fibres of the ripe fruit of the cotton plant.

Some plants are dangerous to eat – hemlock can be used to make poison.

Plants provide timber. Wood from the oak tree is heavy, hard and strong.

Most plants are able to absorb sunlight by means of a green substance inside them called chlorophyll. They use the energy from the Sun's light to make food by a chemical process called photosynthesis. This results in the production of oxygen, which all plants and animals, including humans, need to live.

## PLANTS OF ALL KINDS

There are about 400,000 different kinds of plant, ranging in size from tiny mosses only a few millimetres long to giant redwood trees, which grow to over 100m tall. Each has adapted to absorb light, find water and minerals and withstand the temperature range in its own habitat. Desert plants such as cacti have long, widely spreading roots to collect water, which they store in their expandable stems. Succulent plants store water in swollen fleshy leaves. Plants in cold places grow in thick, low clumps which protects them from the cold and wind.

## DESIGNED TO CATCH LIGHT

Plants need to catch as much light as possible. Each one has leaves which are shaped and arranged on the stem so they over-shadow the leaves below as little as possible. Tall trees have strong, woody trunks to hold their leaves high above the ground and other plants. Plants like vines climb up through the trees with clinging tendrils. Plants called epiphytes grow entirely suspended in tree branches, never touching the ground.

## OTHER SOURCES OF FOOD

Some parasitic plants, such as mistletoe, obtain extra nourishment by growing into the tissues of larger plants. Other plants, such as the dodder, cannot make any of their own food. The dodder attaches itself to another plant for nourishment. There are also carnivorous (meat-eating) plants, such as the pitcher plant and the Venus flytrap, which can catch and digest insects.

## PLANTS AND PEOPLE

People learned to grow plants as crops about 10,000 years ago. Today, over four fifths of the world's food comes from

## GERMINATION

Inside the seed are all the parts needed to form a new plant. The stage when a seed starts to sprout is called germination. In order to begin the germination process, a seed must have warmth, moisture and oxygen.

First leaves

Stem

Cotyledon

Plumule

Hypocotyl

Seed coat

Primary root

### Stage 1
When a seed starts to germinate, it splits and the primary root is formed from the hypocotyl.

### Stage 2
The stem pushes up through the soil and the cotyledon starts to break out of the seed coat.

### Stage 3
The plumule breaks free of the cotyledon, the stem grows upwards and the first leaves are formed.

## CLASSIFYING PLANTS

Plants are classified according to certain similarities they share. One way is to divide them into ten groups, or divisions. The division Bryophyta is made up of non-vascular plants. These plants do not have the tissues that carry food and water from one part of the plant to another. The other nine divisions are all vascular. The division Anthophyta contains all flowering plants (also called angiosperms), which contain their reproductive cells in flowers. Angiosperms are divided into two classes, monocots and dicots. The basic difference is in the number of cotyledons, or seed leaves. Monocots have one and dicots have two. Monocots, such as grasses, normally have long narrow leaves, whereas dicot leaves are usually broad.

**NON-VASCULAR**

Division BRYOPHYTA

Class
HEPATICAE

Liverwort

Class
ANTHOCEROTAE

Hornwort

Class
MUSCI

Moss

**VASCULAR**

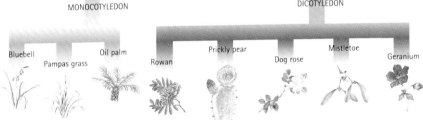

Division
PSILOPHYTA

Division
LYCOPHYTA

Division
SPHENOPHYTA

Division
PTEROPHYTA

Division
CONIFEROPHYTA

Division
CYCADOPHYTA

Division
GINKGOPHYTA

Division
GNETOPHYTA

Division
ANTHOPHYTA

Whiskfern    Club moss    Horsetail    Fern    Pine    Cycad    Ginkgo    Welwitschia

FLOWERING PLANTS

Class
MONOCOTYLEDON

Class
DICOTYLEDON

Bluebell    Oil palm    Rowan    Prickly pear    Mistletoe    Geranium
Pampas grass        Dog rose

plants such as wheat, rice and potatoes. Humans eat a variety of fruits, nuts and vegetables and make drinks from tea, coffee and grains. Plants also provide products such as vegetable oils, cotton, rubber and – perhaps the most useful of all – wood. Many of the drugs we use to treat disease come from plants. Even fuels such as coal are the fossilized remains of prehistoric plants.

## PLANT BREEDING

Most plants we use today are quite different from their ancestors. Using methods such as genetic engineering, plant breeders have made improvements to cereals such as wheat to make them more productive or more resistant to pests.

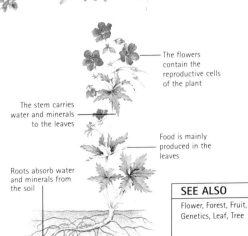

The flowers contain the reproductive cells of the plant

The stem carries water and minerals to the leaves

Food is mainly produced in the leaves

Roots absorb water and minerals from the soil

**SEE ALSO**

Flower, Forest, Fruit, Genetics, Leaf, Tree

# PLASTIC

Plastics are materials that can easily be stretched or moulded into shape. Most are made from the chemicals obtained from petroleum oil.

Plastic replaces many metal and ceramic items because it is light but durable.

Plastics are man-made and consist of long chains of molecules called polymers. The arrangement of these chains gives plastics their different qualities. Hard plastics can be used to replace metals, in cars for example. Soft plastics can be used to create fabrics, leather and even fur.

Many items are wrapped and sealed in plastic rather than paper bags.

## NATURAL INGREDIENTS
In 1862, the British chemist Alexander Parkes showed the first plastic, known as cellulose nitrate, at the London Exhibition. It was later named celluloid and developed by American inventor John Wesley Hyatt. Although celluloid became brittle and changed colour in strong light, it was used to make many objects, from billiard balls to false teeth and photographic film.

Strong and lightweight plastics can replace the metal bodywork in cars.

## CHEMICALLY BASED PLASTIC
The first plastic to be chemically based was a material called Bakelite, invented in 1909. More modern plastics, however, such as polyester and PVC, are lighter and easier to colour. They can also be made flexible and can withstand moisture and strong sunlight.

Polyester is a plastic that is widely used in clothing manufacture.

## HARD OR SOFT
Plastics do not all behave the same way when reheated. Some, called 'thermoplastics', melt and can be reshaped

Instead of wood, boats today are often made of strong, lightweight plastic.

Plastic is used for replacement body parts, such as false teeth.

## PLASTIC MOULDING
Two common methods for moulding plastic are that of injection moulding, in which plastic pellets are heated and then injected into a mould, and hot extrusion, in which hot plastic is forced through openings to make rods or sheets.

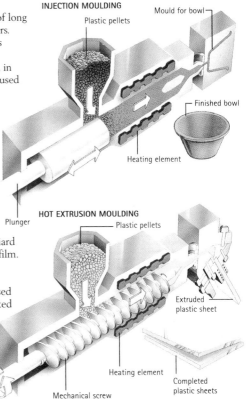

INJECTION MOULDING

Plastic pellets

Mould for bowl

Finished bowl

Heating element

Plunger

HOT EXTRUSION MOULDING

Plastic pellets

Extruded plastic sheet

Heating element

Completed plastic sheets

Mechanical screw

after reheating. Polythene, a material used to make plastic bowls, is like this, which is why it often loses its shape if something hot is placed on it. Other plastics are 'thermosetting'. Once they have cooled and set during manufacture, they cannot be reshaped. In fact, if a thermosetting plastic is heated up, it gets harder. Electric plugs are made of thermosetting plastics, which is why they do not melt if the wires inside them overheat.

◄ Perspex is an ideal plastic for a squash court as it is transparent like glass but much stronger.

| SEE ALSO |
|---|
| Oil |

# POLLUTION

**Pollution happens when a harmful substance is released into the environment in such large quantities that it causes damage to people, wildlife or habitats.**

The control of pollution is a major problem facing the world. Large areas may soon become uninhabitable and many plants and animals may become extinct. Public opinion is now forcing governments and industry to combat pollution.

▲ Liquid waste dumped into rivers may poison wildlife and threaten supplies of drinking water for humans.

### SMOKES AND SMELLS

Car exhausts and factories pump fumes into the air. Some of these gases mix with clouds to form acid rain which kills plants. Carbon dioxide traps the Sun's heat, and may lead to global warming. Other gases, called CFCs, are thought to destroy ozone – the gas barrier that blocks harmful radiation from the Sun. Noise can also be a form of pollution, with traffic or aircraft noise ruining the quality of life.

▲ Smoke and other pollutants can travel thousands of kilometres before falling as deposits or as acid rain.

### OIL SPILL

Oil tankers carry up to 550,000 tonnes of oil, so accidents can be devastating. The oil floats, forming a slick that blocks the sunlight needed by seaweed and other algae. Birds and fish may be trapped or poisoned by the oil, but the sea or coastline usually recovers in a few years.

### A LOAD OF RUBBISH

Rubbish is created in large quantities, and the world is running out of places to put it all. Recycling glass, paper and other waste reduces the need for dumping. Radioactive waste created by nuclear power stations remains dangerous for thousands of years.

### DEAD RIVERS

Industrial waste dumped into rivers can kill all life. Fertilizers can produce growths of algae, which absorb the oxygen in the water, killing fish and plants. International agreements have been drawn up to stop countries dumping waste at sea and to reduce the pollution of lakes and rivers.

| SEE ALSO |
| --- |
| Conservation, Ecology, Habitat |

# PRINTING

Printing is the mass production of identical images of writing or pictures on books, posters, packaging and fabrics. It is used in education, business, art and fashion.

The first attempts at printing were made in China in the eighth century AD. Wooden blocks were carved with characters and pictures, which were then inked and pressed onto paper.

### EARLY PRESSES

The German Johann Gutenberg (c. 1398–1468) invented the first printing press around 1455. Gutenberg used moveable type, with raised pieces of metal for each letter so that words could be rearranged easily. The type was laid on a forme and then covered with ink. A sheet of paper was placed over it, held down by screws to give a clear, even image. Later inventors added mechanisms for automating the printing press. By 1830, a steam press could produce 1,000 sheets per hour.

▲ With the Gutenberg press, books could be printed and circulated on a large scale. As printing became quicker and less expensive, books became cheaper, spreading information to a greater number of people. Printing inventions in the 19th century aided revolutions in science and mechanics.

## MODERN PRINTING

In 1904, the American printer Ira Rubel invented offset lithography printing. He discovered that the inked image from a printing plate could be offset, or stamped, onto a rubber roller, which could then be printed onto paper. In 1930, this system was combined with a method of making pictures up from small dots. When used with four basic colour inks, this made mass-production colour printing possible. Today, many publications are printed from computer-generated pages. Laser printers work by spraying ink onto the page; dot matrix printers form images from tiny dots.

## PICTURE PRINTS

Artists use intaglio to make engravings: they cut a design into the printing plate. Gravure printing uses a copper plate, which is engraved with a picture using a photographic process. Different tones and strengths of colour are produced by engraving deeper or shallower holes.

## OFFSET LITHOGRAPHY PRINTING

Rubber rollers are offset with a printing image, one for each of four basic colours: yellow, magenta, cyan (blue) and black. Paper is then printed with the coloured inks in turn until the complete picture is built up.

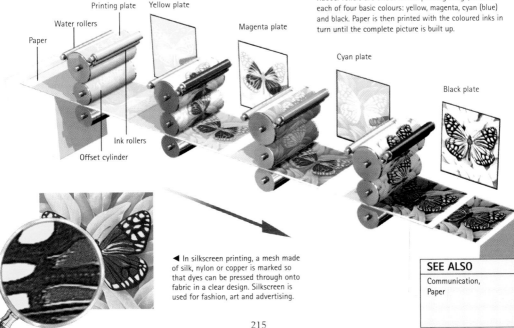

Printing plate  Yellow plate
Water rollers
Paper
Magenta plate
Cyan plate
Black plate
Ink rollers
Offset cylinder

◄ In silkscreen printing, a mesh made of silk, nylon or copper is marked so that dyes can be pressed through onto fabric in a clear design. Silkscreen is used for fashion, art and advertising.

## SEE ALSO

Communication,
Paper

# RADAR AND SONAR

Radar and sonar are systems that locate objects.
They work by sending out waves, detecting echoes
from objects and measuring the distance in between.

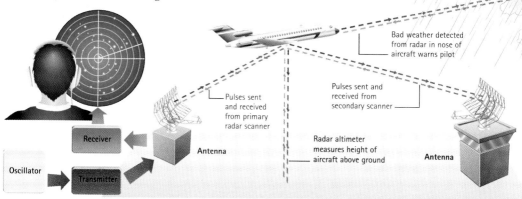

Bad weather detected
from radar in nose of
aircraft warns pilot

Pulses sent
and received
from primary
radar scanner

Pulses sent and
received from
secondary scanner

Receiver

Antenna

Radar altimeter
measures height of
aircraft above ground

Antenna

Oscillator

Transmitter

Radar and sonar are used to find the
location of objects that are difficult to
see. They also help people to judge how
fast objects are moving. Radar is used at
airports to track aircraft in the surrounding
airspace. Boats use sonar to measure the
depth of the sea floor or river bed and to
spot any obstacles under water.

## HOW RADAR WORKS

Radar, which is short for RAdio Detection
And Ranging, works by sending out a
narrow pulse of radio waves. Any car,
aircraft or other large metal object in the
way of this pulse will reflect it, in the
same way that a mirror reflects light. A
receiver on the radar
system picks up

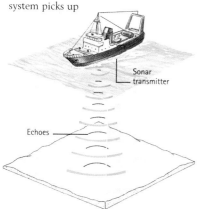

Sonar
transmitter

Echoes

## AIRCRAFT RADAR

Air traffic controllers need to know the height and position of aircraft around busy
airports to prevent collisions between planes. They have small display screens that relay
information they have found. The displays show a realistic map of the area, marked with
objects. Large aircraft have on-board radar to detect other planes and bad weather.

the reflected waves and measures how
long the radio wave took to bounce back.
This information can be used to calculate
the object's distance. Radar is used by
scientists to find out the distance to other
planets and by police to catch speeding
motorists. It is also used to track storm
fronts and forecast the weather.

## HOW SONAR WORKS

Sonar, meaning SOund Navigation And
Ranging, works in a similar way to radar.
Instead of radio waves, it sends out a pulse
of high-pitched sound. Known as
ultrasound, the sound from a sonar system
is so high that humans cannot hear it. The
ultrasound bounces off any dense objects
in its path, such as rocks, shipwrecks and
shoals of fish, back towards the ship.
Hydrophones (underwater microphones)
pick up the reflected sound and use it to
calculate the distance of the objects.

▲ Radar was first used to
detect enemy aircraft
during World War II.
Information was sent to a
central control room,
where it was used to track
enemy action and plot
battle strategies on a map.

◀ Survey ships use sonar to chart the contours of the
seabed. The time it takes sound waves to reflect back to
the ship indicates the depth of the seabed.

### SEE ALSO

Medicine, Navigation,
Sound, Weather,
World War II

# RAINFOREST

These dense, damp forests are mainly found near the Equator. They contain more types of plants and animals than all the other habitats put together.

The world's biggest rainforests are the tropical rainforests of South America, Africa and Southeast Asia, where the climate is always warm and wet. There is no winter at the Equator, so there is nothing to stop the plants growing. The result is a huge variety of trees, ferns, vines and epiphytes (plants that grow on other plants).

## TROPICAL RAINFORESTS
Although they cover only six per cent of the Earth's surface, tropical rainforests contain about three quarters of all known species of animals and plants. Wherever you look, there are always some plants in flower or producing fruit, so there is a constant supply of food for birds, bats, insects, snakes, tree frogs, antelopes, monkeys and a host of other animals. Most of the animals live in the trees.

◄ Tropical forest animals have adapted to life in the trees. The sloth uses its hooked claws to move from branch to branch.

## RAINFOREST LIFE CYCLE
Tropical rainforests are made up of several layers. The main canopy (tree-top layer) is usually 30-50m above ground, where the slender trunks break out into a cluster of branches, but the tallest trees reach 60m. The under-storey, dark beneath the canopy, consists of tree trunks covered with lianas (climbing plants) and laced together by creepers. The forest floor is surprisingly free of clutter. Leaves, fruit, animal droppings and bodies decompose quickly when they fall to the ground, and their chemical building blocks are immediately taken up again by plant roots and used to make new growth. It is nature's most efficient recycling system.

## TEMPERATE RAINFORESTS
Farther from the Equator are temperate rainforests, formed in coastal regions where onshore winds bring constant rain. These lie chiefly in northwestern North America, southern Chile, Tasmania, southeastern Australia and New Zealand. The dominant trees are redwoods and sitka spruce in the Northern Hemisphere and eucalyptus and Antarctic beech in the Southern Hemisphere. Some temperate rainforest trees are even taller than those in the tropical forests, but the animal and plant life is not as rich.

## THREATS TO THE FOREST
Large areas of the Amazon, Congo and Malaysian rainforests have been destroyed by logging for timber. Vast areas have also been cut down to make way for plantations of rubber, coffee, bananas and sugar cane, or to provide pasture for cattle. Rainforests play an important part in keeping the Earth's climate healthy, and they contain many medicinal plants. International organizations are trying to protect the remaining forests before it is too late.

Emergent tree

Canopy

Understorey

Lianas wind around the tree trunks and rafflesias grow on the forest floor

### SEE ALSO
Conservation, Forest, Habitat, Plant

# Rat AND OTHER RODENTS

**Rodents are mammals that have sharp, chisel-like front teeth. They use these for gnawing through food, as well as through anything that gets in their way.**

▲ In order to supply wood for its lodge (nest) and its winter food store, the beaver uses its teeth to trim branches and even to fell small trees.

Black (and brown) rats carry the germs of several diseases, including typhus.

The European red squirrel is one of several species of tree squirrel.

House mice live among people – 'mouse' comes from a word meaning thief.

Most hamsters have large cheek pouches. They use these to carry food in.

Porcupines defend themselves with their sharp, spiny quills.

Found in cold, northern regions, lemmings migrate to prevent overpopulation.

Rats belong to a large group of mammals called rodents. There are about 1,500 kinds of rodent, and they include rats, mice, voles, hamsters, squirrels, beavers and porcupines. The smallest rodent is the harvest mouse from Europe and Asia, which could easily sit in an egg cup. The biggest is the capybara from South America, which can weigh over 75kg. Together, rodents make up about 40 per cent of the world's mammal species.

## SHARP TEETH

All rodents share one important feature – a set of four sharp front teeth, called incisors, which work like chisels. They use these to gnaw their way through their food, to chop up nesting material and to get through anything that blocks their path. Beavers use their incisors to gnaw through solid tree trunks, while rats and mice use them to gnaw through household timber,

▲ Like all rodents, rats have four sharp front teeth. These are self-sharpening, and grow throughout the animal's life.

## WIRE CUTTERS

Both the black rat and the much more common brown rat (shown right) eat almost any kind of plant or animal. With their strong teeth, they are able to cut through materials as strong as wire to get to food. When eating, they often use their front feet to hold their food while their teeth set to work.

food packaging and even electric cables, which can trigger off fires.

## FAST BREEDERS

Compared with many other mammals, rodents can breed very rapidly if they have enough food. A female brown rat can start to breed when just two months old, and may produce as many as five litters a year, with up to 12 babies in each litter. Poisons or traps are often used to keep rats under control, but their fast breeding rate makes this difficult.

### SEE ALSO
Animal, Mammal

# RELIGION

**A religion usually involves a belief in a god or gods. It may have rituals, recognize certain places as holy and recommend a certain way of life.**

There have been, and still are, many religions around the world. Most religions teach that people should lead good lives and behave in certain ways.

Zoroaster (c. 600BC) believed the Earth was fought over by good and evil gods.

## GODS

Gods are thought to be greatly superior to humans, endowed with wonderful powers. The Ancient Greeks had hundreds of gods, each for a different thing – such as the sea, wind or love. This collection of gods is known as a pantheon. Many peoples, such as the Vikings and ancient Egyptians, had a pantheon of gods. Other religions, including Judaism, Christianity and Islam, have only one god.

Siddhartha Gautama (c. 500BC), the Enlightened One, founded Buddhism.

## REVELATIONS

Some religions are based on a revelation – the passing on of sacred knowledge – from a god or gods to a human. Islam is based on the teachings of God as given to the prophet Muhammad in Arabia nearly 1,400 years ago. The Mormon Church of Latter Day Saints is based on visions and a holy book revealed to Joseph Smith in Palmyra, New York in the 1820s.

Confucius (551–479BC) established the way of life now called Confucianism.

▼ In New Guinea, dancers in colourful costume take the roles of spirits during ceremonies.

Jesus Christ (c. 4BC–c. AD30) preached the teachings of Christianity in Palestine.

Abu Bakr (c. 573–634) led Islam after the death of the prophet Muhammad.

## TALKING TO THE GODS

The Ancient Greeks believed that the Oracle at Delphi, dedicated to the Sun god Apollo, could foretell the future. The chief priestess gave answers to questions in a trance. These answers were often ambiguous, but even the government of the day sometimes consulted the Oracle.

## PRIESTS AND TEMPLES

Many religions have priests, who study the holy teachings and make sure that rituals are carried out properly and that holy places are respected. Other religions, such as Islam, have no priests. The Ancient Egyptians built vast temples that were considered to be the home of a god. In many societies, great wealth is lavished on the temple or church. However, Australian Aborigines believe that certain places are sacred to the spirits and should not be built on.

## HOLY COMMUNITIES

The followers of some religions may form a special community and treat non-believers as outsiders. In some religions, people form communities where they follow the teachings of the religion very strictly. Such dedicated communities include the monasteries and convents of Christianity and Buddhism.

### SEE ALSO

Buddhism, Christianity, Hinduism, Islam

# RENAISSANCE

The Renaissance was a revival in arts and sciences which began in Italy around 1350 and spread across Europe. It marked the end of the Middle Ages.

In the late 14th century, Italy was the richest and most populated of all the European countries. However, Italy was not a unified country at this time – the region was divided up into about 250 states, and each state was based around a city and governed by the wealthiest families in that particular area of the country.

Astronomers developed more accurate telescopes to observe the stars.

## THE REBIRTH

The word "Renaissance" means "rebirth". Italy had preserved much of the Ancient Roman civilization, but this had been largely ignored until the 1300s. Then, around 1350, Italian scholars began to copy the old manuscripts and circulate them. These manuscripts contained the history of the ancient (classical) world and passed on its knowledge of architecture, science and art. There was also an influx of Ancient Greek learning from the city of Constantinople after it fell to the Turks in 1453. Renaissance thinkers became increasingly influenced by the way ancient

The invention of printing in 1440 made the spread of learning possible.

scholars studied subjects such as philosophy, literature and science, and wanted to recreate the spirit of the classical age. During the Middle Ages which had immediately preceded the Renaissance, people had been much more concerned with theology (religion).

## POWERFUL BACKERS

The rich noblemen who ruled the Italian cities paid for the classical manuscripts to be copied. In Florence, the powerful Medici family of bankers spent lavishly as patrons of the arts. Lorenzo Medici, who ruled Florence from 1469 to 1492, was called 'The Magnificent' because he attracted the finest scientists and artists to the area. Francesco Sforza, a mercenary who became Duke of Milan in 1450, was another great Italian patron.

## GREAT ARTISTS

Renaissance artists began to paint and sculpt in a completely new style. Instead of stiff, formal poses, they drew people more naturally and put them in real landscapes and rooms. By 1424, Tomasso Masaccio was decorating churches in Florence with beautiful frescos. At the same time, Filippo Brunelleschi was building startling new structures. His masterpiece is the dome on the cathedral in Florence, which he began in 1420. It blends excellent engineering with graceful design and was the largest dome in the world at the time.

◀ Hans Holbein's *The Ambassadors* (1533) typifies the spirit of the Renaissance: the richly robed ambassadors are surrounded by objects from science and the arts.

# FUTURISTIC IDEAS OF FLYING MACHINES

The great minds of the Renaissance, like Leonardo Da Vinci, did not take all their inspiration from the past. His sketch books show a fascination with flight and the possibility of flying machines long before the invention of the first successful aircraft.

▲ A modern artist's impression of Leonardo's flying machine — turning paddles moved the wings.

**LEONARDO DA VINCI**
As well as being a painter (masterpieces include the *Mona Lisa*) and inventor, da Vinci (1452–1519) studied biology, anatomy and mechanics.

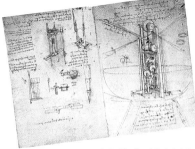

▲ Da Vinci's original sketches

## COMBINING SKILLS

The ability to mix very different skills was typical of the artists and scientist of the Renaissance. Michelangelo Buonarroti is best known for his marble sculptures, such as the famous *Pietá*, but he was also a painter and poet. He even worked as an architect on St Peter's Basilica in Rome in 1547. Most versatile of all was Leonardo da Vinci, who created several great paintings, studied science and designed irrigation systems for farms. Other famous figures of the era include the artists Giotto, Botticelli and Raphael, sculptors Donatello and Ghiberti and the architect Bramante.

Scientists began to make their own detailed observations instead of simply accepting the teachings of the Church. The Polish astronomer Nicolaus Copernicus (1473–1543) realized that the Earth moved round the Sun. However, he was too afraid to publish his findings until he was very close to death, as his thinking opposed the Church view that the Earth was the centre of the universe.

## THE SPREAD OF LEARNING

As the new art and learning developed in Italy, other countries began to take note. The universities of Oxford, Cambridge and Paris became centres of a Renaissance in England and France. Scholars such as Erasmus of Rotterdam in Holland and Thomas More of England developed and spread the ideas. In both Holland and Germany, artists such as the van Eycks, Dürer and Holbein took Renaissance ideals and developed a distinct northern European style. In England, the writers Shakespeare and Spenser began a revolution in poetry and drama. Then, in 1600, Marie de Medici married King Henri IV of France, and took Italian craftsmen, artists and cooks to France, which further spread the new thinking through Europe.

◀ Bramante's Tempietto in Rome reflects classical styles of building.

**DESIDERIUS ERASMUS** (1466–1536) was a Dutch priest and leading Christian humanist whose writings attacked the morals of church leaders.

▲ Michelangelo's statue of Moses, carved in about 1513, is typical of the realistic style of sculpture of the Renaissance.

## SEE ALSO
Astronomy, Invention, Italy, Printing

# REPRODUCTION

Reproduction is the process of producing new organisms so that life continues from one generation to the next. All living things make more of their own kind.

Reproduction is one of the most important functions of all living organisms – from the tiniest microbes to the biggest trees, elephants and whales. It means making more of your own kind, or species. There are two main types of reproduction: asexual and sexual.

▲ Single-celled organisms, such as the amoeba, reproduce asexually by dividing in two – a process called 'binary fission'.

## ONE BECOMES TWO
The simplest form of asexual reproduction is that of organisms consisting of a single cell, such as amoebas or bacteria. These reproduce by simply dividing in two. Each offspring cell grows larger and then also divides, and so on. In conditions that suit them, some bacteria can double their numbers like this every 15 to 20 minutes.

## ONE-PARENT REPRODUCTION
Many plants reproduce asexually by vegetative propagation. A part of the plant grows roots into the soil and sprouts a stem, which then becomes a separate individual. Gardeners make use of this process by slicing off a part of a plant and growing it into a new individual. Some simple animals reproduce in a similar way, by budding. The parent sprouts a 'bud' that grows into a new individual. Hydras, tiny anemone-like water creatures, multiply by budding.

| AVERAGE PREGNANCY TIME FOR MAMMALS: | |
| --- | --- |
| Species | Days |
| Common shrew | 15 |
| House mouse | 17 |
| Horseshoe bat | 45 |
| Cat | 63 |
| Dog | 63 |
| Tiger | 103 |
| Goat | 150 |
| Moose | 245 |
| Gorilla | 260 |
| Human | 266 |
| Horse | 333 |
| Blue whale | 350 |
| Asian elephant | 660 |

## FERTILIZATION
Reproduction is very similar in all mammals, including humans. The female or mother has reproductive organs called ovaries that make hundreds of tiny eggs. The male or father has reproductive organs called testes (testicles) that make millions of even tinier sperm. During mating, the male passes his sperm cells into the reproductive tubes, or tract, of the female. Here, one of the sperm joins with, or fertilizes, an egg. The genes in the egg and sperm come together to create a new individual.

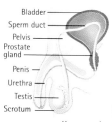

Human male

Bladder
Sperm duct
Pelvis
Prostate gland
Penis
Urethra
Testis
Scrotum

Human female

Fallopian tube
Ovary
Uterus (womb)
Bladder
Vagina
Vulva

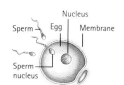

Nucleus
Sperm
Egg
Membrane
Sperm
Sperm nucleus

Cytoplasm
Nucleus

**1** Day 1: a sperm cell penetrates and fertilizes an egg inside the Fallopian tube, forming a zygote.

**2** The zygote divides into two and continues to travel along the Fallopian tube toward the uterus.

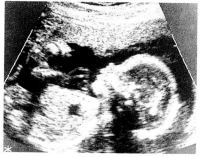

▲ Ultrasound scans, as of this 20-week-old foetus, are used to keep check on a baby's development in the womb.

## DIFFERENT GENES – VARIATION
Most plants and animals breed by sexual reproduction. This requires two parents – female and male. Each parent contributes a unique selection of genes, so the offspring vary in the genes they inherit and grow up to be slightly different from each other. This variation means that at least some offspring will be suited to the world's ever-changing conditions, and so will survive in the struggle for life.

## HAVING BABIES
Some young mammals, such as mice, are born fur-less, with eyes closed, and depend totally on their parents. A human baby is similarly helpless, although it has certain built-in reflexes, such as crying when it is hungry or cold. Other mammal babies, such as whales, giraffes and antelopes, are alert and able to move about within minutes of birth. The number of young born at one time varies. Mother seals, dolphins, bats and humans usually have one baby. Mother dogs, cats and rats have several babies. A mother opossum may give birth to more than 30 babies.

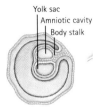
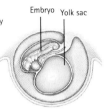
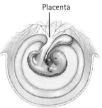

Yolk sac
Amniotic cavity
Body stalk

Embryo  Yolk sac

Placenta

**3** The cells continue to divide until, after 4 to 5 days, a tiny ball of 16 cells has formed.

**4** Day 13: the ball settles into the lining of the uterus, which forms supportive structures.

**5** Day 21: the embryo feeds off the yolk sac and its spine and brain begin to form.

**6** Day 28: the stomach, arm and leg buds have all begun to form and the heart starts pumping blood.

**7** Day 35: bones and muscles start to form, while the arms and legs continue to grow.

## HOW THE HUMAN BABY DEVELOPS

During development, the cells multiply rapidly, move around and change into specialized shapes, gradually forming the basic body organs. This rapid growth is called the embryo stage. As the tiny, tadpole-like body develops, it takes on a recognizable shape. It develops muscles, bones, skin and other features. Eight weeks after fertilization, it is called a foetus. It is nourished by the mother through a specialized organ, the placenta. Finally, it leaves the womb through the birth canal to begin life in the outside world.

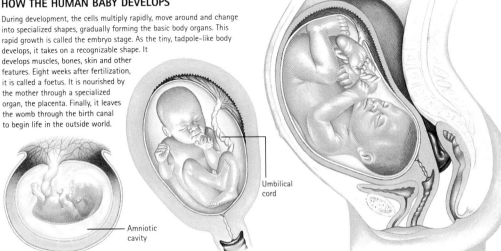

Umbilical cord

Amniotic cavity

**8** Day 56: the 2cm-long foetus has developed its main body parts, including fingers and toes, and some of its muscles and nerves function.

**9** After four months, the baby has doubled in size and has well-developed features such as fingers and toes.

**10** After five months, the lungs and most of the other body organs are working properly. The foetus usually repositions itself, so that at the end of nine months (above) it is ready to be born head first.

## LAYING EGGS

Mammals, some snakes and fish, and a few insects give birth to their young. But the vast majority of animal mothers reproduce by laying eggs, out of which the offspring hatch. On land, the eggs are usually encased in a tough shell for protection and to prevent drying out. Examples are bird and reptile eggs. These contain a yolk, which is the food store for nourishing the baby as it develops. Insects, spiders and similar smaller creatures also lay tough-cased eggs, but without large food stores inside. The offspring must hatch out and feed straight away.

## REPRODUCING IN WATER

Eggs laid in water do not need a waterproof casing. Amphibians' eggs are jelly-like, and the eggs of most fish, crabs and similar creatures have thin walls. On land, the male usually transfers his sperm into the female's body during mating, otherwise the sperm would dry out and die. In water, females can release their eggs, and males their sperm, without the risk of them drying out. Male and female cast their sperm and eggs into the water and fertilization is left to chance. In many fish and crabs, males and females come together and release their eggs and sperm into one place.

### SEE ALSO

Amphibian, Animal, Butterfly and moth, Evolution, Fish, Flower, Human body, Insect, Mammal, Micro-organism

# REPTILE

**Reptiles are air-breathing animals with backbones and a covering of tough scales. Most of them live on land, but some live in the sea or in fresh water.**

▲ The Australian frilled lizard raises its collar in a display of aggression that frightens its attacker away.

When frightened, the poisonous cobra rises and spreads its hood.

The crocodile is a large flesh-eater that seizes its prey with powerful jaws.

Reptiles are usually described as cold-blooded creatures, and this means that their body temperature goes up and down as the air or water temperature changes. Most reptiles live in warm places, but they are found everywhere except in the far north or south. Those living in cooler places have to warm themselves up in the mornings by sitting in the sun. Reptiles are vertebrates (they have backbones), and there are 6,500 different species divided into five main groups: turtles or tortoises; lizards and snakes; crocodiles and alligators; worm lizards; and the tuatara, a species in its own group. The tuatara is described as a living fossil – it has hardly changed in 200 million years.

## TORTOISES – AN ANCIENT GROUP

Reptiles first appeared on the Earth over 300 million years ago, and many different kinds have come and gone since then. The oldest group of reptiles still living are the tortoises and turtles, which have not changed much in 200 million years. They are easily recognized by their shells, which are made of bone and usually have a horny covering. There are about 240 different species. Those living in the sea are usually called turtles and those living on land tortoises. Freshwater species are called terrapins. In the United States, however, the name turtle is often used for all the shelled reptiles. Land-living tortoises feed mainly on plants, but the other species are mainly flesh-eaters.

## SEA-GOING CREATURES

Most reptiles lay eggs. **1** The sea-going marine turtle comes ashore to find a safe place in the sand for her brood. **2** She lays her eggs in a sheltered spot. **3** Weeks later, the hatchlings break out of their shells. **4** They scramble out and race for the safety of the water. **5** Aquatic turtles all have limbs that act as paddles or flippers, which makes them excellent swimmers.

Tortoises have no teeth, and they bite their food with sharp, horny beaks.

## DINOSAUR RELATIVES
The huge dinosaurs that roamed the Earth millions of year ago were reptiles. Their nearest living reptile relatives are the crocodiles and alligators. These dangerous flesh-eaters live in and around tropical rivers. There are 22 to 23 species, and some of them reach lengths of about 9m.

## LIZARDS AND SNAKES
These animals form the largest group of reptiles alive today. There are about 3,750 species of lizard and 2,400 species of snake. Scientists believe that snakes descended from a group of burrowing lizards that gradually lost their legs about 100 million years ago. Some snakes are poisonous and bite with grooved fangs that inject venom from sac-like glands. Lizards nearly all live on land and are mostly very active animals. They include both vegetarians and flesh-eaters. The world's biggest lizard is the Komodo dragon, which lives in Indonesia. Up to 3m long, it eats animals as large as pigs. It is one of the monitor lizards, which have long necks and powerful teeth. Some monitors steal crocodile eggs and even eat young crocodiles. Small lizards feed mainly on insects, slugs and other species of invertebrate animals.

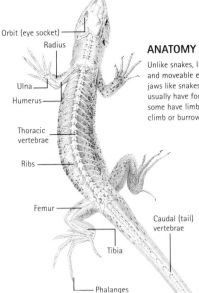

Orbit (eye socket)
Radius
Ulna
Humerus
Thoracic vertebrae
Ribs
Femur
Tibia
Phalanges
Caudal (tail) vertebrae

## ANATOMY OF A TYPICAL LIZARD
Unlike snakes, lizards have an outer ear opening and moveable eyelids. They cannot unhinge their jaws like snakes to swallow large prey. Lizards usually have four well-developed limbs, but some have limbs modified to help them run, climb or burrow. A typical lizard has a long tail.

The slow-worm looks like a snake but is really a lizard without legs.

The tortoise can pull its head, legs and tail into its hard, protective shell.

The gecko can climb walls using sucker-like pads on its feet.

## CHAMELEONS
These are slow-moving lizards, some of which are famous for their ability to change colour. A chameleon surrounded by green leaves is usually some shade of green, but if it is then put among brown leaves or bare twigs it will gradually turn brown. Chameleons feed on insects, which they catch by firing out their long, sticky tongue at great speed. Their bulging eyes are also very unusual because each one can be moved separately: one eye can look forward while the other one looks behind. This is very useful for finding insects and also for spotting enemies.

## A STRANGE SURVIVAL TRICK
Many birds and mammals like to eat lizards, but most lizards run away quickly when they are frightened. Their enemies often manage to grab no more than the tail – and then a surprising thing happens. The lizard snaps off its tail and races away, leaving the predator with just a wriggling tail. The lizard grows a new tail.

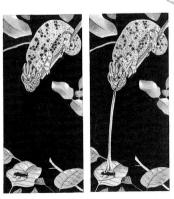

▲ A chameleon lashes out its tongue to catch a hapless insect. Its tongue is almost the same length as its body.

### FAST FACTS
• Some tortoises have been known to live for well over 120 years

• The Gila monster and the beaded lizard can kill people with their poisonous saliva

• The only seagoing lizard is the marine iguana, which lives in the Galapagos Islands

### SEE ALSO
Desert, Ocean and sea, Snake

# REVOLUTION

**A revolution is an overwhelming uprising by the people which aims to destroy the social or political system of a country and replace it with a new system.**

Wat Tyler (*d.* 1381) led the Peasants' Revolt of southern England in 1381.

George Washington (1732–99) led colonial troops in the American Revolution.

Simon Bolívar (1783–1830) led many revolts in South America.

Georges Danton (1759–94) led the republican faction in the French Revolution.

Giuseppe Garibaldi (1807–82) led revolutions in Italy to create a united nation.

Revolutions are unpredictable. They may achieve all their aims or lose sight of the ideals that were fought for. Their leaders may go down in history as heroes or traitors.

## MASS MOVEMENTS
Revolutions occur when most of the people in a country are suffering hardship, or when they want changes to be made. If they cannot gain what they want, anger and the demand for more radical change builds up. However, revolutions need an incident to start them. The uprising of Sicilians against French rulers in 1282 began when a Sicilian stabbed a Frenchman who had insulted his wife.

## REASONS FOR FAILURE
Most revolutions fail. The government has many advantages over ordinary people, including wealth, control of the army and better organization. Revolutions are often disorganized, starting as separate protests

▲ Medieval peasant revolts were generally aimed at abolishing harsh taxes. Rebels often burned the books in which taxes were recorded.

which can be put down by force. Even if rebel forces unite, they often argue later. The revolutions that succeed are those with a clear aim and strong leadership. But even these may fail. In 133BC, the Roman army officer Tiberius Gracchus led the poorer citizens in demands for reform of land and property laws. The revolution failed when noblemen killed Gracchus, his brother and over 300 supporters.

## MEDIEVAL PEASANTS
During the Middle Ages, the peasants of Europe had to pay taxes and work long hours for their masters. Some nobles treated their peasants harshly. In 1381,

## FARMERS AGAINST MERCENARIES
During the American Revolution of 1775 the British hired 30,000 German mercenaries, mostly Hessians. The American farmers and frontiersmen were expert marksmen and won many skirmishes, but, compared with the mercenaries, they were poorly trained. It was only after George Washington began proper training and discipline that the Americans won major battles and, eventually, the war.

the peasants of England demanded an end to such conditions. Although the uprising collapsed, reforms were slowly introduced. In 1524, German peasants launched a violent uprising. They murdered nobles and organized an army. The nobles hired foreign troops and defeated the peasants at Frankenhausen in 1525. Most of the rebels were killed.

● Centres of revolution in 1848

◀ In 1848, people supporting democracy and social reforms rose against the monarchies of Europe. King Louis Philippe was overthrown in France, and major reforms were introduced in Belgium, Denmark and the Netherlands. Elsewhere, the armies and peasants remained loyal to their monarchs. Revolts were crushed in Prussia and Italy, though some reforms were made. Only in Austria, Poland and the smaller German states did the revolutions fail totally.

## THE AMERICAN REVOLUTION
The American Revolution began in 1775 when British colonists protested against being taxed by Britain with no representation in Parliament. At first, the uprising aimed at changing the status of the colonies, but in 1776 the colonies declared independence. After full-scale war with Britain, the new United States established a democratic republic.

## THE FRENCH REVOLUTION
In France, in 1789, the king ruled without a parliament or constitution, spending vast sums on luxuries. Involvement in wars, including the American Revolution, had drained the treasury. At the same time, food prices doubled after the harvest failed,

and many people were close to starvation. The middle classes demanded an end to the injustices. In May 1789, Louis XVI called a meeting of the States General (parliament) for the first time in about 175 years. This body demanded tax reforms. Food riots broke out and mob violence spread. The new government introduced radical measures to please the mob. In 1793, Louis XVI was arrested while trying to flee the country, and beheaded. In the Reign of Terror that followed, almost 20,000 people were executed as enemies of the Revolution. Ten months later, moderates established a new government based on the ideals of the Revolution. ▶

## TO THE BARRICADES
The *sans-culottes*, the working class of Paris, formed the shock troops of the French Revolution. On July 14, 1789 they attacked the royal prison of the Bastille, marking the start of violence. July 14 is now the most important public holiday in France. During fighting, the *sans-culottes* built barricades across the narrow streets of Paris, from which to defy troops and police.

▲ Demonstrations of over one million people in Tehran led to the rise to power of religious leader Ayatollah Khomeini in Iran.

▶ Civilians may take over military weapons in a revolution. The Hungarian Rising of 1956 failed when better-trained Soviet troops invaded.

## REVOLUTION IN RUSSIA

In 1917, Russia was ruled by a tsar, or emperor. The peasants were tied to their land, and the urban poor had no civil rights. In the spring, the tsar was overthrown and replaced by democrats from the middle classes, but many social problems remained. Vladimir Lenin, leader of the Communist Party, took advantage of this to begin an uprising in major cities. The Communist rising spread to become a civil war, which ended in 1921 with complete Communist victory.

## REVOLUTION FROM ABOVE

In 1959, a force of Communist guerrillas united with popular discontent to overthrow the Cuban government. The guerrilla leader, Fidel Castro, then began a revolution from above by overthrowing the economic and social systems of the country in favour of communism.

## VELVET REVOLUTIONS

In 1956, the Hungarians launched a peaceful uprising to overthrow their Communist government. But this uprising was crushed by Soviet troops. By 1989, however, Russia was too weak to interfere in Eastern Europe. Massive peaceful protests began in Poland, East Germany, Czechoslovakia, Bulgaria and Hungary. Known as 'velvet revolutions', these movements replaced communism with democracy within a few months.

## STORMING THE PALACE

Taking key buildings and communication centres is vital to any successful revolution. On October 25, 1917, Russian Communists and supporting troops seized government buildings, including the famous Winter Palace in St Petersburg. Within days, the government of Russia was communist.

▲ Government symbols may be destroyed by revolutionaries, as was this portrait of Stalin by Hungarians in 1956.

### SEE ALSO

Communism, France, Russia and the Baltic States, USA

# RIVER

When water falls as rain and snow over the land, it eventually flows back to the seas and oceans. Usually, it flows back in the form of a river.

A river that flows quickly down a steep slope, over hard rocks, cuts a deep gorge in the land.

When a river flows more slowly over softer rocks, the valley is worn back into an open V-shape.

▲ Waterfalls occur when a river tumbles over the edge of a steep cliff or ledge, as in the powerful Dettifoss Falls in Iceland.

| WORLD'S LONGEST RIVERS | | |
|---|---|---|
| Name | Outflow | Length |
| Nile | Mediterranean Sea (Egypt) | 6,690km |
| Amazon | Atlantic Ocean (Brazil) | 6,570km |
| Missouri | Mississippi River (USA) | 4,090km |
| Chang Jiang | East China Sea (China) | 5,980km |
| Yenisey | Kara Sea (Russia) | 5,870km |
| Amur | Tartar Strait (Russia) | 5,780km |
| Ob-Irtysh | Gulf of Ob (Russia) | 5,410km |

A river goes through many stages in its development. First, water falls as rain on hills and mountainsides and seeps into the ground until the soil and rock are completely saturated with it – so full that they cannot hold any more. The top level of this saturated zone is called the water table. When the water table reaches the surface of the soil, as on a steep slope, water pours out, and forms into a spring. Water from the spring runs downhill as a stream, and in time, many streams flow into one another to form a river.

## YOUNG RIVER

When a river is young, it runs swiftly down the hill or mountainsides. High up, close to the springs, the falling water is full of energy and may even carry rocks and boulders with it. This rocky debris scrapes and crashes along the bed of the river, carving out a deep V-shaped valley or a gorge. This constant erosion is typical of a river in its early stage, and waterfalls and rapids (fast currents) are common here.

## MATURE RIVER

In the second stage of the river's development, some of the rocky debris begins to settle out in a process called deposition. However, erosion continues to take place. The river valley becomes broad and flat, and the river winds, or meanders, around in it. When the course of the river swings towards the valley's edge, the sides are worn back, and the valley becomes even wider. At the same time, rocks and sand are deposited on the valley floor, forming what is known as a flood plain. This whole area can be under water during flooding. As it flows, the river constantly changes direction, and eats into the sediment (solid matter) which has already been dropped, lifting it and depositing it elsewhere.

▼ Rivers are used all over the world to move goods and people. This river market in Zaire is part of a river trade route, where people travel by boat to buy and sell goods.

## LOOPING CURRENTS

When a river flows round in a loop, its current is faster on the outside. The faster current can erode more quickly than the slower current on the inside, so the outside bank of the loop is worn back. In the meantime, sand and pebbles are deposited by the slower current, and build up the inside bank. The loop gradually becomes more pronounced, and the course of the river changes.

## OLD MAN RIVER

In its final stage of development, the river becomes so slow that there is no erosion anywhere, only deposition. The river is now a long way from its source high up in the mountains, and is meandering slowly across a flat plain. The river overflows its banks during times of flood,

depositing fertile sediment on the plains as the water slows down away from the main current. The banks are often built up so that the river may actually flow at a higher level than the plain around it. Such a river alters its course continually during flooding, spreading valuable fertile soil on the plain, but making the water difficult to manage.

## MEETING THE SEA

Eventually, the river reaches the sea at its mouth. If there are no sea currents at this point, the rest of the river's sediment is deposited as sand banks. These sand banks may even form islands, and the river water splits up into individual streams between them, forming a delta. More often, the sediment is carried away, and the river has a broad tidal mouth called an estuary.

When the channel of a river flows in a snake-like pattern across its valley, it is said to meander.

1 Some meanders swell to broader loops than others.

2 The neck of the loop then becomes very narrow.

3 The old channel is cut off to form an oxbow lake.

Glacier — Meltwater — Waterfall — Rapids — Stream — Tributary stream — River — Oxbow lake — Meander — Estuary — Flood plain — River mouth

## THE IMPORTANCE OF RIVERS

Although rivers make up only a tiny percentage of the Earth's surface water, they are very important. Rivers form the landscape and provide natural barriers. They also provide vital links from seas to inland areas, and are used for trading goods. Most inland villages, towns and cities began as settlements around rivers; when bridges were built, the settlements grew. Rivers supply food, and water for drinking, washing and crop irrigation.

## SEE ALSO

Mountain and valley, Transport, Water

# ROCK

Rocks are the solid substances that make up the surface of the Earth. There are three types of rock, each of which forms in a different way.

Granite is a coarse-grained igneous rock that has formed slowly underground.

Igneous rocks are formed from heat. Sedimentary rocks are formed underwater from layers of soil and organic remains. Metamorphic rocks are the result of changes made to existing rocks.

▲ Basalt is an igneous rock formed from volcanic lava. It cools very fast, often producing these pencil-like columns.

Pumice is a light igneous rock that often forms in a volcanic eruption.

## ROCKS FROM HEAT
Hot molten magma from inside the Earth can break out at the surface through a volcano as lava. It then cools and solidifies quickly, forming very fine rock such as basalt. Or, it may cool slowly underground, forming big, coarse, mineral crystals. Granite is a rock formed in this way. In both cases, the rock is igneous – formed from fire.

Marble is a medium-grained rock that forms in metamorphic terrains.

## ROCKS FROM WATER
Loose material, such as sand or mud, can build up in layers at the bottom of the sea. These layers, or beds, may eventually be buried, compressed and cemented into a

Slate is a dense, fine-grained metamorphic rock that splits into thin slabs.

solid mass. The resulting rock is called a sedimentary rock – built from layers. The layers may consist of small fragments such as sand, creating sandstone. Or they may be built from minerals dissolved in the sea water, such as limestone, or built up from things that were once alive, such as coal. We find fossils in sedimentary rocks.

## NEW ROCKS FROM OLD
The third kind of rock forms when a rock that already exists is heated or squeezed. This may occur in the heart of a mountain chain when it is being pushed up, as the heat and pressure change the minerals that it contains. This produces a metamorphic rock – a rock of change. Great heat gives a rock with an even, crystalline structure, such as marble. Great pressure produces a rock in which the crystals are all twisted and deformed, such as schist.

Limestone is a sedimentary rock that often contains tiny fossilized remains.

Sandstone is a sedimentary rock made of fine or coarse grains cemented into beds.

## ROCK CYCLE
New rock is constantly being pushed up towards the Earth's surface, where it is broken down by the elements and deposited at the bottom of lakes, rivers and seas. These sedimentary layers are compressed into new rock, which may later be uplifted or sink to depths where it melts to form igneous rocks again. It can also become so roasted and compressed that it forms metamorphic rock.

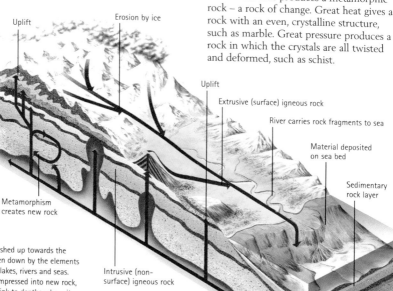

Uplift

Erosion by ice

Uplift

Extrusive (surface) igneous rock

River carries rock fragments to sea

Material deposited on sea bed

Sedimentary rock layer

Metamorphism creates new rock

Intrusive (non-surface) igneous rock

Buried rock layer

## SEE ALSO
Earth, Fossil, Mineral and gem, Oil

# ROMAN EMPIRE

The Romans ruled the Mediterranean and much of Europe for nearly 400 years. Many modern law codes and government systems are based on those of Rome.

▲ The territory of the Roman Empire expanded rapidly during wars with Egypt, Carthage and Greece. After AD117, remote areas, such as Mesopotamia, were abandoned.

Julius Caesar (c.100–44BC) was a dictator, taking power from the Senate.

Caligula (AD12–41) ordered many executions and may have been insane.

Hadrian (76–138) ordered the building of defences along the Empire's borders.

Septimius Severus (146–211) reformed the Empire into a military state.

The cruelty of Commodus (161–192) plunged the Empire into civil war.

Constantine the Great (c.280–337) was the first Christian emperor.

The Roman Empire was built up by the people of Rome from about 250BC and lasted until AD476. The Romans were good at organization and were feared for their powerful army and navy. The Empire had one language, one economy and one government.

## THE REPUBLIC

According to legend, Rome was founded in 753BC, and in 509BC became a republic. Rome's main rival was the city of Carthage in North Africa, and in 218BC the two went to war. The Carthaginian leader, Hannibal, wiped out the main Roman army at Cannae in 216BC, but he could not capture Rome, and Carthage was later defeated. By 44BC, Rome had conquered Greece and large areas of the Near East, North Africa, Spain and France.

## AGE OF AUGUSTUS

As the Roman Empire grew, patricians, or noblemen, gained vast wealth and the ordinary citizens, or plebeians, lost political power. The army was more loyal to successful commanders than to the government. These tensions led to a series of civil wars from 49BC to 30BC. The wars were won by Octavian, nephew of the dictator Julius Caesar. He took the title Augustus, meaning 'the sacred one', and established a new type of government, giving power to the emperor.

## CITIZENS OF ROME

Being a citizen of Rome had many advantages. Citizens could vote, stand in elections or work in the government. At first only people from Rome were citizens, but gradually men from other cities or who had served in the army for 30 years became citizens. Finally, in AD212, every free man in the Empire became a citizen of Rome.

## THE ROMAN ARMY

The Roman army was organized into legions of about 6,000 armoured infantry, with a few archers and cavalry. In battle, the legion was trained to fight in tight formations, such as the *testudo*, or tortoise (below). The army built roads and forts to guard the frontiers. Each legionary had to carry all his equipment, including weapons, cooking pot, blanket and tools (right).

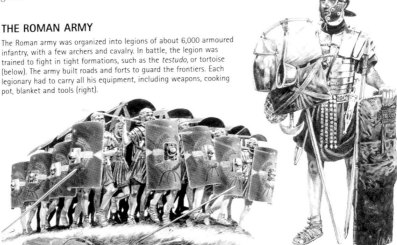

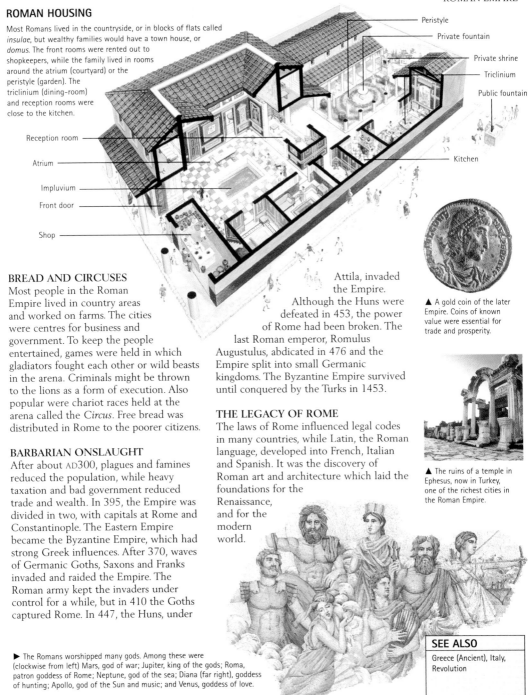

# ROMAN HOUSING

Most Romans lived in the countryside, or in blocks of flats called *insulae*, but wealthy families would have a town house, or *domus*. The front rooms were rented out to shopkeepers, while the family lived in rooms around the atrium (courtyard) or the peristyle (garden). The triclinium (dining-room) and reception rooms were close to the kitchen.

Peristyle

Private fountain

Private shrine

Triclinium

Public fountain

Reception room

Atrium

Impluvium

Front door

Shop

Kitchen

▲ A gold coin of the later Empire. Coins of known value were essential for trade and prosperity.

## BREAD AND CIRCUSES

Most people in the Roman Empire lived in country areas and worked on farms. The cities were centres for business and government. To keep the people entertained, games were held in which gladiators fought each other or wild beasts in the arena. Criminals might be thrown to the lions as a form of execution. Also popular were chariot races held at the arena called the *Circus*. Free bread was distributed in Rome to the poorer citizens.

## BARBARIAN ONSLAUGHT

After about AD300, plagues and famines reduced the population, while heavy taxation and bad government reduced trade and wealth. In 395, the Empire was divided in two, with capitals at Rome and Constantinople. The Eastern Empire became the Byzantine Empire, which had strong Greek influences. After 370, waves of Germanic Goths, Saxons and Franks invaded and raided the Empire. The Roman army kept the invaders under control for a while, but in 410 the Goths captured Rome. In 447, the Huns, under Attila, invaded the Empire. Although the Huns were defeated in 453, the power of Rome had been broken. The last Roman emperor, Romulus Augustulus, abdicated in 476 and the Empire split into small Germanic kingdoms. The Byzantine Empire survived until conquered by the Turks in 1453.

## THE LEGACY OF ROME

The laws of Rome influenced legal codes in many countries, while Latin, the Roman language, developed into French, Italian and Spanish. It was the discovery of Roman art and architecture which laid the foundations for the Renaissance, and for the modern world.

▲ The ruins of a temple in Ephesus, now in Turkey, one of the richest cities in the Roman Empire.

▶ The Romans worshipped many gods. Among these were (clockwise from left) Mars, god of war; Jupiter, king of the gods; Roma, patron goddess of Rome; Neptune, god of the sea; Diana (far right), goddess of hunting; Apollo, god of the Sun and music; and Venus, goddess of love.

## SEE ALSO

Greece (Ancient), Italy, Revolution

# RUSSIA AND THE BALTIC STATES

The Russian Federation is the largest country in the world. Its western neighbours – Estonia, Latvia and Lithuania – are known as the Baltic states.

**ESTONIA**
Area: 45,100 sq km
Population: 1,450,000
Capital: Tallinn
Language: Estonian
Currency: Kroon

**LATVIA**
Area: 64,600 sq km
Population: 2,449,000
Capital: Riga
Language: Latvian
Currency: Lats

**LITHUANIA**
Area: 65,200 sq km
Population: 3,703,000
Capital: Vilnius
Language: Lithuanian
Currency: Litas

**RUSSIA**
Area: 17,075,400 sq km
Population: 196,909,000
Capital: Moscow
Language: Russian
Currency: Rouble

▶ Riga, on the Western Dvina River, is Latvia's capital city and its main industrial centre.

Western Russia is mostly flat and low-lying, and is separated from the east by the Ural mountains. In the east, Siberia consists of tablelands and ridges while to the south, the landscape is mountainous. Much of the north is tundra – treeless land where the soil is frozen below the surface. The north is bounded by the world's longest Arctic coastline. Estonia is flat and almost half of it is farmland, while Latvia has low, forested hills. Lithuania's coast of white sand dunes is popular with tourists.

## WINTER AND SUMMER

Most of Russia has long, cold winters, with half the country covered by snow for six months. Summers are mild or warm, but short. In winter, most northern ports, such as St Petersburg, are closed by ice. Rivers such as the Volga, Don and Dnieper are an important part of the transport system and are joined at many points by major canals.

▲ Russian ballet became internationally famous in the 1800s. The Moscow Academic School of Choreography is one of the training grounds for children.

## RICH IN RESOURCES

Russia's rich resources include coal, oil, gas, iron, copper, gold and platinum. Many of these reserves, however, are in remote areas and their use is hampered by the harsh climate and by transport problems. The railway system radiates out from Moscow and St Petersburg, around which industry is concentrated. Three quarters of the population lives in towns and cities. Agricultural output ranges from cattle and

miles
0        500

0     500
km

ARCTIC OCEAN

N

cotton to barley, maize, sunflower seeds, tobacco, wine and reindeer. The main exports of the Baltic States are foods, chemicals and manufactured goods.

## PEOPLE AND RELIGION

Russians account for 87.5 per cent of the population of Russia. Important minorities include Tatars, Ukrainians and Germans. There are 130 different nationalities in all. Despite over half a century of campaigns by communist governments against religion, many people are strongly loyal to the Russian Orthodox Church. In the Baltic States, most people belong to either the Lutheran, Roman Catholic or Russian Orthodox Churches. Average levels of education are high, although researchers, especially in technology and medicine, have been held back by shortages of funds.

## RUSSIA'S EXPANSION

The Russian state grew up around Moscow, which was founded in 1147. Its rulers took the title of tsar. Peter the Great, tsar from 1682 to 1725, introduced Western European culture and technology

and founded a new capital, St Petersburg. By conquering Estonia and Latvia, he began a programme of expansion which his successors extended to Lithuania, Belarus, Ukraine and the Crimea. Russian settlement of Siberia began in the 18th century and in the 19th century Finland, the Caucasus and Central Asia were added to the Russian Empire. ▶

▼ Lake Baikal in Siberia is the world's deepest lake.

▲ Like Latvia and Lithuania, Estonia became independent in 1991. It had been taken into the Soviet Union in 1940.

▲ President Boris Yeltsin came to power after Mikhail Gorbachev resigned in 1991.

▲ Long, harsh winters are an accepted part of life in Siberia. Local people use sledges to carry shopping.

## LIMITATIONS AND DEVELOPMENTS

Russia was held back by its very size and its limited skills. It consisted of a vast mass of uneducated peasants ruled by a tiny class of officials. Russian achievements, nevertheless, included the development of modern ballet, the music of Tchaikovsky and the writings of Tolstoy and Chekhov.

## RUSSIAN REVOLUTION

Revolution finally came in 1917, in two stages. Alexander Kerensky – a moderate – was brought to power, then overthrown by the Bolsheviks, led by Vladimir Ilyich Ulyanov (Lenin). Lenin ruthlessly led the Bolsheviks to victory and, in 1922, established the communist-run Union of Soviet Socialist Republics (USSR), or Soviet Union. This covered almost all of the former Russian Empire, except Finland and the Baltic States.

## SOVIET CONTROL

After Lenin's death in 1924, Joseph Stalin ruled as a brutal dictator. He took the peasants' land to create government-run farms and built up heavy industry, dams, railways and an electric power system. After World War II, the USSR gained control over much of

Eastern Europe, either by forcing countries to become Soviet republics or by controlling their governments. After Stalin's death in 1953, Soviet life was dominated by the Cold War between the Soviet-led communist countries and the US-led Western democracies.

## TOWARDS DEMOCRACY

Mikhail Gorbachev became Soviet leader in 1985 and introduced political reforms. He encouraged other Eastern European countries to do the same and many of these abandoned communism. The Soviet Union broke up at the end of 1991 and countries including the Baltic States became independent. Gorbachev gave way to Boris Yeltsin. He was the first Russian leader to be elected.

▶ The Kremlin, in Moscow's Red Square, was originally a fortress. Under communist rule, it became the government headquarters.

### SEE ALSO
Asia, Cold War, Communism, Europe, Revolution

# SATELLITE

Satellites are objects that move in orbit around other objects of greater mass. A satellite may be natural, like the Moon, or artificial, like an orbiting spacecraft.

Spacecraft orbiting high above the Earth can be used to relay messages over very long distances. Some satellites are used to send television signals around the world or to track the movement of hurricanes and large weather fronts. Communication satellites are used to pass on telephone conversations and computer data. These satellites receive signals from a transmitting station on Earth, amplify them, and beam the signals down to another Earth station, which may be thousands of kilometres away.

▲ *Sputnik 1*, the world's first artificial satellite, was launched by Russia on October 4, 1957. It was used to broadcast scientific data and orbited the Earth for six months.

▼ Satellites can sometimes give us a clearer picture of activity on the Earth's surface than we can get from the ground. The Earth is surrounded by craft designed specifically for different purposes.

## GEOSYNCHRONOUS ORBIT
Most communication satellites move in a special orbit known as a geosynchronous orbit, which is about 35,900km above the Equator. This orbit allows the satellite to remain over the same point on the Earth's surface at all times.

## ASTRONOMICAL SATELLITES
By carrying telescopes and other instruments above the Earth's atmosphere, astronomical satellites can see distant objects, such as stars, nebulae and galaxies, much more clearly than we can from the ground. They can also pick up types of waves, such as infrared, ultraviolet, X-rays and gamma rays, which are partly or totally blocked by the atmosphere. For example, X-ray satellites have helped scientists to study black holes and dense, remote binary (double) stars.

## SURVEYING THE EARTH
Remote-sensing satellites, equipped with powerful cameras and other equipment, provide valuable information about our planet's natural resources. They can reveal changes to the polar ice caps or the rate at which human beings are destroying the rainforests. Weather satellites can track the movement of hurricanes and supply data that allows accurate weather forecasts several days in advance.

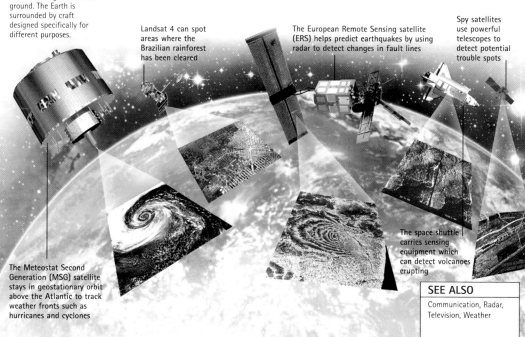

Landsat 4 can spot areas where the Brazilian rainforest has been cleared

The European Remote Sensing satellite (ERS) helps predict earthquakes by using radar to detect changes in fault lines

Spy satellites use powerful telescopes to detect potential trouble spots

The space shuttle carries sensing equipment which can detect volcanoes erupting

The Meteostat Second Generation (MSG) satellite stays in geostationary orbit above the Atlantic to track weather fronts such as hurricanes and cyclones

## SEE ALSO
Communication, Radar, Television, Weather

# SCANDINAVIA

**Scandinavia consists of the neighbouring north European countries of Denmark, Norway, Sweden, Finland, Iceland and the Faeroe Islands.**

**DENMARK**
**Area:** 43,094 sq km
**Population:** 5,301,000
**Capital:** Copenhagen
**Language:** Danish
**Currency:** Krone

**FINLAND**
**Area:** 338,145 sq km
**Population:** 5,153,000
**Capital:** Helsinki
**Languages:** Finnish and Swedish
**Currency:** Markka, Euro

**ICELAND**
**Area:** 103,000 sq km
**Population:** 274,000
**Capital:** Reykjavik
**Language:** Icelandic
**Currency:** Krona

**NORWAY**
**Area:** 323,877 sq km
**Population:** 4,432,000
**Capital:** Oslo
**Language:** Norwegian
**Currency:** Krone

**SWEDEN**
**Area:** 449,964 sq km
**Population:** 8,872,000
**Capital:** Stockholm
**Language:** Swedish
**Currency:** Krona

▶ Stockholm, capital of Sweden, is built on 14 small islands connected by about 50 bridges.

The name Scandinavia refers to the large peninsula made up of Sweden and Norway. Often included in this term are the neighbouring countries of Denmark and Finland, as well as Iceland and the Faeroe Islands, which have cultural and language links with the region. Danish, Swedish, Norwegian and Icelandic all come from a common ancestor language, but Finnish is quite different.

### THE FAEROE ISLANDS
These 21 islands in the North Atlantic Ocean have a population of about 47,000. They were ruled by Norway until 1380, and many of the inhabitants are of Norse origin. For the last 600 years, they have been under Danish control, and in 1948, Denmark allowed them to become self-governing. The representatives of their parliament, or *Lagting*, hold seats in the Danish parliament in Copenhagen.

### LONG SUMMER DAYS
Due to their northerly location, the countries of Scandinavia have long, cold, snowy winters. In Iceland and in the northernmost parts of Finland, Norway

▲ Norway's coast is famous for its many fjords – long, narrow inlets of the sea that make fine natural harbours.

and Sweden around the Arctic Circle, it is light for 24 hours a day around midsummer and dark for most of the day towards the end of December.

### RICH IN RESOURCES
Flat Denmark is famous for its agriculture, Finland for its lakes, Sweden for its forests, Norway for its spectacular coastal fjords (inlets) and Iceland for its dramatic geysers (hot springs) and volcanoes. The region is rich in natural resources, including oil, gas, iron and timber. Since oil was discovered in the North Sea in the 1960s, Norway has become self-sufficient in natural gas and oil, and expert at oil rig construction. Sweden is the most industrial of the Scandinavian nations and is one of the

ARCTIC
OCEAN

• Tromsø

LAPLAND

Bodø

ARCTIC CIRCLE

RUSSIA

Skellefte

• Oulu

SWEDEN

FINLAND

Trondheim •
Ålesund

NORWAY

Lillehammer •
• Bergen

Oslo

• Stavanger

Tampere •
• Lahti

Turku

■ Helsinki

Uppsala •
Örebro
Stockholm
Norrköping

ESTONIA

Lake
Vänern
Lake
Vättern
• Göteborg

Gotland

BALTIC SEA

miles
0                250

0                250
km

NORTH
SEA

DENMARK   Århus

Copenhagen ■ • Malmö
Odense

GERMANY

wealthiest countries in Europe. Fishing
and ship-building have been important
industries for the whole region. Modern
Scandinavian styles of architecture and
design, especially of furniture, metalwork
and glassware, are influential worldwide.

## NORTHERN PEOPLES

Most Scandinavians are descendants of
Germanic peoples who moved into the
area around 2,000 years ago, while most
Finns migrated around the same time from
western Russia. North of the Arctic Circle
are the Sami – descendants of the earliest
inhabitants of Sweden and Finland. Today,
a small number of Sami live a traditional
way of life herding reindeer, which they
keep for their meat, milk and hides. But
most earn a living from farming, fishing or
mining. Since 1993, the Sami have had
their own council called the *Sameting*.

▼ In Denmark, surrounded as it is by sea, both fishing
and ship-building are important. Danish fishing fleets
bring in mackerel, herring, cod, shrimp and flatfish.

## SCANDINAVIAN POLICIES

Norway, Denmark and Sweden are all
constitutional monarchies, but Finland and
Iceland are republics. The Scandinavian
countries have traditionally been strong
supporters of international organizations,
human rights, health and welfare
programmes and conservation. Many of
these efforts are co-ordinated by the
Nordic Council, founded in 1953.

## NORSE MYTHOLOGY

In pre-Christian times, early Scandinavian
and Germanic peoples shared a common
mythology, known as Norse mythology.
The myths, originally passed on by word
of mouth, were first written down in the
1200s. Four of the early Norse gods – Tiw,
Odin, Thor and Freya – are remembered
in the days of the week, Tuesday,
Wednesday, Thursday and Friday. Today,
Lutheran Protestant Christianity is the
main religion in all Scandinavian countries.

▲ Found in Arctic regions,
reindeer migrate several
hundred kilometres a year
in search of food.

## SEE ALSO

Arctic, Europe, Vikings

# SEASHORE

There are many types of seashore, from rocky cliffs to sandy beaches. Each habitat has its own creatures and plant life, specially adapted to live there.

Tidal pools contain plants and small marine animals.

Rocky cliffs are a favourite nesting place for kittiwakes.

Many salt-resistant grasses thrive on sand dunes.

The narrow zone where land and sea meet, the seashore, is one of the most varied and fascinating habitats on Earth. It contains creatures that have evolved to live half their lives on land and half at sea.

## BEACHES
The most common type of shore is the sandy beach, made of tiny particles of rock (sand) worn down by being constantly rolled together by waves. Plants can't grow in the loose sand between high- and low-water marks, but just below the surface, sand-worms and burrowing shellfish feed on tiny food particles washed in with the tide. Sandy and muddy shores are favourite feeding places for shorebirds.

## CLIFFS
Where waves hammer against hard rocks, a steep cliff may form. Here, the tiny ledges

and cracks are home to specialized plants that can survive the salt spray and cold winter winds. Cliff ledges also provide nesting places for many seabirds such as gulls, guillemots and gannets, while puffins live in burrows in the soil on the cliff top.

## ROCKY SHORES
Rocky coasts are home to a huge variety of red, brown and green seaweeds, some like long leather belts, some like mosses. The seaweed fronds provide a cool, damp hiding place for sand-hoppers, crabs, barnacles, winkles and limpets. Rock pools provide another place in which sea creatures can survive while the tide is out. Some molluscs, such as mussels and limpets, attach themselves to rocks.

## SANDY SEASHORES
A vast array of birds, plants, molluscs and crustaceans live around the world's seashores. Crashing waves constantly change the shape of sandy beaches, so all forms of life must be adaptable – most shore plants and animals are able to live in and out of water. Shorebirds feed on worms, fish and other small creatures.

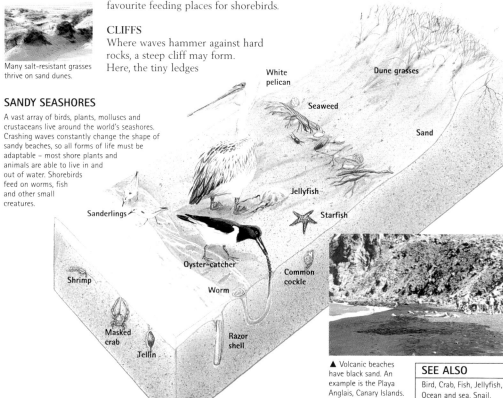

White pelican

Dune grasses

Seaweed

Sand

Jellyfish

Starfish

Sanderlings

Oyster-catcher

Common cockle

Shrimp

Worm

Masked crab

Razor shell

Tellin

▲ Volcanic beaches have black sand. An example is the Playa Anglais, Canary Islands.

### SEE ALSO
Bird, Crab, Fish, Jellyfish, Ocean and sea, Snail, Starfish, Volcano

# SEASON

As the Earth orbits the Sun, the tilt of its axis causes changes in the length of day and the temperature. This creates what we call the seasons.

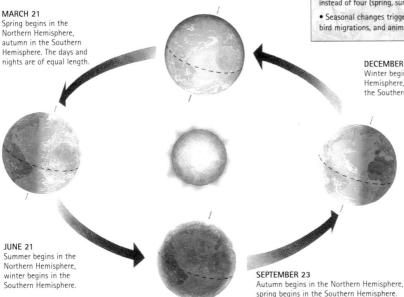

**MARCH 21**
Spring begins in the Northern Hemisphere, autumn in the Southern Hemisphere. The days and nights are of equal length.

**DECEMBER 21**
Winter begins in Northern the Hemisphere, summer begins in the Southern Hemisphere.

**JUNE 21**
Summer begins in the Northern Hemisphere, winter begins in the Southern Hemisphere.

**SEPTEMBER 23**
Autumn begins in the Northern Hemisphere, spring begins in the Southern Hemisphere. Days and nights are of equal length again.

▲ December in Alberta, Canada brings the typically snowy and cold weather of a Northern Hemisphere winter.

The seasons affect everything we do. They determine when we plant our crops and harvest them, what kind of clothes we wear, what we eat, how much energy we use for heating and lighting, and even how we feel. The seasons are caused by the tilt of the Earth's axis during its yearly journey around the Sun.

## THE EARTH'S TILT
The Earth is always spinning, tilted at an angle of 23.5°, so that the North Pole tilts towards the Sun for part of the year. In the Northern Hemisphere, the Sun is high in the sky and the days are long and warm, resulting in summer. At the same time, the South Pole is tilted away from the Sun, and the Southern Hemisphere has its winter.

## THE SOLSTICES
As the Earth orbits the Sun, its axis points towards the same spot in space, so that six

months later, the North Pole tilts away from the Sun. It is now winter in the Northern Hemisphere and summer in the Southern Hemisphere. In the Northern Hemisphere, the longest day (the summer solstice) is June 21, and the shortest day (the winter solstice) is December 21. For the Southern Hemisphere, the longest day of the year is December 21 and the shortest day is June 21.

## THE EQUINOXES
Halfway between the solstices are the autumn and spring equinoxes. On March 21 and September 23, the tilted Earth is sideways-on to the Sun, and day and night are of equal length. Spring in the Northern Hemisphere begins on March 21, when the Southern Hemisphere has autumn. On September 23, the Northern Hemisphere autumn begins, and it is spring south of the Equator.

▲ Southern Hemisphere areas like Green Island Beach, Australia enjoy the beginning of their summer season in December.

**SEE ALSO**

Climate, Earth, Hibernation, Sun, Weather

241

# SIGHT

**Sight is the ability to detect light and form it into an accurate view of the shapes, colours and distances of surrounding objects.**

Sight is the most important sense for most animals, providing over half of all the information that enters the brain. Animals use their eyes to look for food and mates and to watch for danger. Most invertebrates (creatures without backbones) have simple eyes, able to give only a rough picture of their surroundings.

Insect compound eyes have a mosaic of cells which build up an image.

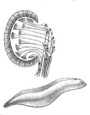

Flatworms have cupped organs able to detect the direction of a light source.

### ADVANCED VISION

Animals with backbones (vertebrates) have eyes that are able to see clearly. At the front of the eye is a transparent area, known as the cornea, through which light enters. Behind the cornea is a coloured ring of muscle, the iris, with a central hole, the pupil. The iris changes shape to make the pupil wider in dim light, so that more light enters the eye, for clearer vision. Behind the pupil is the lens, which focuses light rays. A ring of ciliary muscles changes the shape of the lens to adjust the focus.

### THE HUMAN EYE

The human eyeball, about 25mm across, is set into a bowl-shaped socket in the skull. Six small muscles move the eye up, down and sideways. The eye's whitish outer layer, the sclera, is strong and tough. Inside is the choroid layer, soft and blood-rich, which nourishes the inner parts of the eye. The main bulk of the eyeball is filled with clear jelly, or vitreous humour, which keeps it firm.

▲ Cats' eyes stand out in poor light (left) as they have an extra layer, the guanine, which reflects light back past the retina. The guanine allows cats to see clearly in poor light (right), although they cannot distinguish colours.

### LIGHT TO NERVE SIGNALS

Light rays focused by the lens shine onto the retina. This contains millions of light-sensitive cells, called rods and cones, which send nerve signals to the brain where they are translated into a picture. The rods are sensitive in dim light and detect movement and the contrast between black and white. The cones, which are clustered in one small area, see colour. Only humans and a few other types of animal can see in full colour.

### TWO EYES

Most animals have two eyes, which help to judge distance in two ways. Each eye sees an object from a slightly different position. The brain compares the view it receives from each eye and, the more different they are, the nearer the object. The brain also measures how much the eyes swivel inwards to look at an object that is very near.

▲ Nerve cells on the retina react to light. They send signals along the optic nerve to the brain.

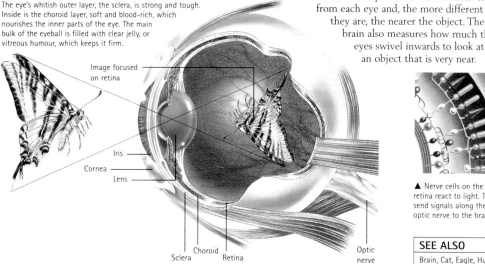

Image focused on retina

Iris

Cornea

Lens

Sclera

Choroid

Retina

Optic nerve

### SEE ALSO

Brain, Cat, Eagle, Human body, Insect, Lens, Light

# SKELETON

**The strong framework of more than 200 bones called the skeleton gives the body shape, support and protection, and allows it to move.**

The body's firmness, shape and strength are due to its skeleton. The skeleton has two main parts. The skull, backbone, and ribs form the central, or axial, skeleton, and the arms and legs make up the appendicular skeleton. This system of 206 tough, rigid parts, called bones, forms the body's internal framework and protects delicate organs such as the brain, heart and lungs. Bones are linked to each other at joints and are anchored to muscles, which pull on them to move the body.

A bird's skeleton is very light in weight, making flight easier.

Large mammals such as cows need strong bones to carry their body weight.

Fish have spiny bones to support fins and flexible backbones for swimming.

## BONE STRENGTH

Each bone's size, shape and strength depend on how it supports its part of the body and its muscle attachments. Bones are stiff because they contain crystals of minerals such as calcium and phosphate. But they are also slightly flexible, because they contain fibres of the body protein collagen, so that they bend slightly under stress, rather than crack.

## INSIDE A BONE

Bones are pale yellow and have their own blood vessels and nerves. They are a combination of living cells and minerals. Bone cells, called osteocytes, produce tiny rod-like structures of bone minerals, called osteons (Haversian systems). Most bones have a strong outer layer of compact bone, with the osteons packed together. Inside this is a layer of spongy, or cancellous, bone.

## BONE MARROW

In the middle of some bones is jelly-like marrow. This makes new cells for the blood, producing millions every second. All of a baby's bones contain marrow, but by adulthood, marrow is found mainly in the breast bone, backbone, ribs and skull.

### THE HUMAN SKELETON

The skull is made up of eight bones joined together; the face has 14 bones. Inside each ear are three of the body's tiniest bones called ossicles. The backbone has 26 bones called vertebrae; 12 pairs of ribs join the breast bone at the front of the chest. Each shoulder and arm has 32 bones, including eight carpals in the wrist. Each hip and leg has 31 bones, including seven tarsals in the ankle.

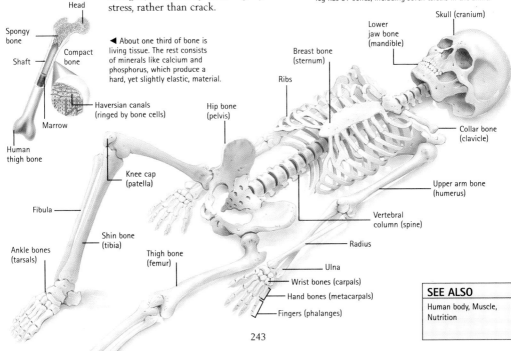

Head

Spongy bone

Shaft

Compact bone

Marrow

Human thigh bone

◄ About one third of bone is living tissue. The rest consists of minerals like calcium and phosphorus, which produce a hard, yet slightly elastic, material.

Haversian canals (ringed by bone cells)

Skull (cranium)

Lower jaw bone (mandible)

Breast bone (sternum)

Ribs

Hip bone (pelvis)

Collar bone (clavicle)

Upper arm bone (humerus)

Knee cap (patella)

Vertebral column (spine)

Fibula

Shin bone (tibia)

Thigh bone (femur)

Radius

Ankle bones (tarsals)

Ulna

Wrist bones (carpals)

Hand bones (metacarpals)

Fingers (phalanges)

### SEE ALSO

Human body, Muscle, Nutrition

# SKIN AND HAIR

Skin protects our delicate insides from wear, knocks, dirt, germs and rain. It also helps to cool or warm the body, and gives us our sense of touch.

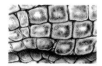

Reptiles such as lizards have dry, scaly skin.

Pigskin: only mammals' skin is covered with hair.

Slug skin: glands secrete slime on the skin.

Skin is our all-over, hard-wearing, living overcoat, covering an area of about 2m square. It weighs around 4kg and varies in thickness from 0.5mm on the eyelids to 5mm on the soles of the feet; the average thickness is 1–2mm. Skin is continually growing and renewing, and with pressure and wear, it becomes thicker and tougher.

## THE OUTER LAYER

The skin's surface, the epidermis, is dead, but just underneath it is one of the body's busiest parts, the dermis. Microscopic cells at the base of the epidermis continually multiply, which pushes old cells upwards. Over about four weeks, these cells fill with the tough body protein, keratin (which also makes up hair and nails), flatten and die. The dead cells then reach the surface, and rub and flake off with daily wear and tear.

## GETTING UNDER YOUR SKIN

There is an outer and inner layer of skin. The outer layer is the epidermis, underneath is the thicker dermis. This contains fibres of stiff collagen and stretchy elastin, making it strong yet flexible. In the dermis are sweat glands, hair roots, tiny blood vessels, and microscopic nerve endings for our sense of touch. Each hair is anchored in a follicle. It has a sebaceous gland that makes a natural wax or oil called sebum.

When skin is damaged, a scab forms to protect the body from germs while new skin develops under it.

1 Broken blood vessels become narrow to stop blood loss. White blood cells destroy bacteria.

2 Substances in the blood called platelets cause it to clot. This clot hardens into the scab.

3 In the dermis, cells called fibroblasts produce new tissue. When healed, the scab falls off.

## SKIN COLOUR

Our melanocyte cells produce tiny flecks of dark brown melanin (pigment). More active melanocytes make more melanin and thus produce darker skin. We inherit our normal level of melanocyte activity, and therefore our skin colour, from our parents. However, strong sunlight makes melanocytes more active to protect the body from the sun's ultraviolet rays – and this produces a sun tan.

## COOLING SWEAT

Skin helps to control our temperature. If the body is too hot, tiny blood vessels in the dermis widen, allowing more blood to lose heat to the air. The microscopic sweat glands also ooze sweat through the pores (tiny holes) onto the skin. As this dries, it draws more warmth from the body.

## HAIR AND GOOSEBUMPS

If the body is too cold, the blood vessels narrow, to reduce heat loss. The erector muscle, attached to a hair, pulls it upright. This traps air near the skin's surface which keeps warmth in, and causes goosebumps. Hairs are long rods of dead, keratin-filled cells. The only living part is the hair bulb inside the follicle.

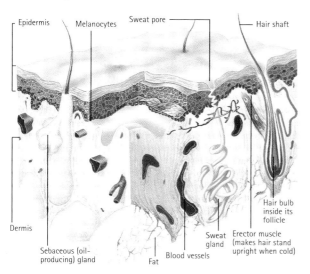

Epidermis  Melanocytes  Sweat pore  Hair shaft

Dermis

Sebaceous (oil-producing) gland

Fat

Blood vessels

Sweat gland

Erector muscle (makes hair stand upright when cold)

Hair bulb inside its follicle

### SEE ALSO

Amphibian, Blood, Cell, Human body, Snail, Touch

# SNAIL AND OTHER MOLLUSCS

Molluscs are soft-bodied invertebrate animals that have no bones and no legs. They include snails, slugs, clams, cockles, limpets, oysters, octopuses and cuttlefish.

The great black slug (which can be orange) has a tough skin flap on top.

The common mussel, a bivalve, has a shell in two parts, hinged at the front.

The spiny murex, a type of sea snail, is a univalve – it has a single, coiled shell.

Cuttlefish, octopuses and squid are among the most active and mobile molluscs.

Most molluscs are protected by hard shells. Snails have a one-piece shell that is usually coiled; bivalves, such as cockles and mussels, have a two-piece shell hinged along one side. Cuttlefish and squid have a shell that grows inside their body and some slugs have a small, flat shell under the skin. A few kinds of mollusc, like octopuses and some kind of slugs, have no shell at all, just a tough skin cover protecting the organs.

## SLIMY TRAILS

A snail moves from place to place by gliding along on a muscular part of its body called the foot. It lubricates its path with slime poured out from glands near the front. The head is at the front and carries one or two pairs of feelers or tentacles. Land snails have eyes at the tips of their tentacles, sea snails' eyes are at the base.

▲ A baby leopard slug emerges from a pearl-like cluster of eggs. It takes about 30 days for the eggs to hatch.

## THOUSANDS OF TEETH

Land snails are usually active at night or in damp weather. They feed mainly on plants. A snail's tongue, called a radula, carries thousands of tiny teeth and it works like a strip of sandpaper to shred up the stems and leaves of the plants. The tongues of some sea snails are so strong that they can drill through the shells of other animals.

## MOLLUSCS WITH HINGED SHELLS

Bivalves all live in water, most of them in the sea. Some are fixed to rocks and never move, but others can burrow in sand and mud. They feed by drawing a current of water into the open shell and filtering small particles of food from it, taking oxygen from the water at the same time.

## LIFE SUPPORT BACKPACK

Molluscs have a skin-like mantle that makes the shell. Most of the snail's internal organs are in its coiled hump, which stays inside the shell. When it is alarmed, the snail can pull its head and foot right inside its shell as well.

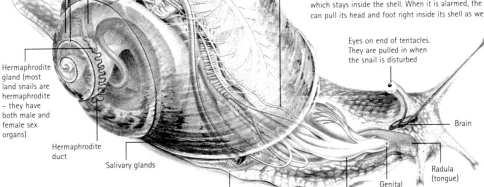

Heart

Intestine

Kidney

Stomach

Digestive gland

Mucous glands

Hermaphrodite gland (most land snails are hermaphrodite – they have both male and female sex organs)

Hermaphrodite duct

Salivary glands

Foot

Penis

Genital pore

Eyes on end of tentacles. They are pulled in when the snail is disturbed

Brain

Radula (tongue)

### SEE ALSO
Animal, Evolution, Ocean and sea

# SNAKE

Snakes are slender reptiles with no legs and, like all reptiles, they are covered with scales. There are about 2,800 species and all of them prey on other animals.

▲ Snakes regularly shed their skins (epidermis), including the scale covering their eyes (the brille), in order to grow.

Although they have no legs, snakes can slither surprisingly quickly over the ground. Most of them move by throwing their bodies into curves and pushing backwards against the ground. Some also push themselves along by digging their belly scales into the ground. Many snakes can even climb trees in this way. Snakes are generally inactive and are seldom seen except when they are hunting or disturbed.

Most snakes live alone, but rattlesnakes and corn snakes hibernate in groups.

## HUG OF DEATH

A snake finds its food largely by smell. It picks up scent particles from the air by flicking out its forked tongue, and it homes in on the scent of its prey. Some snakes merely grab their prey in their jaws and swallow it live. Others poison or suffocate their prey first. Snakes that suffocate their prey are called constrictors. They include boas, pythons, and the anaconda – the largest snake, which can grow to 9m long. They coil their powerful bodies around their victims and squeeze.

The bright yellow eyelash viper is well camouflaged in the golden palm fruit.

## DEADLY INJECTION

Poisonous snakes, which include vipers and cobras, inject venom into their prey through large teeth called fangs. The venom of around 270 snakes is harmful or fatal to humans. The saw-scaled viper of Africa, Indian cobra and Australian taipan are among the world's most dangerous snakes.

## SWALLOW IT WHOLE

All snakes swallow prey whole since they have no broad back teeth for crushing and cannot chew. A snake can swallow animals larger than itself because it can open its mouth extremely wide. And, as its ribs are not joined together, they open out to let the food pass along the body.

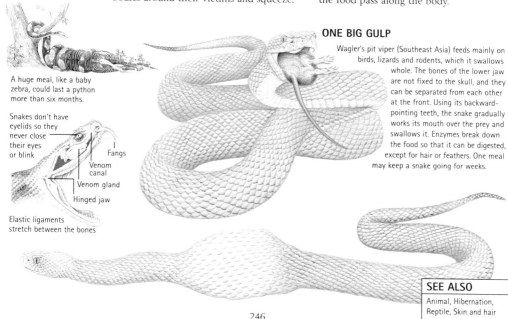

A huge meal, like a baby zebra, could last a python more than six months.

Snakes don't have eyelids so they never close their eyes or blink

Fangs

Venom canal

Venom gland

Hinged jaw

Elastic ligaments stretch between the bones

## ONE BIG GULP

Wagler's pit viper (Southeast Asia) feeds mainly on birds, lizards and rodents, which it swallows whole. The bones of the lower jaw are not fixed to the skull, and they can be separated from each other at the front. Using its backward-pointing teeth, the snake gradually works its mouth over the prey and swallows it. Enzymes break down the food so that it can be digested, except for hair or feathers. One meal may keep a snake going for weeks.

## SEE ALSO
Animal, Hibernation, Reptile, Skin and hair

# SOLAR SYSTEM

Our solar system is made up of the Sun and the objects that orbit it. These include the nine planets and their moons, as well as asteroids, comets and meteors.

| THE PLANETS | |
|---|---|
| Distance from Sun (million km) | Average time to orbit Sun |
| Mercury | |
| 58 | 88 days |
| Venus | |
| 108 | 225 days |
| Earth | |
| 150 | 1 year |
| Mars | |
| 228 | 1.9 years |
| Jupiter | |
| 778 | 11.9 years |
| Saturn | |
| 1,427 | 29.5 years |
| Uranus | |
| 2,870 | 84 years |
| Neptune | |
| 4,498 | 164.8 years |
| Pluto | |
| 5,900 | 247.7 years |

The Sun is at the centre of the solar system and has a mass 740 times greater than all the planets combined. It is this mass that holds the planets and other objects in their orbits through gravity.

## ROCKY WORLDS AND GAS GIANTS
Most of the matter from which the planets formed consisted of hydrogen and helium. The planets nearest the Sun – Mercury, Venus, Earth and Mars – were too warm to hold on to these plentiful light gases and instead became small worlds of rock and metal. Farther from the Sun, where temperatures were very low, the planets attracted huge amounts of hydrogen and helium. They became the gas giants – Jupiter, Saturn, Uranus and Neptune.

## ASTEROIDS AND COMETS
Between the orbits of Mars and Jupiter is a band of space where asteroids – rocks as big as mountains – are common. This is the asteroid belt. Occasionally asteroids collide. When this happens, bits break off that may eventually arrive on Earth as meteorites. A vast cloud of frozen comets is thought to lie much farther from the Sun than Pluto. This cloud, which may be 100 times farther from the Sun than the Earth is, marks the outer edge of the solar system.

## HOW THE SOLAR SYSTEM FORMED
The Sun was born about five billion years ago out of a great cloud of gas and dust in space. Scientists believe that the planets, as well as the asteroids and comets, gradually formed out of this spinning cloud.

**1** Material that was left over from the cloud of dust and gas formed a disc that circled the Sun.

**2** As particles within the disc collided, they began to stick together, forming larger objects.

**3** The objects grew into planets, moons, asteroids and comets, which often collided.

**4** Eventually, the remaining objects circled the Sun in orbits that rarely crossed.

◄ The planets of our solar system drawn to scale:
1 Mercury; 2 Venus;
3 Earth; 4 Mars; 5 Jupiter;
6 Saturn; 7 Uranus;
8 Neptune; and 9 Pluto.

| SEE ALSO |
|---|
| Astronomy, Comet, meteor and asteroid, Earth, Galaxy, Gravity, Planet, Sun, Universe |

# SOUND

**Sound is a form of energy that can be heard. It is caused by vibrations and travels in waves through solids, liquids and gases.**

▼ When you tap a tuning fork against a hard surface, it starts to vibrate rapidly, giving out a constant pitch. When the prongs vibrate outwards, they compress the air near them, creating high pressure. When they vibrate inwards, the air expands, leaving an area of low pressure.

Air compressed

Air expanded

We normally think of sound travelling only through air, but it can also move through other substances. If you put your head under the bath water, for example, you can still hear sounds in the room around you. That is because sound can travel through water – or any other liquid. Noisy neighbours are a problem because the sounds they make can travel through walls and floors – solid materials.

## MAKING SOUND

You can make a sound in air if you hit together two objects, such as a pair of saucepan lids. The objects create sound because you give them some energy, making them vibrate (shake). As the objects vibrate, they squash, then release the air each side of them, over and over again. This makes the air pressure around them rise and fall repeatedly.

## THE HUMAN VOICE

The human voice produces sound when air from the lungs is forced past the vocal cords. How high or low the voice is depends on how quickly or slowly these cords vibrate. The diaphragm controls the flow of air in and out of the lungs. The muscles around the mouth turn the noise produced by the vocal cords into recognizable sounds. The cavities in the nose, throat and chest help the sounds to resonate.

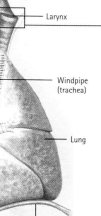

Nasal cavity
Mouth
Epiglottis
Larynx
Windpipe (trachea)
Lung
Diaphragm

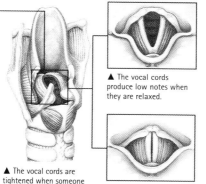

▲ The vocal cords produce low notes when they are relaxed.

▲ The vocal cords are tightened when someone speaks or sings. Breathing out makes the cords vibrate and produce sound.

▲ The vocal cords produce high notes when they are taut.

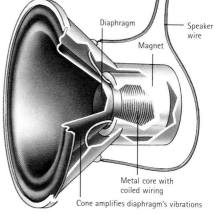

Diaphragm
Speaker wire
Magnet
Metal core with coiled wiring
Cone amplifies diaphragm's vibrations

▲ Loudspeakers turn electrical signals back into sounds. The signals cause a diaphragm inside the speaker to vibrate, and this motion reproduces the original sound.

## AIR VIBRATIONS

Sound is caused by only tiny changes of air pressure. When someone nearby talks to you, they make the air pressure rise and fall by about 1/10,000 of normal air pressure. That is roughly the pressure change you feel when you put a single sheet of paper in your palm. As air vibrates, it shakes a thin membrane in our ear called our 'ear drum'. That is why we can hear the vibrations as sound. Our ears can not pick up all kinds of vibration. The vibrations have to be loud enough for us to hear. They also have to happen at a rate that our ears can detect – in other words, they have to be the right frequency.

## SPREAD OF SOUND

When an object vibrates, sound waves spread out from it. The farther you are from the object, the more the energy from it has spread, so the quieter it is. Sound waves bounce off hard objects such as brick walls or windows. When you listen to someone speaking in a room, for example, you hear both the sound that has come directly from their voice and the sound that has bounced off the walls, ceiling and floor. This effect is called 'reverberation'.

## LOUDNESS

The harder you hit something, the louder the sound you make with it. That is because it vibrates more, creating a greater pressure change in the air around it. Our

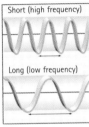

▲ The pitch of a sound – whether it is high or low – depends on its frequency or wavelength. Long waves have a lower frequency and pitch than short waves.

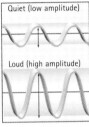

▲ A sound's loudness depends on the height of its waves, called its amplitude. Quiet sounds have a smaller amplitude than loud sounds.

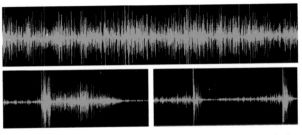

▲ A visual display of three different sounds: a symphony orchestra in full swing (top); the spoken word 'hello' (above left); and two hand claps (above right). Rich, complex sounds involve thousands of waveforms, of differing amplitudes and frequencies, all intermingling at the same time to make up the waveform shapes above.

ears can pick up a wide range of pressure changes. At best, they can detect sounds made by pressure changes that are a mere 5 billionths of normal air pressure. A pin drop is this quiet. At the other extreme, our ears can detect pressure changes about one fifth of normal air pressure. A road drill is this loud.

## FREQUENCY AND PITCH
Whistles and women's voices make sounds that are much higher in pitch than bass guitars and men's voices. That is because

## BREAKING THE SOUND BARRIER
When a vehicle, such as the British jet car Thrust SSC (below), travels at the speed of sound, pressure waves build up in front of the vehicle and form a shock wave. As the car accelerates through the sound barrier and travels faster than sound, the shock wave breaks away and can be heard, after the car has passed, as a sonic boom. You cannot hear a vehicle approaching at supersonic speeds.

they make sounds that have a higher frequency, or shorter wavelength. Frequency is measured in hertz (Hz). Our ears can only pick up sounds that are between 20 Hz and 20,000 Hz. A car horn makes a sound with a frequency of about 200 Hz, women can sing notes as high as 1,200 Hz and men can sing notes as low as 60 Hz.

## SPEED OF SOUND
On a warm day, sound travels through air at about 330m per second. On colder days, it travels more slowly. Sound travels at different speeds through other materials. It travels four times faster through water than air. Sound travels through solid concrete (such as the concrete partition between two offices) over ten times faster than it travels through air.

### LOUDNESS SCALE
Loudness is measured in decibels (dB). As the sound energy increases ten times, the decibels go up by the number ten. The following table shows the loudness of some sounds.

| | |
|---|---|
| • Rocket lift-off | 150–190 dB |
| • Jet take-off | 120–140 dB |
| • Thunder | 95–115 dB |
| • Motorbike | 70–90 dB |
| • Vacuum cleaner | 60–80 dB |
| • Orchestra | 50–70 dB |
| • Talking | 30–60 dB |
| • Whispering | 20–30 dB |
| • Falling leaves | 20 dB |

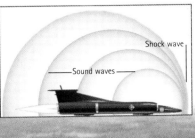

Shock wave

Sound waves

### SEE ALSO
Hearing, Musical instrument, Radar and sonar

# SOUTH AFRICA

Occupying the southernmost tip of the African continent, the country of South Africa consists mostly of a vast plateau, 1,200m above sea level.

**Area**: 1,221,037 sq km
**Population**: 41,402,000
**Capital**: Pretoria
**Languages**: Afrikaans and English
**Currency**: Rand

South Africa's high, flat-topped hills are surrounded by fertile, low-lying coastlands varying from 55km to 240km across. The spectacular Drakensberg Mountains rise to 3,482m and, in the north, the Limpopo River marks much of the country's northern boundary. The separate, mountainous kingdom of Lesotho is entirely surrounded by South African territory. The climate is mostly dry and sunny, averaging 17°C.

## DESERT, GRASSLAND AND SCRUB
In the north, the Kalahari Desert stretches into neighbouring Botswana. Most of the vast central plateau is occupied by an area of coarse grassland called the Highveld. The Middleveld, in the northwest, is more suited to livestock than crops because of its poor soil, owing to erosion and little rain. The northeast of the plateau is the Transvaal basin, where farmers grow citrus fruits, maize and tobacco. Elephants, lions, leopards and great herds of antelope and zebras live on Transvaal's thorny scrub and are protected in the Kruger National Park.

▲ Apartheid forced many blacks to live in sprawling slums, or townships, such as Soweto – South Africa's largest black residential area.

## PRECIOUS RESOURCES
South Africa has a vast wealth of natural resources, in particular minerals. It exports more diamonds than any other country, and is the world's largest producer of gold, platinum, chrome and manganese. It also has large reserves of gas, coal, copper, iron, asbestos, silver, nickel and uranium. It is Africa's most industrial country and could be one of the world's richest nations. It can provide enough of its own grain and meat to feed its population, and a quarter of its wealth comes from industries such as chemicals, textiles and machinery.

▲ The Drakensberg mountains form a long line of sharp cliffs where South Africa's high central plateau drops down towards coastal lowlands.

▶ For many visitors, the first sight of South Africa is Cape Town, set against the dramatic backdrop of Table Mountain, at the southern tip of the country.

## POLICY OF APARTHEID

The wealth of South Africa's natural resources has benefited only a minority of the population. This is because a policy of apartheid (separateness) was introduced in 1950 by the white government, which separated blacks from whites and refused blacks equal rights. With black people making up almost three quarters of the population, millions of people were left in abject poverty. Many other countries protested against the cruelty of apartheid, and imposed sanctions which limited South Africa's overseas trade.

## THE AFTERMATH OF APARTHEID

The process of apartheid began to collapse in 1990, under the presidency of F.W. de Klerk. In 1994, the first multi-racial elections were held in South Africa, bringing to power a majority black government. Although this struck a blow for equality, the new democracy still faces enormous problems: two million children have no schooling at all; half the population still lives in homes without electricity; 12 million still need clean water supplies and a third of the population is unemployed. The great gap between rich and poor creates a major problem of violent street crime.

▲ The elections of 1994 brought to power the African National Congress (ANC), headed by Nelson Mandela. Between 1964 and 1990, Mandela had been imprisoned for his opposition to the apartheid regime.

## FIGHTING FOR TERRITORY

The first South Africans were the San and the Khoi peoples. From about AD300, Bantu-speaking peoples such as the Zulus, Xhosa and Sesotho moved into the region. From 1652, Dutch settlers came by sea, soon followed by other Europeans. In 1806, the British took over the coastal areas, where the Dutch farmers (called Boers or Afrikaners) had settled. In order to keep their independence and claim new land for themselves, the Afrikaners made a 'Great Trek' inland in 1834–38, during which time they founded Transvaal and the Orange Free State. The discovery of gold and diamonds on Afrikaner territory led to two wars between the Boers and the British. Final Afrikaner defeat in 1902 led to a united South Africa in 1910.

## PLANS FOR THE FUTURE

South Africa's population is 77.4 per cent black, 12.2 per cent white, eight per cent of mixed descent and 2.4 per cent Asian. The government intends to build a 'rainbow society' where all peoples can live in harmony. South Africa's public holidays celebrate Human Rights, the Family, Freedom, Workers, Youth, Women, Heritage, Reconciliation and Goodwill.

▲ One of the main peoples of South Africa is the Zulus. About 7 million of them live here, mostly in the province of Natal.

### SEE ALSO

Africa

251

# SOUTH AMERICA

Covering 12 per cent of the planet's land area, South America is the fourth largest continent. Its people make up six per cent of the world's population.

South America's varied landscape includes the rocky islands of Tierra del Fuego (belonging to Argentina and Chile) and the immense grasslands of Argentina and Venezuela. There are also snow-capped mountains and active volcanoes. The Andes, running along the Pacific coast for 8,000km, form the longest mountain range in the world. Aconcagua in Argentina is the continent's highest peak.

▲ Ecuador's Cotopaxi (5,897m) is the continent's highest active volcano. Here it is seen from the volcano Illiniza.

## WET AND DRY

The Amazon River basin holds half of the world's fresh water. It occupies two fifths of the continent and is the world's largest tropical rainforest. The Amazon River is second only to the Nile in length. Quibdo in Colombia is South America's rainiest place, receiving more than 8900mm of rain a year. The Atacama desert in Chile is one of the world's driest places – the port of Arica in northern Chile averages less than 1mm of rain a year – but the hottest temperatures are recorded in the Gran Chaco region of northern Argentina.

## CLIMATIC DIFFERENCES

The great range of climates is due to the fact that there is a wide variation in the distance of the different countries from the Equator, and in the height of different areas above sea level. Lake Titicaca, between Bolivia and Peru, is the highest lake in the world, 3,812m above sea level.

## COASTAL CITIES

High mountains, dense forests and vast distances make overland transport difficult and costly. Most major cities lie along the coast or on large rivers, where they can be served by shipping. Only a tenth of all

▲ Venezuela's Angel Falls has a longer drop (979m) than any other waterfall in the world.

▶ In Bolivia, llamas graze high up in the Andes and are kept for their wool and meat. They are also able to carry heavy loads.

▲ The giant tortoise is one of the many unusual forms of wildlife on the Galapagos Islands, which lie 960km off the coast of Ecuador.

CARIBBEAN SEA

PANAMA

Lake Maracaibo
Caracas
Georgetown
VENEZUELA
Paramaribo
Quibdo
Angel Falls
Kourou
Bogotá
Cayenne
San Agustin
SURINAM
GALAPAGOS IS.
(Ecuador)
COLOMBIA
FRENCH GUIANA
(France)
Quito
ECUADOR
Amazon
Cotopaxi
B R A Z I L

Andes
BOLIVIA
Lima
Brasilia
Lake Titicaca
La Paz (seat of government)
Arica
Sucre (legal)
São Paulo
PACIFIC OCEAN
Rio de Janeiro
GRAN CHACO
ATACAMA DESERT
PARAGUAY
Asunción
ARGENTINA
URUGUAY
Aconcagua
Buenos Aires
Montevideo
Santiago
ATLANTIC OCEAN
CHILE
N

miles
0        500
0        500
km

FALKLAND IS. (U.K.)
Stanley
SOUTH GEORGIA (U.K.)
Tierra del Fuego

SOUTH SANDWICH IS. (U.K.)

roads are paved, and in rural areas, donkeys and carts drawn by oxen, or horses are used to carry goods. Aviation has developed rapidly since about 1950, especially in Brazil, which has 1,500 airports and landing grounds.

## UNIQUE WILDLIFE
South America's isolation from the rest of the world has led to the evolution of many unique forms of wildlife. These include the rhea (a large flightless bird), the capybara (the world's largest rodent) and the llama. Other South American creatures include the tapir, armadillo, jaguar, condor, iguana, giant anteater, tree sloth, vicuña, piranha fish, manatee and many varieties of parrot and monkey.

## PLANTS AND PRODUCTS
The Amazon region contains more kinds of plants than anywhere else in the world, including 2,500 types of tree and hundreds of species of orchid. South American plants yield products such as rubber, quinine, sisal and chocolate and woods such as mahogany and balsa.

▼ The Pan-American highway, which runs through the Atacama Desert, links most South American countries to each other and to North America.

## VARIED DESCENT
The native peoples of South America came from Asia by way of North America. From 1500 onwards, Europeans came to settle, mostly from Spain and Portugal. Many intermarried with local peoples, producing children of mixed race known as *mestizos*. In Andean countries such as Bolivia and Peru, native peoples still make up a large proportion of the population. Argentina's population is largely white, with many people of Italian, German or British descent, while Brazil's population includes many descendants of African slaves brought to work on sugar plantations. Since 1940, South America's population has tripled.

▲ Sugar cane is Guyana's most important crop. It is grown near the coast.

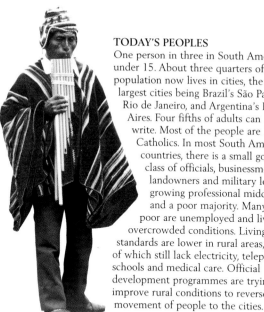

## TODAY'S PEOPLES
One person in three in South America is under 15. About three quarters of the population now lives in cities, the three largest cities being Brazil's São Paolo and Rio de Janeiro, and Argentina's Buenos Aires. Four fifths of adults can read and write. Most of the people are Roman Catholics. In most South American countries, there is a small governing class of officials, businessmen, landowners and military leaders, a growing professional middle class and a poor majority. Many of the poor are unemployed and live in overcrowded conditions. Living standards are lower in rural areas, many of which still lack electricity, telephones, schools and medical care. Official development programmes are trying to improve rural conditions to reverse the movement of people to the cities.

▲ Indians make up much of the population in Bolivia. Many wear traditional clothes, especially for festivals. Panpipes are a popular local instrument.

## SPORT AND LEISURE
Soccer has passionate fans throughout the continent – Brazil's Pelé has been called the world's greatest footballer of all time. Bullfighting is still popular in Colombia, Venezuela and Peru. South America has

▲ Brazil produces a third of the world's coffee. The beans must be washed in order to remove the outer skin.

produced many popular forms of music and dance such as the tango and samba. Colourful fiestas (festivals) are held on national and religious holidays. South American writers who have won the Nobel Prize for Literature include Chilean poets Gabriela Mistral and Pablo Neruda, and Colombian novelist Gabriel Garcia Marquez.

## MINERAL RESOURCES
Since European settlement began, South America has developed as a supplier of raw materials. At first this meant gold and silver, then timber, sugar, coffee and

▼ Bolivia is rich in tin. Local people sift through the mountains of slag for tin ore.

rubber and, after the coming of railways and steamships, beef, wheat and wool. Venezuela is rich in oil and iron, Brazil in manganese and bauxite. Colombia has emeralds and coal and Chile has copper as well as guano (bird droppings) and nitrates – used as fertilizer and to make explosives. Mineral exports pay for imports of manufactured goods, but modern mining is highly mechanized and creates few jobs.

## INDUSTRIALIZATION

Brazil is the most industrialized South American country, producing vehicles, light planes, televisions and machinery for the rest of the continent. Shortages of money and skills hold back industry in other countries, but most now produce basic items such as clothes, shoes, furniture and drinks for local use, reducing the need for imports.

## NEW VERSUS OLD

Brazil and Argentina both have vast plantations and ranches. Large-scale forest clearance has created environmental problems, as well as disturbing the traditional way of life of tribal peoples, who live by hunting and gathering. Offshore fishing is a major industry for both Chile and Peru.

## EUROPEAN SETTLEMENT

During the 1400s, the Inca built up a great empire in the Andes. In the early 1500s, European settlers from Spain and Portugal – greedy for gold and silver – enslaved or killed many Indians, and brought with them diseases

▲ Paraguay's capital city Asunción was built by the Spanish, who arrived in the 1500s and ruled the country for 300 years.

unknown to the continent, which wiped out millions of others. Missionaries introduced Christianity to replace traditional beliefs. The Napoleonic Wars in the early 1800s, however, weakened the hold of Spain and Portugal on their South American colonies.

## TO INDEPENDENCE

Revolutions in the early 1800s brought independence. The leading revolutionary figures were Simón Bolívar and José de San Martín. The former Spanish colonies became republics, but Brazil was ruled by emperors until 1889. South American trade remained tied to Europe and, from the late 1800s onwards, increasingly to the United States. Centuries of European influence are clearly shown in the Spanish-style architecture of many older cities.

## STONE STATUES

Some 300 stone statues have been found in the hills near San Agustin in Colombia. They are at least 1,000 years old and appear to mark burial sites. Colombia was originally home to many groups of indigenous people, some living in rainforest settlements, others wandering the open plains.

## MILITARY RULE

Many South American countries have been ruled by dictators – usually backed by the military – and changes of government by revolution have been common. Since the 1980s, civilian rule has been restored in countries such as Argentina, Brazil and Chile.

▲ *Ariane IV* is one of a number of rockets launched from the Kourou Space Centre in French Guiana.

## SEE ALSO

Aztecs, Continent, Incas, Maya

# SPACECRAFT

There are three main types of spacecraft: artificial satellites, unmanned probes and manned spacecraft. All require powerful rockets to lift them into space.

▼ Two minutes after launch, the booster rockets fall away; six minutes later, the main liquid-fuelled tank drops away. The boosters splash down in the Atlantic Ocean and are retrieved by ships.

Unmanned spacecraft that orbit the Earth are satellites. They are used for surveying our planet, communication, forecasting the weather or, as in the case of the Hubble Space Telescope, investigating the universe. They carry a variety of equipment, including radio receivers and transmitters, measuring instruments, cameras and computers. The energy needed to run the onboard equipment comes from solar panels that convert sunlight into electricity.

The shuttle launches its cargo ▲ into orbit – here, a satellite. The shuttle's speed at the time of launch is crucial: if it is too fast, the satellite will fly off into space; too slow and it will drop to Earth.

## GETTING THERE

A space shuttle takes off like a rocket, lands like a plane and can reach speeds of 28,000km/h. The launch in 1981 of the first space shuttle, *Columbia*, by NASA meant that a reusable vehicle could launch craft into space instead of having to build a new rocket for each mission.

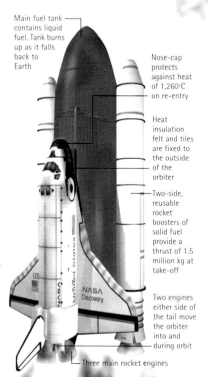

Main fuel tank contains liquid fuel. Tank burns up as it falls back to Earth

Nose-cap protects against heat of 1,260°C on re-entry

Heat insulation felt and tiles are fixed to the outside of the orbiter

Two-side, reusable rocket boosters of solid fuel provide a thrust of 1.5 million kg at take-off

Two engines either side of the tail move the orbiter into and during orbit

Three main rocket engines

## ROBOTS IN SPACE

Robotic spacecraft called probes have been sent to fly past, orbit or land on other planets. They carry cameras and instruments to gather scientific data which is sent back to Earth as a stream of radio signals. Space probes have small rocket engines which are fired to alter course or slow down before they enter orbit. Some probes send a lander down to a planet's surface, where it soft-lands using rocket-braking and parachutes.

## MANNED SPACECRAFT

Early spacecraft able to carry people include the 1969 *Apollo* craft that carried the first astronauts to the Moon. Later came orbital space stations, and the space shuttle. Manned spacecraft must carry enough air, food, and water to keep their crew of astronauts alive and working for what may be months in space. Fresh supplies can be brought from Earth by unmanned vehicles that dock with the manned spacecraft. In this way, permanent space stations can be maintained in orbit.

## ROCKETS

To gather enough speed to go into orbit around the Earth, or to escape from Earth's gravity, spacecraft need rocket launch vehicles. These usually come in three parts, or stages. As one stage runs out of fuel, it falls away, and the next stage fires.

*Sputnik* (USSR), the first satellite, launched in 1957, orbited for six months.

*Mir* space station (USSR, 1986) was almost continuously occupied.

*Luna 9* was the first craft to land on the Moon and send back pictures, in 1966.

The European Space Agency's *Ariane* rocket was first launched in 1981.

### SEE ALSO

Planet, Satellite, Solar system, Space exploration

# SPACE EXPLORATION

Space exploration began in 1957 with the launch of the first artificial satellite. By 1961, people were orbiting the Earth. Most major planets have now been investigated.

▲ A dog named Laika was the first astronaut, sent into orbit in *Sputnik 2* in 1957. It stayed up for two weeks.

Unmanned *Luna 2* (USSR) was the first spacecraft to reach the Moon, in 1959.

Five unmanned *Surveyor* craft (USA) landed on the Moon in the 1960s.

Radio-controlled *Lunokhod* (USSR) travelled on Moon's surface in 1970 and 1973.

The Moon, being nearest to Earth, was the first target for space probes. In 1959, Russia's *Luna 1* flew past the Moon at a distance of 5,955km. Later that year, *Luna 2* crash-landed on the Moon and *Luna 3* went around it, to send back the first pictures of the 'far side' – not visible from Earth. In the 1960s, several US and Russian probes landed on the Moon and sent back pictures of its surface. These, and a series of manned orbital flights to practise docking the spacecraft, prepared the way for manned landings, beginning with *Apollo 11* in 1969. Altogether, the six successful Apollo missions brought back 381kg of lunar rock and dust.

## HOT VENUS

Although Venus is the planet closest to the Earth (about 41.4 million km away), its surface is always hidden by thick clouds, so it's hard to get a clear picture of it by telescope or spacecraft. In 1967, the Russian probe *Venera 4* parachuted down through the gaseous clouds and sent back information about their make-up.

## SEARCHING PROBES

During the 1970s, several Russian probes landed on Venus and took measurements of their surroundings. But in scorching temperatures of over 450°C, none of the spacecraft survived for more than about an hour. Maps of Venus have been made by probes using radar. ▶

*APOLLO* COMMAND MODULE

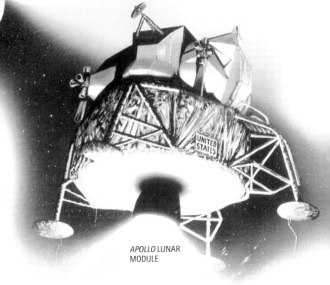

*APOLLO* LUNAR MODULE

## A GIANT LEAP FOR MANKIND

In 1969, US astronaut Neil Armstrong made history when he stepped from *Apollo 11*'s lunar module onto the Moon. Later missions, like this fourth US landing in 1971, used lunar rovers to explore and collect soil samples. The lunar module took them back to the orbiting command module.

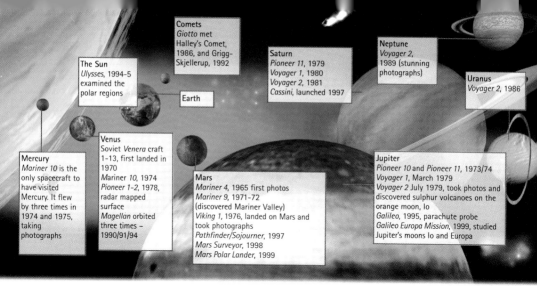

**The Sun**
*Ulysses*, 1994-5 examined the polar regions

**Comets**
*Giotto* met Halley's Comet, 1986, and Grigg-Skjellerup, 1992

**Earth**

**Saturn**
*Pioneer 11*, 1979
*Voyager 1*, 1980
*Voyager 2*, 1981
*Cassini*, launched 1997

**Neptune**
*Voyager 2*, 1989 (stunning photographs)

**Uranus**
*Voyager 2*, 1986

**Mercury**
*Mariner 10* is the only spacecraft to have visited Mercury. It flew by three times in 1974 and 1975, taking photographs

**Venus**
Soviet *Venera* craft 1-13, first landed in 1970
*Mariner 10*, 1974
*Pioneer 1-2*, 1978, radar mapped surface
*Magellan* orbited three times – 1990/91/94

**Mars**
*Mariner 4*, 1965 first photos
*Mariner 9*, 1971-72 (discovered Mariner Valley)
*Viking 1*, 1976, landed on Mars and took photographs
*Pathfinder/Sojourner*, 1997
*Mars Surveyor*, 1998
*Mars Polar Lander*, 1999

**Jupiter**
*Pioneer 10* and *Pioneer 11*, 1973/74
*Voyager 1*, March 1979
*Voyager 2* July 1979, took photos and discovered sulphur volcanoes on the orange moon, Io
*Galileo*, 1995, parachute probe
*Galileo Europa Mission*, 1999, studied Jupiter's moons Io and Europa

The *Mars 96 Penetrator* (USSR) has a 6-m long spike full of instruments to monitor soil composition.

Artist's impression of the *Magellan* radar-mapping spacecraft orbiting Venus in 1994.

Earth-controlled exploring robot designed to roam Mars or the Moon and send back images.

▲ Unmanned probes have now been sent to all of the major planets – only faraway Pluto has yet to be explored. Recent ventures include further deep-space missions and the 1999 *Mars Polar Lander*, which carried a CD-ROM full of children's names from around the world.

## MAPS AND PHOTOS

The most accurate maps of Venus came from the *Magellan* probe, which went into orbit around Venus in August 1990. It discovered the longest canyon in the solar system and a landslide that happened while the craft was taking measurements. The probe *Mariner 10*, which skimmed past Venus in 1974, also flew by Mercury, sending back the first clear photos of this small world's heavily cratered surface.

## LIFE ON MARS?

One of the most exciting moments in space exploration came in 1971 when the American probe *Mariner 9* photographed what looked like dried-up riverbeds on Mars. This suggested that millions of years ago, Mars had water and a thicker, warmer atmosphere, and therefore may have supported life. In 1976, the American spacecraft *Viking 1* and *Viking 2* went into orbit around Mars, named the 'Red Planet', after the colour of its soil. Probes descended to the surface by parachute. Each lander collected samples of the Martian soil and ran tests to see if they contained any life. Results were uncertain.

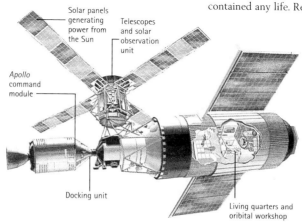

Solar panels generating power from the Sun

Telescopes and solar observation unit

Apollo command module

Docking unit

Living quarters and oribital workshop

◀ *Skylab*, launched in 1973, was built by NASA as a laboratory in space. It lasted until 1979, when it broke up and fell back to Earth. Some astronauts lived and worked in orbit for a year at a time on the Russian space station, *Mir*. *Mir* fell back to Earth in 2001.

## IS ANYONE OUT THERE?

| Planet | Probability |
|--------|-------------|
| Mars | Top runner among scientists who suspect life could exist underground |
| Titan, Saturn's moon | Orange, nitrogen-rich atmosphere |
| Europa, Jupiter's moon | Pictures have hinted at a possible ocean beneath its crust and tests suggest oxygen may be present |
| Jupiter | Scientists say a chemical pre-life form could exist in its clouds |
| Comets | Some scientists suggest dust fragments in a comet's tail contain pre-life forms and viruses |

◀ The Mars *Global Surveyor*, launched in 1996, orbited Mars (the Red Planet) taking photographs, assessing the planet's geology and finding a landing site for the next mission due to land there.

## RETURN TO THE RED PLANET

In 1997, *Mars Pathfinder* made the most unusual landing of any spacecraft so far. Parachutes and small rocket engines helped to slow it down. It bounced along the Martian surface using big balloons until it finally came to rest. The probe released a roving vehicle, *Sojourner*, which analyzed rocks and returned 550 images.

## DEEP SPACE

Beyond Mars lie the giant planets Jupiter, Saturn, Uranus and Neptune. These are much more remote worlds and it was only in 1973 that the first probe to Jupiter, *Pioneer 10*, flew past its target. Its sister craft, *Pioneer 11*, used the gravity pull of Jupiter to swing it on to an encounter with Saturn. This 'sling-shot effect' was also used by the later probes, *Voyager 1* and *Voyager 2*. In 1979, *Voyager 2* swung past Jupiter on its way to Saturn in 1981, Uranus in 1986 and Neptune in 1989.

Like the three earlier deep space probes, *Voyager 2* is now heading out of the solar system. In 1995, the *Galileo* spacecraft went into orbit around Jupiter. It released a probe that dropped by parachute through Jupiter's clouds and sent back details on the weather conditions and make-up of the atmosphere before burning up.

## MANNED EXPLORATION

More than 345 astronauts have flown in space, and 12 have set foot on the Moon. The next target for manned exploration is Mars. A craft to make this journey could be built in space, by astronauts working at an international space station orbiting the Earth.

▼ *Huygens* will take two-and-a-half hours to parachute to Titan's surface, sending back information about the moon's atmosphere to *Cassini*, which will relay it to Earth.

## TO SATURN AND BEYOND

Launched in 1997, NASA's *Cassini* spacecraft will take seven years to reach Saturn, where it will orbit and circle round the planet for four years. It will take around 30,000 colour photos and carry scientific instruments to study Saturn's rings and moons. A robot probe, *Huygens*, will attempt to land on Saturn's moon, Titan. If the probe survives the landing and can still send a signal back to *Cassini*, it will send back measurements from the surface.

**SEE ALSO**

Planet, Satellite, Solar system, Spacecraft, Sun

# SPAIN AND PORTUGAL

Spain and Portugal lie in the most southwesterly part of Europe, in an area known as the Iberian Peninsula. The countries have a linked history.

**SPAIN**
**Area:** 505,992 sq km
**Population:** 39,371,000
**Capital:** Madrid
**Languages:** Spanish, Catalan, Galician, Basque
**Currency:** Peseta, Euro

**PORTUGAL**
**Area:** 91,982 sq km
**Population:** 9,968,000
**Capital:** Lisbon
**Language:** Portuguese
**Currency:** Escudo, Euro

▲ Forests of cork oak trees in central and southern Portugal are stripped of their bark to provide large quantities of cork, a major product.

▶ Spain has about 1,400 castles and palaces. The fortified Alhambra Palace in Granada was built in the 1200s and 1300s.

Much of the Spanish mainland is a huge plateau called the Meseta. The country's high mountains include the Sierra Nevada and the Cantabrian ranges. The Pyrenees separate Spain from France. The Mediterranean coastline consists of fertile plains and, together with Spain's Balearic Islands, it attracts many tourists. The Canary Islands in the Atlantic are also popular with tourists and Spain's highest peak, Pico de Teide (3,718m), lies on the island of Tenerife. Central Spain has hot summers, reaching 42°C, and cold winters, but the coasts have a more moderate climate. Portugal is also mountainous, with high cliffs along its sandy Atlantic coastline. It has a milder climate than Spain. Its territory includes the islands of the Azores and Madeira in the Atlantic.

## KEY CITIES
Spain's capital city, Madrid, is in the centre of the country. Other major cities include the industrial ports of Barcelona, Valencia, Malaga and Bilbao, as well as the historic fortress-cities of Granada, Cordova, Seville and Murcia. Portugal's capital city, Lisbon, stands on the River Tagus, which divides the country. Lisbon

▲ Traditional costume, like that of these women and children from Seville, is still worn by many Spanish people for festivals and other celebrations.

was rebuilt after being destroyed by an earthquake in 1755. Portugal's other major city, Porto, is the centre of the port wine trade. Two thirds of the Portuguese people live in rural villages.

## TOURISM AND TRADE
In Spain, tourism and industry have grown rapidly since the 1950s, alongside traditional activities such as crafts, winemaking, fishing, and growing fruits and vegetables. Portugal's main products are wine, fish, cork and marble. Portugal also depends heavily on tourism. Many Portuguese work abroad, sending money back home. A fifth of the country's adults cannot read or write.

## THE SPANISH LANGUAGE
Southern Spain was ruled by Moors – Muslims from North Africa – from AD711 to 1492. Moorish civilization left its mark on language, architecture, food and music.

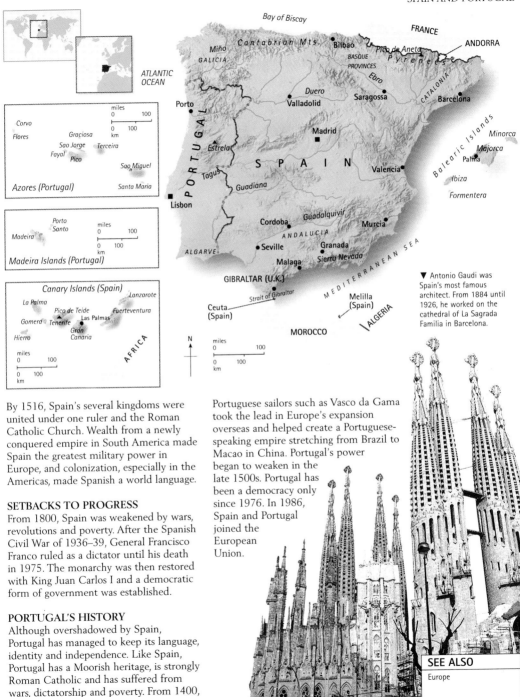

Bay of Biscay

FRANCE

ANDORRA

Cantabrian Mts.

Miño
GALICIA

Bilbao

Pico de Aneta

Pyrenees

BASQUE
PROVINCES

Ebro

CATALONIA

ATLANTIC
OCEAN

Duero

Saragossa

Barcelona

Porto

Valladolid

Madrid

Balearic Islands

Minorca

Majorca

Palma

Estrela

S P A I N

Valencia

Ibiza

Tagus

Formentera

Guadiana

Lisbon

Cordoba

Guadalquivir

Murcia

ANDALUCIA

Granada

Seville

Sierra Nevada

MEDITERRANEAN SEA

ALGARVE

Malaga

GIBRALTAR (U.K.)

Melilla
(Spain)

Strait of Gibraltar

Ceuta
(Spain)

ALGERIA

N

MOROCCO

miles
0          100

0        100
km

**Azores (Portugal)**

Corvo

Flores

Graciosa

Sao Jorge    Terceira

Fayal    Pico

Sao Miguel

Santa Maria

miles
0          100

0        100
km

**Madeira Islands (Portugal)**

Porto
Santo

Madeira

miles
0          100

0        100
km

**Canary Islands (Spain)**

La Palma

Lanzarote

Pico de Teide    Fuerteventura

Gomera    Tenerife

Las Palmas

Hierro

Gran
Canaria

AFRICA

miles
0          100

0        100
km

▼ Antonio Gaudi was
Spain's most famous
architect. From 1884 until
1926, he worked on the
cathedral of La Sagrada
Familia in Barcelona.

By 1516, Spain's several kingdoms were united under one ruler and the Roman Catholic Church. Wealth from a newly conquered empire in South America made Spain the greatest military power in Europe, and colonization, especially in the Americas, made Spanish a world language.

### SETBACKS TO PROGRESS
From 1800, Spain was weakened by wars, revolutions and poverty. After the Spanish Civil War of 1936–39, General Francisco Franco ruled as a dictator until his death in 1975. The monarchy was then restored with King Juan Carlos I and a democratic form of government was established.

### PORTUGAL'S HISTORY
Although overshadowed by Spain, Portugal has managed to keep its language, identity and independence. Like Spain, Portugal has a Moorish heritage, is strongly Roman Catholic and has suffered from wars, dictatorship and poverty. From 1400,

Portuguese sailors such as Vasco da Gama took the lead in Europe's expansion overseas and helped create a Portuguese-speaking empire stretching from Brazil to Macao in China. Portugal's power began to weaken in the late 1500s. Portugal has been a democracy only since 1976. In 1986, Spain and Portugal joined the European Union.

### SEE ALSO
Europe

# SPIDER AND SCORPION

Spiders and scorpions are invertebrates (animals with no backbone) belonging to a group called arachnids. They have four pairs of legs – insects have only three.

All spiders and scorpions are predatory animals, feeding mainly on insects. Some of the big tropical spiders eat both lizards and mice and even take baby birds from their nests.

The wind scorpion (or Sun spider) uses the wind to run and has huge jaws.

Mites, like this giant desert mite, are members of the arachnid family.

Unlike spiders, harvestmen have just one body section and eight slender legs.

A scorpion has large claws at the front to crush prey, and a sting in its tail.

## WEB OF DEATH

Spiders are famous for the silk webs they spin to trap their prey. There are lots of different web designs, the best-known being the circular orb webs. These have sticky spiral threads fixed to a set of radial threads that look like the spokes of a bicycle wheel. They are designed to catch flying insects. Other webs are designed to trap insects that scuttle over the ground.

## HUNTING OR TRAPPING

The Australian dinopis spider spins a net, and holding this in its front legs, waits for an insect to pass by. Then it throws the net over the insect. But not all spiders make webs. Wolf spiders run after their prey, and crab spiders usually sit on plants, seizing insects that come within range.

## POISONOUS FANGS

A spider kills its prey with poison, which is injected with a pair of needle-like fangs close to its mouth. The poison also starts to digest the prey, making it liquid, so the spider can suck the juices into its tiny mouth. It

◄ Crab spiders use their colours to hide in the centre of flowers, ready to pounce on pollen-hunting bugs.

Spiders have two body parts – an abdomen (back end) and a cephalothorax (head and chest). The legs are joined to the cephalothorax

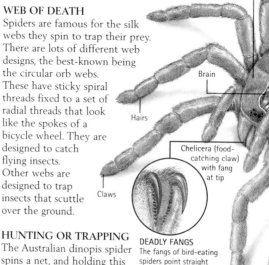

Sucking stomach
Heart
Ovaries
Brain
Hairs
Claws
Chelicera (food-catching claw) with fang at tip
Silk glands

### DEADLY FANGS
The fangs of bird-eating spiders point straight down. In other species, they point sideways.

### SILK SPINNERS
All spiders have spinnerets to make silk, even if, like the bird-eating spider, they don't make webs.

## BIG, HAIRY BIRD-EATER

Bird-eating spiders are among the largest spiders in the world, with a leg-span of up to 25cm and 6cm-wide bodies. Despite their eight eyes, they have poor eyesight and use their sense of touch and body hairs to detect vibrations. They leave trails of silk to help would-be mates find them, to help them climb and to wrap their eggs.

cannot eat solid food. Some spider poisons are powerful enough to kill people, but only about 30 of the 30,000 or so species of spider are really dangerous. They include the black widow and the funnel-web spiders. The most venomous spider known to humans is the wandering spider from Brazil, and there is still no antidote for the bite of the recluse spider, also found in South America. The fangs of most spiders are too small or weak to pierce human skin.

▲ Scorpions are fluorescent. Their outer shell glows bright green when an ultraviolet light is shone at it. This helps scientists to spot them at night when they are most active.

## STICKY TRAPS

Spiders have a variety of ways to trap prey. The orb-web spider (like many common garden spiders) creates a circular web in which unsuspecting flies get stuck. Bolas spiders 'fish' for prey using a sticky line of silk which they throw at nearby insects. Trap door spiders lurk in tunnels with little trap doors. They dart out to catch passing insects and drag them below.

## SCORPIONS

There are about 1,200 species of scorpion and all live in hot countries. Many of them live in deserts, where they can survive the high temperatures without ever needing a drink. Scorpions range from 2–20cm in length, the largest being the imperial scorpion of West Africa. All scorpions and spiders moult or shed their skin around five to ten times as they grow.

## A STING IN THE TAIL

Scorpions have large pincers – pedipalps – at the front and use them to catch lizards, insects and other small animals. A scorpion also has a sting at the end of its slender tail. The sting is used mainly for defence and some species are dangerous to people. The fat-tailed scorpion, found in parts of north Africa and the Middle East, is one of the most venomous scorpions. Its sting can kill a human in six to seven hours.

## SENSITIVE HAIRS

Each leg of a spider has seven segments. Most species have three claws at the tip of the leg and a pad of hairs that helps them stick to surfaces. The legs are covered with three kinds of sensory hairs. On most spiders, the hairs are irritants that can be rubbed off onto attackers. They are also used to taste (by detecting chemicals in the surroundings), to feel and to 'hear', picking up vibrations either on the ground or in the web. A male spider often drums on a female's web as a mating signal.

## A DANGEROUS COURTSHIP

Mating can be dangerous for many arachnids. The male spiders are mostly smaller than the females and often risk being mistaken for prey and eaten when they approach a would-be mate. In fact, the female often eats the male after, or even during, mating. The male nursery web spider gives his partner a gift of an insect wrapped in silk. As she eats the insect, he can mate safely.

## EGGS IN SILK BAGS

A female spider wraps her eggs in silk bags, or sacs. Wolf spiders carry these around with them, and even carry their babies on their backs for a while. Some spiders, such as the pink-haired bird-eating spider, lay 3,000 eggs in one batch – the hatched spiderlings are bigger than many fully-grown species.

▶ A scorpion's sting is at the end of a long flexible tail which it can quickly flick over to inject venom into its prey. The poison comes from two glands at the base.

Common garden spiders spin sticky, circular orb webs between branches.

Water spiders make a tent of silk underwater, using air bubbles to breathe.

Trap door spiders make a silk-lined tunnel in the ground with a lid on top.

### SEE ALSO
Animal, Insect

# SPORT

Sport is a game or activity involving physical skills, usually in competition. It is enjoyable as a form of exercise and also provides big-business entertainment.

Sports can be played either in teams or individually, on a professional or an amateur basis. Most sports are competitive and winning may be decided in a number of ways: by timing speeds (running or swimming events), measuring distances (jumping or throwing events), scoring points (most ball games) or judging performances (diving, boxing and gymnastics).

In ice hockey, players reach speeds of 48km/h and drive a hard, disc-shaped puck over the ice at 160km/h.

In scrambling, strong, light bikes with chunky tyres race across rough and hilly cross-country terrain.

A discus thrower spins around one-and-a-half times before releasing the discus from the hand.

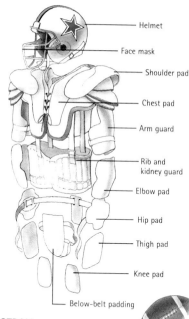

Helmet
Face mask
Shoulder pad
Chest pad
Arm guard
Rib and kidney guard
Elbow pad
Hip pad
Thigh pad
Knee pad
Below-belt padding

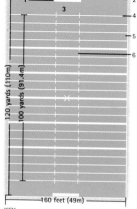

Goal post

120 yards (110m)
100 yards (91.4m)
160 feet (49m)

**KEY**

| | |
|---|---|
| 1 Goal post | 4 Goal line |
| 2 End line | 5 Sideline |
| 3 End zone | 6 Hash marks |

## AMERICAN FOOTBALL

American football evolved from English soccer and rugby. Professional sides have squads of up to 45 players divided into three teams: one for offence, another for defence and the third for taking kicks. The team in possession (offence) has four plays, or 'downs', to advance the ball 10 yards (9.1m) by running with it or passing it. If successful, the team has another series of plays. If it fails, the opposition takes possession of the ball. All plays start on or between the hash marks. Six points are awarded for a touchdown, plus an extra point for converting the ball over the crossbar. Place kicking the ball over the crossbar from anywhere in the field gains three points. The defence also scores two points from a 'safety' either by tackling the ball carrier in his own end zone or if the carrier steps out of the back or side of his zone.

## TENNIS

The modern game of lawn tennis was developed in Britain in the 1860s. The object of the game is to score points by hitting the ball with a racket over the net into the opponent's court so that it cannot be returned. The ball may be struck either before it has hit the ground or after one bounce. Tennis is played in sets, usually the best of three or five. A set is won when one side wins six games, with a lead of at least two games. A game's scoring goes from 'love' (0) to 15, 30, 40 and 'game'. If the score reaches 40–40 ('deuce'), it continues until one side leads by two clear points.

◀ Success in men's tennis depends greatly on having a powerful serve, as Pete Sampras of the USA demonstrates.

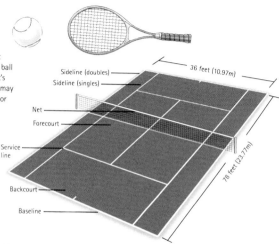

Sideline (doubles)
Sideline (singles)
36 feet (10.97m)
Net
Forecourt
Service line
78 feet (23.77m)
Backcourt
Baseline

# SOCCER

Professional soccer is played 11-a-side, with three substitutes allowed, and consists of two 45-minute halves. The object of the game is to kick or head the ball into the opponents' net to score a goal. The team with the most goals at the end of play wins. Players can move the ball with their feet, head or body, but not their hands or arms. Only the goalkeeper may handle the ball, and then only inside his penalty area. A free-kick is given if a player commits a foul or is off-side. A player is off-side when fewer than two defending players are positioned between him and the goal-line as the ball is being passed forward to him.

▼ Brazilian defenders attempt to tackle Cobi Jones of the USA in the 1994 World Cup competition. Brazil went on to beat Italy in the final.

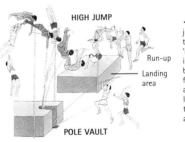

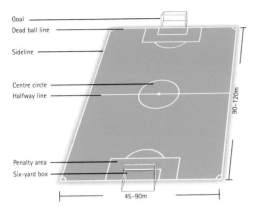

Goal
Dead ball line
Sideline
Centre circle
Halfway line
90–120m
Penalty area
Six-yard box
45–90m

# TRACK AND FIELD EVENTS

Outdoor running events, except for the marathon, take place on the 400m track. They include the 100m, 200m and 400m sprint. The longest middle-distance track race is 10,000m (25 laps), and other running events include the steeplechase and relay. Field events include: high, long and triple jump; hammer, discus and javelin throwing; pole vaulting; and shot putting. Combined track and field events include the ten-event decathlon and seven-event heptathlon.

HIGH JUMP

Run-up

Landing area

POLE VAULT

◄ Leading high jumpers use a technique called the 'Fosbury flop'. This involves clearing the bar head first, followed by the back, and, last of all, the legs. In pole vaulting, the pole may be of any length or width.

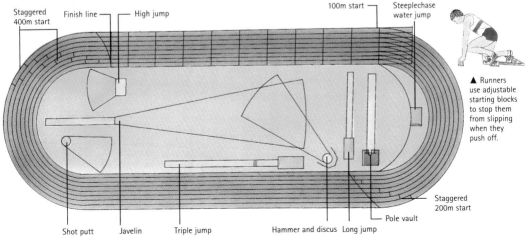

Staggered 400m start
Finish line
High jump
100m start
Steeplechase water jump

▲ Runners use adjustable starting blocks to stop them from slipping when they push off.

Staggered 200m start

Shot putt    Javelin    Triple jump    Hammer and discus    Long jump    Pole vault

An old Scottish game, golf is now one of the most popular sports worldwide.

Horse-racing can either be flat racing or racing over jumps, and is a major betting sport.

Skiing is a snow sport that includes downhill, slalom (obstacle course), ski-jumping and cross-country.

## BASKETBALL

Basketball was invented in Massachusetts, USA, in 1891, and is now one of the most popular team sports worldwide. It is played by two teams of ten, although only five players may be on court at any one time. The object of the game is to score points by throwing the ball into the opposition's basket. Players move the ball around with their hands by passing, dribbling and shooting. Running with the ball is not allowed. Baskets may be scored from any part of the court and are worth three points from outside the three-point arc, two from inside it and one from a free throw.

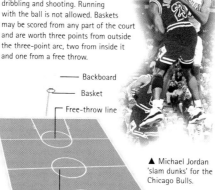

— Backboard

— Basket

— Free-throw line

▲ Michael Jordan 'slam dunks' for the Chicago Bulls.

— Sideline

— End line

Centre circle

## FENCING

As a combat practice, fencing dates from the Middle Ages. Three weapons are now used – the épée, sabre and foil. The object of fencing is to touch your opponent on the target area with your sword to score a hit. The fencers are wired up so that any hit can be registered electronically. Only the point of the weapon may be used in épée and foil, but with the sabre the edge of the blade also counts.

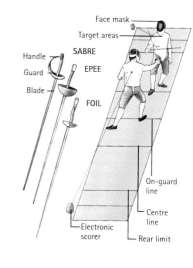

Face mask

Target areas

SABRE

Handle

Guard

Blade

EPEE

FOIL

On-guard line

Centre line

Electronic scorer

Rear limit

## CRICKET

Organized cricket began in late 17th-century England, although its origins probably go as far back as 1300. The modern game is played 11-a-side. At each end of the pitch is a wicket, which is defended by a batsman. The object of the game is to get the opponents' side out with the least number of runs. A side's innings end when ten batsmen have been dismissed, caught or run out. Any member of the fielding side may bowl an 'over', consisting of six balls. After each over, another bowler starts from the other end of the pitch. A run is scored when a batsman hits the ball with the bat and both batsmen run to the opposite end of the pitch without being dismissed. A hit over the boundary scores four runs, or six runs if it does not touch the ground first.

▲ The possible fielding positions for a right-handed batsman (only 11 fielders allowed):
1 Bowler; 2 Wicket-keeper; 3 First slip; 4 Second slip; 5 Gully; 6 Point; 7 Cover point; 8 Extra cover; 9 Silly point; 10 Silly mid-off; 11 Mid-off; 12 Deep mid-off; 13 Long-off; 14 Long-on; 15 Deep mid-on; 16 Mid-on; 17 Mid-wicket; 18 Silly mid-on; 19 Deep square-leg; 20 Square-leg; 21 Forward short-leg; 22 Backward short-leg; 23 Leg slip; 24 Short extra cover; »25 Backward point; 26 Short third man; 27 Third man; 28 Deep mid-wicket; 29 Deep extra cover.

Batting glove

Bails

Leg pad

Stumps

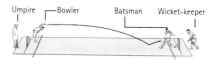

Umpire — Bowler      Batsman      Wicket-keeper

# BASEBALL

Baseball probably developed from games such as cricket and rounders. It was first played in 1846 in New Jersey, USA. It is played nine-a-side on a square field called the diamond, within a larger outfield. At one point of the diamond is home plate, where the batter stands, and at the other points are first, second and third bases, each of which is defended by a baseman. The pitcher throws the ball from a mound in the centre of the diamond. To score a run, the batter moves around the bases to reach home plate. He may do this with one hit or on hits of succeeding batters. Each side has nine turns at batting. The fielding side must get three batters out to close an inning and take its next turn at batting.

Outfield

Centre field

Left field    Right field

Shortstop

Foul line

Pitcher

Infield

Batter and catcher

1 First base; 2 Second base; 3 Third base; 4 Home plate

Fielder's glove

Catcher's mitt

Baseball bat

Baseman's glove

Catcher

Batter

Umpire

Pitcher

# GYMNASTICS

After its birth in Ancient Greece, gymnastics was revived in the late 18th century and was held at the first modern Olympic Games in 1896. In competition, gymnasts are marked out of ten by a panel of judges. The classic events involve floor exercises, high bar, parallel bars, pommel horse, rings and vault. Rhythmic gymnastics is performed to music and involves ballet steps and hand apparatus. Its individual exercises include twirling, throwing, catching, rolling, bouncing or swinging the apparatus. Sports acrobatics, for individuals or teams, includes somersaults and springs.

WOMEN'S VAULT

Handspring

Landing

Springboard

Horse

# SWIMMING AND DIVING

The earliest swimming races took place 2,000 years ago in Japan. Today, they involve four main strokes – front crawl, backstroke, breaststroke and butterfly – as well as freestyle. There are also separate diving events, either from a highboard or springboard, which involve specific somersaults, twists and turns while in the air.

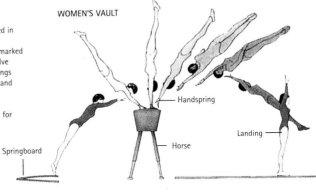

Dive

Recovery

Turn

## SEE ALSO

Olympic Games

# Starfish and other echinoderms

Starfish are star-shaped, marine invertebrates with between five and 40 arms. Other echinoderms include brittle stars, sea urchins and sea cucumbers.

A sea cucumber can grow up to 50cm. It uses its suckered feet for climbing.

A brittle star has no suckers. It uses its long arms to pull itself along.

A rock urchin grows up to 6cm and has sharp spines. It scrapes up algae to eat.

A violet heart urchin has furry spines on top. It burrows in sand and mud.

Echinoderm means 'spiny-skinned' and all members of the group have a rough or spiny skin to protect them. All live in the sea, although brittle stars often live at great depths, while most starfish and sea urchins live in fairly shallow water. There are about 1,700 different kinds of starfish, ranging in size from about 1cm to 1m.

## POWERFUL SUCKERS
Using its suckers, a starfish can move in any direction it chooses. It feeds on other small animals, including fish and worms, and can even open the shells of cockles and other bivalves with its powerful suckers. The starfish wraps its arms around a shell and grips with its suckers, which gradually pull the two halves of the shell apart. The starfish then pushes its stomach through the crack and digests the soft body inside.

## DRIFTING YOUNGSTERS
Starfish do not mate. The males and females release clouds of sperms and eggs into the water and fertilization takes place there. The young starfish (or larvae) are

▲ A starfish digests a mussel. It turns its stomach inside out and pushes it into the shell to eat the soft body.

blob-like with no arms and, instead of living on the sea bed, they float near the surface of the sea so they spread to new areas. They alter shape as they grow, and metamorphose (change) into adults.

## SLENDER RELATIVES
Brittle stars look like starfish, but their arms are more slender and are clearly separated from the central disc. Some brittle stars catch small animals with their arms, but most species shovel mud into their mouth and digest any tiny creatures living there. Sea cucumbers have feeding tentacles around their mouth to filter food from the water. Some sea urchins also feed like this.

## SYMMETRICAL STAR
Like all echinoderms, the starfish is built on a circular plan, with no head or brain, although it has a simple network of nerves in its body. The mouth is on the underside. Common starfish have five arms, which can regrow if they are cut off.

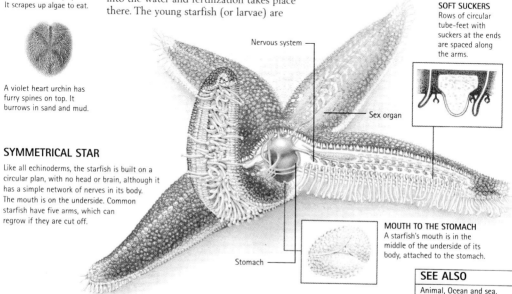

Nervous system

Sex organ

**SOFT SUCKERS**
Rows of circular tube-feet with suckers at the ends are spaced along the arms.

Stomach

**MOUTH TO THE STOMACH**
A starfish's mouth is in the middle of the underside of its body, attached to the stomach.

### SEE ALSO
Animal, Ocean and sea, Seashore

# SUN

The Sun is the closest star to Earth. It is a globe of hot gas, mostly hydrogen, and lies at the centre of our solar system. It contains no solid material.

The Sun is so big that more than a million Earths would fit inside it. It looks different from other stars because it is so much nearer to Earth. At the Sun's core, high temperatures and pressures cause nuclear reactions to take place in which hydrogen is turned into helium. This process releases huge amounts of energy, which eventually finds its way to the Sun's surface, called the photosphere. From there, it escapes into space as light, heat and other radiations.

## EVER-CHANGING

Cooler areas of the Sun form dark patches on the Sun's surface known as sunspots. From these, releases of energy, called solar flares, send bursts of radiation into space. Other eruptions, known as prominences, reach into the Sun's inner atmosphere, the chromosphere, and into its outer atmosphere, the corona. From the corona, there is a constant stream of particles into space, called the solar wind.

## GOOD AND BAD RAYS

Without the warmth and light of the Sun, life on Earth would be impossible. But the Sun also gives off other kinds of radiation, including ultraviolet rays and X-rays, which can be harmful. We are shielded from most of this damaging radiation by the ozone layer of the Earth's atmosphere, but enough ultraviolet radiation penetrates to the surface to be able to cause sunburn.

## LIFE STORY OF THE SUN

The Sun was formed about five billion years ago from a cloud of gas and dust. In another four or five billion years, its supply of hydrogen will run out and the core will collapse. The outer layers will swell as it becomes a red giant, then it will end its life as a slowly cooling white dwarf star.

## THE SUN'S ENERGY

The Sun's energy is produced in the core. It flows out as radiations, through the radiative zone to the convective zone. The energy reaches the visible surface of the Sun (the photosphere) by a churning motion called convection. Hot gas rises to the surface, gives off its energy and cools, then sinks back. The surface gives off the energy as light and heat.

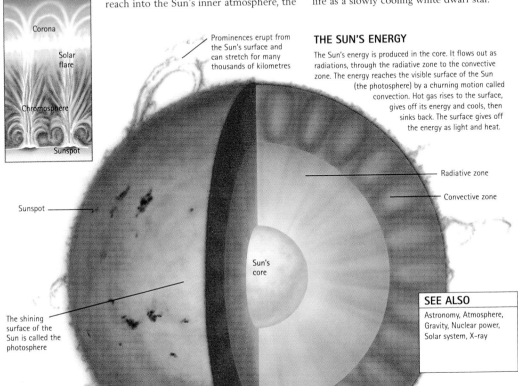

▼ Solar flares occur over sunspots. They can disturb Earth's magnetic field and interfere with radio transmissions on Earth.

Corona

Solar flare

Chromosphere

Sunspot

Prominences erupt from the Sun's surface and can stretch for many thousands of kilometres

Radiative zone

Convective zone

Sunspot

Sun's core

The shining surface of the Sun is called the photosphere

# SWAMP AND MARSH

Swamps, marshes, bogs and fens are all varieties of
wetlands, in which the soil is permanently waterlogged
or even completely covered with water.

A swamp is a wetland area dominated
by trees and shrubs – a kind of
permanently flooded forest. Waterlogged
areas without trees are called marshes.

## UNDERWATER ROOTS

The species found growing in swamps are
those that can withstand having their roots
permanently under water. Some of the
world's largest swamps are found in
southern Asia. Here, mangrove swamps
form a tangle of tall, stilt-like roots along
thousands of kilometres of coast. Strange
fish called mudskippers scurry about on
exposed areas of mud and archer fish spit
water to knock insects off overhanging
branches. Other creatures include crab-
eating frogs and monkeys, and some of the
world's most poisonous water snakes.

## MARSHLAND

Marsh vegetation consists mainly of grasses
and sedges. Dense patches of reeds and
rushes surround patches of open water,
which may contain water-lilies, rooted
to the bottom but with their
leaves floating on the surface,
or true 'floaters' such as the
water hyacinth and
duckweed. Many of
Europe's big rivers

have marshlands alongside them, providing
homes for a huge variety of birdlife – from
herons, egrets and avocets to tiny reed
warblers and bearded tits. Salt marshes are
common around the coasts in temperate
regions. They contain a variety of grasses
depending on how saline (salty) they are
and whether they are permanently
flooded. Like freshwater marshes, they
contain huge numbers of insects, snails
and frogs and are vital breeding and
feeding areas for waterbirds.

## BOGS AND FENS

The term 'bog' is usually used for a
waterlogged area consisting of thick layers
of peat. There is usually no water on the
surface, but the ground is soggy, and the
surface usually covered with spongy
sphagnum moss. The peat is so acidic and
contains so little oxygen that 2,000-year-
old bodies have been found in it, perfectly
preserved. Less acidic wetland areas are
often called fens.

## THE EVERGLADES

The Florida Everglades in the USA are the best known
Northern Hemisphere swamps, extending over 7,000 acres.
The region is essentially a river filled with coarse grasses
and rushes and scattered with dense stands of cypress,
red maple and gum trees, draped with Spanish moss.

Rough
green
snake

Pileated
woodpecker

Zebra butterfly

Raccoon

Roseate spoonbill

Green
tree frog

Mississippi
alligator

Mangrove roots

Terrapin

Oxeye tarpon

### SEE ALSO

Bird, Fish, Habitat, Insect,
Snake, United States of
America

# SWITZERLAND AND AUSTRIA

Switzerland and Austria lie north of Italy, in Europe, with Liechtenstein sandwiched between them. The Alps cover a large area of the two countries.

**AUSTRIA**
**Area:** 83,859 sq km
**Population:** 8,078,000
**Capital:** Vienna
**Language:** German
**Currency:** Schilling, Euro

**SWITZERLAND**
**Area:** 41,284 sq km
**Population:** 7,106,000
**Capital:** Bern
**Languages:** German, French, Italian and Romansch
**Currency:** Swiss franc

▲ Switzerland is famous for its beautiful lakes, including Lake Geneva.

▲ Swiss banks are probably the most secure banks in the world. Gold bars are stored in their vaults.

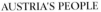

Two of Europe's greatest rivers, the Rhine and the Rhône, both start in the Swiss Alps within 25km of each other, while the mighty Danube flows through Austria. The mountainous landscape of both countries attracts many tourists.

## ALPINE INDUSTRY
Switzerland is one of the richest countries in Europe, despite its lack of natural resources and flat farmland. Its wealth has come from banking, tourism and industry – it produces cheese, chocolate, medicines, machinery and watches. Over a third of Austria is forested, supplying timber and paper. Austria's mountain waters feed hydroelectric plants that provide two thirds of the nation's power.

## SWISS GOVERNMENT
Switzerland is divided into 26 regions, or cantons, but central government controls the army, railways and post, and links with foreign countries. Over 150 international organizations have their headquarters in Switzerland, including the Red Cross, founded there in 1864. Through all the wars of modern history, Switzerland has remained neutral, but all Swiss men must train as soldiers. About one sixth of the population was born outside Switzerland, nearly a third of them in Italy.

## AUSTRIA'S PEOPLE
Until 1918, Austria ruled Europe's sprawling Austro-Hungarian Empire from Vienna. Vienna is Austria's capital city today and almost a fifth of the population lives there. The majority of Austrians are Roman Catholic and keep up old customs and festivals. Many country people wear traditional dress, such as leather breeches.

## POPULAR PASTIMES
Austria has a rich musical history as the home of the waltz and of the composers Mozart, Schubert and Strauss. Favourite Swiss and Austrian pastimes include folk dancing, yodelling, shooting and cycling.

▲ Skiing is a popular pastime in both countries and attracts many tourists. In Austria, there are more than 50 resorts.

### SEE ALSO
Europe

# TASTE AND SMELL

Taste and smell are two of our five main senses. They warn us of harmful fumes or rotten food – and also allow us to enjoy a delicious meal.

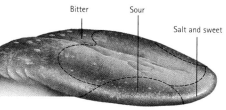

▲ Taste has only four main kinds of flavours: sweet, salty, sour and bitter. Each is detected by a certain part of the tongue, with the tip most sensitive to sweetness.

Bitter / Sour / Salt and sweet

Smell and taste are called chemosenses as they both work by detecting tiny particles of chemicals. In the case of smell, these particles, called odorants, float in the air that we breathe. In the case of taste, they are flavour particles in food and drinks.

## DETECTING SMELLS

When odorant particles land on the sticky liquid, or mucus, at the top of the nose, they touch the hairs of the smell cells. Different smells have differently-shaped particles and the hairs have differently-shaped pits or holes, called receptors. If an odorant particle fits exactly into a receptor, this triggers the smell cell to generate a nerve signal. This passes along the olfactory nerve to the brain, where it is analyzed and identified.

Unlike other senses, smell has direct nerve connections with the parts of the brain that deal with memory and emotion. This is why certain aromas, such as seaside air, can arouse strong memories and feelings.

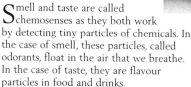

▲ A snake uses its tongue to pick up scents in the air, so it can tell whether a mate, a meal or an enemy is near.

## DOWN IN THE MOUTH

The tongue's upper surface has pimple-like protrusions called papillae, which help to grip and move food during chewing. It also has 10,000 microscopic taste buds, scattered mainly between and on the sides of the papillae. A taste bud is a tiny pit containing a ball-shaped cluster of 20 to 30 gustatory (taste) cells, which are arranged like segments of an orange. Flavour particles dissolve in saliva (watery fluid) and, as in the nose, probably fit into receptors on the hairs of the gustatory cells. This triggers nerve signals that travel along two main nerves to the taste centre of the brain for analysis and identification.

## TASTING SMELLS

When we eat, the mouth mainly tastes the food, but we also smell it. This is because some odorant particles in the mouth float around the back of the roof of the mouth up into the nasal cavity. There, they are smelled in the same way as odorant particles breathed in through the nose.

## NOSE AND MOUTH CELLS

Inside the nose is a two-part chamber called the nasal cavity. The roof of each part has a thumbnail-sized patch of lining which contains about 12 million microscopic olfactory (smell) cells. The tip of each of these cells is covered with 10 to 20 tiny hairs, called cilia. These stick into the thin mucus (sticky liquid) that coats the nasal cavity lining. The gustatory (taste) cells of the tongue's taste buds also have tiny hairs, projecting into the saliva (watery fluid) that coats the tongue.

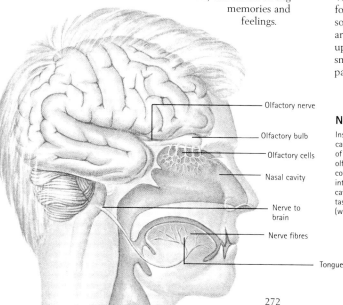

Olfactory nerve

Olfactory bulb

Olfactory cells

Nasal cavity

Nerve to brain

Nerve fibres

Tongue

## SEE ALSO

Brain, Cell, Food, Human body

272

# TEETH

Teeth are hard, bone-like, enamel-coated structures embedded in the jawbones of animals, including humans. They are used mainly for biting and chewing.

Teeth are extremely strong and hard-wearing, and are covered with the body's hardest substance – enamel. But to prevent toothache, tooth decay and gum disease, they need regular cleaning.

Meat-eaters such as the hyena have sharp teeth for tearing and crushing.

The male African elephant's tusk is the largest incisor tooth of any animal.

Snakes have teeth that curve backwards to help pull prey into the throat.

A spider's fangs are hollow and filled with poison for paralyzing its victims.

A shark's teeth are serrated and are regularly replaced as they fall out.

## TYPES OF TEETH

Our four main kinds of teeth do different jobs. Incisors at the front are thin and square-tipped, like a chisel or spade, to slice and bite off food. Next are canines, or eye teeth, which are taller and more pointed in order to tear and rip. Premolars and molars, or cheek teeth, at the back of the mouth, are broad and wide-topped for powerful grinding and chewing.

## FIRST SET OF TEETH

Humans grow two sets of teeth. The first set – baby, milk or deciduous teeth – numbers 20. It begins to appear about six months after birth, and is complete by the age of three. Baby teeth consist of two incisors, one canine and two premolars in both the left and right halves of the upper jaw, and the same in the lower jaw.

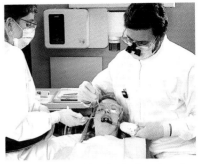

▲ A dentist looks after his patient by diagnosing and treating diseases of the teeth and gums. Regular visits to the dentist help detect problems early.

## SECOND SET OF TEETH

From the age of about seven, a child's first teeth loosen and fall out naturally, to be replaced by 32 permanent, or adult, teeth. In each half of each jaw there are two incisors, one canine, two premolars and three molars. The rear molars, or wisdom teeth, are usually the last to erupt, or grow, above the gum, which happens at around the age of 20. In some people they never erupt, staying small and hidden in the jawbone.

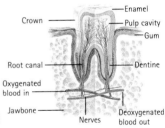

Crown — Enamel
Pulp cavity
Gum
Root canal — Dentine
Oxygenated blood in
Jawbone — Deoxygenated blood out
Nerves

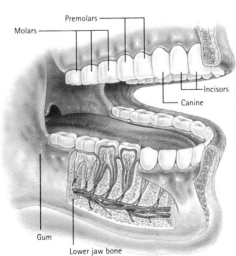

Premolars
Molars
Incisors
Canine
Gum
Lower jaw bone

## INSIDE THE TOOTH

All teeth have the same basic structure. The upper part, or crown, of the tooth shows above the gum, and the root is in the jawbone. At the base of the crown, soft gum tissue (gingiva) joins to the neck of the tooth. In between the crown and root is the pulp cavity. This contains tiny blood vessels to nourish the tooth, and nerves to detect pressure, temperature and pain. The vessels and nerves pass into the jawbone through a tiny hole, the root canal, at the root's base.

### SEE ALSO

Horse, Human body, Snake, Spider and scorpion

# TELEVISION

Television (TV) is the transmission of pictures and sound from one place to another. It is one of the most important means of mass communication in the world.

John Logie Baird's 1926 television system used lenses set in revolving discs to scan a picture.

Large-screen televisions use a back projection system with mirrors to enlarge the image.

Television began in 1937 when public broadcasts were made from Alexandra Palace in London. Several scientists had worked on developing television, including the Scot John Logie Baird and Americans Vladimir Zworykin and Philo Farnsworth.

## IN THE PICTURE

Television pictures and sounds are made up of electronic signals produced by a camera and recreated by a television set. A TV camera has lenses which focus the picture onto a surface that converts light to electronic signals, which can be recorded on video tape. The signals can be turned into radio waves, to be broadcast from radio transmitters, beamed via a satellite or sent along cable networks directly to the TV sets in homes.

▲ A Serb army officer stops a TV news crew from filming during the Bosnian crisis of 1995. Television is a powerful media tool which many governments try to control.

## MAKING A TV PROGRAMME

Producing a TV show is a team effort. Camera operators take the pictures, while mike boom operators keep microphones in position. The director in a control room cuts from one camera to another. There are also script writers, make-up artists, costume designers, caterers, lighting crews, post-production teams and technical staff.

## INTO THE FUTURE

Liquid crystal displays are used for flat screens in camcorders, and high-definition television with 1,125 lines gives a highly detailed picture. Televisions which use digitized signals to give sharper sound and pictures are also now becoming available. In the future, 3-D television may be possible.

## HOW TELEVISION WORKS

A TV camera has a lens which focuses the picture onto light detectors, which convert light to electronic signals for broadcasting. The main part of a TV is a large, funnel-shaped glass tube with a screen at one end. The inside of the screen is coated with strips of a chemical called phosphor, which light up when electrons hit them. A beam of electrons is fired at the screen from electron guns at the back of the tube. Focusing plates, controlled by the TV signal, target the beam on the screen, creating the picture. A mask blocks any stray electrons. Colour TV sets have three electron beams – one each for red, green and blue.

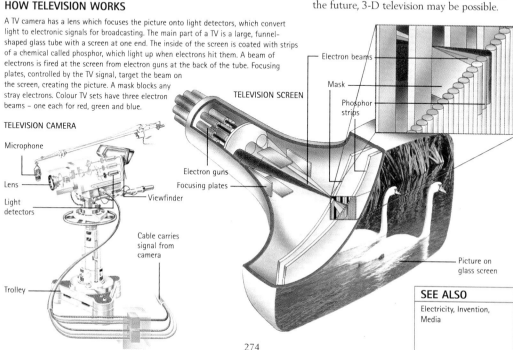

TELEVISION CAMERA

Microphone
Lens
Light detectors
Viewfinder
Electron guns
Focusing plates
Cable carries signal from camera
Trolley

TELEVISION SCREEN

Electron beams
Mask
Phosphor strips
Picture on glass screen

### SEE ALSO

Electricity, Invention, Media

# TIGER AND OTHER BIG CATS

Tigers, lions and leopards belong to a group of the cat family known as 'big cats'. The cat family also includes many smaller wild cats, as well as the domesticated cat.

▲ Although not classed as a 'big cat', the puma is as big as a leopard. Also known as the cougar, mountain lion and panther, it ranges through the Americas and eats a varied menu, from deer to rabbits and birds.

The cheetah is the only cat to outrun its prey rather than stalk it.

Tigers belong to the cat family (*Felidae*). So do six other kinds of big cat – lions, cheetahs, jaguars, leopards, snow leopards and clouded leopards. The cat family also includes about 28 kinds of smaller wild cat, from the puma, bobcat and lynx down to the smaller margay, kodkod and sandcat. The black-footed cat of southern Africa is even smaller than a domesticated cat.

## CAT FEATURES

All cats are meat-eaters, members of the carnivore group. They live by hunting, although a few scavenge dead meat. They have keen senses, with excellent sight even at night-time, and amazing balance for climbing. Long whiskers feel the way in

The black panther is a natural variation of the leopard with very dark fur.

darkness. The cat's body is lithe and agile, with stealthy movements. The fur is striped, spotted or patterned for camouflage, so the cat can creep silently and unseen. Long claws grip, scratch and slash, and can be pulled or retracted into the toe-tips, keeping them sharp. Long, sharp teeth bite and tear flesh.

## BIGGEST OF THE BIG CATS

Tigers live across India, on some islands of Indonesia, and in South China and Manchuria. Siberian tigers of Manchuria are huge and powerful predators, up to 4m long from nose to tail and weighing more than 300kg. Like most cats, tigers live alone. They are only together when mating, or when a mother is with her cubs.

The lynx is a wild cat that lives in the forests of Asia, Europe and North America.

## NIGHT HUNTER

Like other cats, the tiger hunts mainly at twilight or night. It prefers dense, swampy forest and ambushes deer, wild pigs, wild cattle, and the occasional baby elephant or rhino. Very rarely, a tiger preys on people. The record-holding 'man-eater' killed over 400 people.

▲ Lions are the only cats that live and hunt in groups (or prides). The lionesses do the hunting, usually at night. One lioness stalks the prey, driving it towards the other lionesses who lie in wait. The adult male does not join in, but claims a share of the kill. Lions sleep during the day.

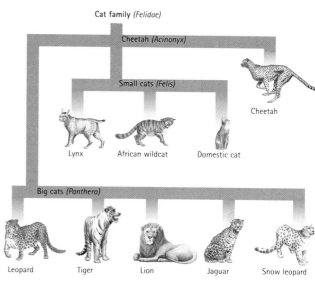

Cat family *(Felidae)*

Cheetah *(Acinonyx)*

Small cats *(Felis)*

Cheetah

Lynx    African wildcat    Domestic cat

Big cats *(Panthera)*

Leopard    Tiger    Lion    Jaguar    Snow leopard

## THE LEOPARD

The leopard is the most widespread big cat, ranging across Africa and Southern Asia, into China and Indonesia. It is adaptable, too, living in high hills, deserts, scrub, rainforests, and even near towns and villages. Leopards eat a wide variety of prey and will drag a carcass into a tree to store it away from scavengers. The rare snow leopard, or ounce, lives in the Himalayas and nearby mountains. It has long, thick, pale fur for warmth and camouflage in the snow. The clouded leopard is the smallest big cat, weighing just 20–30kg. It lives in India and Southeast Asia.

## THE CHEETAH

This lean, long-legged big cat is the fastest land animal. It sprints at almost 100km/h after swift prey such as antelope, hares and even young ostriches. It has spotted fur and a long tail to help it balance and turn at speed. The cheetah is the only cat that cannot retract its claws. For this reason, it is classed on its own in the cat family.

## THE LION

Prides of lions were once common in Europe, Africa and Asia, but now can be found only in protected areas south of the Sahara Desert in Africa and in the Gir forest, a wildlife sanctuary in India. They live in open, grassy plains where

## THE CAT FAMILY

The cat family is divided into three groups, with the cheetah forming a group of its own. The group known as *Felis* includes the domestic cat, as well as about another 27 types of small cat. The big cats belong to the *Panthera* group, which includes six big cats – the five shown here and the clouded leopard.

water is available and are territorial, fiercely protecting their hunting ground, where they stalk zebras, wildebeest and antelope.

## THE JAGUAR

The only American big cat, the muscular jaguar is found in the southern USA and in Central and South America. With its spotted coat, it resembles a leopard, but is larger and more powerful, weighing about 100kg. Jaguars like thick forests with swamps, lakes and rivers. They swim well.

▼ The leopard has a full body length of about 150cm. As with most cats, the males are larger than the females, at 60–70kg. The leopard's larger spots are not single black patches, but circular groups, or rosettes.

### SEE ALSO
Animal, Cat, Mammal

# TIME

We use time to track the passing of days, in hours, minutes and seconds. In addition to natural units of time, people have invented other ways to measure it.

**One day**

One day is exactly the time it takes for the Earth to revolve on its axis once.

**One year**

One year is approximately the time it takes for the Earth to orbit the Sun.

**One lunar month**

A month is based roughly on the time it takes the Moon to orbit the Earth.

When you need to know the time, you look at a watch or clock. This tells you how many hours and minutes it is since noon (midday) or midnight. For example, if your watch says the time is exactly 3:30 ('half past three') in the afternoon, you know that three hours and thirty minutes have passed since noon. If your watch is very precise, it may also tell you how many seconds have passed.

## DAYS

The measurement of time is based on the position of the Sun in the sky. Every day, the Sun seems to rise at dawn, move across the sky, then set at dusk. This happens because the Earth is continually spinning around. Each place on Earth can only see the Sun for part of the day; when the Sun is out of view, it is night-time in that part of the world. The Sun appears to rise as it comes into view and set as it disappears again. At one moment in the day, each place faces the Sun directly. When this happens, the Sun is highest in the sky and the daylight is brightest (on a sunny day).

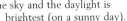

**THE AZTEC CALENDAR**

▲ The Greenwich Observatory, England, is the place where astronomers first devised the Greenwich meridian in 1866. This is the line at zero longitude that divides east from west; time zones are still calculated from it.

## HOURS

As early as 2400BC, the Babylonians divided the day into 24 equal parts, called hours. The modern day starts at midnight, a time when the sky is dark in most areas. A few hours later, the Sun rises. Twelve hours after midnight it is noon, the time when the Sun is highest. In another 12 hours, it is midnight again.

## CALENDARS

Every civilization has used some kind of calendar to keep track of years, months, weeks and days. Calendars are used to plan planting and harvesting, but also to mark special holidays and festivals. The Julian calendar was instituted by Julius Caesar in 46BC. Pope Gregory XIII (1502-85) adjusted it in 1582, and his Gregorian calendar is still used in Western countries today. The Chinese calendar is lunar, with a 60-year cycle, but the Chinese use the Western calendar, too. The Jewish calendar is a complex combination of solar and lunar cycles, with 12 or 13 months.

## CALENDARS OF THE AMERICAS

The Aztecs of Central America made a calendar in the ground from a huge stone shaped liked the Sun. The face of the Sun god, Tezcatlipoca, was carved in the middle, and signs for the days were carved around the edges. The Maya – also of Central America – used a calendar with two interlocking cog-wheels to represent circular time. Native American tribes in North America kept track of time by watching the seasons and phases of the Moon.

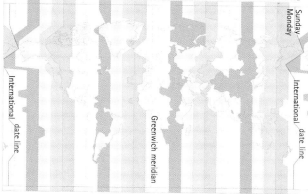

Hours -12 -11 -10  -9  -8  -7  -6  -5  -4  -3  -2  -1   0  +1 +2 +3 +4 +5 +6 +7 +8 +9 +10 +11 +12

International date line

Greenwich meridian

International date line

Sunday
Monday

## TIME ZONES

Because the Earth is spinning, different places on Earth face the Sun at different times of day. When it is midday in London, UK, it is dawn in New York, USA, and in Adelaide, Australia, it is still night. If people read the time directly from the Sun's position, watches worldwide would be set to thousands of different times. Chaos would result; for example, it would be impossible to write accurate train timetables.

▲ The world is divided into 23 full, and two half, time zones, starting at the prime meridian at Greenwich, UK. Each zone west of the meridian is an hour earlier than the last; each zone to the east is one hour ahead.

## GREENWICH MEAN TIME

To get around this timing problem, governments approximate time by dividing the world into 24 time zones. These zones follow the Earth's longitude lines, and are based on Greenwich Mean Time (GMT), the time at Greenwich, UK. Tokyo, Japan is nine hours ahead of GMT, so when it is 2:00 am in Greenwich, it is 11:00 am in Tokyo.

## THE FOURTH DIMENSION

All objects have three dimensions: width, height and breadth (the dimensions of space). Scientists believe that objects also have a fourth dimension: time. Every day, we move through the four dimensions (called space time). We can move in all directions through space (up and down, or from side to side); however, it is believed that we can only move forward through time. Many science fiction writers have played with the idea that time travel into the future (or into the past) is possible.

▲ H. G. Wells' (1866–1946) remarkable science fiction novel, *The Time Machine* (1895), tells the story of a man who builds a machine that carries him into the future. In the 1960 film above, the machine vanishes forward in time without its maker.

▲ The giant Sun clock in New Delhi, India tells the time as the Sun casts shadows on graduated markings.

▼ Stonehenge in England (begun c. 2700BC ) is a stone circle thought to have been used as an astronomical observatory and calendar. Its axis was aligned with midsummer sunrise (June 21), which suggests it was used to track the movements of the Sun, Moon and planets.

## SEE ALSO

Astronomy, Earth, Moon, Navigation, Season, Sun

# TOUCH

**Touch is one of the body's five main senses. It allows us to detect not only physical contact, but also temperature, pressure, heat, cold and pain.**

Touch can distinguish between light and heavy pressure and between things that are soft and hard, cold and hot, dry and wet, rough and smooth, still and moving. From this variety of information, we build up an impression of what our skin comes into contact with – from a cold, slippery ice cube to a warm, furry kitten.

▲ Touch sensors are packed closer together in places such as the lips and fingertips, with hundreds in a pin-head-sized area. These body parts are most sensitive to touch.

## TOUCH SENSORS

There are millions of microscopic sensors in the skin. Each is the specialized ending of a nerve fibre. When stimulated, the sensor sends bursts of nerve signals along its fibre to the brain. Touch sensors are all over the body in the skin. Hairs are mostly dead, so they cannot feel. But touch sensors are

▲ Braille is a special raised-dot type system that enables blind people to read with their fingertips. The system was invented by Louis Braille (1809–52).

wrapped around each hair root. When the hair is rocked or tilted, the sensors send out nerve signals. Similarly, nails are dead but have touch sensors in the skin underneath.

## TYPES OF SENSOR

There are different types of touch sensor. Merkel sensors are tiny discs in the base of the skin's upper layer, or epidermis. Meissner sensors are slightly larger and egg-shaped, in the upper part of the skin's lower layer, or dermis. Krause sensors, also egg-shaped, and Ruffini sensors, larger and sausage-like, are in the middle of the dermis. Pacini sensors are multi-layered, like onions. At up to 1mm long, they are the largest sensors and are just visible to the naked eye. The most numerous sensors are free nerve endings, each one resembling a tiny, many-branched tree.

## WHAT DO THEY DETECT?

Some types of sensor respond better to certain kinds of touch. Meissner and Merkel sensors detect light touch, while Pacini sensors respond better to heavier pressure. Ruffini sensors pick up vibrations well. But in daily life, most types of sensor respond to most kinds of touch. Free nerve endings, which are the most widespread, respond to almost any kind of touch, including heat and cold, as well as the great pressure and damage that cause pain.

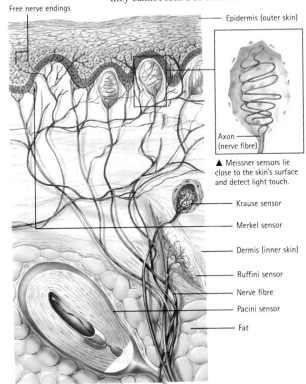

Free nerve endings

Epidermis (outer skin)

Axon (nerve fibre)

▲ Meissner sensors lie close to the skin's surface and detect light touch.

Krause sensor

Merkel sensor

Dermis (inner skin)

Ruffini sensor

Nerve fibre

Pacini sensor

Fat

---

**SEE ALSO**

Brain, Skin and hair

# TRANSPORT

**Transport is a means of carrying people, animals or goods from one place to another. This can be by land, water or air, or through space.**

Britain's *Flying Scotsman* made the world's longest non-stop run in 1928, from London to Edinburgh.

▲ The Japanese inter-city Bullet train can travel over 210km/h and provides smooth and noiseless transport for thousands of commuters daily.

Humans have always needed transport, to move from place to place and to carry their goods. This is why the earliest civilizations were built alongside rivers. Eventually, people began to ride on horseback to cover long distances more quickly. They also used pack animals and carts to carry goods.

## TRADE BY WATER

As civilizations developed, the need for transport continued to grow. Any trading centre close to water built a harbour and began to send heavy goods to other centres by boat. At the same time, vehicles with wheels also became important. But few roads were strong enough to support

heavily laden carts. For this reason, right up to the 19th century, water transport, in the form of ships and barges, developed more quickly than land transport, and most of the world's trade went by sea.

## STEAM ENGINES

At the end of the 18th century, the first practical steam engine was invented. This gave birth to the steamship and, in the 1820s, railway transport. Railways became so successful that they soon put inland

## ON THE ROAD

The first travellers had to carry or drag their belongings. Then they trained animals to carry loads and drag sleds. Around 3500BC, the Sumerians began to use wheeled carts. From that time and for hundreds of years, people travelled in various types of carriages pulled by animals. However, for many years there were no roads. Since the invention of the motor car, a vast network of roads and motorways has run across countries.

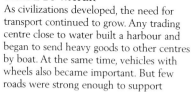

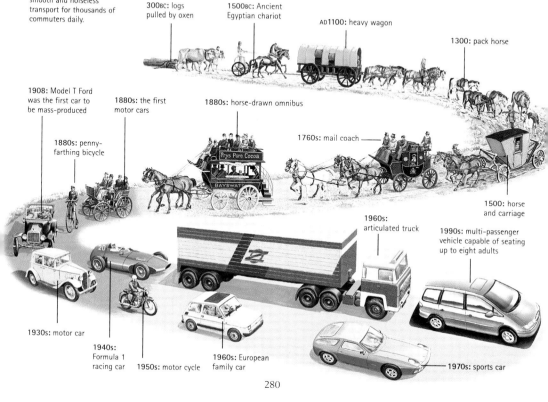

300BC: logs pulled by oxen

1500BC: Ancient Egyptian chariot

AD1100: heavy wagon

1300: pack horse

1908: Model T Ford was the first car to be mass-produced

1880s: the first motor cars

1880s: horse-drawn omnibus

1760s: mail coach

1880s: penny-farthing bicycle

1500: horse and carriage

1960s: articulated truck

1990s: multi-passenger vehicle capable of seating up to eight adults

1930s: motor car

1940s: Formula 1 racing car

1950s: motor cycle

1960s: European family car

1970s: sports car

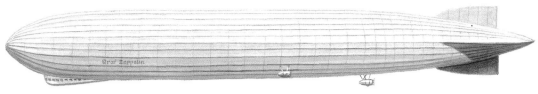

▲ Rigid airships, such as the German Zeppelin, were a successful form of transport in the early 1900s. With a length of 120–240m, they could reach speeds of up to 130km/h.

canals out of business. At the same time, larger, faster steamships were carrying more and more passengers and goods across the oceans.

## TRADE BOOM
This progress had the effect of further boosting trade. By the end of the 19th century, the world's major ports were huge places employing thousands of people, and the railways in most countries had been fully extended. Also, networks of metalled (hard-topped) roads were being built. This meant that goods could be delivered from the ports and railway yards directly to the front doors of shops and houses, and people could travel to work. The development of the roads was aided by two inventions: the pneumatic (air-filled) tyre and the internal combustion engine, which, between them, led to the invention of the modern motor vehicle.

▲ Modern jet airliners can carry up to 500 passengers and fly around the globe in less than three days.

## MOTOR TRANSPORT
Roads quickly became the most useful form of transportation. Anyone with a motor vehicle could travel almost anywhere, for business or pleasure. At first, few people could afford a car of their own. During the 1920s, however, cheap motor cars began to be mass-produced, and heavy lorries became much more efficient. By about 1950, road transport had taken a great deal of business away from the railways. In addition, by this time, air transport, with the development of bigger planes and jet engines, was attracting passengers away from ocean-going liners, which had become too expensive to run.

## MERCHANT SHIPPING
Today, most short-distance transport – of people or goods – is by road, while almost all long-distance transport is by air and sea. Heavy cargo is usually transported by merchant shipping, which consists of specially built cargo carriers, such as oil tankers, bulk carriers and container ships.

## DEATH OF THE RAILWAYS
An increase in air traffic has meant that the role of the railways in many countries has been reduced to carrying people to and from work in city centres. However, the growth of electric underground train systems in many large cities has helped take the strain off street buses and trams, as well as cut down on city pollution.

▲ The daily congested road traffic in cities such as Los Angeles, USA, has become a real global problem because of the pollution it creates and the damage this does to the ozone layer.

Great ocean liners had six or more decks with luxury extras for passengers such as lifts, suites, ballrooms and swimming pools.

The bicycle still remains one of the most efficient means of short-distance transport and in addition causes no pollution.

## SEE ALSO
Horse

# TREE

A tree is a large, upright plant with a single, woody main stem. The biggest trees are among the largest, heaviest and longest-living organisms on Earth.

Trees come in all shapes and sizes, but most are over 6m tall. Some, such as oaks, have a short main trunk that divides into huge, spreading branches. Others, such as redwoods, are tall and conical, with trunks 100m high and 9m thick at the base.

## CLASSIFYING TREES

The two main tree families are the conifers, or softwood trees, and the deciduous trees, or hardwoods. Scientists refer to conifers as gymnosperms (meaning 'naked seeds'), because their seeds form on the woody scales that make up their cones. Deciduous trees are called angiosperms ('enclosed seeds'), because their seeds are enclosed inside fruits. Pines, firs, spruces, larches and hemlocks are all conifers – also called evergreens because most keep their thin, needle-shaped leaves throughout the year. Deciduous trees, such as oak, ash, maple, beech, elm and horse chestnut, shed their leaves in the autumn.

## TREE PARTS

The three main parts of a tree are its roots, trunk and leaves. The roots take in water and nutrients from the soil. The trunk supports the tree and carries water and nutrients to the leaves through tubes, and food from the leaves back down to the rest of the tree.

The silver birch has pure white bark, often pocked with black marks. It has a tall and elegant shape.

Like the sugar maple, the silver maple is tapped for its syrup. Its five-lobed leaves are deeply toothed.

▶ Acorns are the fruits of the oak tree. On the English oak, they are attached to stalks.

— Oak leaf

Acorn

The bark of the oak tree is fissured (ridged) and brownish-grey in colour.

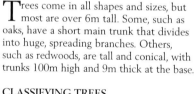

Blossom

Conker

▲ The horse chestnut has spreading branches, and pink or whitish blossom clusters in spring. Its seed, the conker, is covered in a spiky shell, and its leaves have 5–7 leaflets.

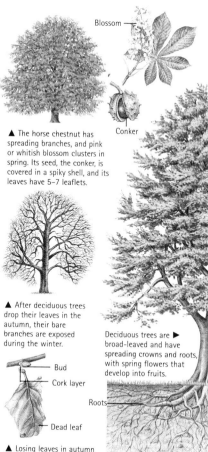

▲ After deciduous trees drop their leaves in the autumn, their bare branches are exposed during the winter.

— Bud

— Cork layer

— Dead leaf

▲ Losing leaves in autumn helps deciduous trees to conserve water in winter. The leaf is sealed off from the stem's food supply near the bud; it dies and falls.

Deciduous trees are ▶ broad-leaved and have spreading crowns and roots, with spring flowers that develop into fruits.

Roots

▲ Many species of oak grow in the Americas and Europe. Most are deciduous, such as the English oak, which can survive for 1,000 years. Its trunk is stout and burred.

▲ The banyan tree, native to India, has branches that hang down to the ground and root themselves. On one banyan in Sri Lanka, over 3,300 trunks were counted.

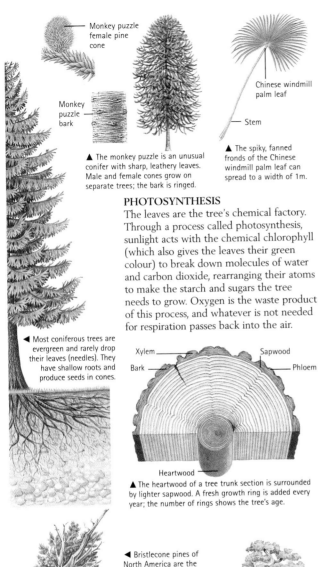

— Monkey puzzle female pine cone

Monkey puzzle bark

▲ The monkey puzzle is an unusual conifer with sharp, leathery leaves. Male and female cones grow on separate trees; the bark is ringed.

Chinese windmill palm leaf

— Stem

▲ The spiky, fanned fronds of the Chinese windmill palm leaf can spread to a width of 1m.

▲ Deciduous trees produce vivid and beautiful autumn colours in North American woodlands. Leaves may change from green to all shades of red, orange and gold.

◀ Most coniferous trees are evergreen and rarely drop their leaves (needles). They have shallow roots and produce seeds in cones.

## PHOTOSYNTHESIS

The leaves are the tree's chemical factory. Through a process called photosynthesis, sunlight acts with the chemical chlorophyll (which also gives the leaves their green colour) to break down molecules of water and carbon dioxide, rearranging their atoms to make the starch and sugars the tree needs to grow. Oxygen is the waste product of this process, and whatever is not needed for respiration passes back into the air.

Xylem — Sapwood
Bark — Phloem
Heartwood —

▲ The heartwood of a tree trunk section is surrounded by lighter sapwood. A fresh growth ring is added every year; the number of rings shows the tree's age.

## USES OF TREES

Trees were among the first natural resources used by people. They provided fuel for fires; wood for shelters, tools and weapons; and fruits and nuts for food. Today, two billion people in developing countries still rely on wood for fuel. The industrial world also uses huge amounts of lumber, plywood and hardboard. Wood pulp is used to make paper and fibres.

## TREES AND THE ENVIRONMENT

Trees help to keep the atmosphere healthy, because they remove carbon dioxide from the air and give off oxygen not used during photosynthesis. Trees also protect the land from erosion. Their large canopies of leaves and branches absorb heavy rainfall; their roots bind the soil and prevent it from being washed away. This is why it is important to preserve rainforests in Brazil and Indonesia. In parts of Africa, where natural forests have been cut down, fast-growing trees are being planted to help prevent the desert taking over.

◀ Bristlecone pines of North America are the world's oldest trees. Some are over 6,000 years old.

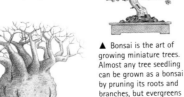

▶ The baobab tree is native to Africa and Australia. It has a wide, bulbous trunk with thick, short branches.

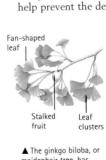

▲ Bonsai is the art of growing miniature trees. Almost any tree seedling can be grown as a bonsai by pruning its roots and branches, but evergreens are the most popular.

Fan-shaped leaf

Stalked fruit

Leaf clusters

▲ The ginkgo biloba, or maidenhair tree, has remained unchanged for 160 million years. The tree was cultivated for centuries in Chinese temple gardens.

### SEE ALSO

Conservation, Ecology, Forest, Fruit, Habitat, Leaf, Plant, Rainforest

# UNITED KINGDOM

England, Scotland and Wales lie on the island of Great Britain in northwest Europe. Together with Northern Ireland, they are governed as a United Kingdom.

**UNITED KINGDOM**
**Area:** 242,900 sq km
**Population:** 59,055,000
**Capital:** London
**Languages:** English and Welsh
**Currency:** Pound sterling

Much of England is lowland, with the flattest areas in the east. Upland regions include the Lake District and the Pennines. Scotland, Wales and Northern Ireland are more mountainous than England. Scotland's Ben Nevis (1,343m) is the United Kingdom's (UK's) highest peak. Loch Neagh, in Northern Ireland, is the UK's largest lake, and the Severn (354km), which runs through Wales and the west of England, is the UK's longest river. In most parts, summers are generally cool and winters mild, with rainfall all year round.

### TOWN AND COUNTRY
The UK is a crowded nation. Four out of every five British people live in cities and towns. England – especially the southeast around London – is the most densely populated country. London is one of the world's greatest cultural centres. The UK has an extensive road system with many motorways, and London's Heathrow is the world's busiest airport for international traffic. Since 1994, the Channel Tunnel, under the English Channel, has physically linked Great Britain with France.

▲ Many commuters use London Bridge, over the river Thames, to reach the City of London, the heart of the capital's business community.

### INDUSTRY AND FARMING
Natural resources include oil and natural gas deposits in the North Sea. The UK's many rivers provide drinking water, as well as water for crops. Much of the countryside is farmed and the crops include wheat, sugar beet, potatoes and oil-seed rape. Dairy cattle and sheep are raised as well as pigs and poultry. Manufacturing industries include aerospace, chemicals, telecommunication and electronics. Scotland also produces fine woollens and Northern Ireland is famous for its pure white linen. Service industries such as banking, publishing and tourism are also important.

▲ Northern Ireland has been the scene of violent conflict between Catholics and Protestants. Here the Protestant Orange Order celebrate the anniversary of the victory of William of Orange over Catholic king James II in the Battle of the Boyne in 1690.

► Wales is a land of green valleys, grassy plains, hill farms and mountains. Its castles include Carreg Cennen in the southwest, shown here.

The word *loch* means 'lake' in Gaelic. Loch Tulla is one of many lakes lying between Scotland's peaks.

## FROM CONQUEST TO KINGDOM

The Romans conquered lowland Britain from AD43. After the Romans came Anglo-Saxons, Vikings and Normans. The United Kingdom of Great Britain and Ireland was formed in 1801. It became the United Kingdom of Great Britain and Northern Ireland in 1922, after the southern part of the island of Ireland became independent.

## WORLD POWER

During the 18th century, Britain colonized large parts of North America, Africa and Asia. Wealth from the colonies supplied money for the Industrial Revolution to begin at home, and factories and machinery were built. By 1900, the British Empire had become the biggest empire in the world, defended by the biggest navy.

## DECLINE OF EMPIRE

In the first half of the 20th century, two world wars caused loss of life and economic strain. From the 1950s, the UK's wealth and power declined as many of the colonies became independent and

▲ England's south coast, including Dartmouth Quay in Devon, is popular with tourists for its scenery and climate.

Britain's traditional manufacturing industries such as coal, iron, steel and ship-building declined.

## THE UK TODAY

Today, the UK is still a major player in finance and in the service industries, and plays a leading part in world affairs through the United Nations, the Commonwealth and the European Union. The UK is a constitutional monarchy, which means the king or queen is head of state but political power is controlled by parliament. The Isle of Man and the Channel Islands are largely self-governing but some of their laws are made by parliament. In 1997, some power was devolved to a regional parliament in Scotland and an assembly in Wales.

▲ Tower Bridge, across the River Thames in London, is a moveable bridge. The two halves of its roadway are raised for passing tall ships.

### SEE ALSO

Europe, Industrial Revolution, Middle Ages, United Nations, World War I, World War II

# UNITED NATIONS

The United Nations is an international organization based in New York City. Its member nations meet there to discuss problems and try to find solutions.

The United Nations flag features the world surrounded by the olive branch, a symbol of peace.

### UN AGENCIES

World Health Organization (WHO)

Food and Agricultural Organization (FAO)

International Monetary Fund (IMF)

UN Educational, Scientific and Cultural Organization (UNESCO)

International Civil Aviation Organization (ICAO)

World Bank

United Nations Children's Fund (UNICEF)

Founded in 1945 by the allies after World War II, the United Nations (UN) has grown to include 185 of the nearly 200 independent states on Earth. The UN sponsors negotiations between disputing members, and its many agencies carry out humanitarian work.

## GENERAL ASSEMBLY
Each UN member country has one vote in the General Assembly, which meets in New York City, USA. The General Assembly approves UN work, debates important issues and decides how to spend its money. The 15-member Security Council is responsible for peace and security. It can send a peace-keeping force to any country, and may condemn aggressive action. Five countries are permanent members: the USA, Russia, Britain, France and China.

## HUMANITARIAN WORK
The UN works to promote trade, health education and cultural understanding. This work is carried out by the bodies of the Economic and Social Council (ESC), which pays for aid projects in poor

countries, encourages health care and promotes the rights of minorities. UNICEF (UN Children's Fund) promotes the welfare of children in poor countries. In 1991, the UN held an Earth Summit in Rio de Janeiro, so that world leaders could discuss environmental problems.

## PROBLEMS IN THE UN
Problems have beset the UN in recent years. In the 1990s, civil wars in Rwanda and Bosnia continued despite UN efforts. The USA, Russia, Japan and the UK pay half of UN costs, but are regularly outvoted by poorer nations. The USA has accused the UN of corruption and of bias against developed nations, and it has refused to pay its share until reforms are made.

▲ United Nations forces are stationed in many parts of the world, such as Cambodia, to help keep the peace. Here, a UN soldier talks to a Cambodian woman and her child.

◀ The United Nations General Assembly meets for three months every autumn to decide important issues. It can hold a Special Session during an emergency, such as the Soviet invasion of Hungary in 1956.

### SEE ALSO
World War II

# UNITED STATES OF AMERICA

The United States is a republic in the continent of North America and is made up of 50 states. It is rich in natural resources and advanced in technology.

**Area:** 9,363,520 sq km
**Population:** 270,299,000
**Capital:** Washington, D.C. (District of Columbia)
**Language:** English
**Currency:** US dollar

▼ The Statue of Liberty stands at the entrance to New York Harbor. It was a gift from France in 1884 and represents freedom for the American people.

The United States (US) is the third largest country in the world in population and the fourth largest in area. Two states sit apart from the others. Alaska, lying west of Canada, includes Mount McKinley (6,194m), the highest peak in the US. The state of Hawaii is made up of a group of islands in the Pacific Ocean.

## THE EASTERN STATES
In the eastern US, rocky, forested New England centres on Boston, famed for universities such as Harvard. Also in the east are the historic cities of Philadelphia and New York City and the industrial cities of Detroit and Cleveland. Spectacular Niagara Falls and the country's largest lake, Michigan, are in the north. The southeast includes the federal capital of Washington, D.C., booming cities such as Atlanta, sunny Florida with its rich wildlife in the Everglades swamps, and historic settlements such as Charleston.

## ACROSS THE COUNTRY
The north-central part of the US is known as the Midwest. It is a rich farming region and has mighty rivers, including the longest river in the US, the Missouri (4,090km) which is part of the Mississippi-Missouri river system.

▲ New York City is the largest city in the US. One of its key symbols is the yellow taxi, a common sight on the streets of Manhattan and the other four boroughs.

There are also huge grasslands known as prairies. Farther west are the Rocky Mountains, the geysers of Yellowstone National Park, ski resorts and bustling cities such as Denver. The south has scorching deserts in Arizona and business centres such as Houston and Dallas in Texas. The far west is dominated by the most populous and richest state, California. Los Angeles, in California, is the second largest city in the US and home of the Hollywood film industry. ▶

▲ The Grand Canyon lies in the state of Arizona, in the warm, dry southwest. It is one of the most spectacular gorges in the world, carved from the desert rock by the Colorado River.

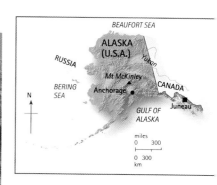

▲ The Trans-Alaska pipeline carries oil from the north of Alaska to its south coast. The state of Alaska has a cold climate and is thinly populated.

## THE PEOPLE

Since 1940, the population of the United States has more than doubled. Native Americans, who lived in North America for thousands of years before Europeans began arriving, now make up just under one per cent of the population. About half of all Americans are Protestants and nearly a third are Roman Catholics. About two per cent of the population are Jewish, and about the same percentage are Muslim.

## SETTLEMENT AND REVOLUTION

Permanent European settlement of what was to become the US began with a British colony founded in 1607 at Jamestown, Virginia. British colonists spread along America's east coast. In the south, they grew tobacco, cotton and indigo on plantations worked by slaves shipped from Africa. In the north, timber and furs were key products and fishing was a major industry. French and Spanish explorers and colonists began to settle other territories to the west. Disputes between Britain and its 13 colonies

▲ The casinos and nightclubs of Las Vegas, in the state of Nevada, attract thousands of visitors. Neon signs light up the city.

over trade, taxes and defence led to the American Revolution (1775–83) and on July 4, 1776, a group of colonial leaders signed the Declaration of Independence. The war ended in victory for the colonists, led by General George Washington.

## THE NEW REPUBLIC

The colonies united to form a republic. In 1787, the US Constitution was written, dividing power between a central, federal government and the ex-colonies, which became separate states and were given powers of self-government. National laws were to be made by the president together with Congress, which is made up of the House of Representatives and the Senate.

▶ About 80 per cent of Americans are white or Hispanic. African Americans form about 12 per cent of the population and Asians, Native Americans and other groups make up the remaining eight per cent. This classroom reflects the multicultural make-up of the United States.

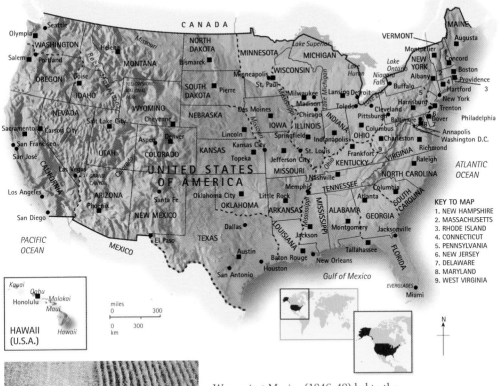

KEY TO MAP
1. NEW HAMPSHIRE
2. MASSACHUSETTS
3. RHODE ISLAND
4. CONNECTICUT
5. PENNSYLVANIA
6. NEW JERSEY
7. DELAWARE
8. MARYLAND
9. WEST VIRGINIA

▲ Wheat is harvested on the prairies – the vast grasslands of the Midwest.

## GROWTH OF A NATION

George Washington was the first president and a new national capital was founded and named in his honour. In 1791, a Bill of Rights was added to the Constitution, guaranteeing the rights of all US citizens. In 1802, President Thomas Jefferson bought vast western territories claimed by France, doubling the size of the new nation. In 1804, he sent an expedition to explore the continent from east to west.

War against Mexico (1846–48) led to the conquest of the southwest and Pacific coast. Lured by the discovery of gold in California in 1848 and by the prospect of free land on the prairies, Americans headed west. Washington Irving and other writers helped create a new national identity and Noah Webster compiled the first dictionary of American English.

## WAR AND PEACE

From 1861 to 1865, America was torn by civil war which made the south poor but boosted industry in the north. Peace brought a boom in railway building. By 1869, the railway joined the east and west coasts. San Francisco, Chicago and St Louis grew from frontier posts into great cities. ▶

▼ Surfing and other water sports are popular on all the Hawaiian islands, including Oahu, where 80 per cent of Hawaii's population lives.

▲ Like baseball and basketball, American football is a popular national sport.

▲ The White House, in Washington D.C. has been the home of US presidents since it was built in 1800. It was rebuilt after a fire in the War of 1812.

## INDUSTRY AND IMMIGRATION
Millions of Europeans moved to the US and Native Americans were driven from their traditional lands. America grew rich from its farms and factories. By 1900, the average American was better off than the average European. Half of all Americans still lived on farms, but cities were booming. Inventions made in America, such as the light bulb, elevator, skyscraper and aeroplane, were to change the world.

## A WORLD POWER
In 1867, the United States bought Alaska from Russia. In 1898, it took over the Pacific islands of Hawaii and also went to war with Spain. This led to independence for Cuba and American rule over the Philippines. The US developed a great navy. In 1917, the country joined in World War I to help Britain and France to defeat Germany and its allies.

## BOOM, BUST AND WAR
In the 1920s, the US was the first country in which millions of people drove cars, listened to radio and enjoyed the movies, but the 'roaring twenties' ended in a business collapse in 1929, with millions out of work. President Franklin D. Roosevelt used government money from taxes to create new jobs. Following Japan's attack on the US naval base at Pearl Harbor (Hawaii) in 1940, Roosevelt led the country into World War II, but died just before the German surrender in 1945.

## SUPERPOWER
War boosted industry in the US and left the country as a superpower, armed with atomic bombs and with a new role as leader of the democratic world. American wealth helped Europe recover from war damage. Today, the US is the world's most powerful nation and US culture has spread across the world.

▲ In 1620, English Puritans who called themselves Pilgrims sailed to America and founded a colony in Plymouth, Massachusetts. A recreation of their settlement now stands on the site of the original colony.

◀ In the early 1900s, jazz emerged in New Orleans and developed as a new and distinctly American style of music. Today, the New Orleans jazz festival is world famous.

### SEE ALSO
Bridge, Cold War, Habitat, Native Americans, North America, World War I, World War II

# UNIVERSE

The universe is made up of stars, planets and other matter scattered throughout space. It may contain up to 100 billion galaxies with 100 billion stars in each.

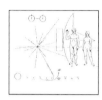

▲ NASA sent a diagram of humans into space, so that it could be found by intelligent life elsewhere in the universe. The dumb-bell represents a hydrogen atom; the symbols below it represent the solar system.

Most scientists believe that the universe began with an enormous explosion called the Big Bang, which happened about 15 billion years ago. During this event, all the matter and energy that would ever exist was created in a fraction of a second, in an area smaller than the size of a grape. Ever since the Big Bang, the universe has been expanding outward into space.

## SEEING INTO THE PAST

A galaxy that is five billion light years away is seen by astronomers as it was five billion years ago. Therefore, looking at very remote objects gives us a way of seeing the universe when it was much younger than it is today. The most distant objects ever seen are newborn galaxies or galaxies that are still being formed. At even greater distances and earlier times, astronomers can detect only faint radio waves, which come from all parts of space. These are the cooled-down remains of the fireball that erupted out of the Big Bang.

## MYSTERIES OF THE UNIVERSE

Scientists ask: will the universe go on expanding forever, or will it eventually begin to shrink and end in a Big Crunch? At present, the answer is unknown, but it seems that the universe may be delicately balanced between the two options. Another question is: does life exists elsewhere in the universe? Again, the answer is not yet known, but the evidence suggests that life may be common throughout space. Space probes sent to other planets search for water, the main ingredient that supports life as we know it. Over 90 per cent of the universe consists of dark matter, which cannot be seen. The composition of this remains another great mystery.

### SEE ALSO
Astronomy, Galaxy, Planet, Solar system, Star

# VIKINGS

The Vikings were a warrior people from Norway, Sweden and Denmark, who invaded much of northern Europe during the ninth and tenth centuries.

▲ Viking trade and expansion routes in the ninth and tenth centuries ran east through Russia, as far south as Seville and Pisa, and, by AD1000, to North America.

Thor was the Viking god of thunder and war. Thursday is named after him.

In battle, Vikings often used a spear made of ash wood with an iron head.

A Viking silver amulet in the shape of Thor's hammer and decorated with a face.

During the eighth century, the population of Scandinavia rose dramatically, but there was not enough land there for farming. At about the same time, the Vikings developed the longship, which gave them the means to reach other lands.

## EARLY RAIDS

The first Viking raids were carried out by one or two longships. They would land on the coast, raid a village or two and escape with their loot. In 793, a Viking force destroyed the monastery on Lindisfarne, in northern England. Within a few years, raids were made on the coasts of Scotland, Wales, Ireland and northern France.

## FIERCE RELIGION

Viking gods were fierce and warlike. The Vikings told stories of the gods and heroes in long poems called sagas. They believed the world would end in a mighty war between the gods and giants at Ragnarok, meaning the 'twilight of the gods'. Odin was their chief god. Men who died bravely in battle were thought to be collected by the Valkyries, 12 handmaidens from Odin's court, and taken to Valhalla, a great hall, to spend eternity feasting and fighting.

## INVASION OF ENGLAND

In 851, Vikings arrived in England with a great army and 350 ships. They invaded Kent, destroying Canterbury. In 866, an even larger Viking army, led by Halfdane and Basecg, invaded Kent. Within five years nearly all of England had been defeated and conquered. The victory of King Alfred the Great (849–99) over Guthrum's Viking army at Edington in 878 saved southern and western England.

## VIKING SETTLEMENTS

Large numbers of Vikings sailed to England and settled in the conquered lands as farmers and traders. York, Lincoln and Derby became Viking towns. In Ireland, the Vikings founded Dublin and Waterford as trading cities. A large section of northern France – later known as Normandy (from Norsemen) – was captured by Earl Rollo and settled by Vikings. Some Vikings sailed east to travel up the rivers of eastern Europe. At Kiev, they founded a kingdom called the Russ, or Russia.

◄ Like the Ancient Egyptians, Vikings believed that there was life after death and that people would need some of their possessions in the after-life. The greatest possession a Viking warrior could take with him was his longship – and many Vikings were either buried or burned in their longships, along with some everyday possessions.

▲ Swords were highly valued by the Vikings and were often richly decorated with gold and silver.

## FEARLESS RAIDERS FROM THE SEA

From the 8th to the 11th centuries, fearless Viking warriors from the Scandinavian countries of Norway, Sweden and Denmark made several raids on the coasts of Christian countries, inflicting great terror on the local inhabitants. They plundered monasteries and churches, killing, burning houses and driving away the cattle.

### OCEAN VOYAGES

The Vikings were skilled navigators. By studying the stars and the Sun they could travel accurately across vast distances of open sea. In about 825, they reached and settled the Faeroe Islands. Fifty years later, they reached Iceland. There, they founded an assembly – the Althing – to discuss and decide communal matters. The Althing still meets and is the oldest parliament in the world. In 982, the first Viking settlements on Greenland were established. About the year 1000, a Viking named Leif Ericsson travelled to Newfoundland in search of

timber, which was scarce in Greenland. Although they continued to visit North America for many years, the Vikings never settled there.

### VIKING TWILIGHT

By 900, the great Viking raids were over. Wars between Viking settlements and surrounding kingdoms remained common, but most Vikings settled down to a more peaceful existence. The Viking kingdoms in England and Ireland were taken over by the native kingdoms by 970.

### CHRISTIAN CONVERTS

Vikings and English lived side by side and, for a time, England became part of the Scandinavian empire, under Cnut (1016–35). A last attempt at conquest was made by the Norwegian Viking Harald Hardrada when he invaded England in 1066, but he was defeated and killed. From then on, most of the Vikings adopted Christianity and turned to farming and trading, abandoning raiding and conquest.

▲ A Viking man and woman dressed in everyday clothes.

| SEE ALSO |
| --- |
| Religion |

# VOLCANO

When lava bursts through an opening in the Earth's crust, a volcano forms. The word 'volcano' comes from Vulcan, the Roman god of fire and metalworking.

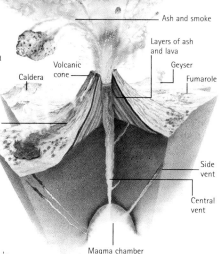

Ash and smoke

Layers of ash and lava

Volcanic cone

Geyser

Caldera

Fumarole

Lava flow

Side vent

Central vent

Magma chamber

▲ Volcanic activity has formed the whole landscape of Iceland. The terrain is littered with hot jets of boiling water, called geysers.

The Earth's surface is continually moving through the action of plate tectonics, as sections of the Earth's crust are moved along by currents in the molten rock below. There are two types of volcano: basaltic volcanoes, found where new plate material is being created, and andesitic volcanoes in areas where plates are being destroyed.

## BASALTIC VOLCANOES

Where new crust forms along oceanic ridges, the molten material from the Earth's mantle wells up and spreads out, pushing the plates apart. This usually happens at the bottom of the ocean, but in Iceland it has risen above the ocean and produced a whole island. The molten material, or lava, that erupts from these basaltic volcanoes is very runny and flows a long distance before becoming solid. Basaltic volcanoes are also found a long way from the edges of the plates. The Hawaiian islands were formed as basaltic material pushed its way up through the plate from the Earth's mantle. These so-called 'hot-spot' volcanoes have produced many other islands of the Pacific, such as the Galapagos Islands and Fiji.

## INSIDE A VOLCANO

A typical volcano has a crater and a cone of solidified lava and ash. Eruptions take place through a chimney-like vent. Far below the surface is a chamber of magma (molten rock), containing bubbling gases that make some volcanic rock frothy. A caldera forms when a violent eruption empties the magma chamber that feeds it. The roof then collapses, leaving a hole. Fumaroles are openings that let out only gas and steam, and geysers sometimes shoot fountains of boiling water high into the air.

## VIOLENT ERUPTIONS

Andesitic volcanoes are found where plates are being drawn beneath one another and destroyed. Molten plate material rises through the overriding plate and bursts through at the surface. These andesitic volcanoes occur in the great mountain chains, and in island arcs around the edges of oceans, close to deep ocean trenches. The lava of an andesitic volcano is stiff and sticky, and when it erupts, it does so explosively. Mount St Helens, in Washington, USA, and the island of Montserrat are recent examples of such violent and destructive eruptions. Because of accurate forecasting, few people were killed, but the hot ash from Mount St Helens destroyed trees up to 30km away.

Vulcanian eruption

Plinian eruption

Hawaiian eruption

Volcano cones created by Hawaiian eruptions slope gently, because the lava flow is quite runny

A vulcanian eruption, after Vulcano in Italy, throws out almost solid magma during its rare explosions

Plinian eruptions, such as the one that destroyed Pompeii in AD79, explode with great clouds of ash and pumice

## SEE ALSO
Earth, Earthquake, Mountain and valley, Ocean and sea, Rock

# WATER

Water is the most common substance on Earth. It is the main ingredient in all living organisms – without water, life on the planet could not exist.

## WATER FACTS

• The average person drinks over 60,000 litres of water in a lifetime

• Human beings will die if they lose more than 20% of the body's normal water content

• It takes about 10 litres of water to flush a toilet; 140 litres to fill a bath tub; nearly 40 litres to wash the dishes; and up to 120 litres to run an automatic washing machine

• The wettest place on Earth is Cherrapunji in India, with an average annual rainfall of 10,820mm

▲ Three quarters of the world's fresh water is frozen in glaciers and polar ice caps.

Water vapour condenses and forms clouds

Rain and snow

Transpiration from plants

Water vapour in atmosphere

River flows back to oceans

Water vapour in atmosphere

Evaporation from seas and lakes

Water vapour cools and forms rain

Groundwater runs off

## THE WATER CYCLE

Water is constantly being recycled. When the Sun heats the Earth's surface, water evaporates into the atmosphere. Over 80 per cent of this comes from oceans, but some comes from plants giving off water vapour (transpiration). As water in the atmosphere cools, it condenses to form clouds. Some of this water falls again as rain.

| | |
|---|---|
| Water vapour | 0.05% |
| Moisture in soil | 0.2% |
| Rivers and lakes | 0.35% |
| Salt water lakes and inland seas | 0.4% |

22% Groundwater

Ice caps and glaciers 77%

Fresh water 3%

Sea water 97%

▲ Of the three per cent of the world's water that is not in the sea, 77 per cent is in ice and glaciers.

Water exists naturally in three different forms: solid (frozen as ice), liquid (water) and gas (water vapour in the air). It can dissolve more substances than any other liquid. The force of natural water power has shaped the world's mountains, valleys, coastlines and plains.

## UNIVERSAL SUBSTANCE

Water covers 70 per cent of the Earth's surface – over 1.4 billion cubic kilometres. But only a tiny fraction is of any use to humans. Almost 97 per cent of the world's water is sea water, containing up to 35kg of dissolved mineral salts in every 1,000kg. That is eight times too salty to drink or to use for watering crops. Only about three per cent of the world's water is fresh – and three quarters of that is locked up in polar ice caps and mountain glaciers. Every living thing on Earth depends on the small amount of fresh water (less than one per cent of the total) that falls as rain and fills our rivers and lakes.

## WATER FOR LIVING

Life began in the sea 3.5 billion years ago, and water is still essential for all life forms. The human body is made up of about two thirds water. People need 2.5 litres of water a day to stay alive, but in Western societies, we use about 250 litres each per day for showers, toilets and washing machines. We also use vast amounts of water in industry and agriculture. It takes 400 litres of water to grow enough wheat for one loaf of bread, and 270 tonnes of water to produce a tonne of steel.

## SHAPING THE LAND

Water is the most important force in shaping the land. Rivers and glaciers carve valleys, wear down mountain ranges, and carry gravel, sand, silt and clay onto lowland plains and eventually out into the sea. Even spectacular desert scenery is carved mainly by water from flash floods.

## SEE ALSO

Mountain and valley, Ocean and sea, River, Weather

# WEATHER

**Atmospheric conditions, such as rain, wind and sunshine, make up the weather at a particular place and time. Weather may change slowly or rapidly.**

The weather depends on the way air masses move around the globe. The climate of a place is the average of these weather conditions over a long period of time. Though weather may change within hours, climates change over years.

An anemometer is used to measure the speed of the wind. Its sensitive shells move in the wind's path.

A barograph records changes in air pressure on a rotating drum, using an inked pen to draw a graph.

The psychrometer uses a dry bulb and a wet bulb to measure the humidity in the air.

Thermometers measure air temperature. They are used either inside or outside buildings.

## CAUSES OF WEATHER

The way that air masses are driven depends on factors such as distance from the Equator and the presence of mountains or seas. When an air mass moves from the sea over high ground, it cools, and the water it contains falls as rain. If an air mass moves from the centre of a continent, it contains no water and brings dry weather. If a mass of air rests over tropical waters for a long time, it becomes extremely moist and warm, leading to severe storms.

## REGULAR CYCLES

The weather follows regular cycles. In many areas, the summer has warmer weather than the winter because more solar (Sun) energy is received during long, hot days. In Southeast Asia, the monsoon period is dominated by warm, wet winds from the Indian Ocean, causing heavy rains. Every ten years or so, a phenomenon called El Niño occurs: the temperature of the southeast Pacific Ocean rises slightly, which alters the movements of air masses. This can lead to drought, severe rainstorms and economic disaster.

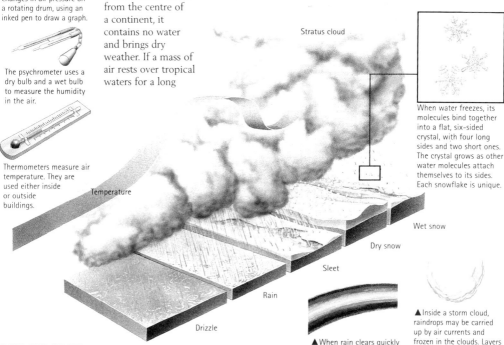

Stratus cloud

When water freezes, its molecules bind together into a flat, six-sided crystal, with four long sides and two short ones. The crystal grows as other water molecules attach themselves to its sides. Each snowflake is unique.

Temperature

Wet snow

Dry snow

Sleet

Rain

Drizzle

▲When rain clears quickly after a shower, a colourful rainbow may stretch across the sky. Sunlight shines on water droplets, and light is bent, or refracted, until it is split into spectrum colours.

▲Inside a storm cloud, raindrops may be carried up by air currents and frozen in the clouds. Layers of ice build up as water vapour freezes onto these icy crystals. The growing hailstones fall to warmer levels, then rise again until they are heavy enough to fall from the clouds.

## RAIN AND SNOW

Two main types of rain occur. In the tropics, rain forms when tiny droplets bump into each other in a cloud, join together and fall. Rain outside the tropics is caused by melting snowflakes. If the base of a stratus cloud is low enough, rain falls as drizzle. Dry snow falls when the ground temperature is cold, but if snow falls into air that is above freezing, sleet (a mixture of rain and snow) occurs.

**1** The Sun heats one area of ground, such as bare soil, more than others. On warm days, bubbles of hot air form over these areas, and rise up through the cooler air around them.

**2** Warm air rises into low-pressure air, then expands and cools. The air cools so much that water vapour condenses into droplets, and a small cumulus cloud is formed.

**3** As it is fed by a series of air bubbles, the cloud grows, and the wind detaches it. Fair-weather cumulus clouds look like cotton balls. They do not carry enough water to cause rain.

## HIGH AND LOW PRESSURE

In most parts of the world, weather is determined by areas of low air pressure (cyclones) or areas of high pressure (anticyclones). Some last for months, for example, the Bermuda High is an anticyclone that appears in the North Atlantic during summer. Others last only a few days or weeks. In tropical areas, belts of low pressure can be massive and move slowly westward. As they suck in warm air, heavy rains and storms are created.

## FRONTS

When a mass of cold air meets a mass of warm air, a front develops. If cold air cuts sharply under warm air, a cold front forms. The warm air rises rapidly, cools and produces heavy rains. If warm air rises slowly, it produces a warm front marked by long periods of gentle rain and drizzle.

## DESTRUCTIVE WEATHER

Although most thunderstorms are harmless, a large storm can produce strong winds, heavy rain, lightning and hail. In 1986, a storm in Gopalganj, India, created a downpour of hailstones weighing 1kg each and killing 100 people in a few seconds. Lightning is thought to kill 200 people a year and to start over 20,000 fires. Tornadoes form when thunderstorms create strong updraughts. The spinning air can reach 500km/h and wreak destruction along a path 1km wide and 100km long.

## FORECASTING

Traditionally, people have forecast weather either by watching the sky or by noticing the behaviour of animals, which is affected by basic weather changes. Modern weather forecasting follows the global movement of areas of low and high pressure and fronts. Satellite photographs of cloud patterns help produce accurate forecasts.

▲ Radiosondes are balloons that carry instruments to measure temperature, air pressure, and humidity in the upper atmosphere.

▲ As water droplets collide in a large cloud, water becomes electrically charged. Positive charges collect at the cloud's top, and negative charges at the bottom. As a negative charge meets a positive charge on the ground, forked lightning flashes; sheet lightning flashes between clouds. Thunder is the sound of hot air expanding.

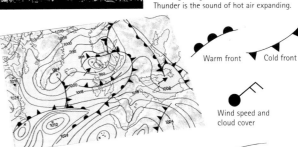

Warm front    Cold front

Wind speed and cloud cover

Isobar

▲ Weather maps, such as this synoptic chart, use standard symbols. Isobars are lines that connect places where air pressure is the same. Winds flow parallel to isobars; the closer together they are, the stronger the wind. Air pressure (in millibars) is shown at centres of low and high pressure. Wind speed, and warm and cold front symbols, are also shown.

**SEE ALSO**

Climate, Ecology, Electricity, Light, Satellite, Season, Water

# WEIGHTS AND MEASURES

**Weights and measures are the standard units that we use to work out how much we have of things. Each form of measurement needs its own kind of 'ruler'.**

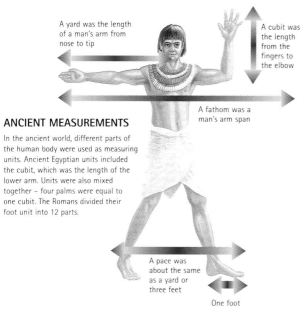

A yard was the length of a man's arm from nose to tip

A cubit was the length from the fingers to the elbow

A fathom was a man's arm span

A pace was about the same as a yard or three feet

One foot

## ANCIENT MEASUREMENTS

In the ancient world, different parts of the human body were used as measuring units. Ancient Egyptian units included the cubit, which was the length of the lower arm. Units were also mixed together – four palms were equal to one cubit. The Romans divided their foot unit into 12 parts.

▲ Units based on the hand included the digit, which was the width of a finger. This later became the inch. A span was the length from thumb to little finger and there was also the palm unit.

Ever since people started making things, trading goods or carrying out experiments, they have needed to measure amounts. Ancient civilizations based their measurements on parts of the body. These would have been standard (the same) only within each civilization. An Egyptian cubit, for example, was different from a Greek or Roman cubit. This caused many problems, especially when people needed to trade with one another. That is why, over centuries, standard measurement systems have come into use.

## IMPERIAL SYSTEM

Until about 30 years ago, most people used the imperial system of measurement. This measured length in inches, feet, yards and miles; and weight in ounces, pounds, stones and tons. The use of the foot as a unit of measurement dates back to Anglo-Saxon times. The inch (three grains of barley laid lengthwise) dates to the 1300s, and the

mile has its origins in measuring thousands of paces. Ounces and pounds are units of the avoirdupois ('goods sold by weight') system, in use since the 1400s. The imperial system was not always easy to use, however, and people who took complex measurements realized they needed a simpler set of units. In the 1790s, the metric system was created in France.

## METRIC SYSTEM

Many countries now use the metric system, or SI (Système International). The units are the metre (length) and the kilogram, (weight). There are many other units with their own special names such as the joule, the newton and the volt. However, scientists can relate most of them to this basic set – one newton (1N), for example, the unit of force, can also be written as one kilogram metre per second per second ($1kg\ m/sec^2$).

## SETTING STANDARDS

A laboratory near Paris holds examples of the SI units – the Standard Metre is the length of a certain number of wavelengths of a specially made laser beam. The Standard Kilogram is the weight of a special ingot of platinum-iridium metal, stored at a controlled temperature.

▲ Scales have been used to weigh objects for sale for thousands of years. In this case, they are being used to weigh dried flower and plant remedies for sale at a herbalist dispensary.

## WEIGHT

**SI units**

| | | |
|---|---|---|
| 1,000 milligrams (mg) | = | 1 gram (g) |
| 1,000g | = | 1 kilogram (kg) |
| 100kg | = | 1 quintal (q) |
| 1,000kg | = | 1 metric ton or tonne (t) |

**Imperial units**

| | | |
|---|---|---|
| 16 ounces (oz) | = | 1 pound (lb) |
| 14lb | = | 1 stone |
| 112lb | = | 1 hundredweight (cwt) |
| 20cwt | = | 1 (long) ton (= 2,240lb) |
| 2,000lb | = | 1 short ton (US) |

**Conversions**

| | | |
|---|---|---|
| 1 gram | = | 0.035oz |
| 1kg | = | 2.205lb |
| 1 metric ton or tonne (t) | = | 2,200lb |
| 1t | = | 0.984 (long) tons |
| 1oz | = | 28.35g |
| 1lb | = | 454g |
| 1 (long) ton | = | 1.02t |

## AREA

**SI units**

| | | |
|---|---|---|
| 100 square mm (mm$^2$) | = | 1 square cm (cm$^2$) |
| 10,000cm$^2$ | = | 1 square metre (m$^2$) |
| 100m$^2$ | = | 1 are (a) |
| 100a | = | 1 hectare (ha) |
| 100ha | = | 1 square kilometre (km$^2$) |

**Imperial units**

| | | |
|---|---|---|
| 144 square inches (in$^2$) | = | 1 square foot (ft$^2$) |
| 9ft$^2$ | = | 1 square yard (yd$^2$) |
| 4,840yd$^2$ | = | 1 acre |
| 640 acres | = | 1 square mile (mile$^2$) |

**Conversions**

| | | |
|---|---|---|
| 1cm$^2$ | = | 0.155in$^2$ |
| 1m$^2$ | = | 10.76ft$^2$ |
| 1 hectare | = | 2.47 acres |
| 1km$^2$ | = | 0.386 square miles |
| 1in$^2$ | = | 6.45cm$^2$ |
| 1ft$^2$ | = | 0.093m$^2$ |
| 1 acre | = | 0.405 hectares |
| 1 square mile | = | 2.59km$^2$ |

## LENGTH

**SI units**

| | | |
|---|---|---|
| 10 millimetres (mm) | = | 1 centimetre (cm) |
| 100cm | = | 1 metre (m) |
| 1,000m | = | 1 kilometre (km) |

**Imperial units**

| | | |
|---|---|---|
| 12 inches (in) | = | 1 foot (ft) |
| 3ft | = | 1 yard (yd) |
| 1,760 yd | = | 1 mile |

**Conversions**

| | | |
|---|---|---|
| 1mm | = | 0.0394in |
| 1cm | = | 0.394in |
| 1m | = | 1.094yd |
| 1km | = | 0.621 miles |
| 1in | = | 2.54cm |
| 1ft | = | 30.48cm |
| 1yd | = | 0.914m |
| 1 mile | = | 1.609km |

## VOLUME

**SI units**

| | | |
|---|---|---|
| 1,000mm$^3$ | = | 1 cubic centimetre (cm$^3$) |
| 1,000cm$^3$ | = | 1 cubic decimetre (dm$^3$) |
| 1,000dm$^3$ | = | 1 cubic metre (m$^3$) |

**Imperial units**

| | | |
|---|---|---|
| 1,728 cubic inches (in$^3$) | = | 1 cubic foot (ft$^3$) |
| 27ft$^3$ | = | 1 cubic yard (yd$^3$) |

**Conversions**

| | | |
|---|---|---|
| 1cm$^3$ = 0.061in$^3$ | 1m$^3$ = 35.3ft$^3$ |
| 1in$^3$ = 16.4cm$^3$ | 1ft$^3$ = 0.028m$^3$ |

## CAPACITY

**SI units**

| | | |
|---|---|---|
| 1,000 millilitres (ml) | = | 1 litre (l) |
| 100 litres | = | 1 hectolitre (hl) |

**Imperial units**

| | | |
|---|---|---|
| 4 gills | = | 1 pint (= 20 fluid ounces) |
| 2 pints | = | 1 quart |
| 4 quarts | = | 1 UK gallon |

**Conversions**

| | |
|---|---|
| 1 litre = 0.22 UK gallons | 1 pint = 0.568 litres |
| 1 UK gallon = 1.2 US gallons | |

The Egyptians used delicate balancing scales to weigh gold and precious stones. Later, the Babylonians (who lived in what is now Iraq) made standard weights from metal to use at markets.

The builders of the pyramids in Egypt had to measure length so that they knew how many stones they needed, as well as how to drive shafts accurately through the huge structures.

The measuring jug is used to measure liquids in fluid ounces (imperial units) and centilitres (metric units). Most wine bottles hold 70 or 75 centilitres (cl) of wine when they are full.

### SEE ALSO

Gravity, Time

# WHALE AND DOLPHIN

Whales, dolphins and porpoises are collectively known as cetaceans, which means 'large sea animal'. They are divided into two groups: toothed and baleen whales.

A white-sided dolphin eats fish and has 92–128 teeth. It is found in big schools of up to 1,000 dolphins.

There are about 37 species of dolphin; 23 species of large-toothed whale; ten species of baleen whale and six types of porpoise. They may look like fish, but whales and dolphins are warm-blooded, air-breathing mammals.

▶ Black right whales belong to the right whale family of three species. They reach 18m in length and are now very rare.

## FROM EARTH TO SEA

Whales first appeared on the Earth over 50 million years ago. Their ancestors once lived on land, but then moved into the water and gradually lost their back legs; their front legs became flippers. The flippers are used for steering and balance, but the power comes from the big tail with its horizontal fins or flukes. The tail is waved up and down to drive the whale forward. (Fish have vertical tail fins, waved from side to side.)

◀ Fin whales belong to the rorqual and humpback family that have grooved throats. They grow to 20m.

▶ Bowhead whales grow up to 18m and their baleen plates can be 3m long. They belong to the right whale family.

A rough-toothed dolphin is a small (up to 2.5m), tropical species known to follow ships.

Common porpoises are one of the smallest types of cetaceans (up to 2m). There are six species.

The adult beluga, or white whale, is pure white, but the young are grey. Belugas have no dorsal fin.

True's beaked whale has a single pair of teeth in the lower jaw. It is found in the North Atlantic.

A male bottle-nosed whale grows up to 9m (females are smaller). It eats squid, cuttlefish and herring.

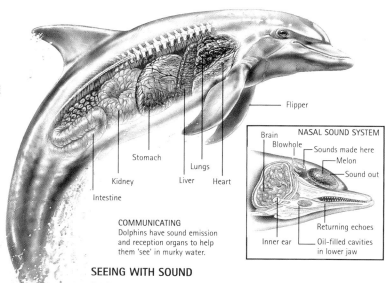

Stomach
Kidney
Intestine
Lungs
Liver
Heart
Flipper

### NASAL SOUND SYSTEM
Brain
Blowhole
Sounds made here
Melon
Sound out
Inner ear
Returning echoes
Oil-filled cavities in lower jaw

### COMMUNICATING
Dolphins have sound emission and reception organs to help them 'see' in murky water.

## SEEING WITH SOUND

Dolphins communicate, find food and navigate using a kind of radar sound system under water. They make high-frequency clicking noises by blowing air through their nasal passages. Then the melon (a waxy cavity in the dolphin's head) focuses the sound into a beam. Sound vibrations travel through the water and bounce off objects. A dolphin receives the sound echoes through an area in its jaw where the bones are thinner. The echoes then travel to the inner ear.

## SIEVE OR BITE

There are two types of whale: baleen whales and toothed whales. Baleen whales are filter feeders that sieve tiny creatures from the water through fringed curtains of a horny material called baleen or whalebone.

◀ Blue whale.

▲ The number and size of teeth varies with species. Dolphins (above) have conical, interlocking teeth, porpoises have spade-shaped teeth and most beaked whales only have two visible pairs.

## THERE SHE BLOWS

Whales come to the surface to breathe. As they breathe out, warm moist air rushes out through nostrils on the top of the head – the blowhole. This 'blow' may reach 10m into the air. They then take a few breaths through the blowhole and dive down for several minutes. Toothed whales have just one blowhole, baleen whales have two.

## FRIENDLY GIANT

The blue whale is the largest animal that has ever lived on Earth. It can reach a length of 30m and a weight of 150 tonnes – as heavy as 20 fully grown elephants. Like most of the other large whales, the blue whale has no teeth. It is a baleen whale that feeds on tiny plankton and krill living near the surface of the sea. Other whales and dolphins have lots of teeth and feed on fish, squid, seals, and penguins.

## SMILING DOLPHINS

Dolphins are small whales with a pointed snout and appear to have a permanent smile. They are playful and intelligent animals. They live in groups called schools and communicate with clicks and whistles. They use sound location to navigate and find fish to eat. An injured dolphin will usually be helped by other members of the school. There are even reports of dolphins helping drowning people. Like all whales, dolphins never come ashore. They mate and give birth to their young in the sea. A mother dolphin feeds her baby on her milk for a year and they often stay together for several years.

▲ Narwhals grow up to 5.5m with no dorsal fin and two teeth. In males, one tooth develops into a 3-m long spiral tusk.

◀ Sperm whales are a family of three species. They are the largest toothed whales (growing up to 20m) and the deepest divers. They eat mostly squid – even giant ones.

◀ Orcas, or killer whales, are dolphins with a tall (2m) shark-like fin. They have long, sharp teeth and eat young whales, seals, squid or fish.

## SEE ALSO

Animal, Conservation, Mammal

# WORLD WAR I

World War I was a terrible war fought between 1914 and 1918 in which millions of people died. It began in Europe, but spread to many parts of the globe.

Kaiser Wilhelm II (1859–1941) of Germany led an aggressive foreign policy against other nations.

Lloyd George (1863–1945), British prime minister from 1916, reorganized the war effort for victory.

Russia's Tsar Nicholas II (1868–1918) backed Serbia against Austria, bringing Russia into the war.

People living at the time called World War I 'the Great War' because no other war had been so widespread nor so destructive. Millions of soldiers were killed and the world economy changed for ever.

## OUTBREAK OF WAR
In 1914, Europe was divided into two major alliances. The Habsburg Empire was allied to Germany to block Russian moves in the Balkans, while France sided with Russia against the growing might of Germany. On June 28, 1914, the Habsburg archduke Franz Ferdinand was shot dead by a Serb terrorist, prompting the Habsburgs to declare war on Serbia. Serbia, in turn, asked for help from the Russians, who then declared war on the Habsburgs. This brought Germany and France into the war. Britain joined the war when Germany invaded Belgium.

## EARLY BATTLES
In the East, Russian armies were smashed by the Germans at Tannenberg, while Habsburg armies were defeated by the Russians in several encounters during the month of September. In the West, the Germans intended to capture Paris and defeat France, but were stopped on the River Marne on September 8, 1914, while the British army blocked outflanking moves to the North. By October, the armies had settled into trenches for the winter.

## NEW WEAPONS
Barbed wire barriers, machine guns and artillery made defence so strong that attacks were almost useless. Troops experimented with poison gas to help attackers, but it rarely had much effect. Tanks, first used by the British in 1916,

Russian Cossacks and other cavalry were used for scouting, but were useless in the trenches.

▲ World War I began after Serb terrorist Gavrilo Princip killed the Habsburg archduke Franz Ferdinand. Princip was sentenced to 20 years in prison, but fell ill and died in 1918.

could defeat barbed wire or machine guns, but they often broke down. Aircraft were more successful, and were used to spy out enemy troops, target artillery shells and drop bombs. The German pilot Manfred von Richthofen, nicknamed the 'Red Baron', successfully shot 80 enemy aircraft down in flames.

## WORLD WAR
In Africa, British and French troops attacked German colonies. In 1915, Australian and New Zealand troops attacked Turkey at Gallipoli, but were badly defeated and sustained heavy losses. At sea, German ships and submarines sank Allied ships, and in 1917 began attacking any ships heading for Allied ports. The United States first protested about these attacks on its ships, and then joined the Allies, declaring war on Germany.

▲ Trench warfare led to small battle fronts. Only on the Eastern Front were sweeping movements made.

Aircraft were a new weapon, used for scouting and fighting.

The small Serb army was driven out of Serbia into Greece in December 1915.

## KEY DATES

**August 1914** War breaks out between the Allies (France, Britain, Russia, Belgium, Serbia and Montenegro) and the Central Powers (Germany and Habsburg Empire)

**November 1914** Turkey joins the Central Powers

**May 1915** Italy joins the Allies

**October 1915** Bulgaria joins the Central Powers

**August 1916** Romania joins the Allies

**April 1917** The USA joins the Allies

**December 1917** Russia makes peace with Germany

**November 1918** Fighting ceases

**1919** Peace Treaties signed at Versailles in France

## FINAL MOVES

In 1917, the Communists took over Russia, and made peace. The German troops, freed from Russia, launched a massive attack in March 1918 in France. American troops helped to stop the attack. But Bulgaria, Turkey and the Habsburgs were close to collapse and Germany asked for peace. A ceasefire was finally agreed on November 11, 1918.

## TRENCH WARFARE

The war in the West was fought from trenches guarded by barbed wire and machine guns. Conditions were appalling, with knee-deep mud, constant shelling, sniping and raids. The battles of the Somme and Verdun in France in 1916 cost over two million casualties, although neither side managed to advance more than a few hundred metres.

## THE WAR ENDS

The cost of World War I was immense. Germany lost 1.9 million men, Russia 1.7 million, France 1.5 million and Britain and the Habsburgs 1 million each, as well as vast amounts of money. The Habsburg Empire was split into Austria, Hungary, Czechoslovakia and Yugoslavia. Poland, Estonia, Latvia and Lithuania became independent. European countries lost economic power as others built up their industries. The world was changed for ever.

Britain had the smallest army in 1914, but it was made up of professionals.

In 1914, the German army was the largest and best trained in the world.

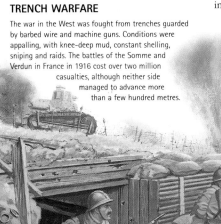

Machine gun post in the French trenches

German troops

## SEE ALSO

Communism, World War II

# WORLD WAR II

**World War II was fought between 1939 and 1945. It involved more countries, cost more lives and caused more destruction than any other war.**

Erwin Rommel (1891–1944) was a daring leader of German armoured units.

Yamamoto Isoroku (1884–1943) planned Japan's attack on Pearl Harbor.

Bernard Montgomery (1887–1976) led the British in North Africa and Europe.

Georgy Zhukov (1896–1974) commanded the Soviet Red Army.

Dwight D. Eisenhower (1890–1969) led the D-Day invasion of 1944.

The dictators Adolf Hitler in Germany, Benito Mussolini in Italy and General Tojo Hideki in Japan wanted to extend the power and territories of their countries. They formed a pact, called the Axis, to gain what they wanted.

## BLITZKRIEG

In September 1939, Germany invaded Poland to regain land it had lost in World War I. Britain and France supported Poland. The Germans used a tactic called *Blitzkrieg* – 'lightning war'. Bomber aircraft began the attack, then tanks, or panzers, plunged deep behind enemy lines, followed by infantry and artillery. Poland was defeated in just five weeks. In April 1940, Hitler invaded Denmark, Belgium, Holland, Norway and France. By July, only Britain had not surrendered. In the Battle of Britain which followed, the Royal Air Force beat off German air attacks.

## INTO RUSSIA

Hitler wanted to expand Germany and create new 'living space' for the German nation. In June 1941, 3.5 million German, Italian, Romanian and Hungarian troops stormed into Russia, capturing vast territories and over a million prisoners. In December, a reinforced Red Army finally stopped the invaders just outside Moscow.

The American B17 Flying Fortress

The Japanese Mitsubishi Ki-67, codenamed 'Peggy'

The German Dornier Do217

The British Lancaster

▲ Small bombers, such as the Dornier and Mitsubishi, were used to destroy battlefield targets, such as tanks and artillery. The Lancaster, Flying Fortress and other heavy bombers pounded cities and factories.

## PEARL HARBOR

Japan wanted to capture large areas of Southeast Asia to secure industrial raw materials. The Japanese hoped that a quick defeat of the USA would persuade the Americans to allow Japanese expansion, so they launched a surprise attack on Pearl Harbor, Hawaii. The USA did not give way, but declared war. The same day, Japan invaded Southeast Asia. By May 1942, Japan had conquered Burma, Malaya, the Philippines and the East Indies.

### THE TIDE TURNS

After three years of war, the Allies had built up their armed forces. In North Africa, German and Italian troops were defeated at El Alamein in October 1942, and in December 1942, the German 6th Army was

◄ On December 7, 1941, 360 Japanese aircraft attacked Pearl Harbor, Hawaii, the base of the US Pacific Fleet. The attack opened the way for Japanese conquests and brought the USA into the war.

▶ The Axis powers – Germany, Japan and their allies – made large conquests in 1939–42. But the greater resources of the Allies were brought into action after 1942, leading to eventual victory.

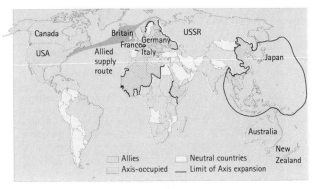

wiped out by the Russians at Stalingrad. The Japanese were halted by British, Australian and American troops in February 1943. The Allies then organized strike forces to reconquer Burma, and to use 'island-hopping' tactics in the Pacific.

## GERMANY COLLAPSES

In June 1944, Germany was caught between the D-Day landings in Normandy, France and the Russian advance in the East. In April 1945, the Russians reached Berlin. On April 30, Hitler killed himself, and two days later Germany surrendered. Allied troops discovered that the Nazis had killed millions, six million of them Jews, in what became known as the Holocaust.

## THE ATOM BOMBS

In April 1945, the Americans attacked the island of Okinawa, from which Japan could be invaded. American casualties were high as the Japanese fought back. US President Harry S. Truman decided to use the atom bomb. The cities of Hiroshima and Nagasaki were destroyed in August with the loss of about 200,000 lives. Japan surrendered on September 2, 1945.

## PEACE AND COLD WAR

The war had cost the lives of some 15 million troops and 35 million civilians. After the war, the world divided into two powerful blocs: the Communist countries, led by the Soviet Union and China and the democratic world, led by the USA. The Cold War had begun.

## D-DAY

At dawn on June 6, 1944, the largest invasion fleet in history landed Allied forces on the coast of Normandy. In all, 1,200 warships and 4,100 landing craft put 132,500 men ashore, while 10,000 aircraft attacked German positions inland. The success of the D-Day invasion allowed American, British and French troops to drive the Germans out of France.

▲ The Allied leaders, Winston Churchill (left), Franklin D. Roosevelt (centre) and Joseph Stalin (right), met at Yalta in 1945 to decide the post-war arrangements for Europe.

## SEE ALSO

Cold War, World War I

# X-RAY

X-rays are a form of energy that can pass straight through many solid materials. We use X-rays to look inside bodies and machines and to kill some cancers.

▲ X-ray radiation was discovered by the German physicist Wilhelm Roentgen (1845–1923), who was awarded the first Nobel Prize for Physics in 1901.

▼ High doses of X-rays can damage body cells. The harmful effects of X-rays are often used to help cure cancers. Powerful beams of X-rays are directed at cells in a tumour, killing them off.

If you break a bone, you will probably go to the hospital for an X-ray. An X-ray image lets the doctor see where your bone is fractured or damaged. A special machine directs a narrow beam of X-rays at the part of your body that needs examining. Unlike light waves, these X-rays can pass right through the soft parts of your body, such as the skin and muscles.

## X-RAY IMAGE
When X-rays come out the other side of your body, they hit a photographic plate, where they form an image. As your bones and teeth are heavy and dense, they block the path of the X-rays. This is why they leave blank patches on the X-ray image. Trained people can look at these blank areas and work out the exact shape of your skeleton.

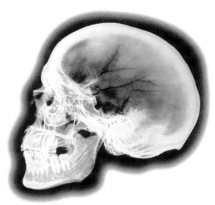

▲ An X-ray image of a human skull found at a Roman burial site, revealing a missing top molar tooth.

## SOFT TISSUE
Sometimes, doctors use X-rays to look at softer, lighter parts of your body, such as the liver or bladder. To do this, they inject you with a special chemical called barium sulphate, which makes these tissues block the path of X-rays. The body gets rid of this chemical naturally after a few hours.

## MACHINES AND CRYSTALS
X-rays are not only used to look inside people. They are also used to examine the insides of certain machines. Aircraft makers, for example, take X-ray images of various machine parts to make sure they have no inner cracks. Chemists take X-ray images of crystals. They use these to study how the X-rays bounce off a crystal's inner structure. This can help them work out how the atoms in crystals are arranged.

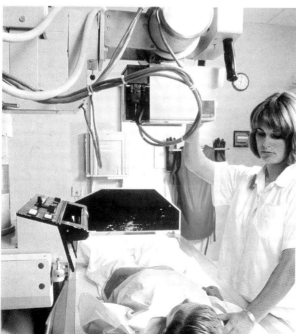

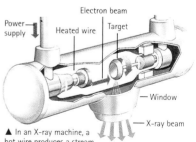

Power supply — Heated wire — Electron beam — Target — Window — X-ray beam

▲ In an X-ray machine, a hot wire produces a stream of electrons. These are fired at a tungsten metal target, giving out X-rays. Some pass through the patient's body, making an image on film or a fluorescent screen.

### SEE ALSO
Astronomy, Atom and molecule, Light, Medicine

# ZOOLOGY

Zoology is the scientific study of all animals – their body structure, how they live, feed, breed, move and behave – in nature or captivity.

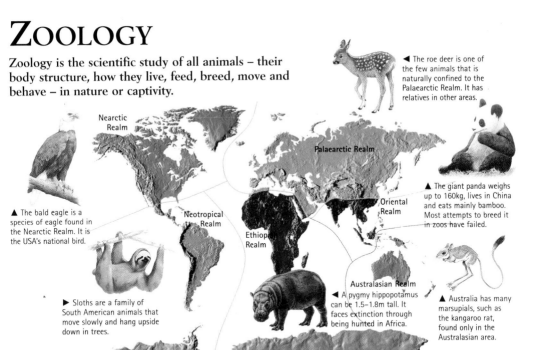

◀ The roe deer is one of the few animals that is naturally confined to the Palaearctic Realm. It has relatives in other areas.

Nearctic Realm

Palaearctic Realm

Oriental Realm

▲ The giant panda weighs up to 160kg, lives in China and eats mainly bamboo. Most attempts to breed it in zoos have failed.

▲ The bald eagle is a species of eagle found in the Nearctic Realm. It is the USA's national bird.

Neotropical Realm

Ethiopian Realm

▶ Sloths are a family of South American animals that move slowly and hang upside down in trees.

Australasian Realm

◀ A pygmy hippopotamus can be 1.5–1.8m tall. It faces extinction through being hunted in Africa.

▲ Australia has many marsupials, such as the kangaroo rat, found only in the Australasian area.

## GROUPING ANIMALS

Zoologists divide the Earth into six distinct regions, or realms, following the work of British wildlife expert, Alfred Russel Wallace, in the 1800s. He first noticed that whole orders or families of animals, birds and freshwater fish may be confined to one region. This map shows the six realms and an example of the animals found only in each area.

The animal kingdom is vast, varied and complicated. Zoology has many specialist branches. These often overlap. Some branches deal with particular groups of animals. For example, entomology is the detailed study of insects. Ichthyology specializes in fish. Herpetology is the study of amphibians and reptiles.

## LEARNING ABOUT ANIMALS

Other branches of zoology deal with the features that animals share. Anatomists study the structure of an animal's body and the parts inside, such as the heart, nerves, guts and kidneys. Physiologists look at how these parts work, such as how worms take food from soil or how fish take in oxygen through gills. Embryologists deal with how animals develop before they are born.

## THE LIVING AND THE DEAD

Some areas of zoology are very wide-ranging. Ethologists watch animal behaviour – their actions and instincts. Ecologists study how a creature fits into its surroundings or habitat. They observe its needs, such as food and shelter, and its predators. Palaeontologists study fossil remains that tell us about prehistoric life, such as dinosaurs. They deal with 'dead' remains, but still need a good knowledge of living animals to reconstruct finds and compare them with other creatures.

## WHAT ZOOLOGISTS DO

Some zoologists are desk-based, writing reports or books. Others work in laboratories, carrying out tests and experiments. Some are based in museums, zoos or wildlife parks and others are in the field – watching, taking notes on and photographing animals in the wild. Many deal with the media: for example, campaigning to save endangered creatures or giving pet advice.

▼ A keeper at Marwell Zoo (UK) bottle-feeds a baby okapi, a very rare African animal. Breeding threatened species such as these is one invaluable role of a zoo. Many breed animals in captivity to help boost their dwindling numbers in the wild.

## SEE ALSO
Animal, Conservation, Evolution, Mammal

# INTERNATIONAL ORGANIZATIONS

## APEC
Asia-Pacific Economic Co-operation Group. Promotes trade between members and the rest of the world. Members are Australia, Brunei, Canada, Chile, China, Chinese Taipai, Indonesia, Japan, Malaysia, Mexico, New Zealand, Papua New Guinea, Peru, Philippines, Russia, Singapore, Korea, Taiwan, Thailand, Vietnam and USA.

## ASEAN
Association of Southeast Asian Nations. Promotes economic, social and cultural co-operation and development. Members are Brunei, Cambodia, Indonesia, Laos, Malaysia, Myanmar, Philippines, Singapore, Thailand, Vietnam.

## CARICOM
Caribbean Community and Common Market. Members are Antigua and Barbuda, Bahamas, Barbados, Belize, Dominica, Grenada, Guyana, Jamaica, Montserrat, St Kitts-Nevis, St Lucia, St Vincent and the Grenadines, Suriname, Trinidad and Tobago.

## CIS
Commonwealth of Independent States. It is made up of 12 of the 15 independent ex-Soviet republics. Members are Armenia, Azerbaijan, Belarus, Georgia, Kazakhstan, Kyrgyzstan, Moldova, Russia, Tajikistan, Turkmenistan, Ukraine, Uzbekistan.

## Commonwealth
A grouping of mainly former British-ruled states, founded in 1949. It has over 50 members.

## European Union (EU)
A political and economic union of 15 members: Austria, Belgium, Denmark, Finland, France, Germany, Greece, Ireland, Italy, Luxembourg, Netherlands, Portugal, Spain, Sweden, UK.

## ECOWAS
Economic Community of West African States.

## EFTA
European Free Trade Association. Promotes the expansion of trade, especially between EFTA and EU member countries. Many former members are now part of the EU. Non-EU members are Iceland, Liechtenstein, Norway, Switzerland.

## Group of Eight (G-8)
An informal group of eight leading nations that meet to discuss economic issues. Members are Canada, Germany, France, Japan, Italy, Russia, UK and USA.

## Interpol
International Criminal Police Organization. Promotes co-operation between police authorities. It has 177 members.

## League of Arab States
Also known as the Arab League. It promotes cultural, political and economic links among Arab states. It has 22 members.

## NATO
North Atlantic Treaty Organization. This military alliance of Western nations was set up to defend Europe and the North Atlantic from military aggression. Members are Belgium, Canada, Czech Republic, Denmark, France, Germany, Greece, Hungary, Iceland, Italy, Poland, Luxembourg, Netherlands, Norway, Portugal, Spain, Turkey, UK, USA.

**OAS** (Organization of American States) It has 35 members, including Cuba, which has been suspended from activities since 1962.

**OAU** (Organization of African Unity) Promotes African unity and co-operation. It has 53 members.

## OECD
Organization for Economic Co-operation and Development. Promotes social and economic welfare in members and co-ordinates efforts on behalf of developing nations. It has 29 members.

## OPEC
Organization of Petroleum Exporting Countries. Co-ordinates oil production and prices. Members are Algeria, Indonesia, Iran, Iraq, Kuwait, Libya, Nigeria, Qatar, Saudi Arabia, United Arab Emirates, Venezuela.

## United Nations (UN)
Formed to maintain international peace and security and to develop friendly relations between nations. By 2001, it had 189 members; its headquarters are in New York, USA. Its main parts include: General Assembly with representatives of all members; Security Council of 15 members, five of which (China, France, Russia, UK and USA) have permanent seats and ten of which are elected for two years; and the International Court of Justice, which sits in The Hague, Netherlands.

The following agencies are self-governing, but have a working agreement with the UN:

## FAO
Food and Agriculture Organization of the United Nations improves production and distribution of food, and the living conditions of rural people.

## IBRD
International Bank for Reconstruction and Development, more usually known as the World Bank. It provides loans and technical help for economic projects in developing countries.

**IMF** (International Monetary Fund) A UN agency which promotes monetary co-operation and the expansion of international trade.

## UNESCO
United Nations Educational, Scientific and Cultural Organization, set up to promote the exchange of information, ideas and culture.

## UNHCR
The United Nations High Commissioner for Refugees. Provides assistance for refugees worldwide.

## UNICEF
United Nations Children's Fund. Set up to help governments to meet the long-term needs of child welfare.

**World Health Organization (WHO)**
A UN agency dedicated to fighting disease and improving health standards.

**World Trade Organization (WTO)**
This UN agency is the main body which oversees international trade, administering trade agreements and attempting to settle trade disputes.

# RECENT WARS AND CONFLICTS

**Afghanistan**
Soviet occupation ended in 1989, but civil war continued between the government and guerilla forces until 1992. Since then, the Taliban, an Islamic fundamentalist group, has seized power.

**Albania**
UN-sponsored peace-keeping forces arrived in 1997 for a few months to end public unrest and violence.

**Algeria**
The FIS, an Islamic fundamentalist group, opposed the government, but its win in the 1991 elections was . declared illegal. It was then banned. Massacres and terrorism followed.

**Angola**
Civil war since the 1970s between government and UNITA rebels (UNITA = National Union for Total Independence of Angola). In 2000, heavy fighting broke out when UNITA attacked government forces.

**Armenia**
Independent ex-Soviet republic fought neighbour Azerbaijan over the disputed territory of Nagorno-Karabakh. Since 1994, an uneasy peace has existed.

**Burundi**
Tribal disputes between the Hutu and the Tutsi since the early 1970s have left hundreds of thousands of people dead. Conditions deteriorated after a military coup in July 1996.

**Cambodia**
Devastated by civil war in the 1970s, which left millions dead. After further disputes with Vietnam in 1980s, the UN sponsored elections in 1993. The re-established monarchy was opposed by the communist party, the Khmer Rouge. Armed violence continues.

**Chechnya**
Republic in southwest Russia with tradition of Chechen nationalism. Fighting began in 1994, when Russian troops invaded to stop a Chechen rising.

**Colombia**
Guerilla wars broke out in 1998 after President Andrés Pastana was elected. In 2000, the US committed itself to back the government over the guerillas and drug trade.

**Congo**
In 1998, Rwanda, Uganda and Burundi launched a civil war in Congo to overthrow President Laurent Kabila. Angola, Namibia and Zimbabwe sent troops to help Kabila. In 1999, a peace agreement was signed. However, conflict continues.

**Eritea**
In 2000, Eritrea and Ethiopia signed an agreement to end all border disputes in Algiers.

**Fiji**
In 2000, rebels seized parliament and held the prime minister hostage. The rebels were arrested and charged with treason. But the entire political system and economy remained in turmoil. The army appointed an interim government to rule until the next general election.

**Israel**
At odds with its Arab neighbours since the foundation of a Jewish state in 1948. In 2000, peace talks between Israel and Palestine failed, mainly over the control of Jerusalem. Violence continues.

**Kashmir**
A predominantly Muslim territory, disputed between India and Pakistan since 1947. Recent ceasefires have fuelled hope of the end of conflict.

**Kosovo**
Trouble between minority Serbs and majority ethnic Albanians led to rioting in this province of Serbia (part of Yugoslavia) in 1998.

**Kuwait**
Invaded by Iraq in 1990 under Saddam Hussein. In 1991, Iraq was defeated by Allied Forces in the Gulf War.

**Mozambique**
Civil war which devastated the country and made five million people homeless was ended in 1992, with elections following in 1994.

**Northern Ireland**
A disputed part of the UK; current terrorism began in the late 1960s, though two cease-fires hold out the promise of a negotiated settlement.

**Rwanda**
After a history of Hutu and Tutsi rivalries, a multi-party democracy was established in 1990. But in 1994, after the Hutu leader and the president of Burundi were killed in an aeroplane crash, massive violence broke out and around half a million people, mostly Tutsis, were massacred. Millions of refugees fled the country. French and UN troops tried to keep the peace and gather evidence of the genocide. Many refugees returned in 1996.

**Yemen**
After two wars in the 1970s, an agreement was reached in 1979 that North and South Yemen should unify. This occurred in 1990, but civil war erupted in 1994, ending when the breakaway southern state was captured by northern troops.

**Yugoslavia**
The break-up of this former federal republic in 1991 caused civil war. Croatia, Slovenia, Bosnia-Herzegovina and Macedonia have all become independent.

# KINGS AND QUEENS OF GREAT BRITAIN

## SCOTLAND

| | |
|---|---|
| Malcolm III Canmore | 1057–1093 |
| Donald Bane | 1093–1094 |
| Duncan II | 1094 |
| Donald Bane (restored) | 1094–1097 |
| Edgar | 1097–1107 |
| Alexander I | 1107–1124 |
| David I | 1124–1153 |
| Malcolm IV | 1153–1165 |
| William The Lion | 1165–1214 |
| Alexander II | 1214–1249 |
| Alexander III | 1249–1286 |
| Margaret of Norway | 1286–1290 |
| INTERREGNUM | 1290–1292 |
| John Balliol | 1292–1296 |
| INTERREGNUM | 1296–1306 |
| Robert I The Bruce | 1306–1329 |
| David II | 1329–1371 |

### HOUSE OF STUART

| | |
|---|---|
| Robert II | 1371–1390 |
| Robert III | 1390–1406 |
| James I | 1406–1437 |
| James II | 1437–1460 |
| James III | 1460–1488 |
| James IV | 1488–1513 |
| James V | 1513–1542 |
| Mary Queen of Scots | 1542–1567 |
| James VI (I of England) | 1567–1625 |

## ENGLAND

### SAXONS

| | |
|---|---|
| Egbert | 827–839 |
| Ethelwulf | 839–858 |
| Ethelbald | 858–860 |
| Ethelbert | 860–865 |
| Ethelred I | 865–871 |
| Alfred The Great | 871–899 |
| Edward The Elder | 899–924 |
| Athelstan | 924–939 |
| Edmund | 939–946 |
| Edred | 946–955 |
| Edwy | 955–959 |
| Edgar | 959–975 |
| Edward The Martyr | 975–978 |
| Ethelred II The Unready | 978–1016 |
| Edmund II Ironside | 1016 |

### DANES

| | |
|---|---|
| Canute | 1016–1035 |
| Harold I Harefoot | 1035–1040 |
| Hardecanute | 1040–1042 |

### SAXONS

| | |
|---|---|
| Edward The Confessor | 1042–1066 |
| Harold II | 1066 |

### HOUSE OF NORMANDY

| | |
|---|---|
| William I The Conqueror | 1066–1087 |
| William II | 1087–1100 |
| Henry I | 1100–1135 |
| Stephen | 1135–1154 |

### HOUSE OF PLANTAGENET

| | |
|---|---|
| Henry II | 1154–1189 |
| Richard I The Lionheart | 1189–1199 |
| John | 1199–1216 |
| Henry III | 1216–1272 |
| Edward I | 1272–1307 |
| Edward II | 1307–1327 |
| Edward III | 1327–1377 |
| Richard II | 1377–1399 |

### HOUSE OF LANCASTER

| | |
|---|---|
| Henry IV | 1399–1413 |
| Henry V | 1413–1422 |
| Henry VI | 1422–1461 |

### HOUSE OF YORK

| | |
|---|---|
| Edward IV | 1461–1483 |
| Edward V | 1483 |
| Richard III | 1483–1485 |

### HOUSE OF TUDOR

| | |
|---|---|
| Henry VII | 1485–1509 |
| Henry VIII | 1509–1547 |
| Edward VI | 1547–1553 |
| Mary I | 1553–1558 |
| Elizabeth I | 1558–1603 |

## BRITAIN

### HOUSE OF STUART

| | |
|---|---|
| James I (VI of Scotland) | 1603–1625 |
| Charles I | 1625–1649 |

### COMMONWEALTH

| | |
|---|---|
| Oliver Cromwell (Lord Protector) | 1649–1658 |
| Richard Cromwell (Lord Protector) | 1658–1659 |

### HOUSE OF STUART (restored)

| | |
|---|---|
| Charles II | 1660–1685 |
| James II | 1685–1688 |
| William III (and) | 1688–1702 |
| Mary II (jointly) | 1688–1694 |
| Anne | 1702–1714 |

### HOUSE OF HANOVER

| | |
|---|---|
| George I | 1714–1727 |
| George II | 1727–1760 |
| George III | 1760–1820 |
| George IV | 1820–1830 |
| William IV | 1830–1837 |
| Victoria | 1837–1901 |

### HOUSE OF SAXE–COBURG

| | |
|---|---|
| Edward VII | 1901–1910 |

### HOUSE OF WINDSOR

| | |
|---|---|
| George V | 1910–1936 |
| Edward VIII | 1936 |
| George VI | 1936–1952 |
| Elizabeth II | 1952– |

# PRESIDENTS OF THE UNITED STATES OF AMERICA

*(D)* Democrat   *(DR)* Democratic Republican   *(F)* Federalist   *(NU)* National Unionist   *(R)* Republican   *(W)* Whig

| | | | | | |
|---|---|---|---|---|---|
| George Washington *(None)* | 1789–1797 | Abraham Lincoln *(R)* | 1861–1865 | Herbert Hoover *(R)* | 1929–1933 |
| John Adams *(F)* | 1797–1801 | Andrew Johnson *(NU)* | 1865–1869 | Franklin D. Roosevelt *(D)* | 1933–1945 |
| Thomas Jefferson *(DR)* | 1801–1809 | Ulysses S. Grant *(R)* | 1869–1877 | Harry Truman *(D)* | 1945–1953 |
| James Madison *(DR)* | 1809–1817 | Rutherford Hayes *(R)* | 1877–1881 | Dwight Eisenhower *(R)* | 1953–1961 |
| James Monroe *(DR)* | 1817–1825 | James Garfield *(R)* | 1881 | John F. Kennedy *(D)* | 1961–1963 |
| John Quincy Adams *(DR)* | 1825–1829 | Chester Arthur *(R)* | 1881–1885 | Lyndon Johnson *(D)* | 1963–1969 |
| Andrew Jackson *(D)* | 1829–1837 | Grover Cleveland *(D)* | 1885–1889 | Richard Nixon *(R)* | 1969–1974 |
| Martin Van Buren *(D)* | 1837–1841 | Benjamin Harrison *(R)* | 1889–1893 | Gerald Ford *(R)* | 1974–1977 |
| William H. Harrison *(W)* | 1841 | Grover Cleveland *(D)* | 1893–1897 | Jimmy Carter *(D)* | 1977–1981 |
| John Tyler *(W)* | 1841–1845 | William McKinley *(R)* | 1897–1901 | Ronald Reagan *(R)* | 1981–1989 |
| James K. Polk *(D)* | 1845–1849 | Theodore Roosevelt *(R)* | 1901–1909 | George Bush *(R)* | 1989–1993 |
| Zachary Taylor *(W)* | 1849–1850 | William Taft *(R)* | 1909–1913 | Bill Clinton *(D)* | 1993–2001 |
| Millard Fillmore *(W)* | 1850–1853 | Woodrow Wilson *(D)* | 1913–1921 | George W. Bush *(R)* | 2001– |
| Franklin Pierce *(D)* | 1853–1857 | Warren Harding *(R)* | 1921–1923 | | |
| James Buchanan *(D)* | 1857–1861 | Calvin Coolidge *(R)* | 1923–1929 | | |

# PRIME MINISTERS OF GREAT BRITAIN

*(C)* Conservative  *(Coa)* Coalition  *(Lab)* Labour  *(L)* Liberal  *(P)* Peelite  *(T)* Tory  *(W)* Whig

| | | | | | |
|---|---|---|---|---|---|
| Sir Robert Walpole *(W)* | 1721–1742 | Earl Grey *(W)* | 1830–1834 | Herbert Asquith *(Coa)* | 1915–1916 |
| Earl of Wilmington *(W)* | 1742–1743 | Viscount Melbourne *(W)* | 1834 | David Lloyd-George *(Coa)* | 1916–1922 |
| Henry Pelham *(W)* | 1743–1754 | Sir Robert Peel *(T)* | 1834–1835 | Andrew Bonar Law *(C)* | 1922–1923 |
| Duke of Newcastle *(W)* | 1754–1756 | Viscount Melbourne *(W)* | 1835–1841 | Stanley Baldwin *(C)* | 1923–1924 |
| Duke of Devonshire *(W)* | 1756–1757 | Sir Robert Peel (T) | 1841–1846 | James Ramsay MacDonald *(Lab)* | 1924 |
| Duke of Newcastle *(W)* | 1757–1762 | Lord John Russell *(W)* | 1846–1852 | Stanley Baldwin *(C)* | 1924–1929 |
| Earl of Bute *(T)* | 1762–1763 | Earl of Derby *(T)* | 1852 | James Ramsay MacDonald *(Lab)* | 1929–1931 |
| George Grenville *(W)* | 1763–1765 | Earl of Aberdeen *(P)* | 1852–1855 | James Ramsay MacDonald *(Coa)* | 1931–1935 |
| Marquess of Rockingham *(W)* | 1765–1766 | Viscount Palmerston *(L)* | 1855–1858 | Stanley Baldwin *(Coa)* | 1935–1937 |
| William Pitt **(The Elder)** *(W)* | 1766–1768 | Earl of Derby *(C)* | 1858–1859 | Neville Chamberlain *(Coa)* | 1937–1940 |
| Duke of Grafton *(W)* | 1767–1770 | Viscount Palmerston *(L)* | 1859–1865 | Winston Churchill *(Coa)* | 1940–1945 |
| Lord North *(T)* | 1770–1782 | Earl Russell *(L)* | 1865–1866 | Winston Churchill *(C)* | 1945 |
| Marquess of Rockingham *(W)* | 1782 | Earl of Derby *(C)* | 1866–1868 | Clement Atlee *(Lab)* | 1945–1951 |
| Earl of Shelburne *(W)* | 1782–1783 | Benjamin Disraeli *(C)* | 1868 | Winston Churchill *(C)* | 1951–1955 |
| Duke of Portland *(Coa)* | 1783 | William Gladstone *(L)* | 1868–1874 | Anthony Eden *(C)* | 1955–1957 |
| William Pitt **(The Younger)** *(T)* | 1783–1801 | Benjamin Disraeli *(C)* | 1874–1880 | Harold Macmillan *(C)* | 1957–1963 |
| Henry Addington *(T)* | 1801–1804 | William Gladstone *(L)* | 1880–1885 | Alec Douglas-Home *(C)* | 1963–1964 |
| William Pitt **(The Younger)** *(T)* | 1804–1806 | Marquess of Salisbury *(C)* | 1885–1886 | Harold Wilson *(Lab)* | 1964–1970 |
| William Wyndham Grenville *(W)* | 1806–1807 | William Gladstone *(L)* | 1886 | Edward Heath *(C)* | 1970–1974 |
| Duke of Portland *(T)* | 1807–1809 | Marquess of Salisbury *(C)* | 1886–1892 | Harold Wilson *(Lab)* | 1974–1976 |
| Spencer Perceval *(T)* | 1809–1812 | William Gladstone *(L)* | 1892–1894 | James Callaghan *(Lab)* | 1976–1979 |
| Earl of Liverpool *(T)* | 1812–1827 | Earl of Rosebery *(L)* | 1894–1895 | Margaret Thatcher *(C)* | 1979–1990 |
| George Canning *(T)* | 1827 | Marquess of Salisbury *(C)* | 1895–1902 | John Major *(C)* | 1990–1997 |
| Viscount Goderich *(T)* | 1827–1828 | Arthur Balfour *(C)* | 1902–1905 | Tony Blair *(Lab)* | 1997– |
| Duke of Wellington *(T)* | 1828–1830 | Sir H. Campbell–Bannerman *(L)* | 1905–1908 | | |
| | | Herbert Asquith *(L)* | 1908–1915 | | |

# PRIME MINISTERS OF NEW ZEALAND

| | |
|---|---|
| Thomas MacKenzie | *1912–1915* |
| William Massey | *1915–1925* |
| Francis Bell | *1925* |
| Joseph Coates | *1925–1928* |
| Joseph Ward | *1928–1930* |
| Georges Forbes | *1930–1935* |
| Michael Savage | *1935–1940* |
| Peter Fraser | *1940–1949* |
| Sidney Holland | *1949–1957* |
| Keith Holyoake | *1957* |
| Walter Nash | *1957–1960* |
| Keith Holyoake | *1960–1972* |
| John Marshall | *1972* |
| Norman Kirk | *1972–1974* |
| Hugh Watt | *1974* |
| Wallace (Bill) Rowling | *1974–1975* |
| Robert Muldoon | *1975–1984* |
| David Lange | *1984–1989* |
| Geoffrey Palmer | *1989–1990* |
| Michael Moore | *1990* |
| Jim Bolger | *1990–1997* |
| Jenny Shipley | *1997–2000* |
| Helen Clark | *2000–* |

# PRIME MINISTERS OF AUSTRALIA

| | |
|---|---|
| Edmund Barton | 1901–1903 |
| Alfred Deakin | 1903–1904 |
| John Watson | 1904 |
| George Reid | 1904–1905 |
| Alfred Deakin | 1905–1908 |
| Andrew Fisher | 1908–1909 |
| Alfred Deakin | 1909–1910 |
| Andrew Fisher | 1910–1913 |
| Joseph Cook | 1913–1914 |
| Andrew Fisher | 1914–1915 |
| William Hughes | 1915–1923 |
| Stanley Bruce | 1923–1929 |
| James Scullin | 1929–1932 |
| Joseph Lyons | 1932–1939 |
| Earle Page | 1939 |
| Robert Menzies | 1939–1941 |
| Arthur Fadden | 1941 |
| John Curtin | 1941–1945 |
| Francis Forde | 1945 |
| Joseph Chifley | 1945–1949 |
| Robert Menzies | 1949–1966 |
| Harold Holt | 1966–1967 |

Bob Hawke sought to increase trade with countries such as the USA, Japan and China.

| | |
|---|---|
| John McEwen | 1967–1968 |
| John Gorton | 1968–1971 |
| William McMahon | 1971–1972 |
| E. Gough Whitlam | 1972–1975 |
| Malcolm Fraser | 1975–1983 |
| Robert Hawke | 1983–1991 |
| Paul Keating | 1991–1996 |
| John Howard | 1996– |

# PRIME MINISTERS OF INDIA

| | |
|---|---|
| Gulzari Lal Nanda | 1964 |
| Lal Shastri | 1964–1966 |
| Gulzarilal Nanda | 1966 |
| Indira Gandhi | 1966–1977 |
| Morarji Desai | 1977–1979 |
| Charan Singh | 1979–1980 |
| Indira Gandhi | 1980–1984 |
| Rajiv Gandhi | 1984–1989 |
| V. P. Singh | 1989–1990 |
| Chadra Shekhar | 1990–1991 |
| P. V. Narasimha Rao | 1991–1996 |
| Atal Behari Vajpayee | 1996 |
| H. D. Deve Gowda | 1996–1997 |
| Inder Kumar Gujral | 1997–1998 |
| Atal Behari Vajpayee | 1998– |

# INDEX

Page numbers shown in **bold** indicate where the main reference to the subject can be found. Numbers in *italic* refer to pages where illustrations can be found.

# ACKNOWLEDGEMENTS

The publishers wish to thank the following for supplying photographs for this book:

### ABBREVIATIONS
(*t* = top; *b* = bottom; *c* = centre; *l* = left; *r* = right)

### PICTURE LIBRARY ABBREVIATIONS
**AKG:** AKG London; **BAL:** The Bridgeman Art Library; **B&C Alexander:** Bryan & Cherry Alexander; **BC:** Bruce Coleman Collection; **EB/JD:** Eye Ubiquitous/James Davis Travel Photography; **FLPA:** Frank Lane Picture Agency; **FS:** Frank Spooner Pictures; **GI:** Getty Images; **HL:** The Hutchison Library; **NHPA:** Natural History Photographic Agency; **OSF:** Oxford Scientific Films; **Panos:** Panos Pictures; **PE:** Planet Earth Pictures; **Popper:** Popperfoto; **RHPL:** Robert Harding Picture Library; **SP:** Still Pictures; **SPL:** Science Photo Library

Cover: GI *(tc)*, *(r)*

Pages: 6: RHPL *(tr)*, NHPA *(b)* 7: SP *(b)* 8: BAL *(tr)*, SP *(tl)*, RHPL *(bl)* 9: RHPL *(tl)*, Allsport *(cr)*, Panos *(bl)* 10: PE *(tr)* 12: NHPA *(tl)*, PE *(tr)* 16: Popper *(tl)*, BC *(cr)*, NHPA *(bl)* 17: NHPA *(cr)*, B&C Alexander *(bc)* 18: SP *(tr)*, NHPA *(bl)*, RHPL *(b)* 19: Panos *(b)* 20: HL *(tl, b)*, FS *(tr)* 21: Panos *(cr, tl)*, BAL *(cl)* 22: SPL *(trt, trb)* 24: SPL *(tl, tr)* 26: PE *(tr)*, OSF *(bc)* 27: PE *(bc)*, NHPA *(br)* 28: Colorific *(tl)*, SP *(bc)* 29: RHPL *(tl)*, Colorific *(tr)*, NHPA *(c)* 32: NHPA *(br)* 34: SPL *(br)* 35: Corbis *(tl)*, SPL *(tr)* 39: Graham Harrison *(tr, cl)*, GI *(br)* 40: BC *(c, bc)* 42: Zefa *(tr)*, RHPL *(b)*, Robert Estall Photo Library *(cr)*, FS *(cl)* 43: Robert Estall Photo Library *(cl)*, RHPL *(br)* 44: Panos *(cr)*, HL *(b)* 45: SuperStock *(br)*, HL *(b)* 49: SPL *(tl, clt, cl, clb, b)* 51: BC *(tr)*, SP *(cl)*, Image Bank *(b)* 52: BC *(b)* 53: GI *(tc, tr, bl)*, RHPL *(br)* 54: Panos *(tr, bl, br)* 55: RHPL *(cr)* 56: Corbis *(b)* 57: RHPL *(cl)*, Zefa *(b)* 58: SPL *(tl, clt, clb, bl)* 59: GI *(tr)* 60: Camera Press *(bl, clb)*, AKG *(br)* 61: GI *(bc)* 62: Corbis *(tr)* 63: SPL *(tl)*, AKG *(tr)* 66 RHPL *(bl)* 67: Popper *(b)* 68: GI *(tl)* 70: The Natural History Museum, London *(c)* 72: FS *(tl)*, SPL *(bl)* 73: Farmers Weekly Picture Library *(br)* 78: Rex Features *(b)* 79: Panos *(tr)*, GI *(b)* 80: Panos *(b)* 81: Panos *(tl)*, GI *(tr)*, Rex Features *(b)* 82: Panos *(br)* 83: Simon Farrell *(tr)* 86: RHPL *(bc)* 88: Popper *(tl, cl)*, Colorsport *(tr)* 90: FLPA *(tr)*, GI *(b)* 91: FLPA *(br)* 92: Zefa *(tl)*, GI *(tr)*, Rex Features *(b)* 93: GI *(tr)*, RHPL *(cl)*, Rex Features *(b)* 96: NHPA *(tr)* 98: NHPA *(bc)* 100: GI *(c)* 101: RHPL *(cl)*, GI *(c)* 102: Telegraph Colour Library *(tr)* 103: GI *(tl)* 105: GI *(tr, br, cl)* 106: FS *(tl)*, Popper *(bl)*, RHPL *(br)* 109: SPL *(tr)* 110: SPL *(tl, clt, clb)* 111: SP *(bl)*, Telegraph Colour Library *(bcl, br)*, GI *(bcr)* 112: Popper *(tr)* 113: Zefa *(tr)*, FS *(cl)*, RHPL *(b)* 114: Popper *(cl)*, GI *(b)* 116 NHPA *(tl)* 117: Corbis *(tl)*, GI *(b)* 118: GI *(tr, b)* 119: Popper *(tl)*, RHPL *(cl)*, Panos *(br)* 121: RHPL *(tr)* 122: NHPA *(tl)*, PE *(tl, bl, bc, br)*, GI *(cr)* 126: FS *(tr)*, GI *(tr)* 127: Image Bank *(tr)*, GI *(br)* 129: FS *(tr)*, GI *(br)*, Panos *(cl, blt)*, EB/JD *(clb, cl, tl)* 131: Image Bank *(tc)* 133: Panos *(tr)*, GI *(b)* 134: Panos *(cr)*, Image Bank *(bl)* 135: Colorific *(tl)*, GI *(tr)*, FS *(b)* 136: OSF *(tl)*, Panos *(bl)* 140: GI *(tl)* 142: RHPL *(tr)*, Panos *(cr)* 143: OSF *(cr, br)* 144: OSF *(tl, clb, bl)*, BC *(br)* 146: FS *(tr)* 147: BAL *(tr)* 148: GI *(cl, bl)*, Houghton's Horses Picture Library *(br)* 147: GI *(tr)* 148: RHPL *(cl)*, GI *(b)* 149: FLPA *(tr)*, GI *(cl)*, Network/Mike Abrahams *(bl)* 150: GI *(tr, b, cl)* 151: FS *(cr)*, John Ferro Sims *(bl)* 152: GI *(tr, b)*, Panos *(cl)* 155: GI *(tr, cl)*, Image Bank *(bl)*, Colorific *(bc)* 157: SPL *(tl)* 158: EB/JD *(tl)*, BAL *(cl)* 161: Zefa *(tr, cr)*, Corbis *(tl)*, Image Bank *(cl)*, OSF *(bl, bc)* 166: SPL *(tl)* 170: Panos *(tr)* 171: Alpha *(tr, bc)*, A.C. Edwards *(bl)* 172: Glaxo Group Research *(bc)* 173: SPL *(tr, bc)* 174: Telegraph Colour Library *(tr)* 175: South American Pictures *(tr)*, Spectrum Colour Library *(cl)*, Panos *(bl)* 176: SPL *(tl, clt, cl, clb, bl)* 177: LEO Electron Microscopy Ltd *(tr)*, Leica Microsystems (UK) Ltd *(bc)*, SPL *(tl, clt, clb, bl)* 179: RHPL *(tr)*, Panos *(b)* 180: HL *(c)* 181: Spectrum Colour Library *(tl)*, FS *(tr)*, HL *(bc)* 185: OSF *(cr)* 191: Edinburgh University *(cr)*, Keith Saunders/LSO with Michael Tilson Thomas *(b)* 192: Corbis *(tr)* 194: FS *(bl)* 195: Spectrum Colour Library *(tc, cl)*, FS *(bl)* 196: Panos *(tr)*, HL *(br)* 197: NHPA *(bl)*, HL *(tr)*, Zefa *(tl)* 199: Popper *(tr)* 200: SP *(tr)* 203: SPL *(tr)* 204: RHPL *(cr)*, Topham *(b)* 205: Topham *(tl)* 206: Allsport *(tr, cr)* 210: Universal/courtesy Kobal Collection *(tr)* 213: ICI *(b)* 214: HL *(b)* 217: NHPA *(cl)* 218: PE *(tr)* 219: HL *(b)* 220: BAL *(bl)* 221: BAL *(cr)* 222: GI *(cr)* 228: Rex Features *(tl)*, Popper *(tr)*, GI *(b)* 229: NHPA *(bl)*, HL *(br)* 231: NHPA *(tr)* 233: Zefa *(crt)*, GI *(crb)* 234: SCR Photo Library/Novosti *(tr)*, RHPL *(b)* 235: HL *(b)* 236: Rex Features *(tl)*, Novosti, London *(cl)*, HL *(bl, br)* 238: GI *(tr, b)* 239: RHPL *(bl)*, FLPA *(br)* 240: GI *(tl, clt)*, HL *(bc)* 241: HL *(cr)*, Spectrum Colour Library *(tr)* 245: OSF *(tr)* 246: NHPA *(tr)* 249: Popper *(b)* 250: RHPL *(cl, tr)*, GI *(b)* 251: FS *(bl)*, RHPL *(cr)* 252: South American Pictures *(tr, cl, b)* 253: HL *(tl)*, South American Pictures *(bl)*, Panos *(br)* 254: Panos *(tl, b)*, South American Pictures *(tr)* 255: South American Pictures *(tr, cr)*, HL *(bl)* 257: SPL *(tr)*, Portfolio Pictures/NASA *(bl)* 258: SPL *(cl, clb, bl)* 260: GI *(tr)*, HL *(cl)*, RHPL *(b)* 261: HL *(b)* 263: NHPA *(cl)* 264: Allsport *(bl)* 265: Sporting Pictures *(tc)* 266: Sporting Pictures *(tr)* 268: NHPA *(tr)* 271: RHPL *(cr)*, Zefa *(tl, bl, br)* 273: Zefa *(tr)* 274: Popper *(tr)* 279: GI *(tr)* 280: SPL *(cl)* 281: FS *(b)* 283: Telegraph Colour Library *(tr)* 284: Popper *(cl)*, RHPL *(tr)*, BTA/Britain On View *(b)* 285: BTA/Britain On View *(tl)*, HL *(bl)*, RHPL *(br)* 286: FS *(tr)*, Popper *(b)* 287: Panos *(tr)*, RHPL *(bl, br)* 288: RHPL *(tl, cl)*, Zefa *(br)* 289: RHPL *(cl, br)* 290: RHPL *(tl, cl)*, Corbis *(cr)*, Redferns *(b)* 291: SPL *(tl)* 294: HL *(tl)* 295: HL *(tc)* 297: SPL *(c)* 298: SPL *(br)* 306: SPL *(tl, bl)* 307: Gaynor Worman/Marwell Zoo *(br)*

- - - - - - - - - -

## Illustrators

Julian Baker Illustration, Julian Baum, Michelle Brand, Andy Burton, Tom Connell, MaggieDowner, Richard Draper, Andrew Farmer, Chris Forsey, Mick Gillah, Trevor Hill, Karen Hiscock, Christian Hook, Kevin Jones Associates, Ruth Lindsay, Ceri Llewellyn, Kevin Maddison, Nicki Palin, Peter Ross, Peter Sarson, Mike Saunders, Ron Tiner, Martin Woodward, *Black Hat*: Kevin Lyles, *Blue Chip*: Keith Harmer, *David Lewis Agency*: Mark Stacey, *J.M. & A*: Steinar Lund, *Linda Rogers Associates*: Peter Dennis, *Linden Artists*: Lindsay Graham, Richard Hook, Sebastian Quigley, Clive Spong, *Specs Art*: Richard Berridge, *Virgil Pomfret*: Luigi Galanti, *W.L.A*: Cy Baker, Derick Bown, Robin Budden, Robin Carter, Barry Croucher, Sandra Doyle, Brin Edwards, David Hardy, Dan Harvey, Philip Hood, Ian Jackson, Bridgette Jones, Rachel Lockwood, Pond/Giles, Jonathan Potter, Steve Roberts, Andrew Robinson, Mike Rowe, Chris Shields, Paul Staveley, Mark Stewart, Mike Taylor, Richard Tibbitts, Chris Turnbull, Simon Turvey, David Woods.

- - - - - - - - - -

## The publishers would also like to thank the following for their help in supplying information used as visual reference:

Pages: 11: Zoological Society of London (fire salamander cutaway); 22-3: W.M. Keck Observatory (Keck observatory); 164-5: Otis plc, Ove Arup & Partners (panoramic lift); 172-3: Picker International Ltd, Siemens Medical Engineering (CAT scanner); 199: Nuclear Electric (nuclear reactor); 203: British Petroleum (platform); 204-5: Olympic Museum; 281: Ford Motor Company (people carrier).

*Every effort has been made to trace the copyright holders of the photographs. The publishers apologise for any unavoidable omissions.*